Cambridge International
AS Level

International history 1870–1939

David Williamson
Series editor: Dr Jo Edwards

For Saul, Jonah and Arthur.

The Publishers would like to thank the following for permission to reproduce copyright material.

Hachette UK's policy is to use papers that are natural, renewable and recyclable products and made from wood grown in well-managed forests and other controlled sources. The logging and manufacturing processes are expected to conform to the environmental regulations of the country of origin.

Orders: please contact Hachette UK Distribution, Hely Hutchinson Centre, Milton Road, Didcot, Oxfordshire, OX11 7HH. Telephone: +44 (0)1235 827827. Email education@hachette.co.uk Lines are open from 9 a.m. to 5 p.m., Monday to Friday. You can also order through our website: www.hachettelearning.com

ISBN: 9781036008956

First published in 2025 by

Hachette Learning (a trading division of Hodder & Stoughton Ltd.)

An Hachette UK Company

Carmelite House

50 Victoria Embankment

London EC4Y 0DZ

www.hachettelearning.com

The authorised representative in the EEA is Hachette Ireland,
8 Castlecourt Centre, Castleknock Road, Castleknock,
Dublin 15, D15 YF6A, Ireland

Impression number 10 9 8 7 6 5 4 3 2 1

Year 2028 2027 2026 2025

Cover photo © Chronicle / Alamy Stock Photo

Illustrations by Newgen Knowledge Works

Typeset by Newgen Publishing UK

Printed and Bound in Great Britain by Bell & Bain Ltd, Glasgow

A catalogue record for this title is available from the British Library.

Contents

Introduction

This book has been written to support your understanding of the key movements, themes, topics and people significant to the study option International history, 1870–1939 for Cambridge International AS Level History (syllabus codes 9489 or 9982). The course offers an education in understanding the changes that characterised the period, and this book supports this. This section gives you an overview of:

- the content you will study for the International option: International history, 1870–1939 structure of the syllabus
- the different features of this book and how these will aid your learning.

1 What you will study

This book is a study of international relations and international history from 1870 to 1939, which is dominated by the emergence of the 'New Imperialism,' the two world wars and the emergence of two new imperial powers, Japan, and the USA. Yet these were also years when there were attempts to create a new international system of peace and security through the League of Nations.

Between 1870 and 1914 the European imperial powers partitioned and colonized Africa, leaving only Liberia and Abyssinia (Ethiopia) independent. The years 1870–1914 saw the development of both Japan and the USA as imperial powers, which began to play important roles in the power politics of the time. The year 1870 was also the date when Prussia defeated France and created the German Reich (Empire), which was to become, for most of the period studied by this book, the dominant power in continental Europe. The tensions created by the emergence of this new great power led to the formation of rival alliance systems and ultimately to the outbreak of war in 1914. The First World War and the Russian Revolution of 1917 were seismic events that influenced the history not just of Europe but of the world for the rest of the century. Although the focus of the war was the European continent, by November 1918 Japan, the USA, and China had been sucked into the conflict and the peoples and economies of the British and French empires mobilised for the struggle. The post-war peace treaties proved deeply flawed and were perceived by the defeated powers as acts of revenge.

In 1924 the USA's new willingness to play a leading financial role in the reconstruction of Germany's economy and the atmosphere of detente opened up the way for the gradual peaceful revision of the Treaty of Versailles and the more effective functioning of the League of Nations. Yet this period was short-lived. The Wall Street Crash and the Great Depression were significant causes of the rise of extremism and nationalism in Germany and Japan, leading to the failure of both disarmament and the League of Nations.

As a consequence of the impact of the Great Depression on the Japanese economy, the influence of the army in the country's politics became dominant. From 1931, with the seizure of Manchuria, until defeat in 1945, Japan was engaged in steadily escalating conflict, first with China and then with Britain and the USA after the attack on Pearl Harbor in 1941. In Germany the Great Depression was instrumental in bringing Hitler and the Nazis to power, whose continued aggression despite the appeasement policies of Britain and France caused the outbreak of the Second World War.

This book covers the following topics:

- Chapter 1 explores the impact of European imperialism on the rest of the world, particularly Africa before 1914, as well as the impact of this imperialism on relations between the European powers. It looks, too, at the emergence of two new world powers, the USA and Japan.

- Chapter 2 analyzes the peace settlements of 1919–20 and their impact on Europe, as well as the attempts to solve the reparations problem and to reconcile France and Germany. It also looks at the aims, membership and development of the League of Nations and efforts to secure global disarmament during the 1920s.
- Chapter 3 is focused on extremism and the road to war. It looks at the impact of the Wall Street Crash and the Great Depression, which fuelled Japanese nationalism and brought Adolf Hitler to power in Germany. The rise of extremism and dictatorship, the failures of the League of Nations, and the causes of the Second World War are the main themes of this chapter.

2 Structure of the syllabus

The information in this section is based on the Cambridge International Education syllabus. You should always refer to the appropriate syllabus document for the year of examination to confirm the details and for more information. The syllabus document is available on the website: www.cambridgeinternational.org.

The Cambridge International AS Level History course will be assessed through two papers: a Historical Sources Paper and an Outline Study.

- For Paper 1, you need to answer one two-part document question on one of the options given. You will need to answer both parts of the question you choose. This counts for 40 per cent of the AS Level.
- For Paper 2, you need to answer two two-part questions from three on one of the options given. You must answer both parts of the question you choose. This counts for 60 per cent of the AS Level.

AS Level topics rotate year on year between Papers 1 and 2 – the prescribed topic for Paper 1 in the June and November series of any given year is not used for Paper 2.

Assessment questions

For Paper 1, there will be two parts to each question. For Part (A), you will be expected to compare two sources on one aspect of the material. For Part (B), you will be expected to use all the sources and your knowledge of the period to address how far the sources support a given statement.

For Paper 2, you will select two questions from the option on International history, 1870–1939. There will be two parts to each question. Part (A) requires an explanation of causes, and Part (B) requires you to consider and weigh up the relative importance of a range of factors. You will need to answer both parts of the question you choose.

Key concepts

The syllabus also focuses on developing your understanding of a number of key concepts and these are also reflected in the nature of the questions set in the examination. The key concepts for AS History are as follows:

Cause and consequence

The events, circumstances, actions, and beliefs that have a direct causal connection to consequential events and developments, circumstances, actions, or beliefs. Causes can be both human and non-human.

Change and continuity

The patterns, processes and interplay of change and continuity within a given time frame.

Similarity and difference

The patterns of similarity and difference that exist between people, lived experiences, events, and situations in the past.

Significance

The importance attached to an event, individual, or entity in the past, whether at the time or subsequent to it. Historical significance is a constructed label that is dependent upon the perspective (context, values, interests, and concerns) of the person ascribing significance and is therefore changeable.

These icons appear next to questions to show where key concepts are being tested and what they are.

Command words

When choosing essay questions, keep in mind that it is vital to answer the actual question that has been asked, not the one that you might have hoped for. A key to doing well is understanding the demands of the question. Cambridge International AS Level History uses key terms and phrases known as command words. The command words are listed below:

Command word	What it means
Compare	Identify / comment on similarities and/or differences
Explain	Set out purposes or reasons / make the relationships between things evident / provide reasons why and/or how and support with relevant evidence

Questions may also use phrases such as:
- How far do you agree?
- To what extent?

Answering assessment questions

It is important that you organize your time well during an assessment. In other words, do not spend too long on one question and leave yourself short of time. Before you begin a question, take a few minutes to draw up a brief plan of the major points you want to make and your argument. You can then tick them off as you make them. This is not a waste of time as it will help you produce a coherent and well-argued answer. Well-organized responses with well-supported arguments and a conclusion will score more highly than responses that lack coherence and jump from point to point.

Answering source questions

For questions that ask you to compare two sources, you should be able to:
- make a developed comparison of the two sources
- identify both similarities **and** differences in the evidence that two sources give about a particular issue
- use contextual knowledge or source evaluation to **explain** the similarities and differences
- evaluate the sources to reach a supported judgement as to how far the sources support the statement.

For questions that ask you to consider how far sources support a view you should be able to:
- identify whether each source supports or challenges the statement in the question
- use each source's content to explain how the source supports or challenges the statement
- use your contextual knowledge to help you understand and analyze the sources
- use the provenance of the sources to help you explain how this affects the extent to which they support the statement.

Answering essay questions

For questions that ask you to explain causes you should be able to:
- consider two or three relevant causes and explain how they were factors
- support each cause with relevant and accurate evidence
- make links between the factors.

For analytical essay questions you should be able to:
- consider a range of different issues and analyze each
- use a balanced argument throughout

- support your argument with relevant and accurate evidence
- reach a relevant and supported judgment which answers the question.

Your essays should include an introduction that sets out your main points. Do not waste time copying out the question, but do define any key terms that are in the question. The strongest essays show awareness of different possible approaches to the question. You will need to write an in-depth analysis of your main points in several paragraphs, providing detailed and accurate information to support them. Each paragraph will focus on one of your main points and be directly related to the question. Finally, you should write a concluding paragraph. All of these skills are developed throughout the book in the Study skills section at the end of each chapter.

3 About this book

Coverage of the course content

This book addresses the key areas listed in the Cambridge International syllabus. The content closely follows the layout and sequence of the Cambridge syllabus, with each chapter covering one of the syllabus topics. Chapters start with an introduction outlining key questions they address. Each key question is accompanied by content that you are expected to understand and use when addressing the key question. Throughout the chapters you will find the following features to aid your study of the course content.

Key terms

Key terms are important terms you need to know to gain an understanding of the period. These are emboldened in the text the first time they appear in the book and are defined in the margin. They also appear in the glossary at the end of the book.

Key figures and profiles

Key figures boxes highlight important individuals and can be found in the margin and within the main text. Some chapters contain profiles, which offer more information about the importance and impact of particularly significant individuals. This information can be very useful in understanding certain events and providing evidence to support your arguments.

Sources

Throughout the book you will encounter both written and visual sources. Historical sources are important components in understanding more fully why specific decisions were taken or on what contemporary writers and politicians based their actions. The sources are accompanied by questions to help you dig deeper into International history, 1870–1939. To help with analyzing the sources, think about the message of the source, its purpose, and its usefulness for a particular line of inquiry. The questions that accompany the source will help you with this.

Extension boxes

Occasional extension boxes will cover additional, related topics that go beyond the syllabus to help further your understanding of the period.

Key debates

Within each key question of the syllabus, one or more key debates summarize different historians' views and opinions of events and individuals.

Activities

Activities and tasks throughout the book will help you develop conceptual understanding and consolidate knowledge.

Summary diagrams

At the end of each section is a summary diagram, which gives a visual summary of the content of the section. These diagrams are intended as an aid for revision.

Chapter summaries

At the end of each chapter is a short summary of the content of that chapter. These summaries are intended to help you consolidate your knowledge and understanding of the content.

Refresher questions

Questions at the end of each chapter will serve as a useful tool to test your knowledge of what you have read. These will serve as prompts and show where you have gaps in your knowledge and understanding.

Study skills

At the end of each chapter you will find guidance on both how to approach writing a successful essay and how to evaluate sources. These pages show you the kinds of questions you might be asked in an assessment. There is also analysis of and comment on sample answers. These are not full responses to the questions. We have written them to help you see what part of good answer might look like.

End of the book

The book concludes with the following sections:

Glossary

All key terms in the book are defined in the glossary.

Further reading

This contains a list of books and websites that may help you with further independent research. At this level of study, it is important to read around the subject and not rely solely on the content of this textbook. The further reading section will help you with this.

Overview

This course is designed to develop understanding of key events in international history from 1870 to 1939 and the substantial forces that shaped nations and affected the world's population over this significant period.

Between 1870 and 1939, the modern international system began to take shape, influencing global events. Nations grew and developed, leading to more advanced diplomacy as they managed conflicts and cooperation. European powers sought new lands, resources, and influence, driven by economic and ideological goals. This competition created significant tensions, which were managed through alliances and efforts to maintain a balance of power. However, the failure of these alliances to keep peace, along with the ambitions of major powers, led to the devastating conflicts of the First World War.

Making a peace deal at the end of the war was very hard. The leaders of the major powers that had won the war had different goals and disagreed on many issues. Some wanted global cooperation, while others, who were badly affected by the war, wanted strict measures to protect their territory. Promises made during the war to gain support from allies made things even more complicated, as those promises had to be kept, which wasn't always possible, causing dissatisfaction and distrust. Some important nations were not included in the negotiations, weakening the process. The peace conferences had to be done quickly, so not all issues were fully discussed. Since 32 nations were involved, it was tough to reach an agreement in the unstable international environment after the war. The resulting changes in international relations and foreign policies, and their successes and failures would affect the whole world in the twentieth century.

This course will cover the causes, sequence, and effects of the new international order as independent topics that provide an overall chronology to structure both knowledge and understanding of the development of international history between 1870 and 1939.

Imperialism and the emergence of world powers c.1870–1918

Our starting point to explore the development of international history focuses on the ambitions of European powers that were attempting to colonize different parts of Africa. We also analyze the circumstances of Japan and the USA in this period, their imperial motivations and actions and their rapid development to becoming global powers.

Since the fifteenth century, European powers had aimed to build empires by colonizing territories worldwide. They conquered North and South America and established settlements in India, Southeast Asia, and Oceania. Europeans also set up trading posts and tried to colonize parts of West and South Africa, driven by developing the transatlantic slave trade and securing global trade routes. By the nineteenth century, the difficulties and costs of maintaining significant overseas territories had become clear. Britain lost control of its North American colonies, and Spain and Portugal were losing control in South America. However, by 1870, a new wave of colonization, known as 'New Imperialism,' emerged, driven by economic, political, ideological, and social motivations.

Seven European powers were involved in the 'Scramble for Africa.' This was driven by their desire to increase wealth through trade, find new markets for their goods, and take raw materials for industry. Politically, they aimed to control key areas for global trade, like rivers and strategic canals. Some nations believed imperialism would benefit their working classes by funding social reforms and keeping employment high. Religious motives and racial ideologies also played a role, as many Europeans believed their language, beliefs, and culture were superior and would bring 'civilization' to the world. This expansion significantly affected African kingdoms and caliphates and increased international tensions.

During this time, Japan and the United States also became world powers. For Japan, the Meiji Restoration started a period of fast modernization and industrial growth. By the early 1900s, Japan was a modern state with a strong military and increasing wealth. Japan became an imperial power itself, looking for its own overseas territories. Japan's victories in wars against China and Russia earned it recognition as a world power, leading other nations to seek alliances with Japan for political, economic, and strategic reasons.

When the USA got involved in international affairs, it quickly became a powerful influence on world relations. Its strength came from its strong industries, so economic reasons were a key reason for its actions abroad. The USA wanted access to overseas markets to make more profits, leading to efforts to control strategic areas like Cuba. Despite some politicians wanting to avoid the costs and risks of overseas involvement, the economic benefits were too tempting. By 1914, the USA had become a key regional power, arguing against critics that its international actions were needed to protect its investments. To support this, the USA expanded its naval power, helping to establish its influence globally.

International relations 1919–29: conflict and co-operation

During the First World War, nations put all their resources, including armies and economies, into the war effort, causing huge human and material losses. After the war, many leaders wanted new international agreements to prevent future wars, focusing on global peace and security through cooperation. Key ideas included collective security, disarmament, and peaceful resolution of disputes. This led to the creation of the League of Nations in 1920, the first permanent international organization for world peace. Despite the USA's major role in its creation, the US Senate chose not to join, which weakened it significantly.

After the war, major powers faced difficulties rebuilding their infrastructure and economies, and recovering from financial losses. Meanwhile, changing ideologies and politics in Europe brought new threats to stability, including the danger of a communist revolution led by the newly established USSR. Old rivalries and new resentments from the peace terms added to the mix, keeping international relations tense.

After the war, the main focus was on quickly negotiating peace settlements. This involved dealing with the problems caused by treaties such as Versailles, Saint Germain, Trianon, and Sèvres. Despite the US president's efforts to create lasting peace, the terms, including territorial losses and restrictions, led to more rivalries and tensions worldwide. These treaties had long-lasting effects, shaping politics for decades.

International history 1929–39: the rise of extremism and the road to war

Our final topic looks at how new ideologies and aggressive actions coincided with a worldwide economic crash and depression, putting stress on the fragile peace. In the 1930s, challenges included the rise of extremist political parties in major nations. In Italy and Germany, fascist regimes imposed authoritarian rule; in Spain and Japan, military dictatorships replaced democratic forces; and in the USSR, Stalin tightened his control over the Communist Party and the Soviet state. The tension between democracy and dictatorship had a dramatic effect on international relations.

This section examines Germany's expansion under the Third Reich, Italy's colonization of Africa, and attempts to create a 'New Roman Empire' around the Mediterranean. It also covers Italy and Germany's involvement in the Spanish Civil War.

The failure of the League of Nations to maintain collective security is discussed, noting its inability to impose sanctions or enforce decisions against aggressive nationalism. Major powers like Britain and France had conflicting interests and focused more on appeasing Germany than supporting collective security. Meanwhile, Japan expanded its influence in Asia, invading Manchuria in 1931 and China in 1937.

Finally, we look at the events that led up to the Second World War. These include rearmament and the formation of new alliances and pacts due to the aggressive expansion policies of Germany, Italy, and Japan. This created a very unstable international environment, leading to the outbreak of war in 1939.

1 Imperialism and the emergence of world powers c.1870–1918

Introduction

This chapter considers the colonization of Africa by European countries, and the emergence of Germany, Japan, and the USA as imperial powers between c.1870 and 1918 under the following headings:

- Why was imperialism a significant force in Africa from 1870?
- What was the impact of imperial expansion on international relations?
- Why did Japan emerge as a world power and what was the impact on international relations?
- Why did the USA emerge as a world power and what was the impact on international relations?

KEY DATES

1870–71	Defeat of France and German unification
1879	Anglo-Zulu War
1882	Defeat of Egyptian nationalists by Britain at Tel el Kebir
1884–85	Foundations of German colonial empire laid
1884–85	Berlin West Africa Conference
1894–95	Sino-Japanese War
1896	Battle of Adwa
1896–97	Ndebele Rebellion
1898	Fashoda incident
1898	US occupation of Cuba, Puerto Rico, and the Philippines
1902	Anglo-Japanese alliance
1904	Anglo-French colonial agreement (Entente Cordiale)
1904–05	Russo-Japanese War
1904–08	Herero War
1905–06	First Moroccan crisis
1908	King Leopold forced to hand over the administration of the Congo to Belgian government
1914 July	Assassination of Archduke Franz Ferdinand, which leads to the First World War
1917 April	US declaration of war on Germany
1918 November	Armistice

1 Why was imperialism a significant force in Africa from 1870?

KEY TERMS

Colonization Taking control of a territory through settlement and military force.

Liberia was founded in the early nineteenth century by the American Colonization Society as a refuge for African-Americans. It was only nominally independent of the US government.

From 1870, European powers sought to control new territories through **colonization**. By 1910 almost all of Africa, with the exception of Ethiopia and **Liberia**, had been colonized by the European powers. Britain controlled Egypt, Sudan, Nigeria, the Gold Coast, most of South Africa, and Uganda and the East Africa Protectorate. France dominated much of West and North Africa, and Belgium dominated the economically valuable Congo. While Germany and Portugal also had substantial territories, Italy controlled a small part of east Africa.

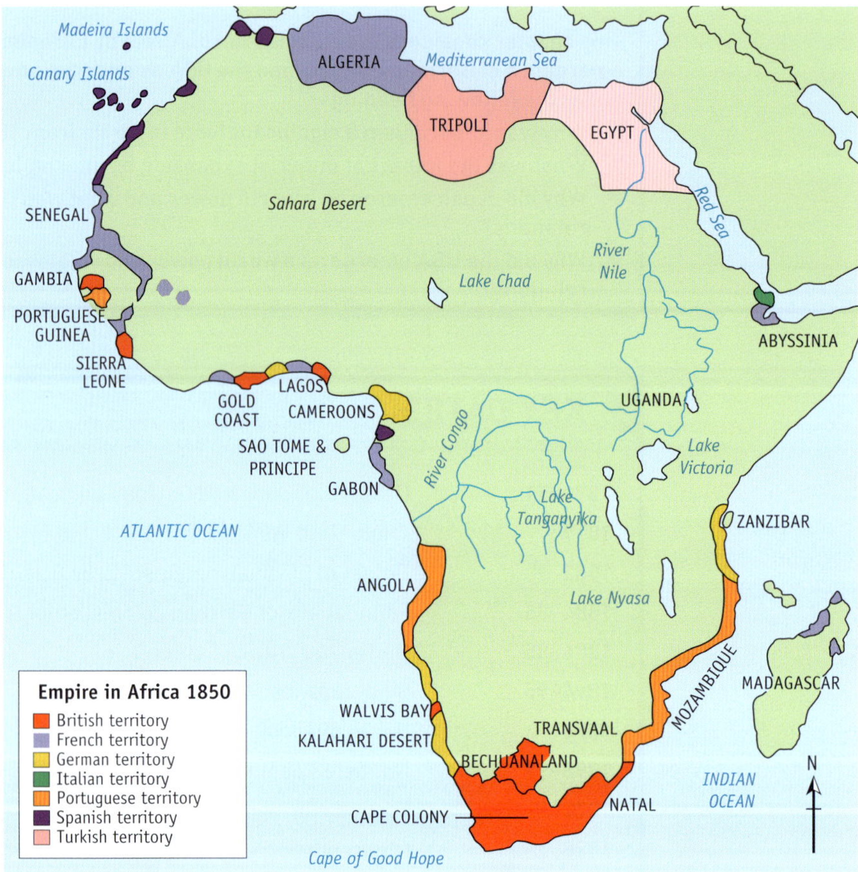

Figure 1.1 Africa in 1850

ACTIVITY

Use Figure 1.1. to describe the colonization of Africa by 1850.

KEY TERMS

Imperialism The policy, carried out by a state, of acquiring and controlling dependent territories.

Partition Dividing up a continent or country into territories controlled by different powers.

Decolonization This refers to the process by which colonies gained independence from their colonial powers, often after years of struggle and negotiation.

The European powers had political and economic reasons for wanting to control new territories. European powers justified the division of Africa as part of the destiny of great powers, dominating other peoples who they considered less civilized than themselves. A consequence of the **partition** of Africa was that Africa became part of a European – and American – dominated world. This meant that Africa adapted to this industrialized world, but this also brought considerable pain and humiliation to its peoples. European powers exploited Africa economically and it was drawn into European conflicts such as the First World War. By the middle of the twentieth century, many African states had regained their independence in a process known as **decolonization**.

Motives for the 'Scramble for Africa' by European countries

There were various reasons why European countries wanted African colonies.

Economic motives

KEY TERM

Tariffs Taxes placed on imported goods to protect the home economy.

European states were expanding their trade and industry and looking for markets for the goods they manufactured, and businesses and investors thought that it would be profitable to invest in the new companies that were being formed to trade in Africa. Also, since more and more countries were introducing **tariffs**, the possession of colonies was seen as the only way of finding and guaranteeing access to vital raw materials needed by modern industrial economies. Businesses in Marseilles, Liverpool, and Hamburg, for example, were constantly pushing their governments into annexing areas where they had important trading interests. There was often an exaggerated belief in the potential wealth of new colonies in Africa.

Religious and cultural motives: the 'civilizing mission'

KEY TERMS

Lutheranism A German variant of Protestantism that followed the teachings of the sixteenth-century theologian Martin Luther.

Polygamy Having more than one wife or husband.

Twin infanticide The practice of killing twins at birth in the belief that they were unnatural and inhabited by evil spirits.

Missionary societies and churches were also keen to convert African people to Christianity. Many of the anti-slave trade and anti-slavery campaigners of the nineteenth century were evangelical Christians, and part of their motivation in stopping enslavement was connected with bringing Christian ideas to Africa. The majority of the missionaries were from Europe and they brought with them their own versions of Christianity – Catholicism, Anglicanism, and **Lutheranism**. They were united in their belief that ultimately the whole of Africa should be converted to Christianity. The missionaries also hoped to eradicate cultural practices such as **polygamy**, female genital mutilation, and **twin infanticide**.

National and strategic rivalry

KEY TERM

Strategic aims Aims intended to gain military or economic security for a state.

The **strategic aims** of the imperial powers also influenced the 'Scramble for Africa.' In South Africa, for example, the discovery of gold in the Transvaal, and the growth of German economic and political influence there, convinced Britain that the Boer republics of the Orange Free State and Transvaal needed to be absorbed into British South Africa before they drew too close to Germany. Strategic considerations motivated Britain to take firm control of Egypt and ultimately of Sudan. Sometimes strategy could also dictate concessions by the imperial powers. In 1890 the German government conceded Zanzibar to Britain in exchange for the return of the important North Sea naval base of Heligoland. Once France recognized British control of Egypt and Sudan, Britain was ready to recognize French claims in West Africa. (See pages 20–26 and 29–35 for a more detailed analysis of the national and strategic rivalries of the imperial powers in Africa and elsewhere.)

ACTIVITY

List the causes of the partition of Africa in this table.

Cause	Explanation	Importance on a scale of 1–6	Reason for awarding this score

Process of colonization of Africa

KEY TERMS

Free trade Trade between nations unimpeded by tariffs.

Indirect government Control exercised by a colonial power indirectly through trading companies or local community leaders.

KEY FIGURES

Sir George Goldie (1846–1925) Founder of the Royal Niger Company, which established British rule on the Niger River.

Franz Lüderitz (1835–86) German merchant and founder of German South West Africa.

Carl Peters (1856–1918) German explorer and administrator, and founder member of the German East Africa Company.

Expansion and government of colonies – direct and indirect

In 1870 ten per cent of the African continent was under European control. France had annexed Algeria and Senegal, and Britain had Cape Colony and Lagos, while Dutch settlers, the Boers, had established settlements in the Transvaal and Orange Free State, and there were small Spanish zones in north-west Africa. Portugal was by far the oldest colonial power in Africa as it had established colonies in Angola and Mozambique as far back as the sixteenth century. At the start of this period, little was known in Europe about the interior of Africa, but despite the hazards of disease and lack of suitable transport, the number of explorations increased. At home, Europeans' interest in Africa was growing due to coverage by the press (newspapers) and newly founded geographical societies promoted journeys across the continent undertaken by explorers.

Trading companies and indirect government

In the middle of the nineteenth century, European governments had little interest in gaining more colonies. In an era of **free trade**, it seemed that political control of overseas markets was unnecessary. In 1865 a parliamentary committee even recommended that Britain should withdraw from its bases on the west coast of Africa. Governments were inclined to stand back and allow trading companies to negotiate commercial agreements with African chiefs. This led to **indirect government** of particular regions of Africa by European states. In 1879 five British companies on the Niger River were taken over by **George Goldie**'s Royal Niger Company (RNC). The RNC dominated commerce in the area, compelling local traders to deal with a British monopoly. Terms of private trading contracts were often made into general treaties by the British government consuls for the area. Goldie was challenged by French traders, and above all the Société française de l'Afrique équatoriale, which was authorized by the French government to set up trading stations wherever the RNC was trading. Germany was also increasing trade activities in Africa. A Bremen merchant called **Franz Lüderitz** had set up a trading station at Angra Pequeña, some 160 miles (260 km) north of the Orange River, and in East Africa **Carl Peters**' Society for German Colonization had negotiated treaties with the local African chiefs.

What attitudes to African people are presented in Source 1.1? Use your knowledge of European reasons for colonization to help explain the portrayals in the source.

SOURCE 1.1

A 'collecting card' showing ivory being traded in Africa. The German company Liebig, which sold beef extracts, produced cards for people to collect that showed various images of Africa. The cards were designed to appeal to the idea of what Africa was like in Europeans' popular imagination.

KEY FIGURES

Leopold II (1835–1909) King of Belgium, 1865–1909, and founder of the Congo Free State.

Pierre Savorgnan de Brazza (1852–1905) French explorer from an Italian family.

The International African Association

In September 1876 **Leopold II**, king of Belgium, set up the International African Association (IAA). Its declared aim was to suppress the slave trade and open up Central Africa to international commerce, but in reality King Leopold was secretly scheming to get, as he wrote to the Belgian ambassador in London, 'a slice of this magnificent African cake,' meaning he wanted to take a large portion of it for his own benefit. In 1879, with Leopold's encouragement, **Pierre Savorgnan de Brazza** and Henry Stanley organized two separate expeditions in the name of the IAA to explore the area to the south of the Congo River. Unknown to Leopold, de Brazza had secret instructions to annex this territory for France. Despite initial successes, he failed, but on his return to France, unsuccessful and bankrupt, de Brazza was greeted as a hero and gained widespread public support for French ambitions in the region around the Congo River.

Study source 1.2. What does it tell you about the nature of colonialization in Africa?

SOURCE 1.2

The treaty between the sultan of Sokoto and the National Niger Company (quoted in Siollun, M., *What Britain Did to Nigeria*, London: Hurst and Co., 2021, pp. 337–8).

Article I

For the mutual advantage of ourselves and people, and those Europeans trading under the name of the 'National African Company (Limited)', I Umaru, King of the Musselmans of the Soudan, with the consent of my Council, grant and transfer to the above people, or other with whom they may arrange, my entire rights to the country on both sides of the river Benue and rivers flowing into it throughout my dominions for such distance from its and their banks as they may desire.

Article II

We further grant to the above mentioned company, the sole right, also among foreigners, to trade in our territories and the sole right, also among foreigners, to possess or work places from which are extracted articles such as lead and antimony.

Article III

We further declare that no communication will be held with foreigners coming from the rivers except through the above mentioned company.

Article IV

These grants we make for ourselves, our heirs and successors for ever, and declare them to be irrevocable.

Article V

The Europeans above named, the National African Company (Limited), agree to make Umaru, Sultan of Sokoto, a yearly present of goods to the value of 3,000 bags of **cowries**, in return for the above grants.

Signed and sealed at Wurno, the 1st June 1885

[Signature of the Sultan in Arabic]

For the National African Company (Limited)

Joseph Thomson FRGS

KEY TERM

Cowrie Type of sea snail or mollusc.

KEY FIGURE

David Livingstone (1813–73) A Scot, who by the age of ten was working in a cotton factory on the banks of the Clyde near Glasgow. Later he studied medicine at the University of Glasgow and became a doctor. He fulfilled his main ambition by becoming a minister of the **Congregational Church** and a missionary.

Activities of European explorers

It was the discoveries of several explorers that revealed the potential of Africa to the European states and played a key part in the first stages of the 'Scramble for Africa.' **David Livingstone** was arguably the most famous of the explorers, but there were others, such as

KEY TERM

Congregational Church A branch of the Protestant Church founded in England in the sixteenth century.

KEY FIGURE

Henry Morton Stanley (1841–1904) Born in Denbigh in North Wales, and baptized John Rowlands, Stanley was abandoned as a baby and grew up in a workhouse. At 17 he went to the USA, where he was befriended by Henry Hope Stanley, a wealthy British cotton merchant, whose surname he took. His work as a journalist took him to Africa, where he became an agent for King Leopold II of Belgium and the IAA. In 1890 in celebrations marking the 25th year of King Leopold's reign, Stanley was honored with a medal, the Order of Leopold, and declared a hero. He retired to Britain, where he became a Liberal MP and was knighted in 1897.

Richard Burton, John Speke, Verney Cameron, **Henry Morton Stanley**, the Germans **Heinrich Barth**, and Gustav Nachtigal.

KEY FIGURE

Heinrich Barth (1821–65) Born in Hamburg, Barth had the benefit of an excellent education. He was fluent in several languages, including Arabic, which helped his research into the history, culture, and languages of some of the peoples he encountered during his explorations in Africa. He was made an honorary professor at the Royal Friedrich Wilhelm University in Berlin in 1863.

David Livingstone

David Livingstone's first visit to Africa was in 1841, when he served as a missionary in South Africa. In 1854–56 he was the first European to cross the African continent. He has been credited as the first European to identify areas around Lake Nyasa and the Zambezi River, which he hoped would become highways for the new steamboats and encourage Africans to trade with Britain. Although he is often believed to have been the first European to see the great Mosi-oa-Tunya Falls ('the smoke that thunders'), it is most probable that they had previously been sighted by Portuguese ivory trader Antonio da Silva Porto, who had been active in the region in the 1840s. Livingstone renamed the falls in honor of Queen Victoria, the reigning monarch of England at the time. Livingstone undertook long and difficult expeditions, traveling with African porters and assistants. He traveled with navigation equipment, medicines, weapons, and scientific instruments, as well as food and water supplies. Livingstone's book *Missionary Travels and Researches in South Africa* was aimed at persuading British public opinion and the government to support his plans for establishing a British colony of settlers in the Zambian Highlands. He was convinced that once this was established it would lead to the whole continent of Africa becoming Christian and, as he saw it, 'civilised.' Livingstone was a dedicated missionary who wanted to spread Christianity to African people for what he believed would be their spiritual salvation. He strongly opposed the slave trade and believed that economic development was key to Africa's progress, hoping it would bring prosperity and stability.

What impression of David Livingstone and his explorations is given by Source 1.3? What does that tell us about European attitudes to Africa? Refer to specific details from the source to support your answer.

SOURCE 1.3

An 1878 painting by an unknown artist, showing David Livingstone (holding a child's hand) with his assistants arriving at Lake Ngami in 1849.

Henry Morton Stanley

As a foreign correspondent, or journalist, for the *New York Herald*, Henry Stanley went on trips to the Ottoman Empire, Ethiopia, Persia and India. In 1871 he was commissioned by the *Herald* to find Livingstone, who had not been heard from since he had started on an expedition up the Ruvuma River towards Lake Tanganyika. He eventually found him at Ujiji, on the northern shore of the lake. When Stanley's story reached Britain and the USA, it dominated newspaper headlines. However, the significance of this event was more than just as a newspaper scoop. In many ways, it was a symbolic meeting of two contrasting philosophies: the **evangelical** Livingstone believed in the spiritual and moral transformation of Africa through Christianity, while Stanley was far more interested in trade and financial profit.

KEY TERM

Evangelical Referring to Christians who are determined to spread their beliefs through the Gospels.

Unlike Livingstone, Stanley believed in using force if necessary to subdue Africa. For example, on another expedition in 1874–75 to explore the central African Great Lakes and Rivers, in revenge for being attacked by local tribesmen, he later boasted of having killed some 30 men and wounding at least 100 more.

By 1878 Stanley was effectively a Belgian agent working for King Leopold II to establish the IAA in the Congo River basin (see page 10).

Heinrich Barth

Heinrich Barth was a very different man from both Livingstone and Stanley. His first journey of exploration was to North Africa, which he was later to write about in a book. After three years as a university lecturer, in 1849, on the recommendation of the Prussian ambassador in London, he joined an expedition led by James Richardson and Adolf Overweg, a Prussian astronomer, to open up trading relations with the states of central and western Sudan. Both Richardson and Overweg died on the expedition, leaving Barth in charge. The expedition trekked across the Sahara to Adamawa and the Cameroons in the south and from Lake Chad in the east to Timbuktu in the west.

ACTIVITY

1 Create a list of the key aims and opinions of Livingstone, Stanley, and Barth. What similarities and differences are there between them?

Barth did not want to convert Africans to Christianity nor to lay the foundations of a business empire in Africa. Instead, he was interested in the history, culture, and languages of African communities and civilizations. As an accomplished linguist, he was able to investigate and research the history of some of the peoples he encountered. He also made friends with several African monarchs and scholars. When he returned home to Germany, he compiled a dictionary of central African languages. Essentially, Barth was a scholar rather than a missionary or an adventurer. He never became a household name as did Livingstone and Stanley.

What does Source 1.4 reveal about the attitudes and motives of the European explorers of Africa? Consider the language and tone of the source. Which words demonstrate their attitudes? Refer to specific details from the source.

SOURCE 1.4

Charles Livingstone accompanied his brother David on his expedition to explore the Zambezi and its tributaries. He served as his brother's general assistant and in effect his secretary. This extract is from *Expedition to the Zambesi and Its Tributaries and of the Discovery of the Lakes Shirwa and Nyassa, 1858–64*, Livingstone, D. and Livingstone, C., London: John Murray, 1865, pp. 352–3.

Now that we had accommodation, Charles Livingstone pursued the same system of attempting to turn the industrial energies of the natives to good account. Cotton was bought and cleaned with cotton gins, and in three months he had collected 300lbs of clean cotton-wool at less than a penny a pound. No great amount, certainly, when compared with the thousand bales which come from other countries; but still sufficient to prove that cotton of superior quality can be raised by native labour alone ...

Influence of the advance of technology and science

Rapid developments in technology and science helped the great powers colonize Africa. For example, the invention of the steamship helped the quick transportation of African produce to Europe and in return troops, settlers, and equipment to Africa. Steamships reduced the time a voyage took from West Africa to Britain from 35 days to 21. They also reduced the cost of shipping products between Africa and Europe because they could take much larger cargoes than the old sailing ships. The **Industrial Revolution** in Europe increased the demand for African products such as palm oil, which served both as a **lubricant** for machinery and as an important ingredient in food and soap. Materials such as rubber, cotton, and copper and crops like coffee, tea, and tobacco, which were grown specially for the European market, were also popular and were imported into Europe in large quantities.

Medical advancements played a crucial role in the colonization of Africa. Notably, the discovery of **quinine**'s effectiveness in treating **malaria** significantly reduced the mortality rate from the disease. Additionally, understanding that Malaria was transmitted by mosquitoes and the use of mosquito nets provided further protection and helped lower death rates.

Other advances in technology, including railways, new road-building methods, and innovative weaponry, helped the colonizers administer and police African territories. Revolts were often brutally suppressed using the **Maxim gun**. Operated by a four-man team and capable of firing 500 rounds a minute, this weapon was devastatingly efficient, being 50 times faster than any other firearm of its time. The use of such overwhelming force caused immense suffering and loss of life among those who resisted.

KEY TERMS

Industrial Revolution The process that enabled the mass production of goods in factories and their transportation by steam-powered trains and ships.

Lubricant A substance used to make movement smoother, on machines, for example.

Quinine A chemical compound derived from the bark of the South American cinchona tree that was first discovered as a malaria treatment in the seventeenth century. In 1820, French chemists managed to isolate and extract quinine and it began to be widely used against malaria. It is still sometimes used as a treatment today.

Malaria A potentially life-threatening disease carried by mosquitoes.

Maxim gun A machine gun invented in the USA by Hiram Maxim and mass-produced from 1884.

ACTIVITY

How were the explorers and their activities in Africa viewed by their contemporaries? Find three examples. Look online for examples in the built environment (statues, memorial plaques) and in material culture (coins, stamps). What attitudes to Africa and its peoples are portrayed in these examples?

Development of the Suez Canal

In 1858 French diplomat Ferdinand de Lesseps formed the Suez Canal Company to raise the necessary money for the construction of the Suez Canal. Building work started the following year and the canal officially opened on November 17, 1869. Extending between the Egyptian cities of Port Said and Suez, the canal created a direct route between the North Atlantic and northern Indian oceans via the Mediterranean Sea and the Red Sea, avoiding the South Atlantic and southern Indian oceans. This reduced the shipping route from the Arabian Sea to London by about 5,500 miles (8,850 km).

KEY TERM

Khedive The title used by the governor and ruler of Egypt and Sudan.

The Suez Canal rapidly became a key link in Britain's communications with India, the wealthiest and most strategically important part of the British Empire. In 1875, when Isma'il Pasha, the **Khedive** of Egypt, needed money because his government was £100 million in debt, British Prime Minister Benjamin Disraeli saw an opportunity.

The Khedive had initially planned to approach the French government to ask for a loan against the security of Egypt's stake in the Suez Canal Company, but Disraeli opened negotiations with him instead to purchase as many shares as he could to stop them falling into the hands of a rival power. He succeeded in securing 44 per cent of the shares for Britain; France had the remaining 56 per cent. The British government then had some say in the running of the canal, including deciding on toll charges and overseeing maintenance. However, Britain did not exercise any political control until it intervened militarily in Egypt.

The canal proved to be of great importance for global trade. Britain especially benefited as 21 per cent of its exports and 16 per cent of its imports went through the canal. It was also important militarily for the British Empire. For example, in 1877–78, during the **Balkan crisis**, when war with Russia seemed imminent, Britain was able to transport a large detachment of Indian troops to Europe via the canal. Similarly, it made it much quicker to send British troops to India or Afghanistan.

KEY TERM

Balkan crisis (1875–78) When revolts against Ottoman rule occurred in Bosnia, Serbia, and Montenegro, Russia threatened to support the rebels and advanced to Constantinople (modern-day Istanbul). This worried Britain, which feared Russia gaining access to the Mediterranean. The crisis was resolved when German Chancellor Bismarck called the Berlin Congress.

Impact of colonialism on Africa

By 1914, Africa was heavily controlled by European powers and changed forever. Most of the continent was ruled from European capitals like London, Paris, and Berlin. Power was exercised by a colonial administration headed by a governor and backed up with military power.

KEY DEBATE

HOW WERE THE EUROPEAN POWERS ABLE TO DEVELOP COLONIES IN AFRICA?

There are a lot of reasons why European colonies were aggressively established in nineteenth-century Africa. These reasons are varied and attempts to explain how the European powers developed colonies are intensely debated by historians.

Some historians argue that European powers were able to dominate other continents because of geographical, environmental, and economic factors. Access to technologies such as gunpowder and mechanised weapons, together with advances in medical science, meant that European colonies could be successfully, if brutally, established. The transport revolution, which resulted in the building of steamships and railways, made commercial activity more effective and encouraged the European powers to extend their 'spheres of influence' as the profitability of their enterprises was proved. Some historians argue that the search for fuels and raw materials for industrial production – the drivers of capitalism and consumerism – was a key motivator.

Other historians focus on the ideological reasons for colonization. They argue that the technological advantages held by the European powers were limited. These historians see the desire to acquire colonies as being shaped by religious and cultural factors. Others dispute the idea of large forces of causation, arguing that individuals and explorers chose to set out to discover new lands as personal projects. These arguments reject the idea that nation states purposely set out to compete with each other in establishing colonies and see colonial expansion as an opportunistic development.

Imposition of arbitrary boundaries by colonizing powers

The European colonizers imposed arbitrary frontiers that did not reflect the natural geographical and cultural boundaries of Africa. To quote the journalist John Gunther in 1955, when most of Africa was still under European control: 'For the most part [the colonial frontiers] mark off where the rule of one white man stops and another begins.' However, different peoples and kingdoms did not correlate with these arbitrary boundaries. For example, the Masai lands were divided between the British East African and German East African territories. There was also the colony of Nigeria, which was formed in 1914 by the joining of two essentially incompatible states – northern and southern Nigeria.

Sir George Goldie, the founder of the RNC, admitted that the two states were 'as widely separated in laws, government, customs and general ideas about life, both in this world and the next, as England is from China' (Siollun, M., *What Britain Did to Nigeria*, p. 320).

Figure 1.2 Africa in 1914

ACTIVITY

Look at Figures 1.1 and 1.2 showing Africa in 1850 and 1914. Note down the key differences. Did anything remain the same? What can we learn from these maps about the colonization of Africa?

Human exploitation and abuse: the Belgian Congo

While atrocities were committed by all the colonial powers in the process of establishing their colonies, some of the most terrible occurred in the Congo Free State and were carried out by the International Association of the Congo, which brutally exploited the local population to harvest rubber and which crushed any resistance. The International Association of the Congo was an organization established by King Leopold II of Belgium in 1876. Supposedly created to promote humanitarian and scientific projects in Central Africa, in reality, it was used to further Leopold's ambitions to control the Congo region. At the trading stations, laborers who returned from the forest with less than their quota of rubber often had their hands or feet cut off. With the maltreatment amplified by the impact of disease and famine, more than a million Africans died due to the actions of the International Association of the Congo.

What was going on was exposed by the African-American lawyer **George Washington Williams**, by missionaries, and above all by the British reformer **Edmund Morel** and by **Sir Roger Casement**, the Irish-born British consul in the Congo Free State. Their reports led to the formation of the British Congo Reform Association, which persuaded the British government to put pressure on King Leopold II of Belgium, who was also facing growing criticism in the Belgian parliament from both conservatives and socialists. In 1908 he was at last forced to hand over administration of the colony to the Belgian government, and the Congo Free State was renamed the Belgian Congo.

Conversion to Christianity, healthcare, and education

Although Islam remained dominant in North Africa, Sudan, and northern Nigeria, the colonization of Africa led to the spread of Christianity as both Catholic and Protestant missionaries set up churches and converted many African people. The following factors helped the spread of Christianity in Africa:

- In areas where the colonial authorities had shown their power, conversion to Christianity was a way for Africans to show loyalty to the colonial regimes and therefore help to protect themselves.
- Christianity taught that all people were equal, which attracted many people, especially those who had been enslaved or who were social outcasts.
- Many missionaries, like Livingstone himself, had medical training, and their ability to treat disease was often seen as confirming the power of the Christian God.
- The missionaries also brought the chance of formal education – for some.

Missionaries had no reservations about equating Christianity with **Western civilization** and attempted to combat what they saw as pagan customs. For example, people in Africa were encouraged to dress like Europeans. Missionaries played a major role in informing European populations about Africa through newspaper articles, books and public lectures. The missionaries believed that through Christianity they were bringing 'civilization' to Africa. Some individual European missionaries exposed the brutality of colonial control and sought to assist local populations and highlight reforms needed to those back at home in Europe. However, the missionaries were also part of the colonial structure of political control, occupation, and exploitation, which included ideas of the supremacy of Western civilization.

Missionaries and education

Some historians have noted that promoting education and literacy was essential to converting locals to Christianity. Western education was seen as a valuable benefit and was sought after by local people. Schools were scattered unevenly over Africa. In 1913 there were 119,000 pupils in Nyasaland (now Malawi) and 83,000 in Uganda but only 2,200 in Kenya. Elsewhere, in French Madagascar there was compulsory education for all eight- to eleven-year-olds and in French West Africa some 10,000 children were being educated. By the early 1900s mission schools in British Africa were being given grants by the colonial governments. In French territories, the French government attempted to exclude the Church's influence from education, but in reality the colonial authorities could not manage without the active participation of missionaries. In Senegal, missionaries and priests became salaried employees of the state rather than ministers of the Catholic Church. In the Ivory Coast the French authorities had no option but to tolerate church schools if education were to be extended to Africans.

In Nigeria and elsewhere in Africa, one of the most complex challenges missionaries and European teachers faced was the huge number of languages they encountered. The missionaries responded by combining the numerous languages and dialects into 'standard' languages into which they translated the Bible. One important consequence of the spread of Christianity was that it produced a new educated African elite, which took the Church's message of equality seriously. It was a Baptist minister, **John Chilembwe**, who led an unsuccessful uprising against British rule in Nyasaland in 1915. Many leaders of the African independence movements in the 1960s had been educated in mission schools.

KEY FIGURES

George Washington Williams (1849–91) A soldier in the American Civil War and a Baptist minister. He wrote a highly critical open letter to King Leopold II about the Congo Free State, which received much attention.

Edmund Morel (1873–1924) A British journalist and politician of French extraction. He founded the British Congo Reform Association and was a pacifist in the First World War.

Sir Roger Casement (1864–1916) An Irish-born British diplomat who drew up a report on the Congo region. He became an Irish nationalist and sought German military support for the 1916 Easter Rising, for which he was executed.

KEY TERM

Western civilization A term used to describe the culture, organization and values of western European countries and the USA.

KEY FIGURE

John Chilembwe (1860–1915) An African Christian missionary in Nyasaland, who led an uprising against British rule in 1915 in protest against Africans being conscripted to fight in German East Africa. He was shot by the police.

Missionaries and healthcare

Missionaries did provide basic medical care for some Africans and brought to Africa the great advances in Western medicine. Livingstone himself believed that one of the most important characteristics of Western civilization was the ability 'to perform surgical operations without pain.' Missionaries set up hospitals and clinics that treated many people's wounds and illnesses. One missionary as early as 1860 was able to remove cataracts from patients' eyes.

KEY TERM

Tsetse fly A large insect that inhabits much of tropical Africa and lives by feeding off the blood of vertebrate animals and humans.

However, they and the colonial medical authorities were powerless to combat epidemics of sleeping sickness spread by the **tsetse fly**. In the first decade of the twentieth century, hundreds of thousands of Africans died of the disease. French and German missionaries developed a drug based on arsenic, which often proved fatal, while the British cordoned off affected groups using coercive tactics to force large numbers to leave their villages, which ultimately stemmed the epidemic. The development of mining in South Africa and Congo led to a sharp increase in tuberculosis rates, and large-scale plantation agriculture led to an increase in mosquito-borne and worm diseases. Again, a large number of Africans died from these diseases, as there was neither health insurance nor an effective medical infrastructure.

ACTIVITY

Find out more details about Christian missionaries from the different European powers. Which churches supported them and how were they funded? What similarities and differences are there between the methods and approaches of Christian missions from different countries and different Christian denominations (for example, Roman Catholic, Lutheran, Methodist)?

Infrastructure development

The creation of new European-dominated states in Africa made the building of roads and railways of vital importance for the colonizing powers. Steamships and the telegraph cable linked these new territories to the European capitals. The telegraph system could provide instant communication to some important administrative centers such as Lagos, Mombasa, and Alexandria. Steamships transported rubber from the regions near the Congo River and palm oil from West Africa to Europe and America, and returned laden with European armies, administrators, guns, and technical equipment. Inside Africa, transport was dependent initially on the rivers, some of which were suitable for steamboats, and on African bearers, but then increasingly on the railways. However, by 1914 large parts of Africa still remained without access to rail links. Colonial administrations were determined to pursue ambitious large-scale railway projects to facilitate communication and control. Cecil Rhodes, prime minister of Cape Colony, was hopeful of establishing a Cape to Cairo rail route to connect the entire continent.

The Sahara remained impenetrable except for trains of camels, but elsewhere bridges were built and tracks or roads upgraded not only for economic reasons but also to enable troops and officials to move around their territories more quickly. This infrastructure was built by forced labor. In British West Africa, for example, the governor of southern Nigeria encouraged his staff to conscript as much forced labor as they needed.

Causes and impact of African resistance

Local populations lacked the large amounts of weaponry needed to resist the modern European armies that sought to colonize their lands. Many Africans organized resistance to the colonizers and there were some significant defeats of European generals and their armies. However, in all cases except for Ethiopia, these represented only temporary setbacks for the European powers. The European forces waged battles that led to people being killed, displaced, or subjugated and their societies being broken up and replaced by systems imposed by the colonizers.

The Anglo-Zulu War, 1879

KEY FIGURE

Sekhukhune (c.1814–82) King of the Bapedi from 1861 until his assassination, believed to have been ordered by his half-brother, in 1882.

In South Africa King **Sekhukhune** of the Bapedi had been successful in blocking the expansion of the independent Boer republic of the Transvaal into his territories. He was aware of the importance of firepower and equipped some of his troops with modern rifles. In 1876 the Transvaal government faced economic collapse as it could not raise enough money to cover the cost of administering the state and equipping an army. There was, therefore, the possibility that Sekhukhune would exploit the crisis and occupy the Transvaal. To prevent what would be a major blow to European prestige, Britain, which controlled Cape Colony,

KEY FIGURE

Cetshwayo (c.1826–84) King of the Zulus from 1873 until his death in 1884.

KEY TERM

Impi A body of Zulu warriors.

KEY FIGURE

General Garnet Wolseley (1833–1913) An experienced general who fought in many campaigns. He served as governor of the Gold Coast (now Sierra Leone) in 1873–74 and was appointed commander of the British forces in the Anglo-Zulu War. In 1884 he led the unsuccessful Nile expedition to rescue General Gordon.

KEY FIGURE

Lobengula (1845–94) The last king of the Ndebele.

seized the chance to expand its territory and annexed the Transvaal in 1877. The chief obstacle to British supremacy in South Africa was now Zululand. The Zulu king, **Cetshwayo**, did not initially want to fight Britain, but during the winter of 1878–79 British forces gathered on the Transvaal–Zululand frontier and invaded in early January. Cetshwayo was able to assemble nearly 30,000 warriors, who ambushed a column of British troops at Isandlwana. Over one thousand imperial soldiers and approximately 2,000 Zulus were killed. One Zulu ***impi*** invaded Natal, but was defeated by British troops at Rorke's Drift. Revenge for Isandlwana was swift. A British force under **General Wolseley**, armed with artillery, defeated the Zulus at Ulundi. Cetshwayo himself was captured and deposed and Zululand annexed. Wolseley went on to defeat the Bapedi and secure the Transvaal.

The Ndebele Rebellion

Once a protectorate had been set up in Bechuanaland (now Botswana) by the British government, Cecil Rhodes was given permission by London in 1888 to form the British South Africa Company. Rhodes' ambition was now to dominate the Ndebele kingdom (a region in Zimbabwe also known as Matabeleland). Its king, **Lobengula**, was coerced into allowing white farmers to settle and prospect for gold, and in protest the Ndebele rose up in October 1893 in what became known as the First Matabele War. The Ndebele's aim was to expel or kill all the Europeans in their lands. However, the uprising had been put down by January 1894.

The First Matabele War was the prelude to a second, longer conflict, which broke out in March 1896. The Ndebele and the neighboring Shona united against the British South Africa Company. Rhodes personally led a group of irregular troops to lift the siege of Bulawayo, where over a thousand women and children had found refuge. He ruthlessly ordered that no mercy should be shown to the Ndebele and Shona. He told one officer to 'do the most harm you can to the natives around you' and ordered another to 'kill all you can' – even those who threw down their arms and begged for mercy. By October 1897, a combination of local settlers and British troops from Cape Town had suppressed the revolt, leaving Rhodes' company firmly in control.

SOURCE 1.5

A painting by Allan Stewart called *To the memory of brave men: The last stand of Major Allan Wilson at the Shangani, Rhodesia*. It depicts the Shangani Patrol, comprising 34 soldiers in the service of the British South Africa Company, which was ambushed by a large force of 3,000 Ndebele warriors in 1893, during the First Matabele War.

Compare and contrast sources 1.5 and 1.6, which depict and describe events in the First Matabele War. What similarities are there between the sources? What differences can you identify about tactics and weapons on both sides?

SOURCE 1.6

A quote from one of Lobengula's indunas (military leaders) describing the effect of the fire from the Maxim guns. Published in The Telegraph on January 1st 1894, and quoted in a 1895 pamphlet advertising the Maxim gun.

I led my men on, but saw them falling like cut corn. We then halted, knelt and fired, but still they fell. We lay down protected by our shields, but most of the remainder were killed, so I crawled away and fled.

CECIL RHODES

1853	Born
1871	Aged eighteen, began working in the diamond trade in Kimberley, Cape Colony
1888	Founded De Beers diamond company
1889	Founded British South Africa Company
1890	Oversaw the colonization of what became known as Rhodesia
1890	Became prime minister of Cape Colony
1896	Forced to resign as prime minister following the Jameson Raid
1902	Died

Cecil Rhodes is one of the most controversial figures of the era of European colonialism. Born in Hertfordshire, England, as the son of a vicar, he was sent to Cape Colony in South Africa at the age of 17. He became a diamond trader and in 1888 created the De Beers diamond company. Having been elected to sit in the Cape parliament as a member of the Liberal Party in 1881, he rose to become prime minister of Cape Colony nine years later.

In 1895 Rhodes encouraged the British government to annex Bechuanaland and then in 1896 he supported the disastrous Jameson Raid, which was an attempt to take over the independent Boer Republic of the Transvaal. This ended in failure and brought an end to his time as prime minister, but the British South Africa Company, which he had formed in 1889, was eventually successful in subordinating Matabeleland. Rhodes aimed to extend British power in South Africa and, ultimately, throughout as much of Africa as possible. He dreamed of constructing a railway from the Cape to Cairo that would never leave British territory. An 1893 cartoon in the magazine *Punch* portrayed him as a colossus astride the African continent.

Rhodes, like so many of his contemporaries, believed passionately in creating what amounted to an economically new Africa that would be powered by large-scale European immigration. He was a firm believer in the supremacy of the white man, and in particular the British, and was often seen as the inspirer of the later **apartheid** system.

KEY TERM

Apartheid The system of racial segregation and discrimination against non-white people in South Africa in the second half of the twentieth century.

The Battle of Adwa

This was the first decisive defeat of a European colonial power by an African state. Since unification in 1861, Italy had sought to establish a colonial empire in Africa. It first occupied the port of Massawa in Eritrea, hoping thereby to control Abyssinia's (Ethiopia's) trade with the outside world. The Abyssinians resented Italy's presence there and a series of clashes between Italian and Abyssinian forces took place. At Dongola, near Massawa, a battalion of about 500 Italian troops was massacred in January 1887. In 1889 after **Emperor Menelik II** ascended the Abyssinian throne, an Italo-Abyssinian treaty of friendship was negotiated, which Italy believed turned Abyssinia into an Italian **protectorate**. Meanwhile Italy continued to expand its coastal territories and annexed part of Somaliland in 1889 and Eritrea in 1890.

KEY FIGURE

Emperor Menelik II (1844–1913) Emperor of Abyssinia (Ethiopia) who did much to modernize Abyssinia and build up its armed forces.

KEY TERM

Protectorate A territory that is controlled and protected by another state without being a possession of that state.

In September 1890 Menelik rejected claims by Italy that it had established a protectorate over Abyssinia. France started building a railway from Addis Ababa to Djibouti in French Somaliland, threatening Italy's position by giving Abyssinia an independent port. Consequently, Italian troops advanced into Abyssinia in 1896 with the intention of turning it into a colony. The invasion united Abyssinia against the Italian invasion – the Ras or lords of Tigre, Gojam, Harar, and Wollo and their followers rallied to the side of the Emperor. The Abyssinian army was also well armed and on March 1, 1896 at Adwa decisively defeated the Italian forces, 5,000 of whom were killed and 2,000 taken prisoner. Italy was forced to make peace and end any claim to a protectorate over Abyssinia.

The Herero War

Rebellion against German colonial power took place in German South West Africa, where the Khoi, Nama and Herero people rose in revolt against German plans, which involved exploiting the labor of the local people. The Herero people rebelled in January 1904, launching a series of attacks on white settlers and their families. German retaliation was ruthless, but it was not until 1908 that German forces were able to re-establish complete control over the colony.

General von Trotha unleashed a campaign of terror; all male prisoners were executed. In total, between 60,000 and 70,000 people were killed and any men who survived, along with all women and children, were driven into the desert, where many either starved or fell prey to wild animals. Those who survived were rounded up and interned in a camp on Shark Island, where they were subject to maltreatment and forced labor. The death rate was calculated at 200 people a month. Initially, von Trotha's firmness was praised in Germany, but as the details of his brutality emerged he was criticized in the German parliament and relieved of his command after two months.

In 1985 the United Nations classified the 1904–08 slaughter in German South West Africa as **genocide**, which the German government accepted in 2015.

KEY TERM

Genocide The deliberate killing of a large number of people from a national, ethnic or religious group with the aim of destroying that group in whole or in part.

KEY FIGURE

General Lothar von Trotha (1848–1920) A German military commander who, having been involved in defeating the Boxer revolt in China (1899–1901), was appointed commander-in-chief of troops in German South West Africa in 1904.

Why was imperialism a significant force in Africa from 1870?

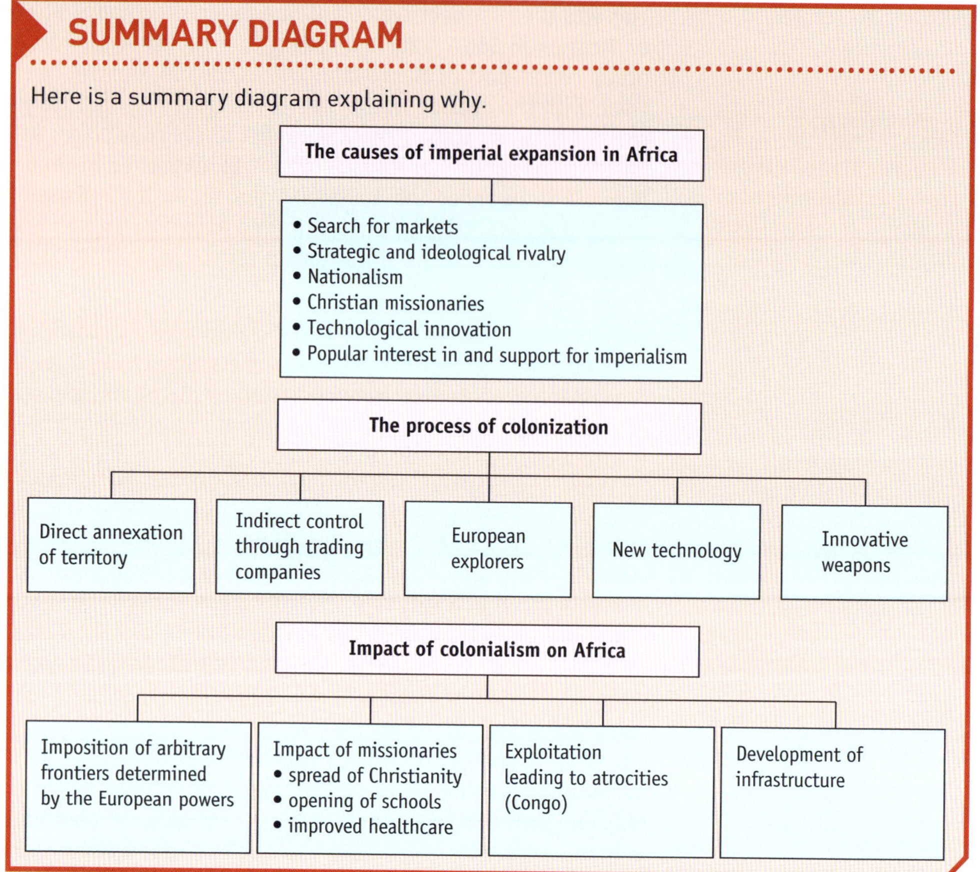

What was the impact of imperial expansion on international relations?

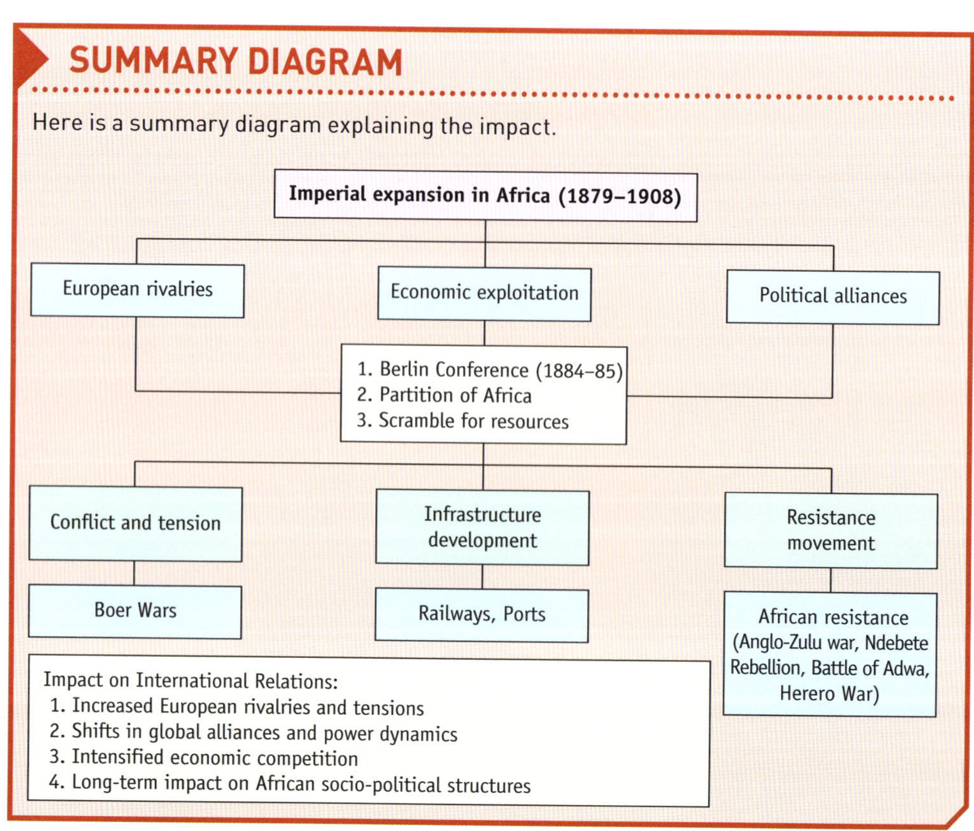

2 What was the impact of imperial expansion on international relations?

The previous section looked at the consequences of European colonization for African peoples. This section examines how the expansion of the major European powers in Africa affected international relations by looking at:

- the Berlin Conference and its outcome
- the rivalry between the colonial powers in Africa
- the various attempts to resolve imperial tensions between the imperial nations after 1900
- the situation in 1914.

The Berlin Conference, 1884–85

The immediate reason for holding the Berlin Conference was to regulate the complex international situation in the Congo basin. As we have seen, in September 1876 King Leopold II of Belgium set up the International African Association (IAA) and, in the face of French opposition, was secretly plotting to secure as much of the Congo basin as he could. France's position in Africa was further threatened by its quarrel with Britain over Egypt. Britain had occupied Egypt in 1882. This angered France, leading them to try to block British ambitions in Egypt and West Africa. Two years later, Britain, alarmed by the prospect of a French advance into the Congo, signed a treaty with Portugal that acknowledged Portugal's claims to the lower Congo while allowing Britain to trade freely there and to have a monopoly of navigation rights on the Congo River. The British government hoped this would provide an effective barrier to any French expansion in the region. France and Belgium both suspected that Britain was using the Anglo-Portuguese Treaty to gain more influence. In response, France asked German Chancellor Otto von Bismarck to pressure Portugal to abandon the treaty.

EXTENSION

The Anglo-French quarrel over Egypt

Egypt was a prosperous self-governing territory within the Ottoman Empire. Cairo was thriving and was linked to Egypt's main cities by a rail network and telegraph system. Egypt's ruler, the Khedive, had his own imperial aims as he wanted to consolidate Egypt's power in Sudan.

Egypt's prosperity relied on foreign loans, but by April 1876 Egypt went bankrupt and could no longer pay the interest on the sums lent by European investors. In exchange for further loans, Britain and France (the majority shareholders in the Suez Canal Company) took joint financial control of the Suez Canal. In 1879, Egypt's finances again deteriorated. Under pressure from other European states, who wished to protect their banks' investments in Egypt, Britain and France were persuaded to set up an Anglo-French commission to run Egypt's finances so that the investors in Europe would get their money back. The Ottoman Empire, the ultimate ruler of Egypt, deposed the Khedive, who was replaced by his son.

In 1882 France and Britain were challenged by a nationalist uprising led by officers in the Egyptian army. As the French parliament vetoed the dispatch of French troops, it was left to Britain to defeat the uprising in the Battle of Tel el Kebir. Britain took control of Egypt and, despite promising to withdraw their troops once order was restored, they did not leave.

OTTO VON BISMARCK

1815	Born
1848	Supported Prussian monarchy during revolts
1851	Appointed Prussian ambassador to the German Confederation in Frankfurt
1862	Became prime minister of Prussia
1866	Established North German Confederation after Austria's defeat
1871	Became chancellor of the newly formed German Reich
1890	Forced to resign as chancellor by the Kaiser (emperor of Germany)
1898	Died

Otto von Bismarck was born into an old, well-established family in Prussia. He entered politics in 1847 and made a reputation for himself as a **counter-revolutionary** when he supported the Prussian king during the revolutionary turmoil of the years 1848–49. As a reward, he was appointed Prussian ambassador to the **German Confederation** in 1851. In this role, he was critical of Austria's attempt to dominate the confederation and at every opportunity urged Prussia to seize the leadership of Germany. He became prime minister of Prussia in 1862 and, after defeating both Austria and France, created the German **Reich** in 1871. Up to 1871 he had been intent on challenging the existing order, but once Germany was unified he was anxious to avoid any further changes that might destroy what he had created.

KEY TERMS

Counter-revolutionary A person who opposes a revolution and wants to reverse its results.

German Confederation A loose grouping of the German states, including Austria, set up in 1815 and dissolved in 1866.

Reich The German Empire, formed in 1871 when the southern German states (not including Austria and Liechtenstein) formed a union with the North German Confederation.

KEY FIGURE

Benjamin Disraeli (1804–81) The Conservative prime minister of Britain in 1868 and 1874–80. He was an ardent imperialist who believed that patriotism and nationalism could overcome class divisions.

KEY TERMS

Social imperialism A policy aimed at uniting all social classes behind plans for creating and expanding an empire.

Pressures on Bismarck

Bismarck was under growing pressure from German imperialists, who wanted to see a German colonial empire in Africa. In 1884–85 he surprised both his own ministers and the other imperial powers by annexing territory in south-west Africa, Cameroon and East Africa (see map, page 10). What persuaded Bismarck so suddenly to create a German empire in Africa?

- German public opinion, influenced by the newly founded German Colonial Union and newspapers, was convinced that Africa was a potential source of enormous wealth.
- North German traders in Hamburg and Bremen, fearing exclusion from African markets, urged Bismarck to recognize Franz Lüderitz's acquisition of a trading post on the south-west African coast at Angra Pequeña.
- Bismarck, like **Disraeli**, the British prime minister, grasped how imperialism could unite people and discourage criticism of the government. Historians call this '**social imperialism**.'

However, Bismarck's main motive was to place himself in a position where he could co-operate with France against Britain in order to distract France from its intention of avenging its defeat by Germany in 1870–71, when France lost the provinces of Alsace and Lorraine. Primarily, he viewed Africa as an area where he could play France off against Britain. The Anglo-French quarrel, which was triggered by the British occupation of Egypt in 1882 and subtly exploited by the German chancellor, accelerated the partition of Africa. In Europe, besides facing threats from France, Bismarck's newly created German Reich also encountered increasing hostility from Russia, which was suspicious of Germany's alliance with Austria–Hungary. Bismarck therefore seized on every opportunity to support French ambitions in Africa that would provoke a clash with Britain and thereby distract France from European issues. Consequently, he refused to recognize the validity of the 1884 Anglo-Portuguese Treaty. Co-operating with France, and overriding British objections, he called an international conference in Berlin of 15 countries, including the USA and the Ottoman Empire, to decide on the future of the Congo basin.

How does source 1.7 explain Bismarck's views about establishing a German colonial empire in Africa and calling the Berlin Conference?

SOURCE 1.7

Bismarck rejects the German acquisition of colonies. Extract from the memoirs of Prince Hohenlohe, the former German ambassador in Paris (from Medlicott, W. and Coveney, D., *Bismarck and Europe*, London: Arnold, 1971, pp. 137–8).

In the evening [of February 22, 1880] I had dinner with Bismarck ... At table we drank much port and wine. Afterwards I sat with the Chancellor and spoke of many things. The Chancellor refuses all talk of colonies. He says that we haven't an adequate fleet to protect them and our bureaucracy [civil service] is not skilful enough to direct the government of such territories. The Chancellor also alluded to my report on the French plans for Morocco, and thought we could only rejoice if France annexed it. She would then be very occupied, and we could let her expand into Africa as compensation for Alsace–Lorraine ...

Intentions of the different powers at the Berlin Conference

KEY TERM

International Congo Society An organization established by King Leopold II of Belgium to further his colonial interests in the Congo.

In November 1884, 12 powers and representatives of the **International Congo Society** (ICS) attended the conference, including Russia, Austria–Hungary, Sweden–Norway, and Denmark, all of which had no colonies in Africa. The powers with the most interest in the conference were Portugal, Britain, France, and Germany, and of course the ICS. The aims of the key powers mentioned above were:

- Britain wanted to loosen French control of the lower Niger River.
- France sought to block further British ambitions in West Africa.
- Portugal hoped to annex territory lying between Angola and Mozambique.
- Bismarck was primarily aiming to widen Anglo-French differences, although he also put forward Germany's colonial claims in western and eastern Africa.

Outcomes of the Berlin Conference

KEY TERM

Free trade zone An area where countries can trade without restrictions.

The conference recognized King Leopold's claim to the Congo region and decided that the area would be administered by the ICS and that direct Portuguese control would be limited to Angola. It also agreed on a treaty that laid down some important ground rules for a huge belt of central African territory stretching from the Atlantic to the Indian Ocean:

- The entire area was to be a **free trade zone** and traders from all states were to have free access to the rivers and ports of this region.
- Religious missions and scientific research were to be protected.
- The slave trade was to be banned by the participating members throughout their colonies and spheres of influence.
- The powers committed – in the words of the treaty – to 'bringing home the blessings of civilisation.'
- The principle of 'effective occupation' was established, setting rules to define and notify other powers when an area was invaded, initially applying only to coastal regions.

How did the principle of 'effective occupation' affect the colonization process as described in Sources 1.8 and 1.9? Write an explanation, using details from the sources. Consider increased organization, competition for land, and impact on the local people.

SOURCE 1.8

Article 34 of the Berlin Conference's final 'General Act'.

Any power which henceforth takes possession of a tract of land on the coasts of the African Continent outside of its present possessions, or which being hitherto without such possessions, shall acquire them and assume a protectorate ... shall accompany either act with a notification thereof, addressed to the other Signatory Powers of the present act, in order to enable them to protest against the same if there exists any grounds for their doing so.

SOURCE 1.9

From a speech by Lord Rosebery, Liberal prime minister of Britain, 1894–95, to the Royal Colonial Institute in March 1893.

It is said that our Empire is already large enough and does not need extension. That would be true enough if the world were elastic but unfortunately it is not elastic and we are engaged at the present moment, in the language of mining, in 'pegging out claims for the future'. We have to consider not what we want now, but what we shall want in the future. We have to consider what countries must be developed either by ourselves or by some other nation, and we shall have to remember that it is part of our responsibility and heritage to take care that the world, so far as it can be moulded by us, shall receive an English-speaking complexion and not that of other nations.

Study sources 1.8 and 1.9. Consider the **provenance** of the sources. Using what you know about the context, decide which source is more important in explaining the 'Scramble for Africa.'

KEY TERM

Provenance The origin or source of a document or artifact. It is important to know a source's provenance so you can assess its authenticity and reliability by considering factors such as who created it, when and where it was created, and why it was created. Identifying and evaluating the provenance of a source will help you assess the value of the source in understanding historical events, by assessing its useful qualities and its limitations.

The general consequence of the Berlin Conference was to speed up the colonization of Africa. The rule that was drawn up for defining how the imperial powers could legitimately claim African territory 'on the coasts' of the continent did not lead to an amicable partition of the rest of Africa. On the contrary, over the next 13 years there was intense rivalry between the colonizing powers. As one French minister put it, the 'scramble' became a 'chase.' Competition for territory, influence and trading rights focused on Sudan, East Africa, and the inland territory of west Africa. This also included the ambitious plans of Cecil Rhodes, the prime minister of the British Cape Colony (see page 14) to create a vast area of British territory between the Transvaal and what later became known as Rhodesia.

ACTIVITY

Write a list of outcomes of the Berlin Conference. Create criteria to make a judgment about how important the consequences of these decisions were. What principles and agreements were established and who gained from them?

Use the impact of events over time in your judgment. You could consider:

- profundity: how deeply people's lives were affected
- extent: how many lives were affected
- durability: for how long people's lives were affected.

Consider political, social, and economic impacts, and which powers and territories were involved.

Rivalries between colonial powers

During the two decades after the Berlin Conference, rivalry between the great powers in Africa intensified, as can be seen by looking at:

- Anglo-German rivalry
- Anglo-French rivalry, particularly in Sudan, which nearly led to war between the two powers
- the Franco-German crises in Morocco, which could have escalated into a major European war.

KEY FIGURES

General Leo von Caprivi (1831–99) A German general and the second chancellor of the Reich, 1890–94.

Lord Salisbury (1830–1903) A Conservative prime minister of Britain who served three separate terms: 1885–January 1886, July 1886–92 and 1895–1902.

KEY TERM

Alliance system A mutual agreement between two or more countries. This might involve members of the alliance agreeing to come to each other's defense in the event of an attack by a non-member.

Rivalry between Britain and Germany

When Bismarck resigned in 1890, his successor, **General von Caprivi**, at first decided to work on a new **alliance system**, or 'New Course,' that would bring Britain into its existing Triple Alliance with Italy and Austria, and so hold in check both Russia and France. In an attempt to achieve this, Caprivi was ready to settle any outstanding colonial disagreements in East Africa, where there was intense rivalry between the German East Africa Company and the Imperial British East Africa Company. However, the problem for Caprivi was that, while the British government was ready to settle colonial disputes with Germany (as eventually it also did with France and Russia; see page 27), it was not prepared to negotiate binding alliances. Berlin refused to acknowledge this and remained convinced that sooner or later French and Russian pressure on Britain's large and vulnerable empire would end in war and would force Britain to turn to Germany for help.

Consequently, in a series of colonial disputes involving the boundaries of Sudan and more importantly the Transvaal in South Africa (see page 22), Caprivi took a strongly anti-British position in the hope that Britain would draw the conclusion that it was better to have Germany as a friend than an enemy. Ultimately, however, this was wishful thinking, as Britain was determined not to join the Triple Alliance, a stance made clear in the observation of **Lord Salisbury**, the British prime minister, that 'the liability of having to defend the German and Austrian frontiers against Russia is greater than that of having to defend the British Isles against France.'

KAISER WILHELM II

1859	Born
1888	Ascended the throne
1890	Forced Bismarck to resign as chancellor
1896	Dispatched the 'Kruger telegram' giving support to the Boers against the British
1897	Supported the construction of a large German navy
1900	Gave personal support to the campaign to crush the Boxer revolt
1905	Made a controversial visit to Tangier in Morocco
1914–18	Played a minor role in the conduct of the First World War
1918	Abdicated two days before the Armistice and went into exile
1940	Congratulated Hitler on the defeat of France
1940	Declined Winston Churchill's offer of asylum in Britain
1941	Died in exile in the Netherlands

Kaiser Wilhelm II ascended the throne in 1888, after the premature death of his father, and almost immediately removed Bismarck. He attempted to gain greater control over the German government, with only partial success, and was an enthusiastic supporter of German imperialism and the German navy. He soon made a name for himself through his rash statements and '**sabre rattling**.' In 1905, for example, he visited Tangier and challenged French claims to Morocco. After Germany's defeat in the First World War, he was forced to abdicate (give up his position of power) in November 1918, and lived for the rest of his life in the Netherlands.

KEY TERM

Sabre rattling Inflammatory statements threatening military action.

Weltpolitik and naval rivalry

After the crisis with Britain over the Transvaal in 1896, the German government drew two conclusions:

- Imperialism and ***Weltpolitik*** were popular with much of the German public and were therefore a way of winning support for the government.
- To gain a substantial empire, Germany would have to build a fleet of warships to challenge the supremacy of the British navy. This decision was to bring about a decisive worsening of Anglo-German relations.

Until the fleet was built, German colonial policy could only be opportunistic. Some historians suggest that German diplomats were stationed near potential trouble spots in order to try to win territory if disputes broke out. This tactic alienated the other powers very quickly. The two Moroccan crises of 1905–06 and 1911 were to illustrate this (see pages 25 and 27).

KEY TERM

Weltpolitik Literally 'world policy', a political strategy designed to turn Germany into a global power.

Consider the content of Source 1.10 and its information about German naval ambition. Then, research Kaiser Wilhelm's appointment of a new Secretary of the Navy in 1897. What can you infer about Kaiser Wilhelm's intentions for the German navy?

SOURCE 1.10

A chart drawn in 1897 by Kaiser Wilhelm II. He heads the chart with 'Germany's new ships [planned and approved since 1893]'. Below, in the right-hand corner, he notes how many ships France (Frankreich) and Russia (Russland) had built during the same period.

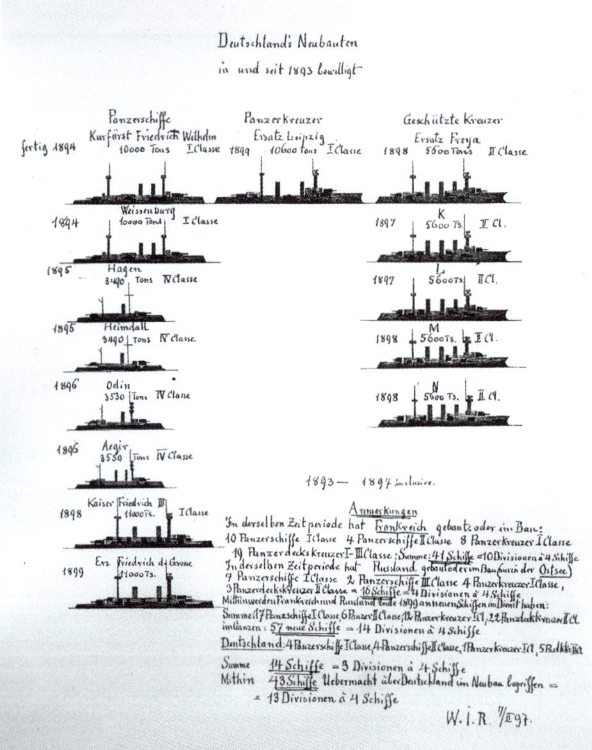

Tension between Britain and Germany over South Africa

South Africa was seen by Britain as vital for the security of its empire, as it lay on the route to India before the Suez Canal was opened in 1869. Initially, the main challenge to British power in South Africa came from the **Boers**. They resented Britain's annexation of Cape Colony from the Dutch in 1814. To escape British control, a large number of Boers migrated between 1836 and 1840 in what was called the 'Great Trek' to found new settlements, which later became the Orange Free State and the Transvaal (see map, page 10). In 1877 both states, which were being threatened by the Zulus, agreed to annexation by Britain. However, once the Zulus were defeated at the Battle of Ulundi in 1879, the Boers began to agitate for independence. This led in 1880 to the First Boer War. The British prime minister, **William Gladstone**, sympathized with the Boers' demands and in the Convention of Pretoria, August 1881, recognized their freedom to run their own affairs, although the British government was still theoretically responsible for their foreign policy.

KEY TERM

Boers Descendants of Dutch settlers who had originally colonized South Africa.

KEY FIGURE

William Gladstone (1809–98) British Liberal politician, who served four separate terms as prime minister between 1868 and 1894.

Germany and the Transvaal

With the German annexation of territory in south-west Africa in 1884, Britain faced the threat of Germany trying to extend its power eastwards to the borders of the Transvaal by annexing the African kingdoms of Bechuanaland and Matabeleland. Cecil Rhodes put pressure on the British government to allow him to take steps against this threat. In 1889 the British government permitted Rhodes' British South Africa Company to colonize and govern the whole area north of the Transvaal and between Mozambique, German South West Africa, and Angola. This region was duly named Rhodesia in May 1895.

The discovery of gold in the Transvaal

The economic significance of the Transvaal was increased by the discovery of gold there in 1886. Over the next five years, large numbers of British prospectors and adventurers poured in. Inevitably, this posed a challenge to the supremacy of the Boer population, and **Paul Kruger**, the president of the Transvaal, began to look to Germany to prevent the absorption of the Transvaal into the British Empire. By 1894 the economy of the Transvaal was dominated by Germany. German bankers controlled the Transvaal's National Bank and some 20 per cent of foreign investment in the state came from Germany.

KEY FIGURE

Paul Kruger (1825–1904) President of the Transvaal, 1883–1900.

The Jameson Raid and the German response

In late 1895 Cecil Rhodes launched a badly planned and unsuccessful attempt to overthrow the Boer government in the Transvaal, the **Jameson Raid**. Germany had to take action in the face of Rhodes' aggression. At first, the Kaiser wanted to declare the Transvaal a German protectorate, send military aid to Kruger, and summon another congress in Berlin to redraw the map of South Africa. However, he was persuaded by his diplomats to send a telegram to Kruger congratulating him on preserving the independence of his country against attack. This caused intense resentment in Britain. Windows belonging to German-owned shops were smashed in British towns and cities and for the first time popular anti-German feeling became widespread and intense. Many British people felt that Germany was interfering in the affairs of the British Empire.

KEY TERM

Jameson Raid An armed intervention in the Transvaal led by Leander Starr Jameson, a British politician in Cape Colony, over the New Year weekend of 1895–96.

Reread Source 1.9 (page 20) and study Source 1.11. What can you infer from Source 1.11 about the potential consequences of expansionist policies as outlined by Lord Rosebery in Source 1.9?

SOURCE 1.11

The Kruger telegram, which was drafted for the Kaiser by the German Foreign Office in early January 1896.

I wish to express my sincere congratulations that you and your people, without asking the help of friendly powers, have succeeded in restoring peace through your own actions against the armed bands which invaded your country as disturbers of the peace, and in preserving the independence of your own country against attack from without.

The Second Boer War and Germany's reluctance to intervene

Four years later, Kruger, who had rebuilt the Boer army and equipped it with modern German artillery, declared war on Britain, believing that France, Germany, and Russia would intervene and force Britain to make concessions. Historians have described this as a great opportunity for the continental European powers to exploit British difficulties in the area. Public opinion in France, Russia, and Germany was decidedly pro-Boer, and the French foreign minister, **Théophile Delcassé**, attempted to co-ordinate a joint intervention by these three powers. Ultimately, he was not successful as neither France nor Russia was ready to intervene against Britain unless they had German backing, but Germany would intervene only if all three powers mutually guaranteed the frontiers of each other's states. France was unwilling to agree to this as it refused to recognize the German annexation of Alsace–Lorraine, and Russia was too distracted by developments in the Far East (see page 44) to undertake fresh commitments in Europe. Britain was therefore able to defeat the Boers in a long-drawn-out war, which ended in 1902.

KEY FIGURE

Théophile Delcassé (1852–1923) French foreign minister, 1898–1905. He was forced to resign by Germany in 1905, but returned to office in 1911 as naval minister and was foreign minister again from 1914 to 1915.

Rivalry between France and Britain over Sudan

Thanks to its control of Egypt, Britain was also responsible for Egyptian possessions in Sudan. In the early 1880s a **Wahhabist** revolution had taken place in Sudan, and the leader of the uprising, the **Mahdi**, was determined to drive the British out. In this he was largely successful. He killed 10,000 Egyptian soldiers led by a British commander at the Battle of Obeid in 1883, and the next year defeated another Anglo-Egyptian force under **General Gordon**, sent to relieve Khartoum. The consequence of this was that a **power vacuum** was created, which the Mahdi, Abyssinia, France, and Italy all competed to fill. In 1896, when Italy was defeated in its attempt to conquer Abyssinia at Adwa, the Mahdi immediately attempted to exploit the situation by attacking the small Italian colony of Kasala. In response to appeals for help, Britain moved troops from Egypt some 200 miles (320 km) up the Nile to threaten the Mahdi's troops in Dongola, the capital of northern Sudan.

KEY FIGURE

General Charles George Gordon (1833–85) British general and governor general of Sudan.

KEY TERMS

Wahhabist Referring to a fundamentalist Islamic reform movement founded by Muhammad ibn Abd al-Wahhab (1703–92).

Mahdi A religious title meaning 'the redeemer of Islam'. The leader of the Wahhabist uprising, Sudanese sheikh Muhammad Ahmad (1843–85), was one of numerous Islamic leaders from the eighth century onwards to claim to be the Mahdi.

Power vacuum A situation in which a territory is left ungoverned after the withdrawal or collapse of the original ruling power.

The Fashoda incident

The French government saw this as the first step in the British reconquest of Sudan and ordered a small military expedition under **Colonel Marchand** to proceed from the French Congo to the Upper Nile. The French government was convinced that occupation of the Upper Nile would enable it to build a huge dam in the swamps. This would control Egypt's essential water supplies, giving them the power to impact Egyptians' lives and the country's economy. In response, Lord Salisbury ordered **General Kitchener**, the commander-in-chief of the Egyptian forces, to reconquer Sudan. Kitchener destroyed the Mahdi's forces at Omdurman in September 1898. However, Marchand had already reached the Upper Nile and hoisted the French flag at Fashoda.

KEY FIGURES

Colonel, Jean-Baptiste Marchand (1863–1934) An officer in the French West African Colonial Infantry, he was a colonel in 1898, was appointed as a general in 1915, and fought in the First World War.

General, Lord Kitchener (1850–1916) As a British army general he defeated the Mahdi in Sudan and played a key role in the Boer War. He then became a politician and was British Secretary of State for War in 1914–16.

Kitchener immediately sent five gunboats down the Nile to challenge him. An armed clash that could have led to war was avoided when he decided not to use force to eject the French troops. Instead, it was left to the two governments to find a diplomatic solution. France, lacking any support from the other powers, had little option but to concede totally to British demands in Sudan.

Arguably, the Fashoda incident was the most serious crisis in Anglo-French relations since the **Battle of Waterloo**, but surprisingly it led to an improvement in Anglo-French relations since influential voices in Paris began to argue that France should forget about Egypt and persuade Britain to support a French annexation of Morocco.

KEY TERM

Battle of Waterloo An 1815 battle in Belgium in which Britain defeated France.

Rivalry between France and Germany over Morocco

France had two 'enemies.' In Europe their main rival was Germany; elsewhere in the world it was the British Empire. In the 'Scramble for Africa' and in the attempts to gain influence and territory in Burma, Siam, and the Pacific islands, there was intense Anglo-French rivalry.

At Fashoda, the two countries came near to war. Yet the realization that France was powerless to challenge Britain's position in Egypt and Sudan persuaded Delcassé, the French foreign minister, to negotiate a far-reaching **entente** with Britain in 1904, the so-called Entente Cordiale. The essence of this agreement was that France would recognize Britain's position in Egypt if, in return, Britain would not object to France maintaining law and order in Morocco and at some future date establishing a protectorate there. The Entente Cordiale was not an alliance, but forceful German intervention in the Moroccan question was to drive Britain and France closer together.

KEY TERM

Entente A friendly understanding between states rather than a formal alliance.

The Moroccan crisis of 1905

KEY FIGURE

Moulay Abd al-Aziz bin Hassan (1881–1943) The sultan of Morocco from 1894 until he was deposed by revolution in 1908.

France lost no time in tightening its grip on Morocco. In November 1905 the French representative in Fez, the Moroccan capital at the time, imposed on the sultan of Morocco, **Abd al-Aziz**, a program of 'reforms' that he should make to the Moroccan banks, police, and army. Two months later a large French mission arrived to oversee the changes, part of which involved installing French officials in all the key roles within these organizations. This made it clear that France was planning to establish a protectorate in Morocco.

The Sultan appealed to Germany for support. The German government had a strong case to intervene, as together with Britain, France, Italy, and Spain, it had signed the Treaty of Madrid, which guaranteed Moroccan independence. Delcassé had secured the agreement of France, Spain, and Italy to increase its influence in Morocco but had ignored Germany. Not only was this a blow to German prestige, but also the German government had been alarmed by the Anglo-French entente, which they feared was the first step towards an Anglo-French alliance directed at Germany. Consequently, the German government decided to intervene in a most dramatic way, hoping that it would humiliate France and irreparably weaken the entente. In March 1905 the Kaiser interrupted his Mediterranean cruise to land at Tangier. By greeting the sultan of Morocco pointedly as an independent ruler, he indicated that Germany did not accept France's position in Morocco. Germany then called for the resignation of Delcassé, to which the French prime minister, Maurice Rouvier, agreed on the grounds that Delcassé had seriously miscalculated in not consulting Germany about France's plans in Morocco. Germany also demanded a conference, which was to meet at Algeciras in January 1906.

How great was the risk of war between France and Germany?

KEY FIGURE

Friedrich von Holstein (1837–1909) Head of the political department of the German Foreign Office.

The Moroccan crisis of 1905 was serious and many historians have seen it as a key turning point in European history. For the first time since 1870, a Franco-German war seemed a real possibility. The German army was ready for war and had begun to develop the **Schlieffen Plan**, which was a strategy for waging a European war on two fronts. **Friedrich von Holstein**, the most influential adviser to the German Foreign Office, was prepared to risk war as the European situation in 1905 was favorable to Germany:

- Russia had been defeated in the Far East by Japan and was paralyzed by revolution at home. Consequently, Russia would be unable to help France against Germany.
- Britain was not ready for a war as its army was still recovering from the conflict against the Boers in South Africa and it was unwilling to commit itself to a conflict on the continent of Europe.

KEY TERM

Schlieffen Plan The German military strategist Alfred von Schlieffen envisaged that any war in Europe would be fought on two fronts, against France and Russia. He therefore created a plan for a swift attack through Belgium to defeat France in one month, allowing Germany's army to then focus on attacking Russia.

KEY FIGURES

J. A. Hobson (1858–1940) An English socialist, economist, and journalist.

Vladimir Lenin (1870–1924) The leader of the Russian Bolshevik Party from 1903. In 1917 the Bolsheviks seized power but were then faced with a bitter civil war, which they won under Lenin's leadership.

KEY DEBATE

WHAT CAUSED THE 'SCRAMBLE FOR AFRICA'?

The explanations for the 'Scramble for Africa' have been the subject of continuous disagreement and debate by historians and economists almost from the time that it occurred.

Until the early 1950s the view put forward by liberal and socialist thinkers was that it was mainly economic factors that triggered the scramble. They were convinced that the imperialist powers were driven into annexing African territory in order to secure guaranteed export markets. The most influential of these writers was **J. A. Hobson**, whose arguments influenced not only **Lenin** and the political left, but also a much wider group of historians and economists.

Other historians developed arguments based on political events and context, arguing that the scramble at the end of the nineteenth century was primarily caused by the dual crises in Egypt and South Africa. The Egyptian nationalist uprising of 1882 and the growing hostility of the Boer republics in South Africa threatened British power in territories that guarded two of the most sensitive points – the Suez Canal and the Cape of Good Hope – on the route between Britain and British India. This argument refuted the notion that the scramble was caused by economic and political factors originating in Europe. Instead, the catalyst for the scramble originated in Africa itself.

This argument that the 'Scramble for Africa' was essentially a consequence of the problems in Egypt and South Africa has met with much criticism. More recently, historians have argued that:

- it was French policies rather than British that lay behind the scramble
- economic pressures were an important factor
- individuals such as Cecil Rhodes, Carl Peters, and King Leopold of Belgium played key roles in triggering the scramble.

ACTIVITY

Create a table like the one below. Look back over this section to fill in as many factors as you can to explain the most important causes of the 'Scramble for Africa'.

Possible cause	How it contributed	Evidence for and against

When you have completed the table, decide what is the most significant reason or combination of reasons and attempt some synthesis. This means bringing together different elements in an analysis. Reflect on these conclusions: are the reasons different depending on the perspective of each of the European powers?

Attempts to resolve tensions between the imperial nations after 1900

Great power rivalry in Africa, the Far East, Europe, and the eastern Mediterranean led to a dangerous increase in tension that might have escalated into a global war. Attempts to resolve these tensions took several forms. Until the formation of the League of Nations in 1920, there was no effective international organization that could solve disputes between the imperial nations, as they were fully sovereign and not bound by any higher authority. Nevertheless, there were often successful efforts to reduce and resolve tensions arising from colonial rivalries, as the Anglo-French entente of 1904 and the Berlin Conference of 1884–85 showed, but these were limited in their scope and ultimately could not guarantee international peace.

The end of Britain's 'splendid isolation'

By the early 1900s, the British Empire was under significant pressure. It took nearly three years to defeat the Boer republics, making it unpopular with continental powers who sympathized with the Boers. Its naval dominance was challenged by the German navy's

KEY TERM

Splendid isolation A term used to describe the determination of British governments from 1815 to 1902 to avoid forming permanent alliances.

construction, and in the Far East, it faced opposition from Russia, France, and Germany in trying to keep Chinese markets open. '**Splendid isolation**' was no longer a viable policy. In 1902 Britain negotiated an alliance with Japan, which covered its interests in the Far East. Britain did not want a formal alliance in Europe, but an entente with France as a reassurance against pressure from Germany was a strategic aim at this stage in British diplomacy.

The Anglo-French entente

The first step in improving relations between France and Britain was the visit by King Edward VII to Paris in May 1903 and the return visit by the French president in July. The British attitude was summed up by Edward's famous statement, 'Providence [luck] has made us neighbours, let us make sure we are friends.' Discussion covering all areas of disagreement between the two countries began in July, and, after detailed and lengthy negotiations, what became known as the Entente Cordiale was signed on April 8, 1904. This agreement settled Anglo-French colonial problems in three main areas:

- France exchanged fishing rights around Newfoundland for territorial compensation in West Africa.
- Siam (present-day Thailand) was divided into two zones of influence and a condominium was set up in the New Hebrides (now Vanuatu).
- France agreed not to block British plans for financial reform in Egypt, provided Britain recognized France's right to maintain law and order in Morocco and to control the country's finances. Secret clauses then made provision for the establishment of a French protectorate over Morocco and a British protectorate over Egypt.

France was increasingly anxious to get the Anglo-French agreement signed as war had broken out between Russia and Japan in 1905. As France was an ally of Russia, and as Britain had concluded a defensive agreement with Japan in 1902, there was a danger that both countries could become involved in the war in the Far East. In August 1907 after Russia's defeat by Japan, the Russian government was ready to sign an agreement with Britain. This entente covered Afghanistan, Tibet, and Persia (Iran). The agreement was welcomed by the French government, who hoped that it would lead to a triple alliance between France, Britain, and Russia.

KEY FIGURE

David Lloyd George (1863–1945) British Liberal politician who was Chancellor of the Exchequer (1908–15), Minister of Munitions (1915–16), Secretary of State for War (1916) and prime minister (1916–22).

The Algeciras Conference

As a concession to forceful German protests about the French handling of the Moroccan crisis of 1905, Delcassé resigned and France agreed to a conference. When the conference opened at Algeciras in southern Spain in January 1906, the majority of states, including the USA, agreed that France had a special economic and security interest in Morocco. Together with Spain, France was therefore entrusted with the supervision of the Moroccan police and the country's finances, although Germany did win the concession that all the powers should enjoy equal economic rights within Morocco.

Read Source 1.12. What is the message of the source? What additional knowledge could you use to consider whether Lord Rosebery's view of the Entente Cordiale was justified?

SOURCE 1.12

Lloyd George recalls in his memoirs that he went to visit the Liberal elder statesman Lord Rosebery on the day the Entente Cordiale was announced:

His first greeting to me was: 'Well, I suppose you are just as pleased as the rest of them with this French agreement?' I assured him that I was delighted that our snarling and scratching relations with France had come to an end at last. He replied: 'You are all wrong. It means war with Germany in the end!'

The Agadir crisis

In May 1911 Germany made a second attempt to assert its influence in Morocco when it became clear that France, contrary to the Algeciras agreement of 1906, was going to occupy Morocco. A German gunboat, the *Panther*, was despatched to Agadir on Morocco's Atlantic coast. Kiderlen-Wächter, the German foreign secretary, hoped that by taking control of territory, the imperial government could change the situation in Morocco, making the setbacks of 1905 obsolete. Initially, France was prepared to make concessions to Germany, as its ally Russia made it clear that in the event of war it would not help. This led to a decisive intervention by the British government, which announced that it would not tolerate German influence in Morocco, as it feared that Germany would build a naval base there, which would be a threat to British sea power. Lloyd George, Britain's Chancellor of the Exchequer, expressed that Britain could not be disregarded in matters where its vital interests were involved. In August the British army drew up plans for an expeditionary force to France should war break out between France and Germany. Britain was anxious to prevent a German success in Morocco, which it feared would destroy the Entente Cordiale, but it was also signalling to France that Britain's interests must not be ignored in any agreement France negotiated with Germany.

The convention of November 1911 that ended the Agadir crisis

In the end, through secret negotiations with Germany in November, France reached an agreement (or convention) over Morocco. Germany agreed to a French protectorate over Morocco provided that Germany was allowed to control a small part of the French Congo and that France agreed that Germany's economic interests in Morocco should be protected.

The Agadir crisis was defused through Franco-German negotiations, but it further strengthened Britain's ties with both France and Russia, and Germany became more isolated. However, at this stage there was no firm British guarantee or formal alliance with France.

ACTIVITY

Following the hostility between Britain and France at Fashoda in 1898, how had they become potential allies by 1911? Make a list of the key events between the Fashoda incident and Agadir and consider to what extent each one signalled improved relations between Britain and France. Which event would you choose as the most important overall in creating change?

EXTENSION

The Hague conferences, 1899 and 1907

In 1898 the great powers began to consider the creation of a more permanent organization for dealing with disagreements between different states. That year the tsar of Russia proposed an international conference to consider disarmament and the peaceful settlement of international disputes. When it met in the Dutch city of The Hague in 1899, there was little agreement on disarmament, but considerable progress was made in resolving future tensions between states through making arrangements for commissions of inquiry and **arbitration**. A permanent court of arbitration was set up to be composed of judges nominated by the states that had signed the arbitration agreement. Its greatest success was the settling of a dispute between Britain and Russia when Russian warships on the way to fight Japan (see page xx) fired on British trawlers in the Dogger Bank area of the North Sea. The second world conference in The Hague in 1907 achieved little apart from banning countries from using force to collect international debts from states that were delaying or refusing payment. Provision was made to call a third conference in 1914, but the First World War intervened.

KEY TERM

Arbitration A form of dispute resolution through mediation by a third party.

ACTIVITY

Write a brief explanation in your own words of the following terms: 'Scramble for Africa,' entente, power vacuum, 'splendid isolation,' Schlieffen Plan, and international law.

The situation in 1914

In explaining the situation in 1914, it is necessary to:

- assess the global extent and influence of the European empires and their roles within the alliances that had been negotiated in Europe
- look at contemporary attitudes to empire at the outbreak of war in 1914.

The extent of European empires

A glance at Figure 1.3 shows the sheer extent of the European empires. The British Empire alone covered around 12 million square miles (31 million square km), while the French Empire covered another 4 million square miles (10 million square km). If all European colonies are taken into consideration, 84 per cent of the world's land mass was under the control of the European powers. In Africa, only Liberia and Abyssinia escaped European control and in the Far East, Siam managed to avoid annexation only by agreeing to the establishment of British and French spheres of interest. In 1900 it even seemed that a 'scramble for China' would lead to partition, but instead the European powers and the USA settled for an agreement that granted themselves special commercial and financial privileges.

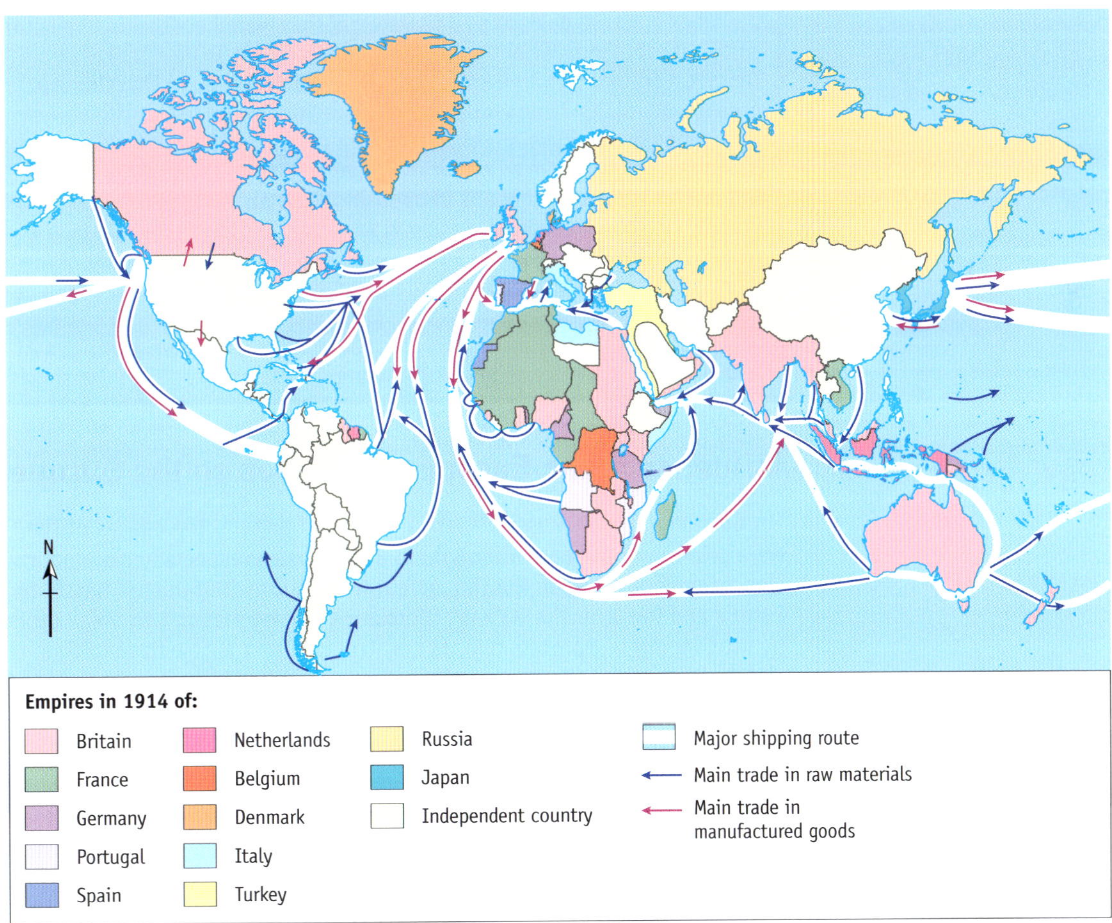

Figure 1.3 The European empires and patterns of world trade, 1880–1914

KEY TERMS

Jiaozhou A bay area on the Shandong peninsula in northern China, seized by Germany in 1897 in revenge for the murder of two missionaries.

Coaling station A base where steamships can be fuelled with coal.

Boxers The English name for The Society of Righteous and Harmonious Fists, a secret Chinese patriotic and nationalist organization, which started an anti-Western uprising in 1899–1901.

Treaty ports Chinese port cities opened up to foreign trade as a result of treaties agreed between Western powers and China.

Triplice An alliance or agreement between three powers.

EXTENSION

European expansion into China

As in Africa, in China rivalry between the great powers was determined by a mixture of political, economic and strategic factors. The Japanese defeat of China in 1895 encouraged the European imperial powers to demand more concessions from China for themselves. As in Africa, Germany was not prepared to play a passive role in China. Like the other European powers, it was attracted by the potential of the huge Chinese market of 450 million people. The murder of two German missionaries in Shandong in 1897 provided Berlin with a convenient reason to seize **Jiaozhou** as a site for a **coaling station** and naval base. This then triggered a series of events, and it looked as if partition of China was about to begin:

- Russia led the way by seizing Port Arthur (modern-day Lüshunkou) and Dalian on the Liaodong Peninsula in December 1897 and forcing China to grant them a 25-year lease.
- Britain insisted on a similar lease on Weihaiwei, which was to run as long as the Russian lease on Liaodong.
- France then demanded a 99-year lease on the Guangzhouwan peninsula in southern China.

Not surprisingly, these demands led to an anti-Western backlash in China, and in the summer of 1900 the **Boxer** rebellion broke out, supported by the Chinese government. In response, at the beginning of August, eight countries – Russia, Japan, Britain, France, Germany, Italy, Austria, and the USA – assembled a force of 54,000 soldiers and within two weeks occupied Beijing, while Russia also marched into Manchuria. China was forced to agree to allow the European powers and Japan to establish further **treaty ports** along the Chinese coast from Manchuria to Guangdong.

To preserve its lucrative trade with China, Britain wanted to avoid dividing China up among the other imperial powers as it feared that they would set tariffs to discriminate against British traders in favor of their own. In October 1900 Britain therefore negotiated the Yangtze Agreement with Germany. The two powers agreed that Chinese unity must be preserved and that China must remain open to foreign trade. The agreement, however, was threatened by the Russian refusal to withdraw from Manchuria. Germany was unwilling to put pressure on Russia to withdraw because it did not want to make an enemy of Russia in Europe. Britain had no means of opposing Russian encroachments in northern China, as France, Germany, and Russia formed what was called the Far Eastern **Triplice**. Effectively, Britain was now as isolated in China as it was in Africa (as a result of the Second Boer War), and Russia was free to pursue its ambitions in Manchuria, Korea, and northern China. It was this threat that brought Britain and Japan together to negotiate the Anglo-Japanese Alliance in January 1902 and also led to Britain improving relations with France and giving up its policy of 'splendid isolation.'

Influence of the European empires on the European alliances

For Germany, France, Russia, Austria, and even Britain, the causes of the First World War were primarily European, although, in Britain's case especially, colonial rivalry with Germany was a significant factor. Russia's defeat by Japan in 1905 forced Russia to turn back to Europe and focus on the Balkans. Germany's clumsy attempt to break up the Entente Cordiale by intervening in Morocco, and its construction of a battle fleet to rival the Royal Navy, clearly emphasized the danger of the German challenge to Britain and made Britain more determined to stop the German domination of Europe.

KEY TERM

South Slavs The main ethnic group in Bosnia and Herzegovina, which Austria had occupied since 1878.

By early 1914, with the Ottoman Empire's decline in Europe, Serbia, supported by Russia, became a major threat to Austria-Hungary. Serbia aimed to free the **South Slavs** from Austro-Hungarian rule (see map xx). The assassination of Franz Ferdinand, the heir to the Austro-Hungarian throne, at Sarajevo on June 28, 1914 by Serb terrorists gave Austria–Hungary a legitimate reason to counter this threat by declaring war on Serbia. The assassination triggered all the built-up tensions among allied powers, leading them to fulfill their obligations to defend each other in the event of one of them going to war. This was how Austria–Hungary's declaration of war on Serbia triggered the outbreak of the First World War.

ACTIVITY

Create a presentation on the relations between Britain, France, and Germany between 1884 and 1914. What changed and what stayed the same? Colour-code events, agreements, and crises to show when relationships between these three key powers became 'colder' and 'warmer.'

The outbreak of the First World War in 1914

The crucial events leading to war were as follows:

- Germany gave Austria–Hungary its unconditional support against Serbia on July 5.
- Austria sent an ultimatum to Serbia demanding that Austria should supervise counter-terrorist measures to be taken by the Serb police. When this was rejected by Serbia, Austria declared war on July 28.
- Russia began to mobilize its army in support of Serbia.
- Germany could not allow its only reliable ally, Austria–Hungary, to which it had been allied since 1879, to be humiliated by Serbia and Russia and declared war on Russia on August 1.
- Once Germany declared war on Russia, France, which was allied to Russia, could not stand back and see Russia defeated. Germany, anticipating this, declared war on France on August 2 and invaded Belgium on August 4.
- Britain, despite initial hesitations, could not afford to run the risk of a German victory and declared war on Germany on August 4.

Contemporary views and verdicts

Assessing contemporary views and verdicts of events is influenced by which sources still remain available to be evaluated by historians. Often, speeches or letters sent to newspapers capture the opinions only of very politically active or well-known people, or those with extreme views. The ideas and opinions of 'ordinary people' are often very difficult to find in the archival records. However, views and attitudes expressed in the popular press, best-selling books, and children's comics and magazines do enable the historian to have some idea of what much of the population was told and read.

Increasingly in the last two decades of the nineteenth century, European governments, apparently backed by public opinion, began to believe that their states could remain great nations only if they had colonial empires that could provide trade and raw materials. By 1900 imperialism had developed into what has been described as a 'mass cult'. The imperial idea was popularized by patriotic and colonial societies, and the new nationalist press. Imperialism also provided excitement and the feeling that one's country and ethnicity were superior to others.

Britain

In December 1884, Lord Derby, the colonial minister, wrote to Gladstone, the prime minister, that 'the British public is just now in a very aggressive and inquisitive mood.' Over the next 20 years the British public's support for what was called the '**New Imperialism**' became greater. Some historians argue that this was essentially a 'defensive' reaction since Britain was facing growing economic and political challenges, particularly from Germany and the USA. In other words, the New Imperialism trumpeted the might of the British Empire just at a time when it was in the early stages of economic decline. There are other reasons for its popularity:

- Many Britons were excited and interested by the stories of empire. The discoveries of the explorers and the victories of the colonial wars were covered in detail in the press.
- The new popular press, particularly the *Daily Mail*, took a strong imperialist line, which to judge by the newspaper's rapidly rising circulation figures must have been influential.
- Many popular adventure books on the British Empire were published: for example, G. A. Henty's stories for the *Boy's Own Paper*; A. E. W. Mason's *The Four Feathers*, set in the Wahhabist uprising; and Edgar Wallace's *Sanders of the River*, a series of short stories about a British colonel serving in South Africa. The excitement of the Empire was also a constant theme in advertisements (see Source 1.1).
- Some political theorists put forward a distorted view of **Charles Darwin**'s ideas on evolution to support the argument that Britain, the northern European nations, and the USA were superior races with a unique right and duty to govern Africa and much of Asia.

KEY TERM

New Imperialism
Intensive colonization by the European powers, Japan, and the USA roughly in the period 1890–1914.

KEY FIGURE

Charles Darwin (1809–82) An English geologist and biologist, who in his *On the Origin of Species* argued that the evolution of life was the result of natural selection – a theory commonly summarized as 'the survival of the fittest.'

What is the message of Source 1.13? Use your knowledge of events to explain the attitude of Lord Salisbury to international cooperation.

SOURCE 1.13

From a speech by the British prime minister Lord Salisbury to the Primrose League at the Albert Hall, London, May 4, 1898.

You may roughly divide the nations of the world as the living and the dying. On the one side you have great countries of enormous power, growing in power every year, growing in wealth, growing in dominion, growing in the perfection of their organisation ... By the side of these splendid organisations there are a number of communities, which I can only describe as dying. For one reason or another – from the necessities of politics or under the pretence of **philanthropy** – the living nations will gradually encroach on the territory of the dying, and the seeds and causes of conflict among civilised nations will speedily appear ... These things may introduce causes of fatal difference between the great nations whose mighty armies stand opposite threatening each other ...

KEY TERM

Philanthropy The desire to help humanity.

KEY TERMS

Anthropologist Someone who studies human beings and their societies, customs, and beliefs.

Jingoism Extreme patriotism in support of an aggressive foreign policy.

'By jingo' was an expression of mild surprise in a popular British song of the 1870s. The term jingoism evolved from this song to describe extreme patriotism.

Critics of the New Imperialism

While support for the New Imperialism in Britain was widespread, there were a number of influential groups and individuals who criticized some of its characteristics and policies. This included some Christian religious groups, who were focused on supporting Christians in Africa. **Anthropologists** were also beginning to study the customs of indigenous African communities on their own terms. The strongest critics of the New Imperialism were the radical wing of the Liberal Party and members of the ILP (Independent Labour Party), but they accepted the Empire as a fact and sought to reform it in the interests of its subject peoples.

When the Second Boer War (see page 23) broke out in 1899, it was welcomed with enormous enthusiasm by supporters of the New Imperialism. Critics of the war, branded as the 'pro-Boers,' were soundly defeated in the general election of 1900. However, the expected speedy British victory did not come. Instead, the Boers waged a guerrilla war, which lasted until 1902. To defeat the guerrillas, the British commander-in-chief, Lord Kitchener, ordered that Boer farmers and their families should be interned in concentration camps, where, through bad food, poor sanitation and overcrowding, over 47,000 people died. When the British press revealed what was happening to the Boers, there was a revulsion against the **jingoism** of the New Imperialism and this was one of the factors that led to the sweeping victory of the Liberal Party in 1906.

Consider Source 1.14. Why do you think this photograph was taken? How is the Barberton camp portrayed in the photograph? Compare this to Source 1.15.

SOURCE 1.14

The Barberton camp in a photograph taken in 1901. Altogether, there were 45 tented camps for Boer internees and 64 for black Africans.

SOURCE 1.15

Emily Hobhouse was a British welfare campaigner, who reported on the suffering of South Africans in British concentration camps. When her findings were published in 1901 the plight of the internees led to public outcry.

In the bell tent, ten or twelve people tried to shelter against the heat of the sun, the dust and the rain. There was no soap. There was no water supply. There were no beds, and rations were extremely poor... it simply meant famine.

KEY TERMS

Battle of Sedan A traumatic defeat of France by Prussia in September 1870.

Elite The ruling class.

Pressure groups Associations formed to promote a particular interest by influencing government policy.

Anarchist A supporter of anarchism, a political theory advocating small, self-governing societies.

France

One of the key reasons for the creation of the French colonial empire was to overcome the legacy of humiliation left by defeats at the battle of Waterloo in 1815 and the **battle of Sedan** in 1870. The acquisition of an empire gave French culture a global role, and awakened national pride as it appeared to make France great again. However, some French nationalists, like **Paul Déroulède**, argued that France's attention would be better concentrated on regaining the lost provinces of Alsace and Lorraine from Germany (see page 19).

Imperialism's most enthusiastic supporters were found in the French **elite**: – army officers, the 'colonial group' of deputies in parliament, and members of the various **pressure groups** and geographical societies outside parliament. Support for the Empire from ordinary French people is harder to assess. The press and parliament swung between resentment at the costs of expansion and outbursts of jingoism and rage when France was outwitted by a rival power, as by Britain at Fashoda in 1898. The politician **Jules Ferry** remarked in 1889 that 'all that interests the French public about the Empire is the dancing.' By this he meant that public opinion was interested only in what seemed exciting in the colonies – in this case, the *raqs sharqi* (a Middle Eastern dance which originated in Egypt). On the other hand, apart from anti-militarists and **anarchists**, the majority of French people accepted that the Empire was a national asset. Even the socialist leader Jean Jaurès, while rejecting the wars of conquest, stressed that the Socialist Party 'has always supported the peaceful expansion of French interests and civilisation.' The imperial drive was fully supported by Catholics, whose missionaries in Africa looked to the French authorities for assistance and protection. In schools throughout France, children were taught about the benefits of French imperialism, but how much impact this had is hard to judge. It was difficult to recruit efficient civilian colonial administrators and, of those appointed between 1900 and 1914, hardly 50 per cent had any secondary education. The French public may have generally approved of the Empire, but probably had little real knowledge about it.

KEY FIGURES

Paul Déroulède (1846–1914) A French politician and co-founder of the League of Patriots.

Jules Ferry (1832–93) French politician and prime minister (1880–81 and 1883–85). He was a strong supporter of French colonial expansion.

Germany

KEY TERM

Ideology A system and set of ideas and theories.

Domestic support for imperialism in Germany was more widespread than in France. To a certain extent, it was a development of German nationalism from earlier in the nineteenth century. German imperialism began to take shape as an **ideology** when two important books were published: Friedrich Fabri's *Does Germany Need Colonies?* (1879) and Wilhelm Hübbe-Schleiden's *German Colonisation* (1881). Both works stressed how important it was for Germany to spread its culture globally through the acquisition of colonies and to ensure that it too had a colonial empire in a world that would increasingly be ruled by great empires. The theories in these books led to the formation of the German Colonial Union, which popularized the idea of a German colonial empire.

It was Bismarck who, with his quick actions, created most of this empire, mainly to support his foreign policy, but as a wily politician he also knew that imperial enthusiasm was building up among the German public. In 1884–85 the German newspapers reported that 'a real fever' for colonies existed among the German public. Ten years later imperialism was not

ACTIVITY

What were the main reasons why imperialism was popular in Britain, France and Germany? Which do you think was the most important reason in each country?

only supported by German intellectuals like **Max Weber** and the German political parties, with the partial exception of the German Social Democratic Party. It began to emerge as an aggressive populist mass movement promoted by such nationalist organizations as the **Pan-German League** and the **Navy League**. These demanded that Germany should acquire new colonies. Germany was a new power, having been united as recently as 1871. Behind its imperialism of the 1890s lay Germany's desire for recognition as a great global power by the other European states.

KEY FIGURE

Max Weber (1864–1920) An eminent German sociologist and economist.

KEY TERMS

Pan-German League A German political society which believed that Germany should extend its frontiers to include all Germans – in Poland, Switzerland, and Austria. It adopted the racist theories of the Anglo-German philosopher Houston Stewart Chamberlain.

Navy League A pressure group which agitated for a large German navy.

Public opinion in 1914

In his *Communist Manifesto* in 1848, Karl Marx argued that the 'working man had no country;' he believed that the key struggle was not between countries and empires but between capital and labor. Socialist parties throughout Europe believed they could stop a war by organizing strikes, but when war broke out the vast majority of workers supported their country and its empire and were ready to fight. The reactions of most people in Europe derived from the history they had been taught at school, the heroic stories they had heard about the past and their countries' achievements, and a simple patriotism. Of course, years of imperialist propaganda had their effect. The threat to the British Empire posed by the German fleet was certainly an influence on public opinion in Britain. In France and Germany the immediate fear of invasion rather than any imperial concerns persuaded public opinion to support the war. However, in the event of victory, imperial ambitions would resurface. In a series of proposals called the 'September Programme' discussed by the German government during the First World War, it was suggested that once Germany won, France and Belgium would be reduced to vassal states and a massive area of German-controlled territory would be created in Africa from the French and Belgian colonies.

3 Why did Japan emerge as a world power and what was the impact on international relations?

By 1918 Japan was the most successful country outside the USA and Europe at modernizing itself and adapting to industrialization. Its transformation into a modern industrial and military power was so effective that in 1905 it became the first Asian state to inflict a humiliating defeat on a major European power: Russia. To understand how this was achieved, it is necessary to look at:

- Japan's relations with the Western powers
- the reasons for its rapid modernization and military development
- international recognition of Japan as a world power
- Japan's role in the First World War and its global position in 1918.

Japanese relations with Western powers in the nineteenth century

KEY TERM

Tokugawa dynasty A powerful Japanese dynasty established in 1603 after a period of civil war and not overthrown until 1868. The Tokugawa dynasty dominated the emperor of Japan, who was in essence their puppet.

Since the early seventeenth century, Japan had been ruled by the **Tokugawa dynasty**, which tried hard to isolate Japan from the rest of the world and to preserve a rigid class system. No foreigners were allowed into the country except for a few Dutch and Chinese merchants whose activities were confined to the port of Nagasaki. Only a handful of Japanese people could speak and read Dutch and consequently have some idea of life outside Japan. They remained a very small minority as Japanese citizens were forbidden to leave the country. In 1825 instructions were even given to coastguards to shoot at any foreign vessels approaching the coast.

Occasionally, ships from western Europe and North America had visited Japanese waters in the early decades of the nineteenth century. During the French Revolutionary Wars, for example, a British frigate had visited Nagasaki. Western powers remained largely uninterested in connecting with Japan – they were far more concerned about trading with China. Britain had a trading station in Guangzhou (formerly Canton), and Japan had no export comparable to Chinese tea, which enjoyed a large market in the West. Until the 1840s for both Europe and the USA, Japan was therefore the most remote of the Far Eastern territories.

KEY TERM

First Opium War A war fought between Britain and China from 1839 to 1842, which was won by Britain. The resulting Treaty of Nanjing granted Hong Kong Island to Britain and forced China to accept free British trade with any merchants in China.

Commodore Perry's mission

In the 1840s, with the opening up of Chinese ports as a consequence of the **First Opium War**, the number of Western ships visiting Japanese ports increased. With the westward expansion of the USA to the Pacific coast and the establishing of the Shanghai–San Francisco shipping route, it now became vital for the USA to set up a coaling station in Japan to refuel its ships on their way to or from China. In 1846 an American squadron sailed into Edo Bay with the demand that Japan open its markets to the West, but this was bluntly refused. However, in 1852 the US government announced, ominously for those Japanese who wanted no contact with the Western world, that a second expedition would be sent.

Read Source 1.16 What attitude does the writer have towards Japanese isolation?

SOURCE 1.16

From an 1852 article published in the quarterly magazine *The Edinburgh Review*.

The compulsory seclusion of the Japanese is wrong not only to themselves but to the civilised world ... The Japanese undoubtedly have an exclusive right to the possession of their territory; but they must not abuse that right to the extent of debarring all other nations from a participation in its riches and virtues.

In July 1853 a US naval squadron of eight ships under **Commodore Matthew Perry** reached Japan bearing a letter from **President Millard Fillmore** to the Japanese emperor demanding the opening up of two ports to international trade and their use by the US navy to take on supplies of water, coal and food. Perry told the Japanese that he would return the following year to receive an answer to the president's letter.

KEY FIGURES

Commodore Matthew Perry (1794–1858) A distinguished naval commander who was called 'the father of the steam navy' for his leading role in modernizing the US navy by building steam-powered warships. In 1852 President Fillmore gave him the task of persuading Japan to open up to American trade. He captained two naval expeditions to Japan, which successfully achieved this objective.

Millard Fillmore (1800–74) The US president from 1850 to 1853. He was previously Zachary Taylor's vice-president, but took over the presidency upon Taylor's death in July 1850.

Who was the intended audience of this source? What impact might this have had on the content, tone and attitudes shown in this source?

Study sources 1.16 and 1.17 again. Compare the attitudes to Japan expressed or implied in each source.

SOURCE 1.17

From President Fillmore's letter of November 13, 1852 to the emperor of Japan (from US Senate, 33rd Congress, 2nd session, 1854–55, Executive Document, Vol. 6, pp. 137–9).

We know that the ancient laws of your Imperial Majesty's government do not allow of foreign trade, except with the Chinese and the Dutch, but as the state of the world changes and new governments are formed, it seems to be wise from time to time to make new laws ...

America, which is sometimes called the New World, was first discovered and settled by Europeans. For a long time there were but a few people, and they were poor. They have now become quite numerous; their commerce is very extensive; and they think that if your imperial majesty were so far to change the ancient laws as to allow free trade between the two countries it would be extremely beneficial to them both ...

These are the only objects for which I have sent Commodore Perry, with a powerful squadron to pay a visit to Your Imperial Majesty's renowned city of Edo [Tokyo]: friendship, commerce, a supply of coal and provisions, and protection for our shipwrecked people.

Although Perry's mission was seemingly peaceful, the Emperor was left in little doubt that in the event of Japan's refusal to co-operate, the USA would eventually use force to achieve its aims. Perry made a great point of showing off his ships' firepower when he ordered 73 cannon shots to be fired in celebration of US Independence Day. He also ordered his ships' officers to conduct survey operations of the coastline and surrounding waters even though the local officials objected to this.

KEY TERMS

Shogun Theoretically the Japanese emperor's military deputy, but in reality the ruler of Japan. Since 1603 the post had been held by members of the Tokugawa dynasty.

Samurai A member of the Japanese ruling class or nobility.

Despite these veiled threats, when the **Shogun** discussed Fillmore's demands there was initially a strong party of **samurai** who argued for defiance of the Americans. However, it was clear that Japan simply lacked the ships and coastal defenses to stand up to foreign pressure. When Perry returned the following February, Japan had little option but to concede and on March 31, 1854 the Treaty of Kanagawa was signed. Under this treaty Japan had to:

- open the ports of Shimoda and Hakodate to the USA
- provide assistance to any shipwrecked American sailors and undertake not to imprison or mistreat them
- permit foreign trade
- grant to the USA any advantages that it might give to another foreign government in the future.

The Harris Treaty

KEY FIGURE

Townsend Harris (1804–78) Merchant and politician and first US Consul General to Japan.

Four years later **Townsend Harris**, the American Consul General to Japan, negotiated a further treaty with the Emperor. The new treaty conceded many more privileges to American and other foreign traders. Two further ports were to be opened for trade, where American citizens would be able to reside, have their own courts and legal system and build their own places of worship. Above all, Japan had to agree to levy only very low tariffs on American imports. When the Emperor refused to sign the treaty, the Shogun ignored him and signed it anyway on the grounds that Japan lacked the military strength to reject it.

The unequal treaties

Soon similar privileges were extended to Britain, France, and Russia. They were all based on the treaties that the Western powers had made with China, and because they gave the Americans and Europeans such privileges, they became known as the 'unequal treaties'. People from overseas were allowed to live and trade under the laws of their own countries, administered through **consular courts** in specially designated ports. To encourage trade, tariffs were to be kept at a very low level.

KEY TERM

Consular courts Courts presided over by foreign officials to protect the interests of their countrymen who were trading or working in a country such as Japan or China. These courts were recognized by treaty.

Reasons for rapid modernization and military development

Between 1868 and the early twentieth century, reforms introduced by the **Meiji regime** transformed Japan into a formidable empire which would hold its own with the Western powers and defeat imperial Russia in 1905.

KEY TERM

Meiji regime The era, from 1868 to 1912, in which Emperor Mutsuhito ruled Japan under the title of Meiji.

The Meiji Restoration

During the Tokugawa period, the Emperor was just a **puppet ruler**. Real power had been delegated to the shoguns, who were all members of the Tokugawa dynasty. The Shogun was effectively the ruler of Japan. This system worked as long as the leading families in Japan supported it. However, by the 1860s Tokugawa rule was coming under increasing pressure. Resentment of the unequal treaties and a desire to revert to the former Japanese policy of seclusion played a key role in the dynasty's unpopularity. In November 1867 the Shogun, **Tokugawa Yoshinobu**, handed over power to the 15-year-old **Emperor Mutsuhito**. This marked the Meiji Restoration, which was confirmed in January 1868.

KEY TERM

Puppet ruler Someone who holds a title that suggests they have authority, but who is actually loyal to or controlled by an outside group or individual.

The revolution started because of a patriotic reaction to unfair treaties, but the Emperor's new advisers believed Japan needed to learn from Western powers to assert itself. This new spirit of openness to outside influences was made clear in the 'charter oath' which the Emperor was persuaded to sign in the presence of his nobles in April 1868 (Source 1.18).

KEY FIGURES

Tokugawa Yoshinobu (1837–1913) The 15th and last Shogun.

Emperor Mutsuhito (1852–1912) Emperor of Japan from 1867 to 1912, also known as Emperor Meiji as he ruled during the Meiji regime.

What can we learn from Source 1.18 about the reasons for the Meiji Restoration and its aims?

SOURCE 1.18

The charter oath taken by Emperor Mutsuhito of Japan on April 5, 1868.

By this oath, we set up as our aim the establishment of the national wealth on a broad basis and the framing of a constitution and laws.

1 Deliberative assemblies shall be widely established and all matters decided by open discussion.

2 All classes, high and low, shall be united in vigorously carrying out the administration of affairs of state.

3 The common people, no less than the civil and military officials, shall all be allowed to pursue their own calling so that there may be no discontent.

4 Evil customs of the past shall be broken off and everything based upon the just laws of Nature.

5 Knowledge shall be sought throughout the world so as to strengthen the foundation of imperial rule.

KEY TERM

Westernizers Those who believed that the Japanese state should modernize along European and American lines.

The Meiji Restoration marked the victory of the '**Westernizers**' and modernizers, who in the course of the next 30 years began to transform the Japanese state.

- A central administration was created; this controlled the local authorities and put in place an effective tax system to provide the government with money.
- A legal system based on Western practice was also introduced.
- In 1890 a new constitution was drawn up with an elected house of representatives and a cabinet.
- There were also significant developments in industry and education.

The constitution of 1890

Although the Japanese constitution of 1890 was influenced by the constitutions of Western countries, compared to US or British parliamentary democracy the powers of the Japanese parliament were restricted. The Emperor had the right to adjourn or prorogue parliament, and parliament's ability to control government expenditure was restricted. The Emperor was also declared 'sacred and inviolable' and was a visible link to and reminder of Japan's past. Fanatical loyalty to the Emperor led to Japan's anti-democratic and nationalistic ideology during the inter-war years.

The armed forces

KEY TERMS

Universal conscription A system in which all people, or all men, of a certain age have to serve for a period of time in the armed services. In Meiji Japan, all men in their twenties had to serve for three years, with a further four years in the reserve (a body of trained soldiers who had left the army but were liable to be recalled in the event of war).

General staff A group of officers responsible for administering the army and planning operations.

A new modern army was created. There was **universal conscription**. By 1883 the army had a wartime strength of 200,000 and a **general staff** based on the German model. The Emperor regularly appeared in a uniform, the design of which was based on the uniform of a Prussian field marshal. Initially, the navy was not expanded as quickly as the army. Given that the unequal treaties had opened Japan's markets to the West, there was now little danger of an invasion by the Western powers as they wanted to trade with, rather than occupy, Japan. It was not until 1888 that a naval officers' training school was set up, but the navy remained relatively small by Western standards. In 1894 it had 28 modern ships and 24 torpedo boats, but after the war with China in 1895 it rapidly increased in size and by 1920 dominated the west Pacific.

Industrialization and the adoption of Western technology

Japan's industrial achievements were unique in scale and effectiveness outside North America and Europe and played an important part in the country's emergence as a great power. Already by the time of the unequal treaties, Japan possessed some of the necessary preconditions for economic growth:

- In some regions of the country, farmers were used to selling their products for money rather than bartering.
- A considerable number of Japanese people were literate.
- Some merchants and farmers were beginning to accumulate capital, which could be invested in modernization projects and new factories.

KEY FIGURE

Iwakura Tomomi (1825–83) A leading political figure in the Meiji Restoration who was instrumental in shaping Japan's rapid modernization during this era.

The unequal treaties brought Japan into contact with western Europe and North America and provided access to markets and new technology. In 1871–73 a mission led by **Iwakura Tomomi** toured the USA and Europe where, in the words of his private secretary, they spent many days 'on noisy trains, with wheels screaming and whistles screeching, amid the smell of iron and belching flames careering through billowing clouds of smoke.' Railways and steam-driven machinery became striking symbols of economic transformation in Meiji Japan.

Growth and modernization were helped by the creation of a centralized state, which enabled the government to encourage and finance key industries and services:

- Rail, postal and telegraph communications were improved. The construction of the railways, initially under government control, meant that by 1877 Tokyo, Osaka, and Kyoto were linked by rail.
- Shipping services were greatly expanded.
- A modern financial system was also introduced, with a national currency regulated by the Bank of Japan, which was set up in 1882.

1874	19
1884	26
1893	44
1895	49
1906	66
1907	72
1911	84
1912	91
1913	100

Table 1.1 Index of industrial output in Japan, 1874–1913 (Source: Statista Research Department, Hamburg)

The unequal treaties prevented Japan from protecting its fledgling industries by placing high tariffs on imported goods. Consequently, efforts had to be made to modernize its industries so that they could withstand competition from the Western world. Japanese workers were trained to operate modern machinery, and steam power was introduced into the new factories. Textiles formed the largest industrial sector in the Japanese economy; between 1868 and 1900 some 70 per cent of Japan's factories were involved in the production of textiles. Silk production expanded rapidly but was mainly carried out on farms and in small workshops. The cotton industry developed on a larger scale and in much bigger units of production or factories, which enabled modern industrial techniques to be used. Heavy industry also made spectacular progress after 1900. Between 1910 and 1925 the production of metals almost quadrupled and chemical, electrical and gas production increased enormously. Coal consumption increased from 2 million tons in 1893 to 21 million tons in 1913. Overall, as Table 1.1 shows, Japanese industrial production was more than five times as great in 1913 as it had been in 1874.

Agriculture remained of vital importance to the Japanese economy, and production more than doubled between 1870 and 1900. The government played an important part in these developments. To improve rice, tea, and silk production, agricultural colleges were set up and a national agricultural society was formed, as well as a model farm where new techniques could be tested.

Education

KEY TERM

Confucian philosophy
The ideas of an ancient Chinese philosopher named Confucius. He wrote rules telling people how to live ethically and maintain a harmonious society.

The Meiji government inherited a traditional system made up of various schools for training young members of the samurai in military skills and **Confucian philosophy**, as well as some 1,500 private schools and temple schools where poorer children could be taught to read and write. Approximately one million Japanese people could read and write. In 1872 the government divided Japan up into eight educational regions, in each of which there was to be one university and 32 secondary schools. By 1880 there were 28,000 primary schools with over 2 million pupils, which amounted to about 40 per cent of children of school age.

In 1885 further reforms were introduced by Mori Arinori, Japan's first minister of education, including extending the time children spent in primary school to eight years. Mori also introduced close government control over all state schools, and private schools were subject to inspection too. Much of the education system was dominated by the teaching of Western skills, and the Education Ministry was advised by Western, mostly American, educationalists.

This education was vital for training Japanese children to live in the modern world, but many traditionalists, while they accepted the need for Western skills, resented the teaching of Western ideas they regarded as subversive, such as democracy. In 1890 they were successful in persuading the government to revise all textbooks in order to remove 'undesirable' foreign influences. Consequently, patriotism and a 'spirit of reverence for the Emperor' were strongly emphasized in the curriculum.

ACTIVITY

Look back over this section and fill in as many factors as you can in this table to explain the modernization of Japan during the Meiji era.

Possible factor	How it contributed to modernization	Evidence against	Links to other factors

When you have completed the table, decide what is the most significant factor or combination of factors and attempt some synthesis. This means bringing together different elements in an analysis. Justify your choices.

Study source 1.19. What does it tell us about the modernization of Japan? What additional knowledge could you use to explain how Japan was industrialized during the Meiji Restoration?

SOURCE 1.19

A Japanese steam locomotive at Sannomiya Station, Kobe, in the early twentieth century.

KEY TERM

Domain lords Provincial noblemen who were in control of large estates and who owed their loyalty to the Emperor.

KEY DEBATE

WHAT WERE THE REASONS FOR JAPAN'S SUCCESSES IN ADAPTING TO A WESTERN-DOMINATED WORLD?

During the Meiji era, Japan experienced an impressive revolution. What back in 1850 had been an isolated and insular feudal state had by 1905 become a modern colonial power capable of defeating Russia. How did this happen? It was not just a consequence of Commodore Perry's expedition and adaptation to Western customs. Japan was less developed than the West, but it was also a stable society. It is easy to dismiss the Tokugawa dynasty as rigid and out of touch, but despite some unrest towards the end of its era it had managed to unite the country. The Tokugawa system, which required **domain lords** to spend every other year at the Shógun's court, may have helped create a sense of national identity that other regions colonized by the West did not have. Japan also had a network of schools attached to temples and government offices, which produced an educated elite capable of absorbing Western culture and technology.

The catalyst was, of course, the decision to open up Japan to foreigners in 1854. This could have resulted in a backlash against modernity, but instead further foreign intervention in 1864 led to a takeover of power by people who believed that there was no option but to modernize Japan. Historians point out that there was still no guarantee that the Meiji regime would succeed, and one writer has observed that the first Meiji years were characterized by a style of government that tried many different things in the hope that something would work. It was by no means clear to contemporaries that the new regime would survive. In 1868 a civil war broke out over the question of modernizing Japan. Many in the West doubted that the regime would survive, but the Meiji leadership won at the cost of some 8,000 casualties, and this victory enabled the modernization of Japan to continue. The success of this process was indicated by the defeat of China in 1895 and Russia ten years later, although these victories were by no means inevitable and arguably were made possible by the international situation at the time. The Meiji achieved a successful blend of modernity and nationalism. This was well expressed in an article in the Japanese newspaper *Nipon* ('Japan'), which praised the excellence of much of the West but warned that Western science, economics and industry 'ought to be adopted only if they can contribute to Japan's welfare.'

International recognition of Japan as a world power

After 1878 the main aim of Japanese foreign policy was to negotiate the modification of the so-called 'unequal treaties' of 1853, in particular the clauses that prevented Japan from setting its own tariffs and allowed overseas nationals working in the treaty ports to be independent of Japanese law (extraterritoriality). The negotiations were long and drawn-out and frequently their lack of success led to outbursts of nationalism in Japan. Only in 1889 was 'extraterritoriality' abolished, and Japan did not obtain complete freedom to set its own tariffs until 1911.

Japanese foreign policy objectives: relations with Korea

Up to 1884, while Japan was still building up its economic and military strength, it pursued a conciliatory policy with its neighbors. However, the status of Korea was an issue that was eventually to cause conflict with China. Japan perceived Korea to be a Japanese satellite even though China claimed ultimate power over it. In 1876 Japan forced Korea to open its ports to Japanese traders and in defiance of China's claims negotiated a treaty with Korea that recognized it as a state independent of China. In December 1884 Korean modernizers, who wanted their country to look more to Japan than to China, attempted to seize control of government. Potentially, this could have caused a war between China and Japan, but neither power was yet in a position to risk conflict. In 1885 by the Tientsin Convention, the two states agreed not to change the status of Korea, but mutual distrust still continued. For example, Japan was suspicious of China's efforts to increase its trade with Korea.

KEY TERM

Donghak A nationalist neo-Confucian movement in Korea that was strongly opposed to Western culture.

Growing economic and military strength led to a change of Japanese policy towards Korea. Japan's chance to strengthen its position in Korea came in 1894, when the followers of the **Donghak** movement attempted to overthrow the Korean government. The King of Korea immediately turned to China for help to crush the revolt. Chinese troops were sent, but Japan argued that this broke the Tientsin Convention and also sent a military force to protect its own position in Korea. Under pressure from the army, the political parties, and patriotic activists, the Japanese government was ready to challenge China. The prime minister, Itō Hirobumi, was also convinced that the political and economic gains from war far outbalanced the international risks.

When Japan refused to withdraw its forces, China declared war. Although the Japanese army was smaller than the Chinese, it was better motivated and organized and was equipped with more modern weapons. The Chinese army was defeated at Pyongyang in northern Korea and its fleet destroyed in the mouth of the Yalu River. The Japanese then went on to take the Pescadores Islands and Taiwan. By April 1895, China had little option but to accept the Treaty of Shimonoseki. The treaty made China recognize Korea's independence and gave Japan control of Taiwan, the Pescadores, and the Liaodong Peninsula, including the important Port Arthur. International pressure and intervention from Russia – backed by France and Germany – forced the return of Port Arthur and the abandonment of the Japanese claim to the Liaodong Peninsula. However, Japanese domination over northern China had been established.

Russia now replaced China as the main challenge to Japanese influence in Korea. Another unsuccessful attempt by Donghak groups to seize power, which led to the murder of the Korean queen and the flight of Korea's king to the Russian embassy, gave Russia the opportunity to strengthen its position in Korea and to send a military mission to Seoul. In 1898, through the Nishi–Rosen agreement, Japan and Russia agreed not to interfere in Korean politics, but this led to only a temporary 'thaw' in Russo-Japanese relations.

ITŌ HIROBUMI

1841	Born
1885	Became the first prime minister of Japan (he served four terms: 1885–88, 1892–96, January 1898–June 1898 and 1900–01)
1888	Became president of the Privy Council (he served four terms: 1888–89, 1891–92, 1903–05 and June 1909 until his death)
1895	Negotiated peace with China
1901	Failed to establish agreement with Russia
1905	Became the first Japanese resident-general of Korea
1909	Assassinated by a Korean nationalist

Itō Hirobumi was the first prime minister of Japan and played a key role in the country's modernization. He was the chairman of the commission that drafted the 1890 constitution. He strengthened diplomatic ties with Germany, the USA, and especially Britain, with whom he negotiated a treaty in 1902. Following Japan's victory over China in 1895, he negotiated a peace that was very favorable to Japan. After Japan's victory over Russia in 1905, Itō became the first Japanese resident-general of Korea. Responding to pressure from the powerful imperial army, in June 1909 he agreed to the total annexation of Korea (which came into effect the following year). Shortly after, he resigned as resident-general and embarked on a fourth term as president of the imperial Privy Council. Four months later he was assassinated in Manchuria by a Korean nationalist.

ACTIVITY

What were the main reasons why Korea was important to Japan?

The Anglo-Japanese Treaty, 1902

The Anglo-Japanese Treaty of 1902 signified that Japan had received recognition as a world power by another world power.

Causes

Japan's victory in 1895 over China caused France, Germany, and Russia to take more vigorous action in China to protect their financial and trading interests. Consequently, each of the three powers established '**spheres of interest**:' France in the territories bordering French Indo-China; Germany in Shandong; and Russia in the Liaodong Peninsula in Manchuria, where it took over Port Arthur, which it had insisted should not be annexed by Japan in 1895. Japan, on the other hand, had its claim to a sphere of influence in Fujian, on the coast opposite Taiwan, rejected outright by China. The subsequent Boxer revolt, in the defeat of which Japan played a major role, provided Russia with the excuse to annex Manchuria with the unconvincing reasoning that the rebellion threatened the Russian railway network there.

KEY TERM

Sphere of interest An area where a great power enjoys special privileges and rights.

The increased foreign intervention in China led, on the one side, to France, Russia, and Germany forming the Far Eastern Triplice and, on the other, to Britain and the USA coming together to support the policy of the 'open door', which aimed to preserve free trade in the Chinese Empire. The only way that Japan could safeguard its interests in China and Korea was to join one or other of these rival groups.

Both of these choices would create problems for Japan. A British alliance would tie Japan to supporting the open-door policy, whereas Japan preferred to carve out its own sphere of influence. On the other hand, co-operation with Russia would be possible only at the cost of accepting Russian domination of Manchuria, Korea, and northern China. Judging that the latter would present a more serious challenge to its interests, Japan turned to Britain with a proposal for an alliance.

The treaty

To protect their interests, Japan and Britain negotiated a defensive alliance. Japan recognized Britain's interests in China, while Britain accepted that Japan was 'in a peculiar degree, politically as well as commercially and industrially' interested in Korea. The two powers then went on to agree in January 1902 that if these interests were threatened, each power should be free to take the necessary action to protect them. In the event of war between Japan and another country, Britain would remain neutral unless a third power came to that other country's assistance. Similarly, if Britain were involved in a conflict in East Asia, Japan would intervene only if a third power declared war against Britain. The advantage to Japan of this agreement was that in any future conflict with Russia, the alliance with Britain would deter intervention by Germany or France.

Summarize the key points of Source 1.20. What additional knowledge could you use to understand the significance of the source?

SOURCE 1.20

From the Anglo-Japanese Treaty, January 30, 1902.

The Governments of Great Britain and Japan, actuated solely by a desire to maintain the status quo and general peace in the extreme east, being moreover specially interested in maintaining the independence and territorial integrity of the Empire of China and the Empire of Korea, and in securing equal opportunities in those countries for the commerce and industry of all nations, hereby agree as follows:

Article I

The High Contracting Parties having mutually recognised the independence of China and Korea, declare themselves to be entirely uninfluenced by the aggressive tendencies in either country. Having in view, however, their special interests, of which those of Great Britain relate principally to China, while Japan, in addition to interests which it possesses in China, is interested in a peculiar degree, politically as well as commercially and industrially, in Korea, the High Contracting Parties recognise that it will be admissible for either of them to take such measures as may be indispensable in order to safeguard those interests if threatened either by the aggressive action of any other Power, or by disturbances arising in China or Korea, and necessitating the intervention of either of the High Contracting Parties for the protection of the lives and property of its subjects.

Article II

If either Great Britain or Japan, in the defence of their respective interests as above described, should become involved in war with another Power, the High Contracting Party will maintain a strict neutrality, and use its efforts to prevent other Powers from joining in hostilities against its ally.

Article III

If, in the above event, any other Power or Powers should join in hostilities against that ally, the other High Contracting Party will come to its assistance, and will conduct the war in common, and will make peace in mutual agreement with it.

Consequences

The Anglo-Japanese Treaty satisfied both Japan and Britain. It recognized Japan's interests in Korea and if war broke out it would stop France supporting Japan's European ally Russia. The main advantage for Britain was that it created a barrier against any further Russian advance in the Far East. Ultimately, the defeat of Russia in the Far East, which the treaty helped to ensure, led to the Anglo-Russian agreement of 1907. Japan was to remain an ally of Britain until the Washington Naval Convention of 1922 (see page 112).

The Russo-Japanese War, 1904–05

KEY FIGURE

Sun Yat-sen (1866–1925)
A leading Chinese nationalist, who played a major role in the Chinese revolution of 1911–12.

It was Japan's victory in the Russo-Japanese War that really marked Japan's emergence as an imperial power. It showed that it could defeat a major world power. It also increased self-confidence among nationalist movements in other Asian countries. The Chinese nationalist **Sun Yat-sen** commented, 'We regarded that Russian defeat by Japan as the defeat of the West by the East. We regarded the Japanese victory as our own victory.'

Japan and Russia's failure to reach an agreement, 1902–05

Under pressure from the Anglo-Japanese Treaty, Russia agreed in 1902 to withdraw its troops from Manchuria in two phases. The first stage was completed on time, but the second stage was delayed. Japan reacted to this by proposing a general settlement, which would involve, as Japan's foreign minister put it, 'exchanging Manchuria for Korea' (that is to say, Japan would accept Russia's presence in Manchuria, and Russia would accept Japan's presence in Korea). This should have been achievable as both the Russian finance minister, Count Witte, and the war minister, Aleksey Kuropatkin, were willing to use negotiation to gain Manchuria. However, Tsar Nicholas II was influenced by **Aleksandr Bezobrazov** and a circle of so-called 'Koreans,' a group of fanatical Russian nationalists who passionately believed that Korea should belong to Russia's sphere of influence. The tsar allowed Bezobrazov to set up a bogus timber company on the Yalu River, which marked the frontier between Manchuria and Korea, where Russian soldiers could be stationed in disguise as lumbermen.

KEY FIGURE

Aleksandr Bezobrazov (1853–1931) A Russian businessman and adviser to Tsar Nicholas II.

Figure 1.4 The Russo-Japanese War, 1904–05

When it became clear by 1904 that Russia would not withdraw troops from Manchuria or cede to Japan a dominant position in Korea, the Anglo-Japanese Treaty gave Japan the confidence to launch a surprise attack on Port Arthur. The subsequent Russo-Japanese War was fought in isolation. Neither Germany nor France, which had just signed the Entente Cordiale with Britain, wanted to intervene in the war as Russia's allies. Both Britain and the USA, however, gave Japan loans to finance the war provided Japan gave a firm commitment to the 'open door' in China.

Initially, there was fighting in Korea and along the coast in the direction of Liaodong. In April, Japan won a naval victory off Port Arthur, gaining control of the seas. This allowed them to move troops by ship to northern Korea, where they crossed the Yalu River and advanced into Manchuria in May. A second Japanese army landed on the Liaodong Peninsula and laid siege to Port Arthur, which fell in January 1905. The way was then clear for a Japanese advance towards Mukden (modern-day Shenyang). The Russian fleet was defeated in the Tsushima straits, having had to sail halfway around the world due to Britain's refusal to let it pass through the Suez Canal. Then, following the defeat of the Russian army at Mukden, the Russian government faced large-scale unrest at home. This led them to agree to mediation by the US president in August 1905.

By the terms of the Treaty of Portsmouth (New Hampshire), Russia ceased to be an immediate threat to either Britain or Japan in the Far East and withdrew from Korea and Manchuria. Russia allowed Japan control over Korea. Japan also took over the Russian lease of Liaodong and the South Manchuria Railway, connecting Port Arthur to Harbin.

Study Sources 1.20 and 1.21. How far do these sources explain Japan's victory over Russia in 1905?

SOURCE 1.21

The sinking of the Russian battleship *Knyaz Suvorov* by Japan during the Battle of Tsushima, May 27, 1905.

ACTIVITY

How similar were the issues Japan faced in its disagreements with China in 1894–95 and Russia in 1904–05? Identify similarities and differences in Japan's strategies in the two wars.

What were the reasons for Japan's victory?

- By initially agreeing to the unequal treaties and then acting cautiously until the 1890s, when it was strong enough to assert its independence, Japan avoided the fate of China – domination by the imperial powers.
- It built up its armed forces and a modern financial and industrial infrastructure.
- It had also inherited the ancient Japanese tradition of loyalty to the Emperor and the state. In 1890 both the Meiji Constitution and the Imperial Rescript (Proclamation) on Education emphasized that subjects of the Emperor should in an emergency 'offer themselves courageously to the state.' General Sir Ian Hamilton, a British observer of the Russo-Japanese war, attributed Japan's success to the fact that they 'have behind them the moral character produced by mothers and fathers who again are the product of generations of mothers and fathers nurtured in ideas of self-sacrifice and loyalty.'
- Above all, the Anglo-Japanese Treaty of 1902 discouraged other powers from becoming involved in the conflict.

ACTIVITY

List the causes of the Russo-Japanese War in this table.

Cause	Explanation	Importance on a scale of 1–6	Reason for awarding this score

KEY TERM

Black Dragon Society (or the Kokuryūkai or Amur Society) An ultra-nationalist association founded in 1901 with the aim of extending Japan's 'imperial mission' to Manchuria, Mongolia, and Siberia. It had close contacts with the Japanese officer corps.

Japanese foreign policy, 1906–14

After the victories of 1905 the Japanese government came under increasing pressure from patriotic societies, particularly the **Black Dragon Society**, to pursue much more aggressive policies, not only in Korea, Manchuria, and China, but also in Mongolia and Siberia. These ideas appealed to the officer corps, who believed that Japan should at all costs preserve its gains from the Treaty of Portsmouth. In 1906 the government rejected the army's demands that in return for a military withdrawal from Manchuria, Japan should retain a number of administrative rights there, which would in fact ensure Manchuria's continued dependence on Japan. The government believed that it was more important to cultivate trade with China and keep good relations with the USA and Britain. This tension between the army and civilian ministers was to become more acute after the end of the First World War.

Although it failed to convince ministers in 1906, the Black Dragon Society continued to push its arguments on the government. As a result, Japan steadily strengthened its positions in Manchuria and Korea up to the outbreak of the First World War. In 1910 a secret agreement between Japan and Russia divided Manchuria into Russian and Japanese spheres of interest: Russian in the north and Japanese in the south. The reason for this was that neither country wanted to open up trade in Manchuria to the other powers. Initially, in 1906 Japan had allowed Korean self-government, subject to overall control from Tokyo, but in the face of growing nationalist opposition in Korea, and Korean attempts to regain their independence, in 1910 it annexed Korea outright.

KEY FIGURE

Yuan Shikai (1859–1916) A Chinese statesman who served as his country's president in the aftermath of the 1911–12 revolution before restoring the monarchy and proclaiming himself emperor in 1915.

The army and the cabinet disagreed about how to react to the Chinese revolution of 1911–12. The army, supported by the Black Dragon Society, aimed to use the revolution's chaos to establish an independent Manchuria under a puppet ruler, which they succeeded in doing in 1932. The Japanese government was more cautious and, once the Chinese politician **Yuan Shikai** was able to establish what promised to be a more stable regime in China, Japan followed the lead of Britain and the USA in supporting it. The reason for this cautious policy was that Japan had built up a considerable economic stake in China. By 1914 some 20 per cent of its exports went there and it wanted to safeguard this trade.

Japan's role in the First World War

To understand Japan's role in the First World War it is necessary to look at both:

- its contribution to the global war
- its role specifically in the Pacific, including the seizure of German possessions.

In order to understand Japan's global position at the end of the war, it is also necessary to examine Japan's intervention in the Russian Civil War.

Contribution to the global war

Most of the fighting of the First World War took place in Europe and the Middle East. Japan refused to send any troops to Europe, but its navy played an important part in helping Britain clear the Pacific Ocean of German warships. The Entente coalition between Britain, France, and Russia was formed by the Franco-Russian alliance of 1894, the Anglo-French Entente Cordiale of 1904, and the Anglo-Russian agreement of 1907. The coalition grew as the war progressed, with Japan joining in 1914, although this was not required by the terms of the Anglo-Japanese Treaty of 1902. Japan declared war on both Germany and Austria-Hungary in August 1914.

KEY FIGURE

Kōzō Satō (1871–1948) A leading member of the Japanese navy who served in the Russo-Japanese War and the First World War and was promoted to the rank of vice-admiral in 1920.

In pursuit of its aims, Japan proved to be a loyal ally of the Entente powers. It refused efforts by Germany to negotiate a separate peace and in July 1916 signed a treaty with Russia whereby the two powers agreed not to make a separate peace. Units of the Japanese navy were sent to the British naval base of Singapore, where Japanese marines helped put down a mutiny by Indian troops in 1915. In February 1917, in response to the German submarine campaign aimed at Allied merchant shipping, Britain urgently asked for Japanese ships to escort convoys bringing food, equipment, and troops to Europe. Two cruisers based in Singapore were sent to South Africa and four to Malta under **Rear-Admiral Satō**. Over the following months Satō's force was strengthened until it consisted of two squadrons of destroyers. Its task was to patrol the eastern Mediterranean and protect Allied shipping from enemy attacks. Japan also constructed merchant ships for Britain and destroyers for France. Three medical teams, each consisting of one surgeon and 20 nurses, were sent to hospitals in Paris, Petrograd, and Southampton.

What can we learn from Source 1.22 about Japan's contribution to the Allied cause in the First World War?

SOURCE 1.22

From the memoirs of a Japanese nurse, Hajimeko Takeda, who was sent to Paris in 1915 as a member of the Japanese Red Cross (JRC) (published in *Stand To!*, issue 122, April 2021).

At the Paris station, there were army surgeons who sent the wounded soldiers, according to their conditions, to various relief corps delegated from various countries. The French army surgeons sent the most seriously wounded to the Japanese relief corps. I want to share with our readers our happiness that they had such confidence in our group. At first the president of the JRC ordered us to ask for the presence of French doctors when operating on any patient, but they came only for the first two or three times and never came afterwards. This is after they witnessed Dr Shiota, our chief surgeon, performing an operation and the nurses tending the wounded. All of us, not only Dr Shiota but our distinguished nurses from the Japanese medical world, felt very proud that the progress of medicine in our country was thus highly appreciated in the West, the greatest authority in the medical world.

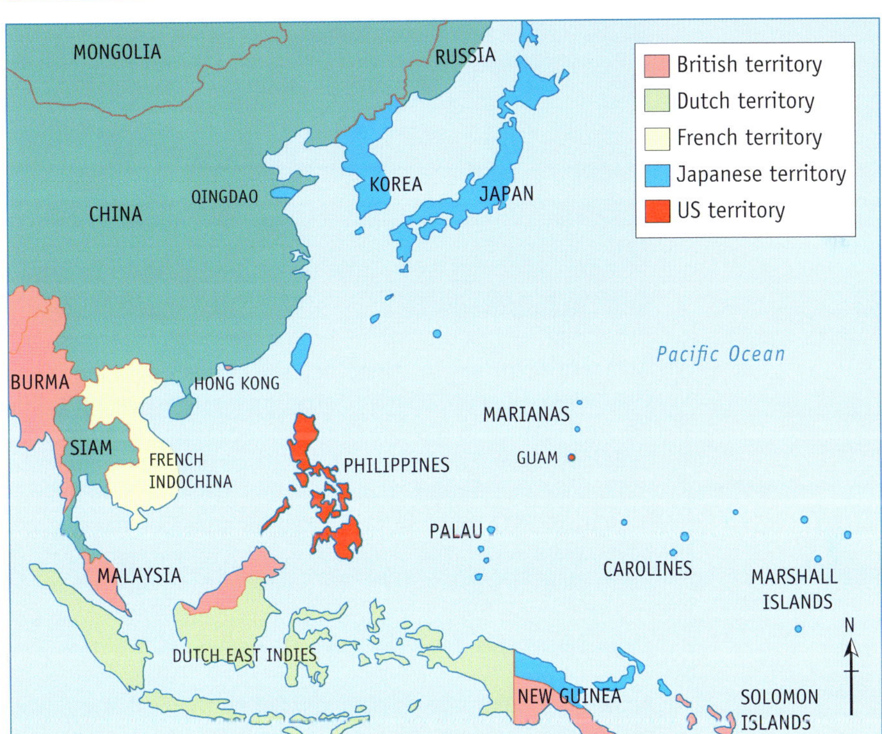

Figure 1.5 The Japanese Empire in 1920

Role in the Pacific

Although the terms of the Anglo-Japanese Treaty did not require Japan to enter the First World War as an ally of Britain, Japan declared war on Germany on August 23, 1914. Japan's primary interest was to strengthen its economic and political hold on China while its rivals were distracted by the war in Europe.

Seizure of German possessions

As soon as Japan had declared war on Germany, its troops, in co-operation with a British contingent, landed in the Chinese province of Shandong and occupied the German concession of Jiaozhou. In October 1914 Japanese soldiers invaded and took control of the German colonies of the Mariana, Caroline, and Marshall Islands. The Japanese navy showed itself to be a highly efficient and effective force. From its seaplane carrier the *Wakamiya* it launched aerial attacks on German targets in Shandong province, and on German, and Austrian naval vessels. These were the world's first attacks by aircraft taking off from a warship.

What can we learn from Source 1.23 about Japan's role in the Pacific?

SOURCE 1.23

A seaplane returning to the Wakamiya after completing an attack. The hoist was used to lift the plane up to the deck of the ship.

Japanese ambitions to strengthen the nation's position in the South Pacific were made clear when Japanese administrators promptly arrived in the occupied Mariana, Caroline, and Marshall Islands to develop their economies and build roads, docks, schools, and public buildings, as well as set up radio stations and telephone networks. Efforts were also made to improve agricultural production, and Japanese immigrants were sent to settle in the islands. In 1917, when Britain asked for increased naval assistance from Japan, the Japanese government seized the chance to get British backing for its claims to the former German possessions in the South Pacific and Shandong that it had seized in 1914.

ACTIVITY

Construct a spider diagram to summarize Japan's contribution to the Allied war effort in the First World War.

China and the Twenty-One Demands

As we have seen, Japan's main aim during the First World War was to strengthen its economic and political hold on China. In January 1915 the Japanese government presented China with the so-called 'Twenty-One Demands,' which would grant Japan exclusive territorial and economic concessions, as well as the right to appoint military, financial, and police advisers to the Chinese government. In the face of Chinese hostility, Japan dropped its demand to appoint advisers, but China was forced by ultimatum to agree to the rest of the demands. Consequently:

- Japan's seizure of the German concessions in Shandong province was confirmed.
- Japan was also able to extend its lease on the South Manchuria Railway Zone to 99 years, and to gain control of the Hanyeping mining and metallurgical plants, which already owed Japan vast sums of money.
- China agreed not to grant any more coastal or island concessions to any power other than Japan.

Further economic concessions were acquired in exchange for a series of loans made to China in 1917 and 1918. In the short term it was hoped that the loans would consolidate the power of the pro-Japanese prime minister **Duan Qirui** and enable him to defeat his rivals. However, the ultimate aim was, in the words of the Japanese businessman **Nishihara Kamezō**, who negotiated the loans: 'to develop the limitless resources of China and the industry of Japan by co-ordinating the two, so as to make possible a plan for self-sufficiency under which Japan and China would become a single entity.'

KEY FIGURES

Duan Qirui (1865–1936)
A warlord who was prime minister of China intermittently between 1913 and 1918.

Nishihara Kamezō (1873–1954)
A businessman sent as a personal envoy by the Japanese prime minister to negotiate loans to China with Duan Qirui.

Japan's global position in 1918

By 1918 Japan was the leading power in East Asia. By a secret treaty in 1916, Russia had recognized Japan's growing mining and railway interests in Manchuria, while Britain, France, and Italy recognized its claims to Germany's former rights in Shandong and the Pacific islands. When the USA entered the war in 1917, it accepted that Japan's geographical position gave it a special interest in China that it was entitled to protect.

Intervention in the Russian Civil War

The Russian Revolution of 1917 represented a significant threat to Japanese influence in Manchuria and China. Anticipating that communist ideals would influence China's revolutionary movement, Japan feared the loss of its economic privileges in China based on the treaty port system. In July 1918 Czech troops, who were originally prisoners of war, seized Vladivostok. Japan agreed with an American proposal that an Allied force should assist the evacuation of the Czech soldiers from Russia. Soon, the aim of the expedition became more ambitious and plans were developed for defeating the revolutionary Bolsheviks with the assistance of the Czech soldiers. Japan sent a force of five divisions. Its intention was to set up an anti-Bolshevik puppet state in Russia's eastern provinces. By November 1919 it was clear that the Bolsheviks were too strong to defeat, and first the USA then Britain, France, and Canada pulled out. Japan only pulled out finally in 1925, when it evacuated the island of Sakhalin.

Complete a chart on the changing power and status of Japan from 1840 to 1918. Consider political, social, economic, and cultural factors in your assessment. Can you identify a particular driver of change or continuity?

Factor	What changed?	What stayed the same?

Why did Japan emerge as a world power and what was the impact on international relations?

SUMMARY DIAGRAM

Here is a summary diagram explaining the reasons and impact.

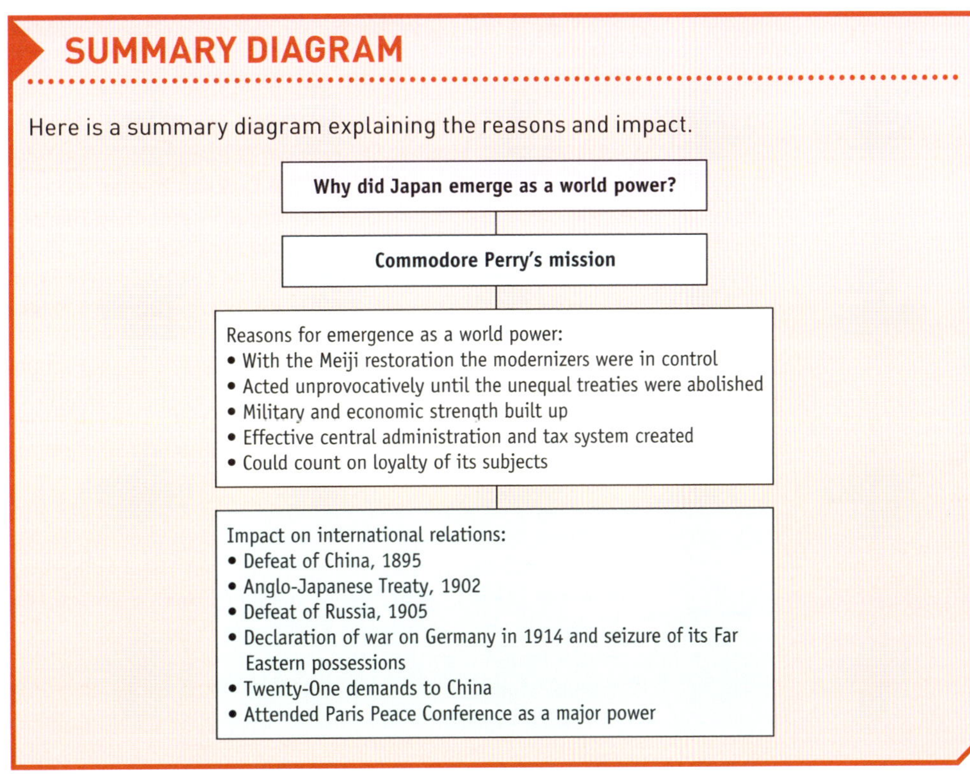

4 Why did the USA emerge as a world power and what was the impact on international relations?

Changing attitudes to overseas expansion

Several factors were responsible for changing US attitudes towards overseas expansion:

- By the 1880s there was no longer land within the USA to be settled by American farmers.
- A powerful US navy had been developed.
- US industry and trade had grown to a point where the country needed new markets.

At the same time the threat of recession and economic competition from Europe emphasized the need for the USA to carve out new markets for itself elsewhere.

Impact of the closing of the frontier on US foreign policy

Since gaining full independence from Britain in 1783, the energies of the USA had been for the most part concentrated on extending its frontier westwards at the expense of the indigenous Americans. By the mid-1890s this process was virtually complete: a network of railroads extended from east to west and some 12,500 square miles (32,000 square km) of land, which had originally been designated as 'Indian territory,' was opened to US settlers. In 1890 the US Census Bureau declared the frontier was now 'closed.' By that it meant that there was no longer a frontier line beyond which the population density was less than two persons per square mile.

Some historians argue that the 1890s marked a turning point in US foreign policy. Like the European powers, between 1898 and 1914 the USA began to colonize territory and protectorates – in Puerto Rico, Cuba, and the Philippines, for example – and show an interest in China.

Others, on the other hand, argue that US foreign policy in the 1890s was merely a logical development from past trends. What cannot be denied, however, is that the 1890s witnessed, as in Britain, an outburst of jingoism in the USA, which was caused by both pride in American achievements and foreboding about the future. In the eyes of some contemporary commentators, the closing of the frontier marked the emergence of the American nation, which according to the Kentucky journalist Henry Watterson was 'destined to exercise a controlling influence upon the actions of mankind and to affect the future of the world.'

An impressive exhibition – the World's Columbian Exposition – was held in Chicago in 1893 to mark the USA's coming of age after Columbus's 'discovery' of America 400 years earlier. At the exhibition a historian, **Frederick Jackson Turner**, gave a lecture, later published under the title 'The Significance of the Frontier in American History,' that caught the imagination of the public. He argued that US democracy had been shaped by the availability of land beyond the frontier in the west, which had enabled generations of US settlers to become sturdy, self-supporting, independent farmers. This became known as the 'frontier thesis'. Although it was a positive explanation of the US national character, it could also be given a more pessimistic interpretation by raising the question of whether the closure of the frontier would undermine the country's unique values and character.

KEY FIGURE

Frederick Jackson Turner (1861–1932)
American historian who taught at the universities of Wisconsin and Harvard. The focus of his work was on the US Midwest.

These fears were further fuelled by threatening developments, which were both internal and external:

- The severe economic depression of 1893 increased unemployment, which led to a wave of demonstrations and strikes that seemed to threaten revolution.
- There were also threats from abroad, with the emergence of Japan and Germany as imperial powers, while the 'Scramble for Africa' and the threat to China showed the dynamism and aggression of European imperialism.
- It was feared that the influx of immigrants from the Mediterranean countries and eastern Europe would dilute the 'traditional' ethnic composition of the USA.
- The rapid growth of great cities, with their social problems and slums, also led to the creation of a new world very different from 'frontier America.'

KEY FIGURE

Henry Cabot Lodge (1850–1924) Republican senator for Massachusetts, 1893–1924.

KEY FIGURE

Captain Alfred Mahan (1840–1914) A US naval officer and naval historian, whose arguments in favor of building up sea power were very influential in both Europe and the USA.

Some historians have suggested that these changes in American society led to a new focus on foreign policy. This interpretation appears to be backed up by an observation by the Massachusetts senator **Henry Cabot Lodge** that this assertive foreign policy could 'knock on the head ... the matters which have embarrassed us at home.' Yet, while the 1890s were indeed an unsettling time for Americans, which the 'closing of the frontier' came to symbolize, there were other factors that also determined US foreign policy during this decade.

Development of naval power

Public opinion and government policy were influenced by **Captain Alfred Mahan**'s influential book *The Influence of Sea Power upon History*, which was published in 1890. This argued that the USA must abandon its '**continentalist strategy**' and instead build up a large navy and **merchant marine** to compete for world trade and acquire colonies for raw materials and bases. In the 1890s the US government followed this advice and began to construct a formidable navy, which gave it the ability to project its power globally. Between 1898 and 1913 the fleet expanded from 11 battleships to 36, and special gunboats were designed to protect US concessions in China.

KEY TERMS

Continentalist strategy A US policy that was primarily concerned with matters occurring on the North American continent.

Merchant marine A fleet of cargo vessels.

The Great White Fleet

To demonstrate America's newly developed naval power, 16 recently constructed battleships, nicknamed the 'Great White Fleet' because their hulls were painted white, were sent on a voyage around the world from December 1907 to February 1909. The voyage was also intended to show Japan, which after its defeat of the Russian navy at Tsushima had emerged as a formidable naval power, that the US fleet could be easily deployed to defend American territory in the Pacific. There were serious tensions between the two countries, which had been caused in part by race riots in San Francisco, where Japanese immigrants had been targeted by hostile mobs. The fleet rounded Cape Horn at the tip of South America and arrived off San Francisco in May. It then went on to Honolulu, New Zealand, Australia, and Japan, where it was well received, despite its unmistakeable message of American naval power. Japanese school children welcomed the fleet by singing in English 'The Star-Spangled Banner' while Japanese destroyers escorted it into Tokyo Bay. The fleet then sailed on to Colombo and returned home via Naples and Gibraltar.

What impression is given by Source 1.24 and what additional knowledge could you use to consider whether this impression is accurate?

SOURCE 1.24

Postcard commemorating the Great White Fleet's visit to Japan.

Rapid economic growth and the need for trade in the late nineteenth century

KEY TERM

Bessemer process
A process to mass-produce steel from molten pig iron, invented in 1856. It worked by removing impurities from the iron by oxidation.

By 1890 the USA had a developed industrial economy as well as a large agricultural sector. The steel industry was revolutionized by the **Bessemer process**, which drastically reduced costs and allowed a huge rise in production volume (see Table 1.2).

Year	US steel production (tons)
1860	13,000
1879	100,000
1900	1,000,000
1920	24,000,000

Table 1.2 US steel production, 1860–1920

Other new industries such as the refining of petroleum and the generation of electricity rapidly developed. By 1891 the long-distance transmission of electricity was possible and enabled the construction of electrical power stations to provide electricity for industry.

KEY TERM

Raw materials
Unprocessed materials such as coal, iron ore and crude oil.

Above all there was a massive expansion of the railways. The amount of track grew from 35,000 miles (56,000 km) in 1865 to over 200,000 miles (320,000 km) by 1900, and the volume of both freight (goods) and passengers tripled from 1877 to 1890. By 1890 the USA was criss-crossed with railway lines, which transported **raw materials** to factories and finished goods to shops and consumers.

How useful is Source 1.25 in explaining why the USA emerged as a world power? What additional information is needed to assess this source?

SOURCE 1.25

Bessemer steel being made at Pittsburgh, Pennsylvania in 1886. The illustration was published in Harper's Weekly, a popular political magazine.

Like their counterparts in Europe, American industrialists and farmers needed markets for their goods and produce. The situation was made even more acute by a series of economic crises in the mid-1880s, which peaked in the depression of 1893–97. Increasingly, manufacturers and industrialists stressed the need both to safeguard traditional markets in South America and to open up new ones. In China, for example, the US government, together with Britain, supported the 'open door' policy that would open up the internal Chinese market to American and European trade.

What can you infer from Source 1.26 about the strength of US industry in the late nineteenth century? What additional knowledge can you use as evidence of the USA's industrial strength?

SOURCE 1.26

From the US business periodical *The American Exporter*, May 1881.

No greater field for commercial enterprise can be found in the vast and underdeveloped markets of China for our manufacturers and farmers ... its vast rivers and canals present unrivalled scope for our steam navigation, and its wide plains and valleys offer matchless facilities for railways ... It stands upon the threshold of the New World and offers to America the greater share of a trade which has enriched every community which has been able to command it.

KEY TERMS

Recession A decline in economic productivity.

Mass industrial production Large-scale production of goods in factories.

The economic cycle and the Panic of 1893

One visitor from France to the World's Columbian Exposition in Chicago was 'speechless ... with wonderment' by the achievements of this 'wonderfully new country,' which was 'well in advance of its age.' Yet the American economy, like the economies of other countries, was subject to an economic cycle of growth and **recession**. Just a month after the Chicago exhibition opened, the failure of a British bank triggered a major economic crisis in the USA, which resulted in some 15,000 bankruptcies and a 17 per cent unemployment rate. This led to a wave of strikes and militancy. For example, in 1894 an 'army' of unemployed people led by Jacob Coxey marched on Washington to demand help from the government.

However, despite the difficulties of the 1890s, by 1912 the USA was a major trading power. Its national wealth doubled between 1900 and 1912, and its investments abroad rose from $700 million in 1897 to $3.5 billion by 1914. It was also a leading global power in technology and manufacturing and had pioneered modern **mass industrial production**.

ACTIVITY

Create a presentation showing the role of different factors in making the USA an expansionist power in the 1890s.

Reasons for, and impact of, the Spanish-American War, 1898

The Spanish-American War has been regarded by historians as a crucial event that marked the USA's emergence as a world power. To understand the reasons for the outbreak of the war, it is necessary to look at:

- the increasing US interest in central and Latin America
- the impact of 'yellow journalism'
- the sinking of the *Maine*
- 'dollar diplomacy'.

KEY FIGURES

Joseph Chamberlain (1836–1914) A British Liberal Party politician, who was a passionate imperialist. He quit the Liberals and founded the Liberal Unionist Party, which worked with the Conservatives.

Grover Cleveland (1837–1908) Democratic president of the USA, 1885–89 and 1893–97.

Increasing US interest in central and Latin America

In the 1890s the USA was beginning to see the rise of European imperialism as a threat to its own independence and prosperity. By the end of the decade the partition of Africa was nearly complete, and it seemed as if the partition of China was about to begin (see page 42). There were also fears that the European powers would next turn their attention to South America. An added worry was **Joseph Chamberlain**'s campaign to persuade the British government to protect its imperial trade by the imposition of tariffs.

In January 1894 **President Grover Cleveland** intervened in an internal conflict in Brazil to protect US trade and sent a fleet of five warships to break a naval blockade imposed by the rebels, who were protesting against the unconstitutional actions of the government. Cleveland feared that Britain would exploit the conflict to strengthen its economic position in Brazil. The rebels rapidly surrendered, and the pro-US government remained in power.

The following year there was a border dispute between Venezuela and British Guiana (now Guyana). The USA again intervened because it feared that Britain might use the dispute to control the Orinoco River and close it to US traders. Richard Olney, the American Secretary of State, justified intervention by quoting the **Monroe Doctrine** and proclaimed that 'the United States is practically sovereign on this continent.' Britain rapidly backed down, and a compromise agreement was achieved that left the Orinoco River under Venezuelan control.

In the presidential election of 1896, William McKinley, the winning candidate, set out an expansionist program for the USA based on the following policy aims:

- making the European powers recognize that South America and the Caribbean were in effect an American sphere of interest
- annexing the Virgin Islands and Hawaii
- winning Cuban independence from Spain.

KEY TERMS

Monroe Doctrine
A US foreign policy position, first expressed in 1823 by President James Monroe, that opposed any intervention in the western hemisphere by colonial powers other than the USA.

Yellow journalism A style of sensationalist and often exaggerated reporting that emerged in the late nineteenth and early twentieth centuries. It was characterized by bold headlines and exaggerated stories. The term originated from the fierce competition between two New York City newspapers, Joseph Pulitzer's *New York World* and William Randolph Hearst's *New York Journal*.

ACTIVITY

Search online for examples of 'Yellow journalism' headlines from Pulitzer's *New York World* and Hearst's *New York Journal*. Find examples of the cartoon strips created by Richard F. Outcault in a series called the 'Yellow Kid.'

Yellow journalism

'Yellow journalism' played a major role in gaining support for a US war against Spain by publishing often misleading reports of Spanish atrocities. The owner of the *New York World*, **Joseph Pulitzer**, instructed his editors to print sensational articles about corruption, crime, and foreign affairs, accompanied by as many eye-catching illustrations as possible. The same technique was followed by **William Randolph Hearst** in the rival *New York Journal*. The term 'yellow journalism' came from a comic strip featuring a character called the Yellow Kid, which appeared in both papers. When the Spanish-American War started in April 1898, it was the first conflict in which media coverage played a key role. The two papers provided the public with sensational reports about the progress of the war and whipped up a jingoistic public opinion.

KEY FIGURES

Joseph Pulitzer (1847–1911) Hungarian-American politician and publisher of the *St Louis Post-Dispatch* and the *New York World*.

William Randolph Hearst (1863–1951) American publisher and politician whose media company, Hearst Communications, owned a string of newspapers, including the *New York Journal*.

ACTIVITY

Write a brief explanation of the following terms: 'yellow journalism', the panic of 1893, naval power, 'closing the frontier', economic recession.

The situation in Cuba

The Spanish-American War was caused by a revolution in the Spanish colony of Cuba. A free trade treaty agreed in 1890 between Spain and the USA caused a short-lived economic boom on the island, but this ended abruptly in 1894 when the USA introduced a tariff that discriminated against Cuban sugar, the island's main product. This caused widespread economic devastation and political unrest, which was quickly exploited by Cuban exiles in the USA, one of whom, **José Martí**, returned to Cuba in 1895 to stir up a revolt against Spain. This led to a prolonged and brutal war of independence between Spain and the insurgents. By 1898, the conflict had stalled. This prompted the USA to intervene militarily because its important trading interests on the island were at risk. In 1897, 87 per cent of Cuba's exports went to the USA, and the value of US investments and trade with the island was $150 million (approximately $2.5 billion in today's prices).

KEY FIGURES

José Martí (1853–95) One of the leading Cuban revolutionaries, who was killed by Spanish troops in the Battle of Dos Ríos.

William McKinley (1843–1901) Republican president of the USA from 1897 until his assassination in September 1901.

William McKinley, who became president in 1897, intended to drive Spain out of Cuba, but initially he hoped to do so without resorting to war. Whether this could have been done is debatable, but two incidents made war between the USA and Spain inevitable. The first was the leaking of a letter from the Spanish ambassador in Washington, which caricatured McKinley as a weak man seeking cheap publicity. It also suggested that Spain's promise to give Cuba greater autonomy was not sincere. The US press seized upon the letter, and one newspaper claimed that it was the 'worst insult to the United States in its history.' The second incident, the sinking of the US warship the *Maine*, had an even greater impact on American public opinion.

Sinking of the *Maine*

In January 1898 the USS *Maine* was sent from the naval base in Key West, Florida to Havana, Cuba. This was described as a courtesy visit, but the real reason for the *Maine*'s presence in Cuba was to show the flag and to protect American interests during the Cuban War of Independence. On the evening of February 15 the *Maine* blew up in Havana harbour. Some 261 sailors were killed, and of the 94 survivors only 16 were uninjured. The disaster was almost certainly the result of a mechanical malfunction, not of Spanish aggression, but the 'yellow press' blamed Spain. 'Remember the *Maine*, to hell with Spain' became a popular rallying cry for action against Spain. Audiences in theatres cheered and wept when patriotic songs were played, and when President McKinley pleaded for calm, effigies of him were burned in the streets. The tragedy acted as a catalyst and accelerated the events that led up to the American-Spanish War, which both the public and **Congress** demanded.

McKinley had little option but to send troops to Cuba. American troops landed at Guantanamo Bay on June 19, 1898, and within a month the Spanish army had capitulated. Congress had not given the US government the authority to colonize the island outright; the **Teller Amendment** specifically forbade its annexation, but not, of course, its subordination to US economic interests.

KEY TERMS

Congress The US parliament, consisting of a lower chamber, the House of Representatives, and an upper chamber, the Senate.

Teller Amendment An amendment (or qualification) put forward in April 1898 by Senator Henry Teller to a joint resolution by the US Congress. The resolution called for American forces to assist Cuba in achieving independence; the amendment prohibited the USA from annexing Cuba.

Read Source 1.27. Take particular note of the language and tone used. Identify examples of words or phrases that show how the *New York Journal* was attempting to influence its readers.

SOURCE 1.27

The *New York Journal* announces that the sinking of the *Maine* was 'the work of an enemy'.

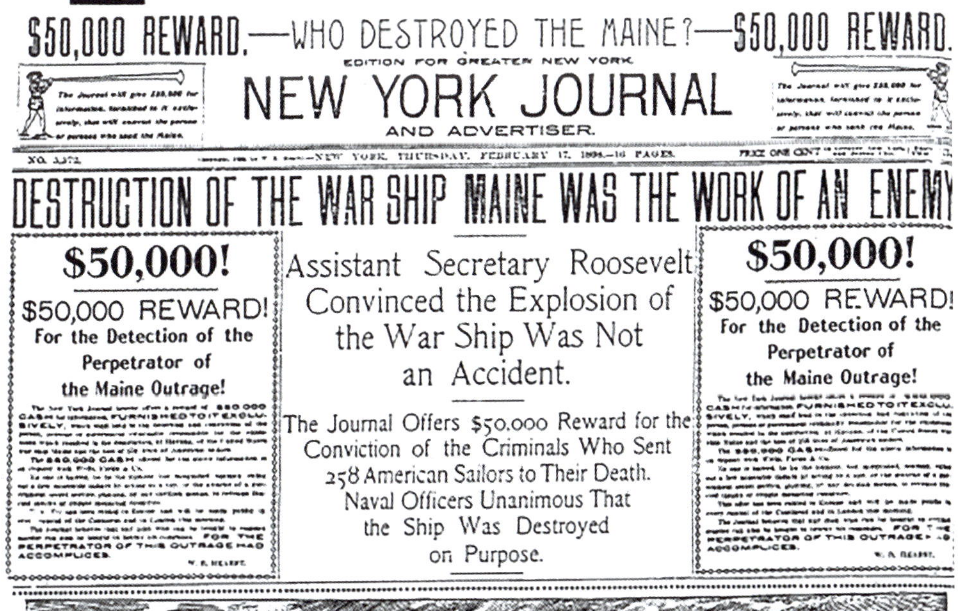

$50,000 REWARD.—WHO DESTROYED THE MAINE?—$50,000 REWARD.

EDITION FOR GREATER NEW YORK

NEW YORK JOURNAL AND ADVERTISER.

DESTRUCTION OF THE WAR SHIP MAINE WAS THE WORK OF AN ENEMY

$50,000!

$50,000 REWARD! For the Detection of the Perpetrator of the Maine Outrage!

Assistant Secretary Roosevelt Convinced the Explosion of the War Ship Was Not an Accident.

The Journal Offers $50,000 Reward for the Conviction of the Criminals Who Sent 258 American Sailors to Their Death. Naval Officers Unanimous That the Ship Was Destroyed on Purpose.

$50,000!

$50,000 REWARD! For the Detection of the Perpetrator of the Maine Outrage!

KEY DEBATE

WHAT MOTIVATED US INTERVENTION IN CUBA?

Historians argue over whether the US intervention in Cuba was an 'aberration' caused by sensationalist reports in the 'yellow press,' which put irresistible pressure on a supposedly weak president, or whether it was the consequence of deliberate US intentions to pursue a more assertive and global foreign policy – in fact to become an imperial power.

It was clear that the USA could not afford to ignore the fighting between the insurgents and the Spanish forces in Cuba as the war threatened US-owned sugar estates, mines, and ranches, as well as the safety of American citizens in Cuba. Some historians stress the importance of this commercial argument and suggest that the USA created an informal empire to try to secure trade.

Other historians believe that the USA was just another imperial power like France, Germany, Japan, or Britain, but that it tried to disguise its imperialistic motives and show it was different from the European colonizers – for example, by stressing its humanitarian reasons for intervening in Cuba.

It is also argued that the USA's emergence as a world power was not planned but was just a response to global events.

What in fact were the forces that compelled the USA to intervene in the Cuban conflict? There was, of course, public opinion, stirred up by the 'yellow press' into outrage over the sinking of the *Maine*, but a complex mixture of other factors was also in play:

- The divided Democratic Party saw US intervention as a cause behind which they could unite.
- This in turn put pressure on the Republicans to pursue a tough line against Spain to head off Democratic opposition.
- The US elites increasingly argued that the USA, as a rising world power, must act to create order in its own 'back yard.'

Certainly, McKinley had very clear aims and during the war declared that 'we must keep all we get; when the war is over we must keep what we want.'

To what extent does this map suggest that the USA had created an empire and emerged as a world power by 1914?

Figure 1.6 US expansion, 1890–1914

ACTIVITY

Why did the USA invade Cuba? Find evidence from this chapter to argue that the invasion came from a desire to create an empire. Find other evidence to argue that the decision was triggered by a more complex combination of factors. Which evidence do you find more persuasive overall?

Taft and dollar diplomacy

The USA was able to strengthen its grip on central America and the Caribbean through '**dollar diplomacy**', backed by military power where necessary. As early as 1903 a reciprocity treaty was signed with Cuba, setting out to tie Cuba closely to the US economy. Honduras, the Dominican Republic, Panama, and Nicaragua were also reduced to economic dependence on the USA and effectively became protectorates, occupied by the US army. When **William Taft** became president in 1909, he wanted to expand foreign trade and pursued dollar diplomacy even further by attempting to eliminate European influence in central and South America. The plan was to provide loans that would enable central and South American countries to pay off their European **creditors** and modernize their economies, which in turn would provide markets for American industry. However, it soon became clear that to work successfully dollar diplomacy needed US military backing. For example:

- Faced with the threat of revolution in the Dominican Republic in 1912, US marines were sent in to stabilize the situation.
- Similarly, in Nicaragua in 1912 a force of 2,700 US marines defeated a rebellion against the government of **Adolfo Díaz**, which had ceded to the USA control of the National Bank and a 51 per cent share in the country's railways.

KEY TERMS

Dollar diplomacy The furthering of diplomatic aims by using economic pressure or incentives, including the offer of loans.

Creditor An individual, organization or country to whom money is owed.

KEY FIGURES

William Taft (1857–1930) Republican president of the USA, 1909–13.

Adolfo Díaz (1875–1964) President of Nicaragua, 1911–17 and 1926–29.

EXTENSION

Dollar diplomacy in Liberia

Liberia, in West Africa, which had been founded in 1847 as an independent state for formerly enslaved people, was similarly subjected to dollar diplomacy when its existence was threatened by civil war and foreign debts. In 1908 a US loan was arranged, a warship was sent to crush the revolt, and a US army officer was given responsibility for building up Liberia's frontier force.

The building of the Panama Canal

The increase in American influence and power across the Pacific made the construction of the Panama Canal a priority because it would enable the US navy to reach Asia without having to take the lengthy and hazardous route around the southern tip of South America. Consequently, the USA pressured Colombia to surrender the Isthmus of Panama. It secretly encouraged Panama to revolt against Colombian rule and sent in warships to prevent Colombian troops from landing in Panama to suppress the rebellion. The architect of the uprising, Philippe Bunau-Varilla, who was also the engineer in charge of the canal project, signed a treaty with the US government that granted it **perpetual sovereignty** over what was to become the canal zone – a strip 10 miles (16 km) wide that ran across the country. Panama became nominally independent but was in reality an American protectorate.

Work started on the Panama Canal in 1904 and was completed in 1914. Historians point out that although Americans saw this as proof of their nation's resourcefulness, in fact it also signified the USA's effective control of Panama.

KEY TERM

Perpetual sovereignty Lasting control, power and authority.

Strengthening US influence in the Caribbean

The construction of the Panama Canal and the creation of the canal zone ensured that Washington continued to exercise close control in the Caribbean and central America through dollar diplomacy, backed up, if necessary, with force. In 1905 **Elihu Root** observed that 'the inevitable result of our building the canal must be to require us to police the surrounding premises.' Even when the Democrat Woodrow Wilson was elected president in 1912 on an anti-imperialist platform, US policy did not change. Faced with political instability in the Caribbean and central America from 1913 onwards, Wilson pursued a policy very similar to McKinley, **Theodore Roosevelt** and Taft. US troops were repeatedly sent to Cuba, Panama, the Dominican Republic, and Haiti.

KEY FIGURES

Elihu Root (1845–1937) Lawyer and Republican politician who served as Secretary of War, 1899–1904, and Secretary of State, 1905–09.

Theodore Roosevelt (1858–1919) Republican president of the USA, 1901–09.

KEY TERM

Civil war in Mexico
A conflict that lasted from 1910 to 1920. It started as a revolt against the regime of President Porfirio Díaz and developed into a multi-sided civil war in which the revolutionaries eventually prevailed.

EXTENSION

US intervention in Mexico, 1916–17

The USA also intervened in the **civil war in Mexico** in an attempt to restore order and to prevent a government hostile to its interests being established. In March 1916, when rebel troops actually attacked the US border town of Columbus in New Mexico, President Wilson sent a 'punitive expedition' to destroy the rebel forces. The two countries came to the brink of war, but in January 1917, after extremely difficult negotiations, the US expeditionary force was withdrawn. Wilson could not afford a war that would need a large number of troops to defeat the rebels at a time when war with Germany was imminent (see page 62).

Reasons for, and impact of, the Philippine-American War, 1899–1902

To understand the causes and consequences of the Philippine-American War, it is necessary to look at:

- US expansion into the Pacific
- the controversy over US motives and actions
- the resistance of the Filipino people.

US expansion into the Pacific

Once war broke out with Spain, McKinley ordered the US fleet to the Pacific. In May 1898 the US fleet destroyed the Spanish naval forces protecting Manila in the Spanish Philippines. When Spain asked for peace terms in August, the USA insisted on the surrender not only of Cuba and Puerto Rico in the Caribbean but also of the Philippines, Guam, and Hawaii in the Pacific. The war destroyed the Spanish Empire and marked the USA's emergence as an imperial world power. Its influence, especially in the Pacific and China, could no longer be ignored by the European powers. This was quickly felt in China, where the USA joined Japan and the European powers to defeat the Boxer uprising. It was also involved in mediating successfully between Russia and Japan and in persuading them to accept the Treaty of Portsmouth in 1905. A key motive for this intervention was fear that a total Japanese victory over Russia would make the Philippines and Hawaii vulnerable to Japanese sea power (see Figure 1.6).

Controversy over US motives and actions

From the late summer of 1898 until well after the presidential election in November 1900, the occupation of the Philippines stimulated a debate in the USA about its role in world affairs. The imperialists pointed out that the Philippines were the 'key to the wealth of the Orient:' not only would they open up markets but they would also provide a base from which the USA would be able to move in on the 'fabled China market.' Imperialists also believed that the USA, on account of its supposedly superior culture, had a duty to educate and 'civilize' the people of the Philippines.

KEY FIGURES

Andrew Carnegie (1835–1919) A Scottish-American industrialist and philanthropist.

E. L. Godkin (1831–1902) An Irish-American journalist and editor-in-chief of the *New York Evening Post*, 1883–99.

Imperialism confronted the USA with a moral dilemma. Could it take part in the rush to establish an empire without violating its own anti-colonial tradition? After all, it was founded as a consequence of a revolt against the British Empire. Anti-imperialist leagues were formed to oppose McKinley's policy. The US industrialist **Andrew Carnegie** argued that annexing the Philippines would be expensive and would damage the US economy. He offered to buy their independence for $20 million. Many believed the USA did not need any more territory, and one journalist, **E. L. Godkin**, joked that 'we do not need any more states until we can civilize Kansas!' Other anti-imperialists opposed the acquisition of the Philippines on racist grounds, arguing that it would 'pollute' the USA racially.

SOURCE 1.28

From the report on the fifth annual meeting of the New England Anti-Imperialist League, November 28, 1903, and its adjournment, November 30.

We used to believe then that we were of a different clay from other nations, that there was something deep in the American heart that answered to our happy birth, free from that hereditary burden which the nations of Europe bear, and which obliges them to grow by preying on their neighbours. Idle dream! pure Fourth of July fancy, scattered in five minutes by the first temptation. In every national soul there lie potentialities of the most barefaced piracy, and our own American soul is no exception to the rule. Angelic impulses and predatory lusts divide our heart exactly as they divide the hearts of other countries. It is good to rid ourselves of **cant and humbug**, and to know the truth about ourselves. Political virtue does not follow geographical divisions. It follows the eternal division inside of each country between the more animal and the more intellectual kind of men, between ... the jingoism and animal instinct that would run things by main force and brute possession, and the critical conscience that believes in educational methods and in rational rules of right.

... The country has ... deliberately pushed itself into the circle of international hatreds, and joined the common pack of wolves. It relishes the attitude ... We are objects of fear to other lands.

KEY TERM

Cant and humbug Hypocritical nonsense.

Compare and contrast the attitudes towards US control in the Philippines in sources 1.28 and 1.29. Look for evidence of similarities in attitude and also for differences. Note down specific details or phrases from each source to support your ideas.

SOURCE 1.29

From President McKinley's parting words to a group of Protestant clergy he was hosting at the White House in Washington, DC, in November 1898 (quoted in Corpuz, O., *The Roots of the Filipino Nation, Volume 2*, Quezon City, Philippines: Aklahi Foundation, 1989).

Before you go, I would like to say just a word about the Philippine business. I have been criticized a good deal about the Philippines but don't deserve it. The truth is, I didn't want the Philippines and when they came to us, as a gift from the gods, I did not know what to do with them. When the Spanish war broke out, **Dewey** was at Hong Kong and I ordered him to go to Manila and he had to; because, if defeated, he had no place to refit on that side of the globe and if the Dons [Spaniards] were victorious they would likely cross the Pacific and ravage our Oregon and California coasts. And so he had to destroy the Spanish fleet and did it! But that was as far as I thought then. When next I realized that the Philippines had dropped into our lap, I confess I did not know what to do with them. I sought counsel from all sides – Democrats as well as Republicans – but got little help ...

And one night late it came to me this way – I don't know how it was but it came: (1) That we could not give them back to Spain – that would be cowardly and dishonourable; (2) That we could not turn them over to France or Germany – our commercial rivals in the Orient – that would be bad business and discreditable; (3) That we could not leave them to themselves – they were unfit for self-government – and they would soon have anarchy and misrule over there, worse than Spain's was; and (4) That there was nothing left for us to do but to take them all and to educate the Filipino people (the people of the Philippines) and uplift and civilize and Christianize them and, by God's grace, do the very best we could by them as our fellow men for whom Christ also died.

... The next morning I sent for the chief engineer of the War Department (our mapmaker) and told him to put the Philippines on the map of the United States [pointing to a large map on the wall of his office]; and there they are, and there they will stay while I am President!"

KEY FIGURE

George Dewey (1837–1917) Admiral of the US navy.

Filipino resistance

Initially, the defeat of Spain in the Spanish-American War was welcomed in the Philippines, who optimistically expected it to lead to independence. Their leader, **Emilio Aguinaldo**, established a provisional government, but this was ignored by President McKinley, who placed the Philippines firmly under US control. He defended this policy by arguing that an American occupation would protect the Philippines from being annexed by Germany or Britain. This was not accepted by Aguinaldo, and the USA was now faced with a war against the people they were claiming to liberate.

The US army had to defeat an enemy in an area of 120,000 square miles (300,000 square km) covering an archipelago of 7,641 islands. Initially, Aguinaldo and his generals attempted to fight a conventional war, but engaging US troops in frontal assaults led to heavy defeats

KEY FIGURE

Emilio Aguinaldo (1869–1964) A Filipino revolutionary, statesman and military leader who fought against both Spain and the USA and is recognized in his own country as the first president of the Philippines.

KEY FIGURE

Jacob Smith (1840–1918) A US general notorious for his brutal treatment of the inhabitants of Samar in the Philippines.

KEY TERMS

Guerrilla warfare Tactics used by small groups of irregular troops, such as sabotage and assassination.

Court martial A court in which members of the armed forces can face trial under military law.

with significant losses. They consequently had no option but to resort to **guerrilla warfare**. In countering this, on the one hand the USA carried out a policy of 'benevolent assimilation,' meaning that they hoped to win over the local population by building helpful infrastructure such as roads, schools, and hospitals. It also established a pro-American political party, which was hoped would Americanize the islands, meaning becoming in line with American attitudes and ideas, adopting American customs, culture, and values, and ensure that they remained effectively US satellites even after they had been given independence. On the other hand, the US army waged a fierce war of counterinsurgency against pockets of resistance. They resettled the population into protected areas to stop sympathizers supplying the guerrillas with food. At times US troops resorted to brutal measures to extract information from prisoners. These included the 'water cure,' in which a large amount of water was poured down a bamboo tube that had been forced into a captive's mouth. In September 1901, after the Balangiga Massacre, in which 48 American soldiers were killed, **General Jacob Smith** ordered the island of Samar to be turned into 'a howling wilderness,' and in the process 2,000 Filipino people were killed. In May 1902 Smith faced a **court martial** for his actions and was ordered to retire from the army.

On July 4, 1902 President Theodore Roosevelt declared victory over the insurgents. The USA had lost 4,000 troops, and almost 3,000 had been wounded. The Filipino casualties were far higher: it was calculated that some 20,000 troops and 200,000 civilians were killed in the fighting. Back home in the USA, criticism and disillusionment with America's imperial mission grew.

In 1916 Congress passed the Jones Act, which promised the Philippines eventual independence and introduced an elected senate there. However, it would be another 30 years before the USA recognized the independence of the Philippines.

Create a presentation giving an overview of the USA as an imperial nation. In what ways had the USA become an imperial nation by 1914 and in what ways had the USA not become an imperial nation by 1914? Conclude your presentation with a judgement based on your criteria.

Reasons for, and impact of, the USA's entry into the First World War

To understand the US declaration of war on Germany in 1917, it is necessary to look at:

- US relations with Germany, Britain, and France
- President Wilson's policy and anti-war pressure groups
- the actions of German U-boats and the sinking of the *Lusitania*
- the Zimmermann telegram
- the impact of the US intervention.

KEY TERMS

Allies An international coalition of countries fighting in the First World War led by Britain, France, and Russia, and also including Japan and Italy.

Central Powers The other coalition fighting in the First World War, consisting of Germany and Austria–Hungary, the Ottoman Empire, and Bulgaria.

US relations with Germany, Britain and France

There were powerful economic factors that were to influence the USA in favor of the **Allies**. Both Britain and France needed to purchase weapons, and Britain also needed to import food, from the USA. Although a British naval blockade stopped the USA trading with the **Central Powers** (Germany and Austria) throughout the war, and was initially very unpopular in the USA, American industrialists were nevertheless delighted with the volume of orders that they received from Britain and France for ammunition and armaments. To pay for these orders, US banks were ready to loan the British and French governments millions of dollars – in May 1916 this amounted to about $10 million a day. In effect, as Wilson's adviser **Colonel House** admitted in the spring of 1915, the United States was economically 'bound up more or less' in an eventual Allied victory.

KEY FIGURE

Colonel Edward House (1858–1938) Diplomat, politician, and adviser to President Wilson. 'Colonel' was a nickname.

Wilson's policy and anti-war pressure groups

When war broke out in Europe in August 1914, the reaction of the majority of Americans was relief that their country was neutral. Although President Wilson and most US elites favored the Allies, many Americans did not. Most German-Americans naturally supported their former homeland, while a deep distrust of Britain was common among Irish-Americans. Many Jewish-Americans whose families had emigrated from Russia as a result of antisemitic pogroms condoned by the authorities hated imperial Russia, which was allied with Britain and France.

Summarize in your own words the message in Source 1.30. After reading pages 60–62 answer the following question: how far does the source explain the reasons for US neutrality?

SOURCE 1.30

From President Wilson's neutrality message to the Senate, August 19, 1914.

The people of the United States are drawn from many nations and chiefly from the nations now at war. It is natural and inevitable that there should be the utmost variety of sympathy and desire among them with regard to the issues and circumstances of the conflict ...

I venture therefore, my fellow countrymen, to speak a solemn word of warning to you against that deepest, most essential breach of neutrality, which may spring out of partisanship, or of passionately taking sides.

WOODROW WILSON

1856	Born in Virginia
1890	Appointed professor of jurisprudence and political economy at the College of New Jersey (renamed Princeton University in 1896)
1902	Promoted to president of Princeton University
1911	Elected as governor of New Jersey
1913–21	Served as president of the USA
1924	Died

As an academic, Woodrow Wilson rose to the position of president of Princeton University. As a politician, he won the 1912 presidential election for the Democratic Party, defeating the Republican incumbent, Taft. During the First World War he pursued a policy of strict neutrality and in 1916 was re-elected on the slogan 'Keep us out of the war.' However, the USA eventually joined the war in April 1917, following Germany's resumption of unrestricted submarine warfare. On January 8, 1918 Wilson issued his Fourteen Points as the basis for a negotiated peace. In 1919 he was welcomed as a hero in Europe, but at the Paris Peace Conference he was forced to compromise his ideas by Britain and France. He was instrumental in the formation of the League of Nations, for which achievement he was awarded the Nobel Peace Prize. However, his ambitions for the League of Nations were undermined by his own country's refusal to join the organization. In 1919 he suffered a stroke while campaigning to win public support for the League, and he was hampered by severe disabilities until his death in 1924.

Many prominent East Coast Americans, often supporters of the Republican Party and representatives of large financial and industrial interests, argued strongly that the USA needed to increase the size of its army and navy, as war with Germany was inevitable. To publicize their arguments they organized parades and published pro-war literature. They also had 'scare films' made, such as *The Battle Cry of Peace*, which featured an invasion of New York by German troops. These arguments were countered by an alliance of pacifists, social reformers and farming interests in the South and Midwest, which believed that US business wanted war only because it could profit from it. Their counter-propaganda included such 'pop' songs as 'I Didn't Raise My Boy to Be a Soldier.' Social reformers such as **Jane Addams** and the journalist **Oswald Villard** believed passionately that peace was vital if they were to achieve their aims of creating better conditions for workers and upholding women's rights.

KEY FIGURES

Jane Addams (1860–1935) American reformer and social worker.

Oswald Villard (1872–1949) Editor of the *New York Evening Post* and civil rights activist.

EXTENSION

Internationalists and isolationists

Internationalists such as the former president William Taft and the statesman Elihu Root believed that the USA could preserve its unique way of life only if it permanently involved itself in world affairs. In the short term this would mean war with Germany, but thereafter some form of **collective security** would have to be sought. Taft even mentioned the possibility of setting up a 'league of nations' and of creating a world parliament. In reaction to this internationalism, there emerged the idea of isolationism, which would preserve America's tradition of non-involvement in foreign affairs and European wars.

KEY TERM

Collective security
Security gained through joining an alliance where each member state agrees to defend the others.

Wilson's position in 1916

By 1916 Wilson was arguing that the US could no longer pursue an isolationist policy and needed to play a leading role in the world to ensure a peaceful future. After winning the 1916 election he unsuccessfully appealed to both the Allies and the Central Powers for 'a peace without victory' and, anticipating the League of Nations, a covenant for an international organization 'to prevent a future war'. Britain responded by presenting a list of conditions which the Central Powers could not accept, while Germany made clear that it would state its aims only at a peace conference to which the USA, as a neutral power, would not be invited, and then started to draw up plans for a ruthless submarine campaign against British shipping.

Actions of German U-boats and the sinking of the *Lusitania*

The only way Germany could halt the steady flow of munitions and vital supplies from the USA to Britain and France was to deploy U-boats (submarines) to sink the cargo ships that were bringing these imports across the Atlantic. For Germany, this ran the risk of sinking US vessels, which could lead to eventual confrontation with Washington. On May 7, 1915 the British liner *Lusitania* was sunk off the Irish coast by a German U-boat, killing 1,198 people, which included 128 Americans. At first Germany responded to Wilson's protests by pointing out quite correctly that the liner had munitions in its hold, but the German chancellor, **Bethmann Hollweg**, realizing that it was more important to keep the USA out of the war than to wage **unrestricted submarine warfare**, promised that no more passenger ships would be sunk without warning. It was only this assurance that kept the USA out of the war.

KEY FIGURE

Theobald von Bethmann Hollweg (1856–1921)
Chancellor of the German Empire, 1909–17.

KEY TERM

Unrestricted submarine warfare Submarine attacks on any ships that were considered to be involved in the war effort, whether naval or merchant, including ships bearing the flags of neutral countries.

The Zimmermann telegram and the US declaration of war

In early 1917 two decisions taken by the German government provoked the USA into declaring war against Germany:

- Bethmann Hollweg was reluctant to risk a rupture with the USA, but in January 1917, against his better judgement, he was pushed by the German high command into sanctioning unrestricted submarine warfare against all ships trading with the Allies, on the optimistic assumption that this would rapidly bring about the defeat of Britain. Predictably, US shipping and commerce suffered severely from the U-boat attacks.

- Any remaining doubts the US government had about abandoning neutrality were removed when, in February, Britain gave Wilson the text of a telegram from the German foreign secretary, **Arthur Zimmermann**, to the German ambassador in Mexico, which it had intercepted. It revealed that if the USA entered the war on the Allied side, Germany would ally with Mexico and encourage a Mexican invasion of New Mexico, Arizona and Texas.

KEY FIGURE

Arthur Zimmermann (1864–1940) German foreign secretary, 1916–17.

On April 6, 1917 President Wilson declared war on the Central Powers as an '**associated power**' rather than ally of the **Entente powers**. This distinction, Wilson hoped, would enable him to pursue, when necessary, a policy independent of Britain and France.

KEY TERMS

Associated power The status which the USA held when it entered the First World War in 1917. It meant that the USA was not bound by any treaties with the Allies and was free if necessary to pursue its own policies.

Entente powers Another term given to the Allied countries fighting Germany and Austria–Hungary: Britain, France, Italy, and Russia.

Compare Sources 1.30 and 1.31 as evidence for the decisive change that occurred in US foreign policy between 1914 and 1917. How do the language and tone differ between the two sources?

SOURCE 1.31

From President Wilson's war address to Congress, April 2, 1917.

We are glad, now that we see the facts with no veil of false pretence about them, to fight thus for the ultimate peace of the world, for the liberation of its peoples – the German peoples included – for the rights of nations great and small and the privilege of men everywhere to choose their way of life and obedience. The world must be safe for democracy. Its peace must be planted upon trusted foundations of political liberty.

We have no selfish ends to serve. We desire no conquests and no dominion. We seek no indemnities for ourselves, and no material compensation for sacrifices we shall freely make.

The impact of US intervention

The US declaration of war was a development of immense importance because the manpower and economic strength of the USA would ultimately become available to the Allies. However, it would take the USA at least a year to train and equip an army that could fight in France. As a result, initially, America's entry into the war did not weaken German power or change Allied strategy. In October 1917, six months after the declaration, the USA had only 80,000 soldiers in France, and they lacked sufficient equipment and training. A German victory was therefore still possible, and in the autumn of 1917 General Ludendorff accordingly advised the German chancellor that the Central Powers were still in a stronger position than the Allies. However, US assistance gave a powerful boost to the confidence of the Allies.

Despite fears from the Allies that Wilson would mediate between the Central Powers and the Allies, he planned to wait until Germany was defeated before proposing his post-war ideas. As he wrote to his chief diplomatic adviser: 'When the war is over, we can force them to our way of thinking because by that time, they will … financially be in our hands.'

The USA and the Russian challenge

Wilson was also confronted with the challenge of the Russian Revolution and its consequences for the Allies. The **February Revolution** of 1917 had swept away the tsarist regime. Russia's new **provisional government** initially promised to fight a '**people's war**' against Germany. It hoped that carrying on the war under a new democratic regime would ignite a great burst of popular enthusiasm. Wilson welcomed the new regime and to encourage it to remain in the war promised it $450 million in aid and sent a 'transportation mission' to keep the key railways functioning. However, the Russian army was in no state to fight. Its morale was low, and discipline was undermined by the Bolsheviks, who seized

KEY TERMS

February Revolution An uprising in Russia February 1917, which installed the Provisional Government. The Bolsheviks seized power later that year in the October Revolution.

Provisional government A temporary government in power only until elections can be held.

People's war A popular war fought by the mass of the people.

power in October and were determined to pull Russia out of the war. This was achieved in March 1918, when Lenin, the Bolshevik leader, signed the Treaty of Brest-Litovsk.

The treaty presented the USA with a major decision: should it join with the Allies in assisting the anti-Bolshevik **White Russians** in a desperate attempt to occupy the ports of Vladivostok and Murmansk so that weapons and supplies could be sent to them to defeat the Bolsheviks and keep Russia fighting against Germany? Wilson initially feared that military intervention would rally support to the Bolsheviks, but eventually in June 1918, when the German army had advanced to just 50 miles (80 km) from Paris, he agreed to send a force of 20,000 troops to Siberia. He wanted to demonstrate his support for the Allies to strengthen his hand when it came to drawing up plans for the post-war world. Another, more cynical reason for this step was to block any Japanese plans for taking over Siberia. However, Allied and US intervention was to achieve little, and by 1921 the Bolsheviks had won the civil war in Russia.

KEY TERM

White Russians The name given to members and supporters of the counter-revolutionary 'White' armies, which fought against the Bolshevik 'Red' army in the Russian Civil War (1918–21).

The Battle of Argonne

KEY FIGURE

General John Pershing (1860–1948) The commander of the US troops in France during the First World War.

The Russian Revolution and the slow arrival of US troops in France gave Germany a chance to launch one final offensive against the British and French in March 1918. US commander **General Pershing** was determined to avoid sending small groups of his troops into the battle early under Allied command. Although American soldiers played a minor part in halting the German advance in the Second Battle of the Marne in July, it was not until the Battle of Argonne, starting on September 26, 1918, that they helped France win the major victory over Germany that hastened the end of the war. It was clear from this point on that the USA would become a major force on the battlefields in France.

The Armistice, November 1918

The USA had emerged as potentially the most powerful of the states waging war against the Central Powers: it bankrolled the French and British war efforts and had more than a million troops in Europe and a further three million being trained. Wilson and his advisers were now ready to exploit this position to ensure what they called a 'just peace.' It was this ideal that had been the driving force behind Wilson's actions since declaring war on Germany. On January 8, 1918 in his Fourteen Points address, he reiterated that the USA wanted 'no annexations' or 'punitive damages.'

By the end of September Germany realized that it could not win the war, and in a desperate attempt to secure a generous peace offer its government embraced the Fourteen Points put forward by Wilson. To convince public opinion in the USA that it was now a democratic country, Germany rapidly created a parliamentary government, which on October 4, asked Wilson for an 'immediate **armistice**' on the basis of the Fourteen Points. Similar requests then came from Germany's allies, Bulgaria, Austria–Hungary, and the Ottoman Empire, all of which faced imminent defeat by Allied forces. However, Germany's immediate hopes of dividing its enemies and achieving an armistice based on the Fourteen Points were dashed when Wilson asked the Allies to draft the details of the armistice agreements. They produced tough terms, which anticipated their key aims at the coming peace conference and, as we shall see in the next chapter, were to contradict the ideals of a Wilsonian peace.

KEY TERM

Armistice An agreement made by opposing sides in a conflict to stop fighting as a step toward negotiating a more permanent peace settlement.

'The First World War greatly enhanced the USA's international power and status'.

In pairs, look through this chapter and find evidence that supports this view. Then find evidence to make a counter-argument to the view.

Does your evidence relate to both elements – power and status – in the statement?

Discuss your ideas and come to a judgment about which side you agree with more overall.

Why did the USA emerge as a world power and what was the impact on international relations?

SUMMARY DIAGRAM

Here is a summary diagram explaining the reasons and impact.

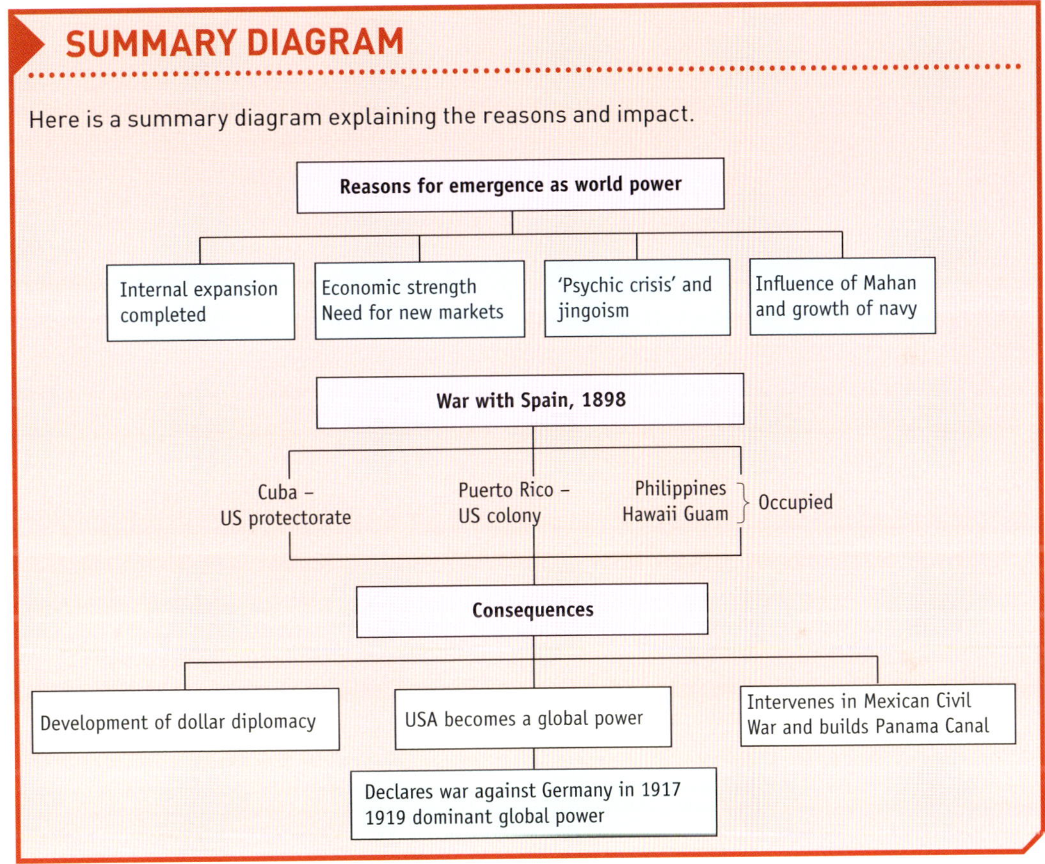

CHAPTER SUMMARY

The years 1870 to 1900 saw the emergence of the 'New Imperialism.' Its causes are complex: economic motives were important, but so too were political factors. Bismarck exploited Anglo-French quarrels in Africa to deflect French attentions from Europe, while France reacted to its perceived humiliation in Egypt by challenging Britain in West Africa. By the 1890s all the great powers of Europe were competing against each other to build up or extend their colonial empires.

The competition for empire, especially in Africa, inevitably influenced relations between the European powers. For example, German intervention in South Africa led to a furious counter-reaction in the British press, while the Moroccan crises of 1904 and 1911 led to close Anglo-French co-operation. There were attempts, particularly at the Berlin West Africa Conference and the Hague conferences, to regulate international rivalries, but they were largely ineffective and were unable to prevent conflict.

In the early twentieth century the European empires were challenged by the emergence of two new powers: Japan, which defeated Russia in 1905, and the USA, which by 1914 was already one of the strongest countries in the world. In 1918 its strength effectively won the First World War for the Allies. Japan managed to avoid colonization by the Western powers and to transform itself into a modern industrial state with a highly effective army and navy while maintaining many of its old national traditions. In 1914 it proved a valuable ally of Britain and played a key role in driving Germany out of the Pacific.

The USA emerged during this period as a potential superpower as a result of its sheer size and industrial strength. Its future direction was a constant subject of debate by Americans: was it going to construct a colonial empire like the European states, or be true to its origins as a successful rebel against colonial power and create what it regarded as a 'better world?' Under McKinley, Roosevelt, and Taft it experimented with colonialism and exerted indirect economic control over the states of the Caribbean, and Central and South America. Wilson continued much of that policy. When the German submarine campaign of 1917 forced the USA to enter the war against Germany as an 'associated power,' Wilson hoped to use his country's financial and growing military strength to build a new world through what would amount to a global government.

REFRESHER QUESTIONS

1. What economic and political motives were behind the creation of the colonial empires, 1870–1919?
2. Why did the 'Scramble for Africa' take place?
3. How popular was overseas expansion in the European states, Japan, and the USA?
4. How did the 'New Imperialism' affect relations between the European powers?
5. How far was British imperial policy up to 1902 based on fear of other European powers?
6. How much progress was made in resolving the tensions between the imperial powers by 1914?
7. What impact did the rise of Japan have on East Asia?
8. How did Japan escape financial and political domination by the West?
9. To what extent did the USA create an empire, 1890–1919?
10. How and why did US foreign policy change during the presidency of McKinley?

Study skills

Source questions

Understanding and interpreting sources

Assessment questions frequently test your understanding and interpretation of sources. Sources can be either written or visual. It is vital that you take time reading each question and studying all the sources carefully.

Comparing sources

Questions on comparing sources will ask you to make a judgment about how far two sources agree and disagree regarding evidence about, or attitudes towards, a historical person, event, or issue. You will need to identify points of similarity and difference by analyzing the sources and provide evidence from the sources to back up your analysis. For example:

> Sources A and B stress different causes of imperialism. Source A indicates that Bismarck, initially at any rate, viewed imperialism as a means of distracting France from reversing its defeat by Prussia in 1870, while in Source B King Leopold of Belgium somewhat hypocritically claims that he wants to bring civilization to a backward area of the world.

You will then need to explain why the sources are similar or different, using your own contextual knowledge.

- First, read the question carefully. Identify the subject of the question – who or what is the question asking you to consider? Does the question want you to consider attitudes towards, evidence about, or responses to events?
- Be careful to compare the correct sources for this question. Tip: write the two source letters down clearly at the start of your plan, and double-check them against the question before you start writing your response.
- Then, read each source carefully. Take notice of the overall message of the source to understand the argument or point of view of the author. This means that the source should be viewed as a whole rather than divided into individual sentences, which, taken alone, might convey ideas that are different from the idea of the whole source.
- Next, consider the provenance. This means the nature (what type of source it is), the origin (who wrote or produced the source), and purpose of each source. This will help you suggest reasons for similarities and differences. You will need to use your contextual knowledge to make this judgment.
- Jot down notes as you read the sources.

Writing your response

- Plan out your answer. Identify at least two points of similarity and difference and the evidence to support each one in brief on your plan. This will make writing your response more straightforward.
- You do not need to provide a summary of the sources or a summary of the historical context.
- Do not write out large sections of the source in your response. This will take up too much of your time. Select the most important parts of the source and write them out clearly. Do not use an ellipsis to quote a whole sentence (for example, 'How ... assembly'), as this does not identify the specific evidence needed. A sufficient selection from the source might need to be only three or four words long. Be precise and concise.
- Structure your response. Start with the similarities and follow with the differences.
- You will then need to develop your comparison. Are there more differences than similarities or more similarities than differences? Why? What explains this? Your response should consider the nature, origin, and purpose of both sources, and relevant contextual knowledge of events, to explain why the points of similarity or difference exist.

ACTIVITY

Read Source A and Source B on page 69, and then highlight two similarities and two differences between the sources.

Then provide a short explanation of where the sources agree or disagree.

Considering how far sources support a view

These questions are looking for a considered judgment about the extent to which all the sources support and/or challenge a particular view that is stated in the question. You will need to judge 'how far' they do so. Some sources might be nuanced and both support and challenge. You must make careful use of all the sources and evaluate them to come to a judgment about which side of the argument is stronger – do the sources mostly support or mostly challenge the view in the question?

Make sure you read the question very carefully before you start to plan your response.

Writing your response

A typical question will take the form of a statement followed by a question that asks how far the sources agree with or support the statement. For example:

Read all of the sources. 'Imperialism greatly increased the tensions between major powers and was the main cause of the First World War.' How far do the sources support this view? (25 marks)

In this question, you need to consider all four of the sources provided. You will have already looked at two of these in depth when completing the activity above.

- Create a brief plan listing sources A–D. Make brief notes as you analyze them. How does the source connect with the view given in the question? Does it agree or disagree? Where is the evidence in the source? Which sources strongly support or challenge the view and which are more restrained?
- In some cases, the source will be nuanced. This means that the source could be used to both support and challenge the view in the question. This could be implicit or explicit in the text or image, and you may need to use your contextual knowledge to recognize the nuance in the source. This might come from your knowledge of key individuals or important events that may have affected the reason for the view in the source.
- You will need to consider how useful the evidence contained within the sources is to your answer with relation to the view stated in the question. This involves thinking carefully about who wrote it, why it was written, and the type of source material it is. For example, a source could be an extract from a diplomatic letter written to a foreign power by the ambassador. If so, what might make this a useful and reliable source of information, and what might make it less useful? Was it written at the same time as key events took place or afterwards? Could this affect how objectively the information in the source is being phrased? Why would this affect its usefulness? Why might official documents be different from private letters? Make sure you include comments on the specific source, not just generic comments on the type of source it is.
- You may be asked to consider a visual source such as a cartoon or a poster. It is important to be able to see its meaning in relation to the issue in the question and consider its nature, origin, and purpose together with contextual knowledge. You will need to consider why it was produced and by whom. Consider the image and what is emphasized – what is the focal point of the image? How is the subject portrayed? Is the portrayal sympathetic or satirical? Is there anything shown in the image (for example, clothing, emblems, flags, or equipment) that has particular symbolic associations (religious, military, or social)?
- You will also need to use your knowledge of events to judge whether the source is stronger or weaker evidence. Does it agree factually with the other sources? Does that match your own knowledge? What important details do you know about the context of events that inform your opinion about whether the source is likely to agree or disagree with a particular view?

The activity below will help you practice identifying key points from sources and to evidence this with information from the source.

ACTIVITY

First, look in detail at the question on page 68 and identify its focus. Then, look at sources A, B, C, and D. Make a copy of the table below. You will see that one part has been done for you. Now complete the table for sources B, C, and D.

Source	What is this source saying about the key issue?	What evidence from the source shows this?
A	*Wish to strengthen relations with France*	Entente shows peaceful agreement possible between imperial rivals
	The Entente concerning Morocco and Egypt has provoked an aggressive German reaction	But has provoked hostile German reaction: 'make mischief'
	British policy not anti-German	Ambiguous use of 'we must maintain the Entente:' could this mean eventual war with Germany?
B		
C		
D		

On the basis of what each source shows about the importance of imperialism, group the sources. Which sources imply that imperialism is the key issue and which suggest that there are other issues? Is there a source which is **nuanced and supports and challenges**?

SOURCE A

From a letter by British Foreign Secretary, Sir Edward Grey, to US president, Theodore Roosevelt, December 1906.

Now a word as to our policy. It is not anti-German. But it must be independent of Germany. We wish to keep and strengthen the Entente with France, who is now very peaceful and neither aggressive nor restless. She plays the game fairly, and as long as she trusts one she is a good friend ...

It is in German diplomacy alone that one now meets with deliberate attempts to make mischief between other countries by saying poisoned things to one about another ...

The long and the short of the matter is that, to secure peace, we must maintain the Entente with France, and attempts from outside to shake it will only make it stronger.

SOURCE B

From David Lloyd George's war memoirs, published in 1938, where he recalls a visit to the Liberal elder statesman Lord Rosebery on the day the Entente Cordiale was announced.

It was in the year 1904 on the day when the Anglo-French entente was announced ... His [Rosebery's] first greeting to me was: 'Well, I suppose you are just as pleased as the rest of them with this French agreement?' I assured him that I was delighted that our snarling and scratching relations with France had come to an end at last. He replied: 'You are all wrong. It means war with Germany in the end!'

... Had anyone told me that before I ceased to hold office in the British cabinet I should ... have witnessed a war between Britain and Germany ... I should have treated such [a] forecast as a ... wild prediction.

SOURCE C

From an article written by Alex Thompson, a socialist, in *The Clarion*, a British left-wing newspaper, October 1, 1898.

There you have the real reason of the world's murderous turbulence. It is the excessive accumulation of capital and then the insatiable greed for profitable investment that causes the bloody and ruthless scramble now threatening to set all Europe by the ears.

SOURCE D

From the Franco-Russian Treaty, 1892.

1 If France is attacked by Germany or by Italy supported by Germany, Russia shall employ all her available forces to attack Germany. If Russia is attacked by Germany or by Austria supported by Germany, France shall employ all her available forces to attack Germany.

2 In case the forces of the Triple Alliance, or of any one of the Powers belonging to it, should be mobilised, France and Russia, at the first news of this event and without previous agreement being necessary, shall mobilise immediately and simultaneously the whole of their forces and shall transport them as far as possible to their frontiers.

3 The available forces to be used against Germany shall be, on the part of France, 1,300,000 men, and, on the part of Russia, 700,000 or 800,000 men.

Essay questions

Understanding the task and planning an answer

When preparing and writing essays, it is important to understand from the outset what the essay question is asking you to do.

How to plan and write your response to causal essay questions

In essay questions that ask you to explain the causes of an event, you will need to show your understanding of the reasons why a specific event occurred or why someone adopted a particular course of action. You should focus on the key issue of causation, analyzing a range of factors to show how they are connected, and reach a supported conclusion about why something happened.

- These questions will focus on causation. This means that you will need to identify a range of causes.
- You need to show detailed knowledge and understanding of the reasons why a specific event occurred or why someone adopted a particular course of action.
- This will be the combined effect of several factors, both long- and short-term.
- You will need to show how these factors are connected.
- Be analytical – identify causes and assess them against each other. Do not write a narrative of events.
- Produce a reasoned conclusion for your explanation.

Planning an answer

Once you have understood the demands of the question, the next step is planning your answer. The plan should define your line of argument. This means that you will need to think about what you are going to argue before you start writing. This should help you maintain a consistent line of argument throughout your answer. It also means that your plan will be a list of reasons about the issue or issues in the question, which will ensure an analytical response. Simply writing down a list of dates would lead you to write a narrative or descriptive answer – instead you will need to be analytical. However, you will need to use your contextual knowledge to evidence your arguments.

'The most important reason for the rise of Japan to the position of an imperial power was its readiness to use force.' How far do you agree? (20 marks)

Consider the question above. Your plan should be structured around issues like:

- Why was force important for Japan?
- What other reasons are there for the rise of Japan?
- Why are these reasons important?
- Are they more or less important than force?
- What is your overall view having looked at the key factor and the other causes?

A plan for this essay might take the following form:

1 Readiness to use force: the building up of its army and navy, which was necessary in a world of imperial rivalry in China, Korea, and elsewhere. When did it use force to increase its power? Make the argument that force was the most important factor in the Sino-Japanese War of 1895, the Russo-Japanese War, and the seizure of German concessions and territory in 1914.

2 Other factors:

 a) The Meiji Restoration, which resulted in legal and financial reforms necessary for the modern state, particularly one with claims to becoming an imperial power.

 b) The increasing desire of the Japanese government to end the unequal treaties of 1853. This was achieved not through war but through diplomacy. Yet to negotiate with the Western powers, Japan needed to modernize and build up its armed forces to be taken seriously by them.

 c) The growth of patriotism and nationalism in Japan.

 d) An increasing understanding of the importance of diplomacy made Japan aware that it needed allies before force could be used – for example, the Anglo-Japanese Treaty of 1902.

 e) The building up of its economy and growing volume of exports to China and the USA – a peaceful extension of influence.

3 The conclusion should weigh up the relative importance of the readiness to use force and bring together interim conclusions in previous paragraphs, perhaps arguing that while Japan was certainly ready to use force as a final weapon, it was not reckless with its use. It modernized itself, developed its economy and also used diplomacy to buy time or divide its enemies.

Planning answers to these questions will help you put together a structured answer and avoid the common mistake of listing reasons, where each paragraph starts with 'Another reason for the rise of Japan was …'.

Structuring an answer will help you focus on the actual question and not simply write about the topic. Under the pressure of time in an assessment, it is easy to forget the importance of planning and just to start writing; but this will usually result in an essay that does not have a clear line of argument or that changes its line of argument halfway through, making it less convincing.

2 International relations 1919–29: conflict and co-operation

Introduction

This chapter considers the peace settlements of 1919–20 and the aims and motives of the participants. It assesses how effective these complex settlements were and what their impact, particularly on Europe and the Middle East, was. It also looks at the aims, structure and record of the League of Nations in the 1920s.

It analyzes these problems by examining the following key questions:

- Why was there such extensive dissatisfaction with the peace settlements of 1919–20?
- Why was the League of Nations created and what challenges did it face in the 1920s?
- How and why did international tensions remain high after the Versailles settlement?
- How and why did international relations improve from 1924–29?

KEY DATES

1919	June 28	Treaty of Versailles signed with Germany
	September 10	Treaty of Saint Germain signed with Austria
	November 27	Treaty of Neuilly signed with Bulgaria
1920	June 4	Treaty of Trianon signed with Hungary
	August 10	Treaty of Sèvres signed with the Ottoman Empire
1921	March	Plebiscite in Upper Silesia
	April	German reparations fixed at 132 billion gold marks
	November	Washington Conference
1922	April	Genoa Conference and Rapallo Pact between Germany and the USSR
1923	January 11	French and Belgian troops occupy the Ruhr
	July 24	Treaty of Lausanne
1924	August	Dawes Plan
1925	December	Locarno Treaties
1926	September	Germany joins the League of Nations
1928	August	Kellogg–Briand Pact
1929	August	Young Plan

1 Why was there such extensive dissatisfaction with the peace settlements of 1919–20?

The peace settlements of 1919–20 were a product of compromise between the wartime Allied powers and the USA. They were imposed on Germany and its allies and were punitive in their content. To understand more fully why there was such dissatisfaction with the settlements, it is necessary to look at:

- the negotiations at Versailles
- the key issues involved in agreeing the treaties
- the aims of the 'Big Three'
- the representation of the other powers
- the key terms of the treaties of Versailles, Saint Germain, Neuilly, Trianon, and Sèvres
- the reaction of both the defeated powers and the victors
- the reparations question.

The negotiations at Versailles

KEY TERMS

Pandemic An epidemic on a global scale.

Dictated peace A peace treaty that is dictated to the defeated party rather than negotiated.

In January 1919 the statesmen of the victorious powers were confronted with a Europe in turmoil. The sudden and complete defeat of the Central Powers had made Europe vulnerable to the spread of Bolshevism from Russia. For much of the winter of 1918–19, Germany seemed poised on the edge of revolution. With the disintegration of the Austro-Hungarian, Ottoman, and Russian empires, there was no stable government anywhere east of the Rhine. Further problems were caused by an influenza **pandemic**, which by the spring of 1919 had caused the deaths of millions of people, and by the near famine conditions in central and eastern Europe.

When the Paris Peace Conference opened in January 1919, there were delegates from 27 states, including China, in attendance, but in reality, power lay with the 'Big Three': Britain, France, and the USA. Neither Russia nor the defeated states were invited to participate in negotiations. In Germany this later gave rise to the bitter accusation that the Treaty of Versailles was a '**dictated peace**'.

Key issues in agreeing the treaties

When the USA, Britain, France, Italy, and Japan gathered in Paris to draw up peace terms with Germany, each victorious power had its own aims and agenda.

KEY TERM

Covenant A general term meaning 'agreement', or the specific document laying out the agreed rules and constitution of the League of Nations.

The aims of the 'Big Three'

The USA

President Wilson of the USA was determined to ensure that the Fourteen Points (see Source 2.1) should be the basis for the coming peace negotiations and to anchor the **Covenant** of the League of Nations in the text of the peace treaties.

Using Source 2.1, construct a spider diagram to summarize different elements of the Fourteen Points. You could organize the diagram to include categories such as: territorial/border issues; diplomatic and colonial factors; world organization; self-determination; and economic matters.

SOURCE 2.1

From Woodrow Wilson's Fourteen Points announced in a speech to Congress on January 8, 1918.

1 Open covenants [agreements], openly arrived at ... diplomacy shall always proceed frankly and in the public view.

2 Absolute freedom of navigation upon the seas, outside territorial waters ...

3 The removal, so far as possible, of all economic barriers ...

4 Adequate guarantees given and taken that national armaments will be reduced to the lowest point consistent with domestic safety.

5 A free, open-minded, and absolutely impartial adjustment of all colonial claims ... the interests of the populations concerned must have equal weight with the equitable claims of the government whose title is to be determined.

6 The evacuation of all Russian territory ...

7 Belgium, the whole world will agree, must be evacuated and restored, without any attempt to limit the sovereignty which she enjoys in common with all other free nations ...

8 All French territory should be freed and the invaded portions restored, and the wrong done to France by Prussia in 1871 in the matter of Alsace–Lorraine ... should be righted ...

9 A readjustment of the frontiers of Italy should be effected along clearly recognisable lines of nationality.

10 The peoples of Austria–Hungary, whose place among the nations we wish to see safeguarded and assured, should be accorded the freest opportunity of autonomous development.

11 Romania, Serbia and Montenegro should be evacuated; ... Serbia afforded free and secure access to the sea; and the relations of the several Balkan states to one another determined by friendly counsel along historically established lines of allegiance and nationality ...

12 The Turkish portions of the present Ottoman Empire should be assured a secure sovereignty, but the other nationalities ... should be assured ... an absolutely unmolested opportunity of autonomous development, and the Dardanelles should be permanently opened as a free passage to the ships and commerce of all nations ...

13 An independent Polish state should be erected which should include the territories inhabited by indisputably Polish populations, which should be assured a free and secure access to the sea ...

14 A general association of nations must be formed under specific covenants for the purpose of affording mutual guarantees of political independence and territorial integrity to great and small states alike ...

KEY TERM

Reparations Compensation paid by a defeated power to make good the damage it caused in a war.

France

Georges Clemenceau, the French Prime Minister, was painfully aware that France, with its reduced birth rate and high casualties of 1.3 million dead and 2.8 million wounded, faced a potentially stronger Germany due to the collapse of Austria-Hungary and tsarist Russia. He therefore wanted to enforce maximum disarmament conditions and **reparation** payments on Germany and to set up strong independent Polish, Czechoslovak, and Yugoslav states, as well as an independent Rhineland state. He also wanted an alliance with Britain and the USA and to continue inter-Allied economic co-operation into the post-war years.

KEY FIGURE

Georges Clemenceau (1841–1929) A French politician whose outspokenness won him the title of 'the tiger'. As prime minister from 1917, he then presided over the Paris Peace Conference of 1919, but lost power in 1920. He foresaw the re-emergence of Germany as a great power and predicted the Second World War.

KEY TERMS

Bolshevism A term associated with the Bolsheviks, a faction of the Russian socialist movement led by Vladimir Lenin. The Bolsheviks believed in radical, revolutionary methods to overthrow the existing government. This ideology laid the foundation for the Russian Revolution of 1917, leading to the creation of the Soviet Union.

War guilt Blame for starting a war.

Dominions Self-governing countries within the British Empire and Commonwealth. At the end of the First World War, the list of British Dominions was as follows: Australia, Canada, New Zealand, Newfoundland, and South Africa.

Britain

In contrast to France, Britain, even before the great powers met in Paris, had already achieved many of its aims: the German fleet had surrendered, German trade was no longer a threat and Germany's colonial empire had already been occupied by Japanese and British imperial forces. Britain's territorial ambitions lay in the Middle East, not Europe. Prime Minister David Lloyd George also recognized that a peaceful united Germany would act as a barrier against the spread of **Bolshevism** from Russia. The logic of British policy pointed in the direction of a peace of reconciliation rather than revenge, but in two key areas – reparations and the question of German **war guilt** – Britain adopted a much harder line. Lloyd George and Clemenceau agreed in December 1918 that Kaiser Wilhelm II should be tried by an international tribunal for war crimes. Under pressure from its **Dominions**, who also wanted a share of reparations, the British delegation at Paris was authorized 'to secure from Germany the greatest possible indemnity she can pay consistently with the well-being of the British Empire and the peace of the world without involving an army of occupation in Germany for its collection'.

What impression of pre-war alliances and agreements compared with wartime alliances is given by Source 2.2? What examples from your own knowledge might support or challenge this view?

SOURCE 2.2

From a speech by Georges Clemenceau to the French parliament on December 29, 1918 (quoted in Jordan, W, *Great Britain, France and the German Problem, 1918–1939*, London: Frank Cass, 1971, p. 37).

There was a system, which seems condemned today and to which I do not hesitate to say that I remain to some extent faithful: nations tried to organise their defence. It was very prosaic. They tried to have strong frontiers ... this system seems condemned today by the very high authorities. Yet I believe that if this balance, which had been spontaneously produced during the war, had existed earlier – if, for example, England, America and Italy had agreed in saying that whoever attacked one of them had attacked the whole world – this war would have never taken place.

DAVID LLOYD GEORGE

1863	Born
1890	Elected to parliament as a Liberal
1908–15	Chancellor of the Exchequer
1916–22	Served as prime minister and inspirational war leader
1922	Resigned and never again held ministerial office
1945	Died

David Lloyd George was born in Manchester to Welsh parents and brought up in Wales. Having qualified as a solicitor in 1884, he was elected to parliament six years later. He was bitterly critical of the Boer War and in 1905 became a cabinet minister. During the First World War he made his reputation as an effective Minister of Munitions, and then from 1916 to 1918 served as prime minister in a Liberal–Conservative coalition government. He remained in office until 1922, when he was forced to resign over the Chanak crisis. After his fall he never returned to power, as he was distrusted by both the Conservative and Labour parties, but he continued to hold his parliamentary seat until he was appointed to the House of Lords shortly before his death.

The aims of Italy and Japan

The Italian prime minister, Vittorio Orlando, was anxious to convince Italian voters that Italy had done well out of the war, and he concentrated initially on attempting to hold the Entente powers to their promise made in 1915 in the **Treaty of London** to give Italy the Austrian territories of South Tyrol and those along the Dalmatian coastline, as well as demanding the former Austrian port of Fiume (modern-day Rijeka) in the Adriatic.

KEY TERM

Treaty of London The 1915 treaty that Britain, France, and Russia made with Italy to ensure that Italy would enter the First World War on the side of the Allies.

Japan's aims were limited to securing recognition of the territorial gains it made in the war and having a racial equality clause inserted in the Covenant of the League of Nations.

Representation of other powers

Besides the 'Big Three', and Italy, and Japan, there were 22 other delegations, consisting primarily of powers that had in the course of the war been occupied by Germany or joined the Allied side. Other delegations, like Poland, Czechoslovakia, and the Serbo-Croat-Slovene group of states (**Yugoslavia**), had emerged as independent nations as a consequence of the defeat of Germany and the disintegration of the Russian Empire following the Russian Revolution and hoped that the conference would confirm their independent status. The British Dominions and India, which had all contributed to Britain's war effort, were represented in their own right.

KEY TERM

Yugoslavia A country that came into existence in 1918 as the Kingdom of Serbs, Croats, and Slovenes and changed its name to Yugoslavia in 1929. In 1992 it was dissolved and replaced by several independent states.

ACTIVITY

Draw a mind map showing what each of the five victorious great powers mentioned above – the USA, France, Britain, Italy, and Japan – hoped to gain from the peace negotiations after the First World War.

The key terms of the Treaty of Versailles

All the peace settlements were to a greater or lesser extent the result of compromises between the Allied powers. Versailles, the treaty with Germany, was no exception. Its key clauses were the result of fiercely negotiated agreements, which were often reached only when the conference appeared to be on the verge of collapse. The first 26 articles (which appeared in all the other peace treaties as well) contained the Covenant of the League of Nations and were agreed unanimously. From the Allies' perspectives the treaties, which some judged to be harsh, were justified by the concept of 'war guilt' (see page 88).

German disarmament

The Allies and the USA agreed on the necessity for German disarmament, but there were differences in emphasis. Britain and the USA wanted to end the tradition of conscription in Germany, which they saw as the cause of German militarism. Instead, they aimed to create a small professional army similar to their own peacetime forces. However, **Marshall Foch**, justifiably, feared that a professional German army would simply become a well-organized core of trained men, capable of quickly expanding when the chance arose. Foch was overruled, and the **Council of Ten** accepted in March proposals for the creation of **inter-Allied commissions** to monitor the pace of German disarmament, the abolition of the general staff, the creation of a regular army with a maximum strength of 100,000 men, the dissolution of the German air force and the reduction of its navy to a handful of ships.

The territorial settlement

France wished to use every opportunity to weaken Germany by taking territory away from it, while Britain sought to preserve a united, but democratic Germany as a counter to Bolshevik Russia. The USA also hoped to achieve a fair settlement along the lines of the Fourteen Points, but supported ceding (handing over) to Poland, France, and Belgium those German territories where the majority of the population was Polish, French, or Belgian. In the end the territorial clauses of the treaty were an uneasy compromise.

Germany's eastern frontiers

In March 1919 the Commission for Polish Affairs, which the Peace Conference had set up, recommended that Danzig, Marienwerder, and Upper Silesia should all be included in the Polish state. This would give Poland access to the Baltic port of Danzig. Much of West Prussia and Posen were also to be awarded to Poland. Lloyd George strongly opposed the inclusion of Marienwerder and Danzig in Poland as he feared that it would cause such resentment in Germany that an embittered German government would look to the Bolsheviks for help. He was successful in persuading France to agree to holding **plebiscites** in Marienwerder and Allenstein. Danzig, a city inhabited and surrounded by a largely Polish population, was to become a **free city**, under the protection of the League of Nations.

Germany's frontier with Denmark

In the 1866 **Treaty of Prague**, Austria had agreed to Prussia's annexation of Schleswig and Holstein. Holstein was mainly German-speaking, while there was a Danish majority in northern Schleswig. Article 5 of the treaty had stated that a plebiscite should be held within six years to give the people of Schleswig the option for a restoration of Danish rule. The plebiscite was never held, and consequently after Germany's defeat in 1918 the Danish government asked for the Allies to organize plebiscites in northern and central Schleswig (southern Schleswig was not included in the plebiscite, as it was considered to be overwhelmingly pro-German). This request was granted, and the plebiscites took place in 1920. Northern Schleswig voted for inclusion in Denmark, while central Schleswig voted to remain part of Germany.

Germany's western frontiers

Along Germany's western borders there was a consensus among the victorious powers that Alsace–Lorraine, which Germany had annexed after the Franco-Prussian War in 1870, should revert to France; **Eupen and Malmedy** should be ceded to Belgium; and the Grand Duchy of Luxembourg should be declared neutral.

KEY FIGURE

Marshal Ferdinand Foch (1851–1929) The commander-in-chief of the Allied armies on the western Front from April 1918 until the end of the war. He played a prominent part in the Paris Peace Conference before retiring in 1920.

KEY TERMS

Council of Ten The controlling committee of the Paris Peace Conference, consisting of the head of government and foreign minister from each of Britain, France, Italy, Japan, and the USA. Known officially as the Supreme Council.

Inter-Allied commissions Allied committees set up to deal with particular tasks set by the conference.

KEY TERMS

Plebiscite A direct vote by the electorate on a single issue.

Free city A self-governing city under the protection of the League of Nations.

Treaty of Prague An 1866 peace treaty between Prussia and Austria, signed at Prague.

KEY TERM

Eupen and Malmedy Western German territories integrated into Belgium in 1925 after the League of Nations consulted the local populations about their wishes.

The future of the Saarland proved more controversial. It was ethnically German, but Clemenceau insisted on the restoration to France of that part of the Saar which was given to Prussia in 1814. He also aimed to detach the German-speaking mineral and industrial basin to the north, which had never been part of France, and place it under an independent non-German administration. Finally, he demanded full French ownership of the Saarland coal mines to compensate for Germany's destruction of pits in northern France during the war. Wilson immediately perceived a clash between the national interests of France and the principle of **self-determination** that he preferred. While he was ready to agree to French access to the Saarland coal mines until the production of their own mines had been restored, he vetoed (refused to accept) outright their other claims on the region. To save the conference from breaking down, Lloyd George persuaded Wilson and Clemenceau to accept a compromise whereby the mines would become French for 15 years, while the actual government of the Saar would be entrusted to the League. After 15 years the people would have the right to decide in a plebiscite whether they wished to return to German rule. In 1935 the plebiscite was duly held and the territory reverted to German control.

KEY TERMS

Self-determination The right of a people to decide its own future. In the post-First World War negotiations this issue related primarily to Europe, but the question of self-determination would later become prominent in the European colonial empires.

Demilitarized Having all military defenses removed.

Over the future of the Rhineland there was an equally bitter clash between Britain and France. To France, the occupation of the Rhine was a unique opportunity to weaken Germany permanently by creating an independent Rhineland state that would look to Paris rather than Berlin. Britain feared that this would merely sow the seeds of another war by creating a permanent source of tension between France and Germany. After heated and bitter arguments, Clemenceau agreed that the Rhineland would remain part of Germany. However, it would be divided into three zones and was to be occupied for a period of 15 years by Allied troops as a guarantee of the execution of the treaty. Each zone was in turn to be evacuated after five, ten, and fifteen years, and thereafter the Rhine was to remain **demilitarized**. Clemenceau was persuaded to agree to this by the offer of an Anglo-US military treaty guaranteeing France against any future German attack.

Figure 2.1 Territorial adjustments to Germany's borders after the First World War

ACTIVITY

Create a list or table of Germany's territorial losses in Europe after the First World War.

Germany's colonies

In May 1919 agreement was reached on the division of the German colonies. This was justified on the grounds that Germany, as a defeated nation judged to be guilty of starting the war, was no longer to be trusted as a colonial power. In reality, of course, the victors were motivated above all by a desire to keep their colonial conquests. Britain, France, and the **Union of South Africa** were allocated most of the former German colonial empire in Africa; Australia, New Zealand, and Japan took control of the scattered German territories in the Pacific. Italy was awarded control of the Juba Valley in East Africa, and a few minor territorial adjustments were made to its Libyan frontier with Algeria. President Wilson insisted that Britain, France, and the Dominions needed to at least pretend they cared about the League of Nations. He made them agree to **mandated status** for the former German colonies. Even though they had not made much effort, Britain, the Dominions, and France still got what they wanted.

KEY TERMS

Union of South Africa A self-governing Dominion of the British Empire, which came into being in 1910 when the Cape, Natal, Transvaal, and Orange River colonies were unified.

Mandated status A status given to former German and Ottoman territories by the League of Nations. It put Allied powers in charge, to govern on behalf of the League of Nations.

Japan and former German territory in Shandong

A serious clash arose between Japan and the USA over the former German concessions in China. Japan was determined to hold on to the ex-German leasehold territory in Shandong, which it had seized in 1914. The Chinese government, however, on the strength of its declaration of war against Germany in 1917, argued that all former German rights should automatically revert to the Chinese state, despite the fact that in 1915 it had agreed to recognize Japanese rights in Shandong. Wilson was anxious to block the growth of Japanese influence in the Pacific and supported China, but Lloyd George and Clemenceau, wanting to protect their own countries in China, backed Japan. A compromise was agreed whereby Japan promised – only verbally – that Chinese control would be restored by 1922. Wilson, already in conflict with Italy over Fiume and facing Japanese threats to boycott the conference and sign a separate peace with Germany, had no choice but to concede. It is arguable that this humiliating defeat did much to turn the US Senate against the Treaty of Versailles.

The Shandong decision outraged China and triggered widespread riots and strikes. In June 1919 the Chinese government refused to sign the Treaty of Versailles.

The peace treaties with Austria, Hungary and Bulgaria

After the ceremony at Versailles the Allied leaders returned home, leaving their officials to draft the treaties with Germany's former allies. President Wilson was more sympathetic to the defeated powers than were the leaders of Britain, France, and Italy, but his European allies firmly stated that Austria and Hungary (the heirs to the former Austro-Hungarian Empire) and Bulgaria should bear their entire share of responsibility 'for the crime which has unchained upon the world such a calamity.' The three powers all had to pay large sums of reparations and almost totally disarm. The Austrian army was reduced to a professional force of 30,000; the Hungarian army to 35,000; and the Bulgarian army to 20,000.

Essentially, the basis of the settlement in south-central Europe and the Balkans was the creation of the new Czecho-Slovak and Serbo-Croat-Slovene states – or Czechoslovakia and Yugoslavia, as they became known.

The Treaty of Saint Germain, 10 September 1919

The Treaty of Saint Germain reduced Austria to a **rump state** of some 6 million German-speaking people and split up the diverse territories that before the war had been part of the Austro-Hungarian Empire:

- Italy was awarded South Tyrol, despite the existence there of some 230,000 people of German ethnic origin.
- Bohemia and Moravia were ceded to Czechoslovakia. Any second thoughts Britain or the USA may have had about changing the nationality of the 3 million Germans who made up nearly one-third of the population of these provinces were quickly stifled by French opposition. France wanted a potential ally against Germany to be strengthened by a defensible frontier and the possession of the Skoda munitions works in Pilsen.
- Slovenia, Bosnia-Herzegovina, and Dalmatia were handed over to Yugoslavia.
- Galicia and Bukovina were ceded to Poland and Romania, respectively.
- Only in Carinthia, where the population consisted of German-speaking Slovene people who did not want to join Yugoslavia, did the great powers consent to a plebiscite. This was held in 1920 and resulted in Carinthia remaining Austrian.
- The French feared that **Anschluss** would create a powerful German state in the middle of Europe. To avoid this, Article 88 of the Treaty of Saint Germain (which was identical to Article 80 of the Treaty of Versailles) stated that only the Council of the League of Nations was empowered to sanction a change in Austria's status as an independent state. This meant that France, as a permanent member of the Council, could veto any proposed change (see the map on page 80).

KEY TERMS

Rump state What is left of a much bigger state after it has been reduced by factors such as annexation, occupation, or, as in the case of Austria after the First World War, the breaking up of an empire.

Anschluss The union of Austria with Germany.

The Treaty of Trianon, June 4, 1920

KEY TERM

Magyar The ethnic Hungarian people.

Hungary, by the terms of the Treaty of Trianon lost over two-thirds of its territory and 40 per cent of its population. Hungary was vulnerable to its neighbors' territorial claims because only its heartland, the Great Hungarian Plain, was predominantly **Magyar**. In November 1918, Serb, Czechoslovak, and Romanian troops occupied the regions they claimed. The negotiation of the treaty was delayed by a communist coup in March 1919 (see page 87), but was resumed after the uprising was defeated. Signed in June 1920, the Treaty of Trianon imposed the following terms on Hungary:

- Most of the German-speaking area in the west of the former Hungarian state was ceded to Austria.
- The Slovakian and Ruthenian regions in the north went to Czechoslovakia.
- The east went to Romania.
- The south went to Yugoslavia.

KEY TERM

Balkan Prussia A descriptive phrase by which Bulgaria was compared to Prussia, which in the eyes of the Allies had an aggressive, militarist reputation.

The Treaty of Neuilly, 27 November 1919

Britain and France regarded Bulgaria as essentially the '**Balkan Prussia**', which needed to be restrained, and were determined, despite reservations from Italy and the USA, to reward their allies, at its expense. Thus, southern Dobruja, with a mere 7,000 Romanians out of a total population of 250,000, was ceded to Romania, and western Thrace, which had provided Bulgaria access to the Aegean Sea, was given to Greece.

Figure 2.2 Central Europe after the peace settlements, 1919–23

ACTIVITY

How does Figure 2.2 explain the fragmentation of central Europe? Note down specific details from the peace treaties to back up your answer.

The settlement with the Ottoman Empire, 1919–23: the Treaty of Sèvres

The Treaty of Sèvres, which was signed in August 1920, was another Anglo-French compromise. Lloyd George hoped to weaken the **Ottoman Empire**, which became Turkey after 1922, not only by depriving it of Constantinople (modern-day Istanbul) and of the control of the Straits, but also by forcing it to surrender all territories where there was no ethnic Turkish majority. He now envisaged Greece, which had entered the war on the Allied side in 1917, rather than Italy, filling the vacuum left by the collapse of Ottoman power. In effect, Lloyd George wanted Greece to become the agent of the British Empire in the eastern Mediterranean. France, on the other hand, concerned with protecting its pre-war investments in the Empire, wished to preserve a viable Ottoman state. Above all, France wanted the Ottoman government to remain in Constantinople, where it would be more vulnerable to French pressure. The end product of this Anglo-French compromise was what many felt to be a harsh and humiliating treaty.

An Allied financial committee took control of the Empire's finances, which would give them responsibility for trade, the Ottoman national bank, the budget, and the tax system. The Ottoman army was reduced to 50,000 soldiers and the navy to just 13 ships, and it was also banned from having an air force.

Constantinople remained the capital of the Ottoman Empire, but Thrace and most of the European coastline of the Sea of Marmara and the Dardanelles were to go to Greece. In the Smyrna region Greece was also given responsibility for internal administration and defense, while an Armenian state was to be set up with access across Turkish territory to the Black Sea. **The Straits** were to be controlled by an international commission. By a separate agreement, zones were also awarded to France and Italy in the southern part of the Empire.

KEY TERMS

Ottoman Empire Centered on modern-day Turkey, an empire that at its height in the sixteenth century extended deep into south-east and central Europe, North Africa, and west Asia. Having been founded in 1299, the Ottoman Empire formally ceased to exist in 1922.

The Straits Two important Turkish waterways – the Bosphorus and the Dardanelles – which link the Black Sea to the Aegean Sea.

The division of former Ottoman territories in the Middle East

In May 1916 Britain and France signed the Sykes–Picot Agreement. By this they committed to dividing up Mesopotamia, Syria, and the Lebanon into Anglo-French spheres of interest once the war against the Ottoman Empire had been won. Britain, however, was the only power with a large army in the Middle East and consequently was able to revise the agreement unilaterally. In 1917, Britain claimed Palestine and also issued the **Balfour Declaration**, supporting the establishment of a national home for the Jewish people in Palestine, while ensuring the rights of existing non-Jewish communities. Through this declaration, Britain secured the USA's backing.

In February 1919, in deference to Wilson's Fourteen Points, Britain and France agreed that they could exercise power over these territories only in the name of the League of Nations. It took several more months of bitter argument before Britain agreed to a French mandate in Syria and also French access to the oil wells of Mosul in Iraq. The frontiers between the British mandates of Palestine and Iraq and the French mandate of Syria were then finalized in December.

KEY TERM

Balfour Declaration A 1917 communication by Arthur Balfour, the British foreign secretary, declaring British support for establishing a national home for the Jewish people in Palestine.

ACTIVITY

Copy and complete this chart briefly to summarize the main terms of the peace treaties with Germany's former allies and your assessment of their international significance.

Treaty	Terms	Your assessment

Figure 2.3 The Near and Middle East after the Treaty of Sèvres

ACTIVITY

Explain the changes in the Near and Middle East after the Treaty of Sèvres, as shown in Figure 2.3.

Difficulties created by the treaties

Instead of creating a peaceful Europe, the treaties led to unsolvable problems that caused years of instability and future points of conflict. To understand why this was so, we need to look at the new boundaries created by the settlements and the inconsistent application of the principle of national self-determination.

The boundaries created by the settlements

The simultaneous collapse of the Austro-Hungarian, Russian, Ottoman, and German empires, and the demands for self-determination by the peoples who had been part of these empires, confronted the Allied and associated powers with the complex task of defining the frontiers for these new nation states.

- In eastern Europe the boundaries for a resurrected Polish state had to be drawn up at a time when Poland was claiming much of Ukraine and also pushing its frontiers as far west as possible.
- The collapse of the Austro-Hungarian Empire effectively meant that four new states had to be created – Austria, Hungary, Czechoslovakia, and Yugoslavia – as well as ceding territory to Romania and Italy.
- The collapse of the Russian and the Ottoman empires also led to the drawing up of arbitrary frontiers both in eastern Europe and the Near East. These borders were vulnerable when Russia and the Ottomans (under the flag of the newly created republic of Turkey) regained some of their former strength. For example, the extension of Greece into Smyrna and the creation of an independent Armenia did not survive the emergence of a strong new Turkish state and a reunited Russia, the **USSR**.

KEY TERM

USSR The Union of Soviet Socialist Republics, the new Bolshevik name for the Russian Empire after 1922.

The inconsistent application of national self-determination

Creating these new nations inevitably resulted in an inconsistent application of the ideal of national self-determination, leading to significant future problems. To take just a few examples: in the Sudetenland in Czechslovakia there were 3 million people who identified as German who were now living in a new non-German state, and there were also large German communities in what was now Poland. Otto Bauer, Austria's foreign minister, also complained that: 'No fewer than two-fifths of our people are to be subjugated to foreign dominion, without any plebiscite and against their indisputable will, being thus deprived of their right to self-determination.'

Reactions of the victors and defeated powers to the peace treaties

While the defeated powers deeply resented the terms imposed on them, the victors too were critical of many aspects of the treaties. The reason for this was that the treaties were compromises in which no power achieved all that it wanted.

Britain and France

Neither Britain nor France received all they had hoped for. French public opinion was convinced that France, particularly in the agreements covering the Rhineland, disarmament, and eastern Europe, had not secured the necessary terms to guarantee its future safety. For this France blamed the 'naïve' idealism of Britain and the USA. Many British people, on the other hand, believed that French attitudes had prevented the negotiation of a moderate and lasting peace. Over the next five years both countries would attempt to bend the treaties to their wishes.

The USA

By January 1920 the Treaty of Versailles had been **ratified** by all the signatory powers with the important exception of the USA. In Washington, crucial amendments had been put forward by a coalition of **isolationists** led by Senator Lodge, rejecting the Shandong settlement with Japan and seriously modifying the Covenant of the League of Nations. In essence, the isolationists feared that if the USA joined the League, it could be committed to defending the independence of other League members from aggression, even if this meant going to war. They therefore proposed that Congress should be empowered to veto US participation in any League initiative that clashed with the USA's traditional policy of isolationism and independence. Wilson felt that these amendments would paralyze the League and so refused to accept them. He failed twice to secure the necessary two-thirds majority in the Senate. The consequences for Europe of Wilson's defeat were serious. Without US ratification, the Anglo-American military guarantee of France lapsed and the burden of carrying out the Treaty of Versailles fell on Britain and France.

KEY TERMS

Ratified Having received formal approval from the legislature.

Isolationists Those who argue in favor of remaining detached from international politics.

Italy

Despite gains for their country in the South Tyrol, many Italian nationalists regarded the peace treaties as a '**mutilated victory**.' Italy had suffered high casualties and not been awarded what it had been promised by the Treaty of London in 1915. This treaty promised Italy not only South Tyrol, but also Istria and nearly half the Dalmatian coastline (see map, page 80), as well as territory in Africa and the Middle East. The Italian prime minister, **Vittorio Orlando**, was desperate to prove to his electorate that Italy could not be dictated to by the great powers. In the Adriatic, Italy had claimed Istria and Dalmatia and insisted also on its right to annex the port of Fiume, in which there was a slight majority of ethnic Italians. However, President Wilson, after compromising over the Saar and Shandong, was stubbornly determined to make a stand on the Fourteen Points in the Adriatic. Orlando and his foreign secretary, Sidney Sonnino, walked out of the conference in protest and did not return until May 9, 1919. It was not until November 1920 that Yugoslavia and Italy agreed on a compromise and signed the Treaty of Rapallo. Istria was partitioned between the two powers, and Fiume became a self-governing free city, while the rest of Dalmatia went to Yugoslavia.

KEY TERM

Mutilated victory An Italian nationalist view of their country's victory in the First World War, which they saw as having been tarnished by the refusal of the Allies to give Italy what it had been promised.

KEY FIGURE

Vittorio Orlando (1860–1952) Italian prime minister, 1917–19.

Japan

Japan came to Paris to achieve certain specific aims:

- to retain the the territory of Shandong province, in China, which had been formerly leased to Germany
- to establish control over the former German islands in the north Pacific
- as far as possible to co-operate with Britain and the USA and support the Fourteen Points.

Although Japan gained much of what it had wanted in the Treaty of Versailles, it viewed the treaty with mixed feelings. Japan did retain Shandong and the former German Pacific islands, but they were made mandates under the League of Nations, which meant that they were administered by the League of Nations until they were deemed capable of self-governance.

KEY TERM

Status quo A Latin term denoting the current state of affairs.

Japan was lukewarm about the establishment of the League of Nations as it feared that this might be an attempt to keep the **status quo** and confine Japan to being a second-class power. Japan wanted to ensure a racial equality clause was included in the League of Nations' constitution if it could not delay the League's creation. When this clause was rejected by the USA and also by Britain as a result of pressure from New Zealand and Australia, the Japanese press reacted very negatively. It was also seen as a great humiliation by all political parties in Japan and contributed to the suspicion that Britain and the USA were in reality intent on limiting Japanese power in East Asia.

KEY FIGURE

Count Makino Nobuaki (1861–1949) A prominent member of the Japanese delegation at the Paris Peace Conference.

Count Makino Nobuaki warned the USA and the Allies that the failure to include the racial equality clause might cause Japan to lose faith in the League. Sadly, he was correct; the rejection of the clause was to be an important factor in turning Japan away from co-operating with the West and instead pursuing aggressive policies in China.

ACTIVITY

Look back at your answer to the activity on page 75 on the hopes of the victorious Allied powers. Now create another diagram on what each power gained from the peace treaties. Which power gained the most of what it wanted? Write a paragraph to explain your judgement.

Germany

On May 7, 1919 the draft peace terms of the Treaty of Versailles were at last presented to the German government, which was given 15 days to draw up its reply. The German government criticized the treaty on the basis that it did not conform to the Fourteen Points and demanded the following significant concessions:

- immediate membership of the League of Nations, from which Germany had been excluded
- a guarantee that Austria and the Sudetenland, which was to become part of the new Czechoslovak state (see page 82), should have the opportunity to decide whether they wished to join Germany (see Figure 2.2)
- the setting up of a neutral commission to examine the war guilt question.

Allied and US concessions

Although these demands were not accepted, Lloyd George, fearful that the German government might reject the treaty, persuaded the French representatives to agree to a plebiscite in Upper Silesia. He failed to limit the Rhineland occupation to five years, but did manage to secure the vague assurance, which later became Article 431 of the treaty, 'that once Germany had given concrete evidence of her willingness to fulfil her obligations,' the Allied and associated powers would consider 'an earlier termination of the period of occupation.'

The signing of the Treaty of Versailles and German resentment

On June 16 Germany was handed the final version of the treaty incorporating these concessions. Not surprisingly, given the depth of opposition to it among the German people, it triggered a political crisis that split the cabinet and led to the resignation of the Chancellor. Yet in view of its own military weakness and the continuing Allied blockade, the Berlin government had little option but to accept the treaty, although it made it very clear that it was acting under pressure. On June 28, 1919 the treaty was signed in the Hall of Mirrors at Versailles, where in 1871 the German Empire had been proclaimed.

To what extent does Source 2.3 express the feeling that Germany had no option but to accept the peace treaty?

SOURCE 2.3

Gustav Bauer, the German chancellor, announces Germany's reluctant acceptance of the Treaty of Versailles.

Surrendering to superior force but without retracting its opinion regarding the unheard-of injustice of the peace conditions, the government of the German Republic therefore declares its readiness to accept and sign the peace conditions imposed by the Allied and associated governments.

Study Source 2.4. Why did France choose the Hall of Mirrors as the venue for the peace signature? What effect did this choice have on the attitude of German people?

SOURCE 2.4

In the Hall of Mirrors in Versailles, French prime minister Georges Clemenceau adds his signature to the Treaty of Versailles on June 28, 1919.

Although some historians argue that the Treaty of Versailles was less harsh than its critics have claimed, it was nevertheless a deeply traumatic blow to Germans of all classes and political parties. They particularly resented in what they perceived to be a dictated peace:

- the war guilt clause
- the burden of reparations, which were considered 'punitive' and would burden the German economy for generations to come
- the loss of land in east Germany to Poland
- the occupation of the Rhineland, particularly in the French zone, by French colonial troops, which was regarded as a deep humiliation.

Although after 1924 the Dawes and Young plans (see pages 119 and 121) eased the burden of reparations and in 1930 Britain and France evacuated the Rhineland, the Treaty of Versailles remained a symbol of national humiliation to Germans, which would later be fully exploited by political movements in Germany.

What can we learn from sources 2.3, 2.4 and 2.5 about the attitude of German people to Versailles? Identify specific words and phrases from each source to evidence your views.

SOURCE 2.5

From a German government proclamation issued on the date of the coming into force of the Treaty of Versailles, January 10, 1920.

The unfavourable result of the war has surrendered us defenceless to the mercy of our adversaries, and imposes upon us great sacrifices under the name of peace. The hardest, however, which is forced upon us is the surrender of German districts in the east, west and north. Thousands of our fellow Germans must submit to the rule of foreign states without the possibility of asserting their right to self-determination ... Together we keep the language which our mother taught us … By all the fibres of our being, by our love and by our whole life, we remain united.

Everything that is in our power to preserve your mother tongue, your German individuality, the intimate spiritual connection with your home country will be done …

Austria, Hungary, and Bulgaria

The immediate reaction to the peace terms in all three countries was one of shock and betrayal. One left-wing Austrian newspaper declared that 'never has the substance of a treaty of peace so grossly betrayed the intentions that guided its construction as is the case with this treaty.' Most Austrians were bitterly disappointed by Article 80, which prevented an *Anschluss* with Germany. Many Hungarian people felt that the Treaty of Trianon was an act of revenge and cruelty by the Allied powers. Until the end of the Second World War the overriding aim of the Hungarian government was to regain the lost territories. In Bulgaria nationalists and the army initially talked of resisting the treaties, but the prime minister, **Aleksandar Stamboliyski**, accepted the new frontiers and rejected the expansionist policies of the past, even coming to terms with Yugoslavia. He believed that the treaty could in time be changed peacefully, and he also wanted to turn his attention to internal reform.

KEY FIGURE

Aleksandar Stamboliyski (1879–1923) Prime minister of Bulgaria, 1919–23.

The Ottoman Empire

When the Allies imposed the Treaty of Sèvres, they took little account of the profound changes in the Ottoman Empire brought about by the rise of Mustafa Kemal, leader of the Turkish National Movement and the founder of the modern Republic of Turkey. Kemal had set up a rebel government in Ankara in March 1920 and was determined not to accept the treaty. While the treaty was still being negotiated, Turkish resentment was growing, particularly at the Greek occupation of Smyrna in May 1919 and advance into the Anatolian interior, which the Allies had encouraged. By the time the treaty was finally signed in August 1920, its terms were impossible to enforce.

MUSTAFA KEMAL

1881	Born in Salonika
1905	Graduated from military college as a staff captain
1908	Supported attempts to modernize the then Ottoman Empire
1915	Led the defeat of Allied troops at Gallipoli
1919	Became leader of a nationalist revolution in Turkey
1920	Ejected the Greeks from Smyrna and forced Britain and France to renegotiate the Treaty of Sèvres
1923	Founded the Turkish republic and served as its first president until his death
1934	Granted the honorary name Atatürk, 'father of the Turks'
1938	Died

Mustafa Kemal had supported attempts to modernize Turkey since 1908. He led the defeat of the Allies when they landed at Gallipoli in 1915. Bitterly opposed to the Treaty of Sèvres, he took back Smyrna from Greece in 1920 and confronted Britain over the imposed neutrality of the Straits. In order to avert further conflict, the Allies agreed to renegotiate the treaty. The resulting Treaty of Lausanne replaced the Treaty of Sèvres and led to the foundation of the Turkish republic in 1923. As Turkey's first president, Kemal modernized Turkey by introducing a Latin alphabet and Western-style dress. Women were granted the right to vote. He started to industrialize Turkey and to reorientate policy away from traditional Islamic loyalties.

The position of Russia

The Russian Empire had no representation at the Paris Peace Conference. Technically, Russia was still an ally of the Entente powers and the USA, as Germany had been forced to renounce the Treaty of Brest-Litovsk when it signed the armistice of November 11. However, by the time of the Paris Peace Conference, Russia was engulfed in civil war. The Bolsheviks had overthrown the government, but faced opposition from the white Russians, who were called 'Whites' as a symbol of the old Russian Empire and in opposition to the 'Red' Bolsheviks. They were supported militarily by the Allies and the USA. Allied military support was insufficient to defeat the Bolsheviks, and the White Russians were divided among themselves. It was therefore difficult to know whether to invite the White Russians or the Bolsheviks or both. Who represented the Russian people? Wilson and Lloyd George were ready to issue an invitation, but this was bitterly opposed by Clemenceau, who feared that a Bolshevik delegation would seize the chance to start revolution in Paris.

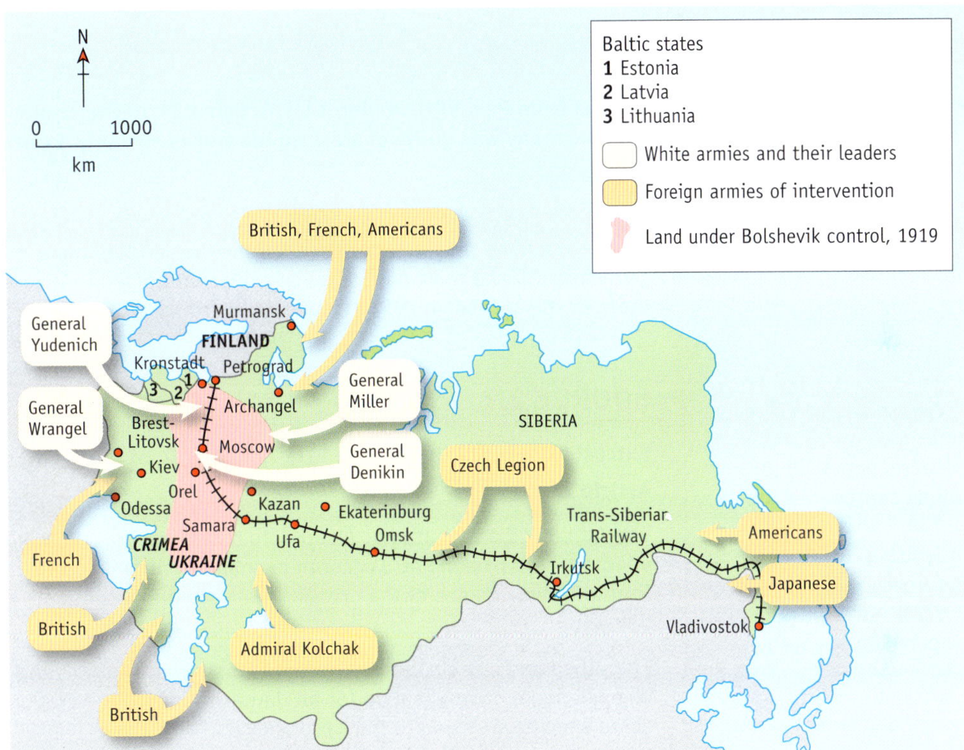

Figure 2.4 The Russian Civil War. The Reds were the Bolsheviks and their supporters; the Whites were Russian supporters of the tsar or those opposed to the Bolsheviks. The White Russians received support from many foreign governments.

Nevertheless, on January 21, 1919 Clemenceau reluctantly agreed to a compromise put forward by Wilson and Lloyd-George that representatives of the conference's Supreme Council (Council of Ten) could meet the Bolsheviks and the other Russian representatives on the island of Prinkipo in the Sea of Marmara, provided that both sides agreed on a ceasefire in the civil war. The Bolsheviks were ready to meet the Allies, but not end the civil war, which they had a good chance of winning. The White Russians, backed by the Conservative Party in Britain and **right-wing** parties in France and Italy, were hostile to the proposal. Negotiations about a possible meeting continued until April, but the communist uprising in Hungary in March 1919 led by **Béla Kun** reawakened suspicions that the Bolsheviks were planning to spread revolution to central and western Europe. Lloyd George was also under pressure from his Conservative **coalition** partners not to recognize a Bolshevik government. On May 23 the Allies agreed to recognize the White Russian regime of **Alexander Kolchak**, provided it agreed to introduce a democratic system of government, but it was already too late as Kolchak faced imminent defeat by the Bolsheviks.

ACTIVITY

Create a spider diagram showing the reaction of each of the defeated powers to their particular peace treaty.

KEY FIGURES

Béla Kun (1886–1938) Hungarian journalist who established a communist regime in his country, which lasted just 133 days in 1919.

Alexander Kolchak (1874–1920) Russian admiral who commanded the Black Sea Fleet during the First World War and led the anti-Bolshevik White Russian regime during the Russian Civil War.

KEY TERMS

Right-wing A general term to describe conservative politicians, parties, and policies. Right-wing politics uphold 'traditional' social hierarchies and argue that some level of social inequality is natural and acceptable. Extreme right-wing beliefs are referred to as 'far-right', and include fascism and Nazism.

Coalition A term commonly used to refer to a government made up of two or more minority parties who agree to work together to form a majority. Following the British general election of December 1918, the Liberal prime minister, Lloyd George, led a Conservative–Liberal coalition in which the Conservatives predominated.

Reparations

The payment of reparations in the form of deliveries of coal or machinery and annual payments of large sums of money for several decades was a key aspect of the peace treaties with the defeated powers. Reparations were intended to provide the funds to help repair the damage that the defeated powers had inflicted on the victors.

The question of 'war guilt'

There was universal agreement among the victorious powers that Germany and its allies were guilty of having started the war. It was this principle of war guilt that was to provide the legal and indeed moral justification for the reparations clauses of the treaty, as was stressed in Article 231 of the Treaty of Versailles (see Source 2.6). War guilt clauses were also included in the treaties with Austria, Hungary, Bulgaria, and the Ottoman Empire.

SOURCE 2.6

Extract from Part VIII, Section 1 [I], Article 231, of the Treaty of Versailles, 1919. The claim that Germany was guilty of starting the war is strongly asserted.

Article 231

The Allied and associated governments affirm, and Germany accepts, the responsibility of Germany and her allies for causing all the loss and damage to which the Allied and associated governments and their nationals have been subjected as a consequence of the war imposed on them by the aggression of Germany and her allies.

Rewrite Source 2.7 in your own words. After reading pages 88–89, study sources 2.6 and 2.7 and answer this question: How far do sources 2.6 and 2.7 agree on German war guilt and reparation payments?

SOURCE 2.7

Extract from Part VIII, Section 1 [I], Article 232, of the Treaty of Versailles, 1919.

Article 232

The Allied and associated governments recognise that the resources of Germany are not adequate, after taking into account permanent diminutions of such resources, which will result from other provisions of the present treaty, to make complete reparation for all such loss and damage.

The Allied and associated governments, however, require, and Germany undertakes, that she will make compensation for all damage done to the civilian population of the Allied and associated powers and to their property.

Size and payment of German reparations

Although there was general agreement that Germany should pay reparations to the victors, there was considerable debate about the amount to be paid, the nature of the damage deserving compensation and how Germany could raise such large sums of money without rebuilding an export trade that might then harm the Allied industries. Essentially, the major issue behind the Allied demands was the need to cover the costs of financing the war. Britain had covered one-third of its war expenditure through taxation; France just one-sixth. At a time of severe social unrest, no Allied country could easily face the prospect of financing debt repayments by huge tax increases and large cuts in expenditure. Initially, it was hoped that the USA could be persuaded to continue wartime inter-Allied economic co-operation and, above all, cancel the repayment of Allied war debts. However, by the end of 1918 it was obvious that this was not going to happen, as Wilson had dissolved all the agencies for inter-Allied co-operation in Washington.

KEY FIGURES

Louis-Lucien Klotz (1868–1930) A French journalist and politician who served as his country's finance minister, 1917–20.

Louis Loucheur (1872–1931) French Minister of Munitions, 1917–18, and Minister of Industrial Reconstruction, 1918–20.

French demands

The French finance minister, **Louis-Lucien Klotz**, backed by the press and the Chamber of Deputies, urged a policy of maximum claims and coined the slogan that 'Germany will pay' (for everything). Behind the scenes, however, **Louis Loucheur**, the Minister of Industrial

KEY TERM

Bond A means for a government or large company to borrow money, which they promise to repay at a fixed rate of interest by a specified date.

KEY TERM

Imperial War Cabinet A co-ordinating body made up of representatives from Britain and the self-governing Commonwealth countries, which met from 1917 to 1919.

Reconstruction, pursued a more subtle policy and informed Germany that, such was the need of the French economy for an immediate injection of cash, his government would settle for a more moderate sum to be raised quickly through Germany selling **bonds** on the world's financial markets. Germany suspected that these gestures were just a way to split Germany from the USA, which the government in Berlin saw as potentially the most sympathetic to the German cause. The USA's reparation policy was certainly more moderate than either Britain's or France's as it recommended that a modest fixed sum should be written into the treaty.

British demands

The British delegation consistently maximized its country's reparation claims on Germany. Some historians explain this in terms of the pressure exerted on the government by the electorate. Lloyd George himself defended the claim by saying that 'the imposition of a high indemnity ... would prevent the Germans spending money on an army.' However, it is arguable that his demand for a high payment by Germany was also motivated by a desire to ensure that there would be money left over for Britain after France and Belgium had claimed their share. To safeguard Britain's percentage of reparations, the **Imperial War Cabinet** urged that the cost of war pensions should be included in the reparation bill. By threatening to walk out of the conference, Lloyd George then forced the US, French, and Italian delegations to support Britain's demands. Later, as reparation debts seemed to paralyze the German economy and hinder global economic recovery, Lloyd George reconsidered his stance on reparations.

The Reparation Commission

The British pension claims made it even more difficult for Allied financial experts to agree on an overall figure for reparations from Germany. Consequently, at the end of April 1919 it was agreed that a commission should be set up in Paris to assess in detail what the German economy could afford. In the meantime, Germany would make an interim payment of 20 billion gold marks and raise a further 60 billion through the sale of bonds. In December 1919 Britain and France agreed that Britain should receive 25 per cent of the total amount of reparations to be paid by Germany, while France would have 55 per cent. Belgium was the only power to be awarded full compensation for its losses and was given priority in payment of the first sums due from Germany, largely because it had threatened to withdraw from the conference at a time when Italy had already walked out and Japan was also threatening to do so. The scope of the commission was later extended to cover reparation payments by Austria, Hungary, and Bulgaria, and oversee the finances of the Ottoman Empire.

In April 1921 the Reparation Commission fixed a global total of 132 billion gold marks for Germany to pay over a period of 42 years. It was this reparations question that was to cause Allied governments the most problems over the next three years.

The reparations of the other defeated powers

Austria, Hungary, and Bulgaria had to accept war guilt clauses and agree to the payment of reparations, of which the amount was to be determined by the Reparation Commission. Reparations were to consist of both money payments and payments in kind.

The Ottoman Empire was spared from paying reparations, but in the Treaty of Sèvres had to agree to Allied control of its finances. This involved allowing the Allies to approve and supervise the national budget, implement financial laws and regulations and totally control the Ottoman Bank. Any future changes to taxes would also need the consent of the Reparation Commission.

Look at the 'payments in kind' listed in Source 2.8. Research online and create a list of the other goods taken as reparations payments.

SOURCE 2.8

Article 127 of the Treaty of Neuilly with Bulgaria.

Bulgaria further undertakes to deliver to Greece, Roumania and the Serb-Croat-Slovene state, within six months from the coming into force of the present treaty, livestock of the description and in numbers set hereunder:

	Greece	Roumania	Serbo-Croat-Slovene state
Bulls (18 months to 3 years)	15	60	50
Milch cows (2–6 years)	1,500	6,000	6,000
Horses and mares (3–7 years)	2,250	5,250	5,000
Mules	450	1,050	1,000
Draught oxen	1,800	4,400	4,000
Sheep	6,000	15,000	12,000

ACTIVITY

Below are four factors that most of the losing powers had to deal with following the peace treaties. For each of the major losing powers, award each factor a mark out of 6 – the higher the mark, the greater the importance. Explain the marks you have given.

Loss of land

Reparations

Loss of military

War guilt

KEY DEBATE

HOW HARSH WERE THE PEACE TREATIES AFTER THE FIRST WORLD WAR?

In the inter-war period the peace treaties were seen by some people as a triumph of democracy, the rule of law, self-determination, and collective security against militarism. Others viewed them as a hypocritical act of vengeance and economic ignorance. Of all the criticisms of the Treaty of Versailles the best-known is by the economist **John Maynard Keynes**. He argued that the Treaty of Versailles would ruin the global economy, which had already been weakened by the war. Later the Treaty of Versailles was also blamed for the rise of Hitler and the outbreak of the Second World War in 1939.

How accurate is this perception? Viewed from the perspective of 1945, when Germany was totally defeated, the Treaty of Versailles does not appear as harsh as it did in 1919. The German army was capped at 100,000 soldiers, but Germany was still potentially a great power. It had lost part of Upper Silesia and much of its eastern territories and Danzig, but it still retained the great industrial center of **the Ruhr**. In fact, given the collapse of the Austrian Empire and the Treaty of Riga, which excluded Russia from central Europe (see page 110), Germany's position was potentially more powerful in central and eastern Europe after the First World War than before it, even though there were considerable German minorities trapped in Poland. It is also important to stress that the schedule of reparations eventually forced on Germany in 1921 was less severe than the one that Germany imposed on France after its defeat in 1870. The total amount of German debt in 1921 was also slightly less than Britain's own national debt in 1921, which was increased by the money it owed to the USA.

The treaties with Austria, Hungary, and Bulgaria were an attempt to give the people of south-eastern Europe a right to self-determination and to secure territorial and strategic advantages for the allies of France and Britain, particularly Romania. The latter aim often overrode the former. Some historians argue that the peacemakers in Paris were faced with an almost impossible task in drawing up the borders of the post-war **successor states** and on the whole managed to navigate different claims fairly evenly, guided by the new concept of ethnic self-determination. Yet the new frontiers interrupted trade and shattered the economic unity that had existed in the pre-war Austro-Hungarian Empire. Perhaps more importantly for the future, many ethnic minorities were left stranded in the new states – for example, the 3 million Sudeten Germans in Czechoslovakia. Hitler's exploitation of the ethnic grievances of German minorities in 1938–39 was a major cause of the outbreak of the Second World War in September 1939.

The Treaty of Sèvres was harsh because of several of the measures it imposed on the Ottoman Empire. Firstly, the treaty forced significant territorial losses, redistributing large portions of Ottoman land to Allied powers such as France, the United Kingdom, Greece, and Italy. It also imposed severe military restrictions, limiting the Ottoman army to just 50,000 troops and prohibiting a navy and air force. Economically, the Allies took control of the Ottoman Empire's finances, taxes, and budget, adding to the strain. Furthermore, their control of the Dardanelles Strait removed strategic control from the Ottomans over this vital waterway. Although specific reparations were not demanded, the economic terms were still burdensome, contributing to the empire's instability. These harsh terms led to widespread resistance and were only improved with the negotiation of a new treaty at Lausanne in 1923, which significantly revised the conditions.

KEY TERMS

The Ruhr Germany's most important industrial region, centered around the Ruhr Valley in the west of the country.

Successor state A new country created when a larger country is divided up. After the First World War successor states such as Czechoslovakia, Yugoslavia, and Poland came into being following the break-up of the German, Austro-Hungarian, and Ottoman empires.

KEY FIGURE

John Maynard Keynes (1883–1946) An influential British economist.

ACTIVITY

Produce a presentation in which you give reasons for arguing, on the one hand, that the peace treaties were fair and, on the other hand, that they were punitive and vengeful.

Why was there such extensive dissatisfaction with the peace settlements of 1919–20?

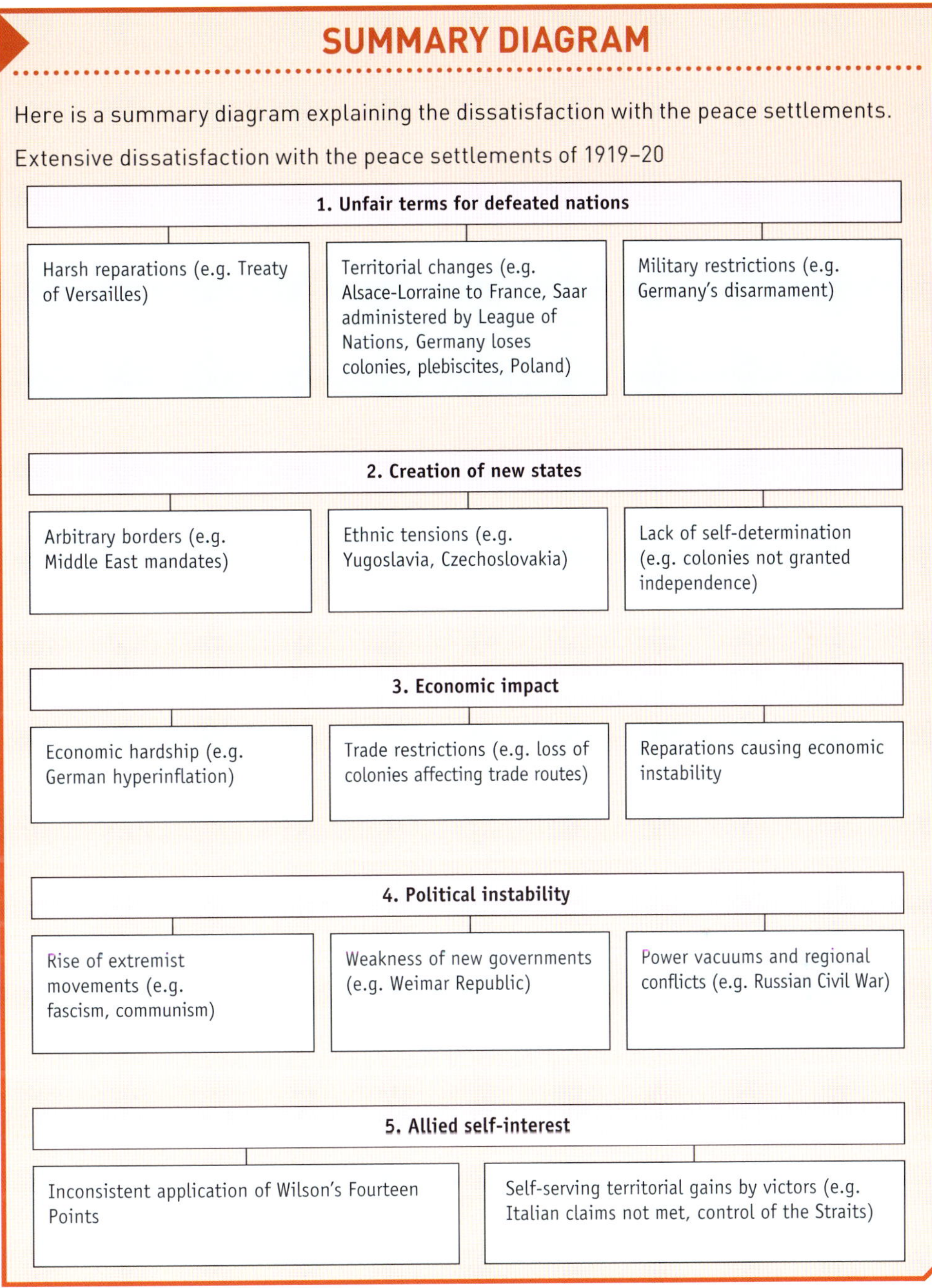

2 Why was the League of Nations created and what challenges did it face in the 1920s?

The League of Nations was a part of the international settlements negotiated in 1919–20, and its ultimate success or failure was dependent on the progress made by the great powers in stabilizing Europe after the First World War. It was clear that the proposals put forward by the Hague conferences of 1899 and 1907 did not go far enough. They had been insufficient to stop the outbreak of war in 1914, although they had devised a framework for settling international disputes by arbitration. The idea of a league of nations was a reaction to the appalling slaughter of the war and the belief that the great powers had slipped into conflict in 1914 by accident.

The creation of the League

To prevent future wars, three key requirements for a proposed league of nations emerged:

- a system of arbitration including some sort of penalty for states that ignored it and used force to achieve their aims
- a regular conference system where international problems could be discussed
- a way of imposing a pause or delay in a dispute to prevent war breaking out before a compromise or solution could be found.

Initially, proposals for an organization embodying these principles were put forward by private individuals and groups such as a meeting of American professors at the Century Club in New York in January 1915 and a study group in London led by **Viscount Bryce** and **Goldsworthy Lowes Dickinson**. In May 1915 a League of Nations Society was founded in Britain, and a month later an American group formed the League to Enforce Peace.

In December 1916 the British government set up a committee under **Sir Walter Phillimore**, a judge with expertise in international law, to enquire into 'various schemes for establishing by means of a league of nations, or other device, some alternative to war as a means of settling international disputes.' In March 1918 the Phillimore committee reported with the following recommendations:

- Signatory states would not resort to war before submitting their disagreement to arbitration or an international conference.
- If a state refused arbitration or ignored the recommendation offered, the other states could ultimately use force to compel acceptance.

In general, Britain was opposed to anything that might lead to the creation of a 'super-state.' It agreed that there should be provision for **sanctions**, but not for the creation of an international police force in any form. Individual states would act independently against an aggressor. In the meantime France drew up plans for a league based on the idea of effective sanctions and the use of an international force to carry them out.

KEY TERM

Sanctions Penalties, usually of a commercial or economic nature, applied to bring pressure on a state that is failing to meet its international obligations.

KEY FIGURES

Viscount Bryce (1838–1922) An academic, lawyer and Liberal politician.

Goldsworthy Lowes Dickinson (1862–1932) A political scientist and philosopher who was associated with the free-thinking Bloomsbury Group of artists and writers.

Sir Walter Phillimore (1845–1929) A British High Court judge.

Wilson's Fourteen Points

Both proposals were sent to Washington for the consideration of President Wilson, who had backed the creation of 'a general association of nations' to guarantee the 'political independence and territorial integrity of all states' in his Fourteen Points. Wilson was critical of both the French and British drafts. He was unhappy with Britain's omission of a guarantee of independence for all states, but equally he disliked the French suggestion of an international force. This was incompatible with the American constitution, according to which only Congress could take the USA into war. If the USA was part of an international force, it might well have to go to war independently of Congress's approval. Optimistically, Wilson believed that once democratic governments were established, the force of public opinion would be powerful enough to stop an aggressive state. It could be argued that this was a naïve approach, but in reality neither American public opinion nor Congress would tolerate subordination to an international power.

The Smuts contribution

KEY FIGURE

Field Marshal Jan Smuts (1870–1950) was a South African military leader who fought against Britain in the Boer War. He later served as Prime Minister of South Africa from 1919 to 1924 and again from 1939 to 1948. He was also an adviser to Winston Churchill during the Second World War. He was the only person to sign the peace treaties that ended both world wars. He strongly believed in white supremacy in South Africa.

Field Marshal Smuts argued in a memorandum published in December 1916 that a league of nations should be more than just a means for settling international disputes. Smuts argued that it should become responsible for stabilizing the new states created in eastern Europe. It would, to quote Smuts, become their 'trustee.' Ultimately, this proposal led to the creation of the mandate system and the economic intervention of the League in Hungary and Austria (see page 111).

The shaping of the League at the Paris Peace Conference

A committee was set up in Paris in 1919 to draft the constitution of the League. It first met on February 4 and consisted of representatives of the five leading powers at the peace conference – Britain, France, the USA, Italy, and Japan – as well as five of the 'smaller states', including Belgium, China, and Portugal. Later, despite British opposition on the grounds that an increase in numbers would only slow down the work of the committee, Czechoslovakia, Greece, Poland, and Romania joined. British fears of long delays proved groundless, and by April the committee put forward its recommendation for the Covenant of the League based on the final Anglo-American draft plan, which was to form the basic structure of the League.

Nevertheless, there were three key disagreements among the committee members:

- The British representative rejected the American insistence that the members of the League should guarantee 'the territorial integrity and existing political independence of all members of the League.' This in fact formed the basis of Article 10, but a compromise was reached that found expression in Article 19 of the Covenant. This provided for the revision of treaties that were no longer relevant.
- The French representative argued that 'covenants without swords' were useless in keeping the peace and wanted an international army. This proposal was defeated by both Britain and the USA. The British feared that France would dominate an international force, while the USA feared that its membership of an international force would be contrary to the US constitution. There was therefore no provision for an international force under the League. This later led to accusations that the League of Nations was just a 'talking shop.'
- The Japanese representative wanted to include in the Covenant a clause guaranteeing racial equality. This met with strong opposition from the USA on the grounds that a state such as itself or Australia could be brought before an international court for discriminating against immigrants on the grounds of race. Japan argued strongly for the insertion of such a clause in the Covenant and was supported by 11 of the 19 committee members, but they could not overcome the opposition of President Wilson. Consequently, it is perhaps not surprising that the first major challenge to the League was to come from Japan in 1931.

ACTIVITY

Draw a spider diagram showing what powers Britain, France, the USA, and Japan thought the League of Nations should possess. Then briefly explain the thinking behind the demands of each of the four states.

The Covenant of the League was finally approved by the Peace Conference on April 28, 1919 and was included in all five peace treaties. However, it did not form part of the Treaty of Lausanne, which was signed with Turkey in 1923 and superseded the Treaty of Sèvres.

The aims of the League

The aims of the League were clearly stated in the Covenant of the League of Nations, which formed the first part of each of the peace treaties. The heart of the Covenant, articles 8–17, was primarily concerned with the overriding question of the prevention of war. The League's long-term strategy for creating a peaceful world was summed up in the first section of Article 8 (see Source 2.9).

SOURCE 2.9

From Article 8 of the Covenant of the League of Nations.

The members of the League recognise that the maintenance of peace requires the reduction of national armaments to the lowest point consistent with national safety, and the enforcement by common action of international obligations.

The process for solving disputes between sovereign powers was defined in articles 12–17. Initially (according to Article 12), disputes were to be submitted to some form of arbitration or inquiry by the League. While this was happening, there was to be a cooling-off period of three months. By Article 13, members were committed to carrying out the judgments of the Permanent Court of International Justice or the recommendations of the Council. Even if a dispute was not submitted to arbitration, the Council was empowered by Article 15 to set up an inquiry into its origins. The assumption in these articles was that states would be only too willing to avoid war by making use of the League's arbitration machinery. If, however, a state ignored the League's recommendations, Article 16 would come into effect (see Source 2.10).

What can we learn from sources 2.9 and 2.10 about the duties of members of the League?

SOURCE 2.10

From Article 16 of the Covenant of the League of Nations.

Should any member of the League resort to war in disregard of its covenants under Articles 12, 13 or 15, it shall ... be deemed to have committed an act of war against all other members of the League, which hereby undertake immediately to subject it to the severance of all trade or financial relations ...

It shall be the duty of the Council in such case to recommend to the several governments concerned what effective military, naval or air force the members of the League shall severally contribute to the armed forces to be used to protect the covenants of the League.

In Article 17 the League's powers were significantly extended by its right to intervene in disputes between non-members of the League.

In theory, the League seemed to have formidable powers, but it was not a world government in the making, with the authority to coerce independent nations. Its existence was based, as Article 10 made clear, on the recognition of the political and territorial independence of all member states. Article 15, for example, recognized that if a dispute arose from an internal issue, the League had no right to intervene. There were, too, several gaps in the League Covenant that allowed a potential aggressor to wage war without sanction. War had to be officially declared before the League could act effectively. Therefore, it had no formula for dealing with acts of guerrilla warfare, for example, which the instigating state could disown. Even in the event of a formal declaration of war, if the Permanent Court of International Justice (see below) or the Council could not agree on a judgment, then League members were free to continue with their war.

The structure of the League

The League of Nations at first consisted of three main organs: the Assembly, the Council, and the Permanent Secretariat. A fourth institution, the Permanent Court of International Justice, was added in 1921.

Assembly

KEY TERM

Deliberative chamber
An assembly appointed to debate or discuss issues.

The Assembly met once a year. It was essentially a **deliberative chamber** where each state, regardless of size, was allotted three representatives. It was a key principle that the smallest state had the right to be heard on international issues.

Council

The Council in 1920 had four permanent members: Britain, France, Italy, and Japan. In 1926 this was increased by one when Germany joined. The smaller states were represented by a changing rota of four temporary members, later increased to seven, who were all selected by the Assembly. As the Council met more frequently than the Assembly (four times a year) and was dominated by the great powers, it gradually developed into an **executive committee** or 'cabinet' of the Assembly and worked out the details and implementation of policies that the Assembly had endorsed in principle. Decisions in both bodies were normally taken by unanimous vote (everyone had to agree). The votes of states involved in a dispute under discussion by the League were discounted when the Assembly and Council voted on recommendations for the settlement of the matter. In this way, they could be prevented from vetoing an otherwise unanimous decision.

KEY TERMS

Executive committee A committee that can take key decisions.

International civil service A permanent administration made up of officials from all the member states.

Permanent Secretariat

The routine administrative work of the League and its agencies was carried out by the Permanent Secretariat, which was staffed by a relatively small **international civil service**.

Permanent Court of International Justice

The Permanent Court of International Justice was set up at The Hague in the Netherlands with the tasks of advising the Council on legal matters and judging cases submitted by individual states.

What can be learned from Source 2.11 about the ambitions of the League of Nations?

SOURCE 2.11

Ambassadors from around the world gather in the Salle de la Réformation, Geneva for the first session of the League of Nations Assembly, November 15, 1920.

Weaknesses of the League

The League was a new experiment in international co-operation, which co-existed uneasily with the traditional system of sovereign states. It had many weaknesses.

Restricted membership

The initial members of the League were the 32 Allied states that had signed the peace treaties and 13 neutral states. Any other state could be admitted to membership by a two-thirds vote of the Assembly. By 1926 all the former Central Powers, including Germany, had joined, but Soviet Russia did not do so until 1934, and the USA never did. The absence of Germany until 1926 and Russia until 1934 weakened the League as both were potentially powerful states. The USA's absence was a huge weakness and was one of the major reasons for the League's ultimate failure.

KEY TERM

Conference of Ambassadors
A standing committee of the principal Allied and associated powers set up to supervise the carrying out of the Treaty of Versailles. It succeeded the Supreme War Council.

Failure to provide international leadership

The League inherited elements of the peace settlement (which it had no role in creating) and often appeared to be answerable to the **Conference of Ambassadors**. It was, for example, responsible for the administration of the Saar and Danzig, which inevitably involved its becoming too closely associated with the policy of the Allies.

The League was dependent on the great powers, none of which was ready to prioritize it over their own interests. Several incidents (see Corfu, page 105, or the Ruhr Crisis, page 106) underlined the continuing self-interest of the major powers and their ability to ignore the League and to take unilateral action when it pleased them. This made it difficult to achieve unanimity (where everyone agrees) in support of a particular policy.

Flawed voting processes

Decisions by the Assembly and Council had to be unanimous, except for procedural matters like electing non-permanent Council members, where a two-thirds majority was sufficient. Similarly, when dealing with the appointment of committees to investigate a particular problem, majority voting was again in order. Also, when either the Council or the Assembly was considering a report on an international dispute, the votes of the parties involved would not be taken into account. However, the unanimity rule could prove a serious handicap, as it was possible for a member of the Council who was accused of threatening or disturbing the peace to prevent any effective action. This happened when Japan invaded Manchuria in 1931 and Italy invaded Abyssinia (now known as Ethiopia) in 1935.

Enforcement difficulties

Given the economic problems many states faced, they were both unwilling and unable to give the League any support in the event of a crisis that might result in war against an aggressor. Collective security struggled to work because it was hard to balance international principles with a nation's desire to maintain its sovereignty.

The League's Covenant provided too many loopholes for war, supported the status quo, which favored the great powers, and lacked the machinery for collective action against an aggressor. In other words, it lacked an army.

Yet even if the League had had a theoretically perfect constitution, would its history have been any different? Ultimately, it was a product of its times and could do only what its members wished.

ACTIVITY

Copy out and complete this table.

League's aims	Structures to carry them out	Weaknesses in structure

Collective security and the League's involvement in the resolution of post-war disputes

Until 1926, when the foreign ministers of Britain, France, and Germany began to attend the meetings of the Council and turn it into a body that regularly discussed the main problems of the day, the League's role in the many post-war crises was subordinated to the Allied leaders and the Conference of Ambassadors. For the most part, it therefore dealt with minor crises only.

In 1920 the inability of the League to act successfully without the backing of the great powers was clearly demonstrated when it failed to protect Armenia from a joint Russo-Turkish attack, as Britain, France, and Italy were not prepared to intervene militarily. One of the French delegates critically observed in the Assembly that he and his colleagues were 'in the ridiculous position of an Assembly that considers what steps should be taken, though it is perfectly aware that it is impossible for them to be carried out.'

Teschen

The border region of Teschen was a source of conflict between Poland and Czechoslovakia, two of the successor states to the Austro-Hungarian Empire, as it contained valuable coal fields and an important railway junction. In January 1919, following an armed clash between Polish and Czechoslovakian troops in Teschen, the Allies dispatched a commission to devise and recommend a solution, which included a plebiscite. Its proposals were not accepted, and neither state agreed to a plebiscite. Consequently, the Supreme Council meeting in Spa in 1920 awarded the coal mines to Czechoslovakia and divided the city of Teschen between the two states. Disagreements over the new frontiers persisted, but were finally resolved in 1924. It was here that the League of Nations played a role as both sides agreed to submit any further disputes to arbitration by the Permanent Court of International Justice unless an alternative means of arbitration were agreed on.

Vilna

KEY FIGURE

General Lucjan Żeligowski (1865–1947)
A Polish general of Lithuanian origin. He fought in both the First World War and the Polish-Soviet War.

In October 1920, in response to appeals from the Polish foreign minister, the League negotiated an armistice between Poland and Lithuania, whose quarrel over border territories was rapidly escalating into war. However, the ceasefire did not hold, as shortly afterwards **General Żeligowski**, with a Polish force that the Warsaw government diplomatically pretended was acting on its own initiative, occupied the city of Vilna and set up the new puppet government of central Lithuania under his protection. The League first called for a plebiscite and then, when this was rejected, attempted unsuccessfully to negotiate a compromise settlement.

In March 1922 Poland finally annexed Vilna province. A year later, after it was obvious that the League could not impose a solution without the support of the great powers, the Conference of Ambassadors took the matter into its own hands and recognized Polish sovereignty over Vilna. By not using the League of Nations to stop Polish aggression, Britain, France, and Italy further marginalized the organization.

The Aaland Islands

In less stubborn disputes, where the states involved were willing to accept a verdict, the League did have an important role to play as a mediator. The League enjoyed a rare success in the dispute between Finland and Sweden over the Aaland Islands. These had belonged to the Grand Duchy of Finland when it had been part of the Russian Empire. Once Finland had broken away from Russia in 1917, the islanders, who were ethnically Swedish, appealed to Stockholm to take over the islands. When Sweden began to threaten to use force, Britain referred the matter to the League. In 1921, the League of Nations decided to maintain the status quo by keeping the Aaland Islands under Finnish sovereignty. However, the League also committed to ensuring the civil rights of the Swedish population on the island itself. Neither government liked the verdict, but both accepted it and, what is more important, made it work.

Albania

In the second half of 1921, the League of Nations helped draw global attention to Albania's urgent plea for assistance against aggression from Greece and Yugoslavia. The Conference of Ambassadors had not yet finalized the borders in south-eastern Europe, so Greece and Yugoslavia took advantage of the situation to occupy as much Albanian territory as possible. The League Council sent a commission to investigate, but it was a telegram from British Prime Minister Lloyd George that spurred the Conference of Ambassadors to set the borders and pushed the Council to threaten Yugoslavia with economic sanctions if it did not comply. When this was successful, the League was then entrusted with supervising the Yugoslav withdrawal. Thus, in this crisis the League had played a useful role, but it was again secondary to the Allied powers. The decision by the Conference of Ambassadors to appoint Italy as the protector of Albania's independence shows that Italy held significant influence and power in the region.

The Upper Silesian coal field dispute

For France, it was crucial that the new Polish state was strong enough to help contain Germany. Therefore, it was important for Poland to control as much of the Upper Silesian coal field as possible, despite Britain's concern that this would create future problems by causing resentment among Germans living in Poland and making Germany more determined to reclaim the territory.

By the end of 1920 the Marienwerder and Allenstein plebiscites had been held, and in both cases the population voted to stay in Germany. Danzig had become a free city under the administration of the League of Nations in November 1920.

However, fixing the Upper Silesian frontiers proved to be very difficult. Upper Silesia had a population of 2,280,000 Germans and Poles, who were bitterly divided along ethnic lines, and a concentration of coal mines and industries that was second in importance within Germany only to the Ruhr.

A plebiscite held in the province on March 17, 1921 produced an ambiguous result that did not solve the Anglo-French disagreement. Britain argued that the result justified keeping the key industrial regions of Upper Silesia German, while France insisted that they should be awarded to Poland. Fearing that British wishes would prevail, Poland seized control of the industrial area, which was still legally German, and an uprising broke out in May 1921. By threatening to occupy the Ruhr, France stopped Germany from intervening, and order was eventually restored by British and French troops in July 1921. As a result of insoluble Anglo-French disagreements, the question of Upper Silesia's borders was handed over to the League of Nations in August.

What impression of the role of the great powers is given by Source 2.12?

SOURCE 2.12

In May 1921 Poland took control of much of Upper Silesia. British troops were sent there to stop the fighting between Polish and German forces. Taken in May 1921, this photo shows a British cavalry squadron arriving in the town of Opole, where they were stationed.

Memelland

The League again proved useful in the protracted dispute over Memelland, an area situated in the far north of the German province of East Prussia. When neighboring Lithuania laid claim to the territory, the Conference of Ambassadors proposed instead to internationalize Memelland, which prompted Lithuania to seize it for itself in 1923. At this point the League was the obvious body to settle the problem. Its decision to grant Memelland to Lithuania but internationalize the port city of Memel was accepted by the Allied powers and Lithuania.

Mosul

In 1924, the League of Nations provided a way for Turkey to resolve its dispute with Britain over Mosul's future, as outlined in the Treaty of Lausanne. The treaty stipulated that the issue would be decided through direct negotiations between the two countries. When these talks broke down in October 1924 and Britain issued an ultimatum to Turkey to withdraw its forces within 48 hours, the League intervened and recommended a temporary demarcation line, behind which the Turkish forces withdrew. It then sent a commission of inquiry to consult the local Kurdish population, which, as total independence was not an option, preferred British to Turkish rule. The League's recommendation that Mosul should become a mandate of Iraq for 25 years was then accepted. As Iraq was a British mandate (meaning that Britain had been given administrative control of Mosul by the League of Nations), this effectively put Mosul under British control.

Greco-Bulgarian border dispute

In October 1925 the League's handling of the Greco-Bulgarian conflict, like its solution to the Aaland Islands dispute, was to be a rare example of a complete success. When Bulgaria appealed to the League, the Council's request for a ceasefire was heeded immediately by both sides. Similarly, the commission of inquiry's verdict also supported Bulgaria.

It was an impressive example of what the League could do, and in the autumn of 1925 this success, together with the new 'Locarno Spirit' (see page 124), seemed to promise well for the future. **Aristide Briand** was able to claim at the meeting of the Council in October 1925 that 'a nation that appealed to the League when it felt that its existence was threatened could be sure the Council would be at its post ready to undertake its work of conciliation.'

The League was not put to the test again until the Manchurian crisis of 1931. Unfortunately, Briand's optimism was then shown to be premature (see pages 155–157). The League could function well only if the great powers were in agreement or if Council members respected the rules of the League.

KEY FIGURE

Aristide Briand (1862–1932) A French politician who between 1909 and 1929 headed 11 French governments, and who was also foreign minister from 1926 to 1932. A dedicated supporter of the League of Nations and Franco-German reconciliation, he was awarded the Nobel Peace Prize jointly with Gustav Stresemann in 1926.

ACTIVITY

List the international incidents you have read about in this section. How did the League deal with each incident? Was this successful or not? Award the League a mark out of 6 for its handling of each incident and explain why you have given this mark.

Incident	Brief details	How the League dealt with this	Success on a scale of 1–6	Reason for awarding this score

Role and impact of the League's agencies

By 1939 it was clear that the League had failed in its central task of peacekeeping, but many people felt that its work in improving economic, social, and health environments had been successful. In addition to its four central bodies, the League formed and oversaw specialized agencies to deal with international issues of particular concern, including the care of refugees, the treatment of harmful diseases, and the protection of workers' rights. These agencies were made all the more effective by their ability to collaborate with non-members such as the USA.

KEY FIGURE

Fridtjof Nansen (1861–1930) A Norwegian diplomat, explorer, and scientist. He was awarded the Nobel Peace Prize in 1922 for his work in helping refugees displaced during the First World War and Russian Revolution.

High Commission for Refugees

Created in 1921, the High Commission for Refugees was largely the inspiration of **Fridtjof Nansen**. In April 1920 he was asked to organize the repatriation of the hundreds of thousands of prisoners of war stranded in Russia by the revolution. One report suggested that up to 200,000 could die in Siberia if they were left there for another winter. He managed successfully to co-ordinate the necessary relief work. Eventually, some 425,000 prisoners were repatriated.

In 1921 the Soviet government withdrew citizenship from all Russian citizens who were living abroad, many of whom had left Russia during the civil war. In response to this, Nansen, as High Commissioner for Refugees, urged the League of Nations to call an inter-governmental conference at Geneva, where it was agreed to issue what were later called 'Nansen passports' to the stateless Russian refugees.

In 1923 the commission was confronted with the problem of the displacement of over a million Greek people from Turkish Anatolia as a consequence of the Greco-Turkish War, and extended the Nansen passport scheme to cover them as well. The League arranged a loan from the Bank of England, which helped Greece settle the refugees in the underpopulated areas of Thrace and western Macedonia.

Defending the rights of minority communities

The League was also the guarantor of the agreements signed by the Allies and the successor states created in 1919 that were aimed at ensuring that minority communities left isolated behind the new frontiers enjoyed full civil rights. By 1922 it was responsible for guaranteeing minority rights in Austria, Bulgaria, Czechoslovakia, Hungary, Poland, Romania, and Yugoslavia.

The League of Nations faced significant challenges in enforcing minority rights. While it could consider petitions from minority communities and sometimes refer them to the Council, it lacked effective ways of enforcing rights. The League primarily relied on persuasion and publicity, hoping to influence governments to comply with minority rights. This approach often proved insufficient, as there were no concrete penalties. Often this did not work. Italy, for example, ignored the League when dealing with its German minority, and in 1934 Poland blocked the efforts of the League Council to intervene in minority matters.

Health Organisation

The League's Health Organisation provided an invaluable forum for drawing up common policies on matters including the treatment of dangerous diseases such as leprosy and malaria, the design of hospitals, and the provision of health education. The League also set up committees to advise on limiting the production of opium and other addictive drugs. The League of Nations took significant steps to combat the trafficking and exploitation of women and children.

Economic and Financial Committees

KEY TERM

Protectionism
Stopping foreign goods by levying tariffs or taxes on imports.

The League was excluded from dealing with the key financial issues of reparations and war debts, but nevertheless in 1922 its Financial Committee was entrusted by the Allied leaders with the task of rebuilding the economies of Austria and then Hungary. Its Economic Committee had the far greater task of attempting to persuade the powers to abolish **protectionism** and create a worldwide free trade zone. It organized two world economic conferences, held in 1927 and 1933, which both the USSR and the USA attended. But not surprisingly, given the strongly protectionist economic climate of the times, which was caused by the Great Depression (see page 127), it failed to make any progress towards free trade.

International Labour Organisation

One of the greatest successes of the League was the International Labour Organisation (ILO). This had originally been created as an independent organization by the Treaty of Versailles, but it was financed by the League. In some ways, it was a League in miniature. It had its own permanent office at Geneva, staffed by a thousand officials. Its work was discussed annually by a conference of labor delegates. Right up until 1939 the ILO turned out an impressive stream of reports, recommendations and statistics, which provided important information for a wide range of industries all over the world. There were reports and recommendations for regulating, for example, the fishing industry, labor conditions on ships and in coal mines, and mechanisms for fixing the minimum wage.

Not all of this was put into effect by the member states, but the recommendations of the League set standards and assisted the trade unions in improving working conditions. These reports were appreciated by the USA, which, despite not being a member of the League, joined the ILO, and Germany and Japan remained members of the ILO even after withdrawing from the League.

What attitudes to the ILO can you infer from Source 2.13? Use features of the source and details from its provenance in your answer.

SOURCE 2.13

A British postage stamp from 1969, celebrating 50 years of the International Labour Organisation.

Slavery Commission

KEY TERM

Inter-tribal slavery
The practice of using captives from a rival tribe for slave labor.

In 1890 a conference in Brussels had approved a global ban on slavery. In 1924 the League set up the Temporary Slavery Commission, and in 1926 a new anti-slavery convention was signed, which the League recommended its members to accept. The League achieved most success in its suppression of slavery in the mandate territories. It also persuaded Abyssinia to abolish slavery and used financial aid and technical assistance to encourage Liberia to stop **inter-tribal slavery**.

Disarmament Commission

By Article 8 of its Covenant the League was committed to reducing the armaments held by each state as far as possible. In September 1920 it set up the Temporary Mixed Commission, composed mainly of military experts, to draw up a plan for international disarmament. It soon became clear that France's demand for security against Germany was a major complication. In September 1922, when the third League Assembly met in Geneva, the French delegates persuaded it to accept Resolution XIV, which emphasized the vital link between disarmament and security. Following the Locarno agreements in 1925, a general improvement in international relations led to the League Council setting up a commission to prepare for a disarmament conference. This did not start work until February 1932.

Mandates Commission

Article 22 of the League of Nations Covenant marked a potentially revolutionary new concept in international affairs.

Summarize in your own words the message in Source 2.14. Explain what was new about it.

SOURCE 2.14

From Article 22 of the Covenant of the League of Nations.

To those colonies and territories, which as a consequence of the late war have ceased to be under the sovereignty of the states which have formerly governed them, and which are inhabited by peoples not yet able to stand by themselves under the strenuous conditions of the modern world, there should be applied the principle that the well-being and development of such peoples should form a sacred trust of civilisation, and that securities for the performance of this trust should be embodied in this Covenant.

When the Allies divided the former German and Ottoman territories after the First World War, they categorized them into three groups based on what the Allied governments described as 'their level of development.' The view at this time was that the most developed were in the Middle East, while the least developed were the former German islands in the Pacific. The League's greatest task was to avoid the mandates being treated as colonies by the powers in temporary charge of them. Thus, mandatory powers were required to send in annual reports on their territories to the League's Permanent Mandates Commission, which rapidly gained a formidable reputation for its expertise and authority.

The League's attitude towards the mandates was by modern standards paternalistic and condescending, but nevertheless it can be argued that the mandate system did help transform the entire climate of colonialism, as it applied moral pressure on imperialist powers to consider the interests of indigenous populations and think about their eventual independence.

Consider sources 2.14 and 2.15. How far do these sources support the view that the League of Nations was more successful in improving the quality of life and addressing social issues than in preventing wars during the interwar period? Pick out specific images and phrases to support your answer.

SOURCE 2.15

'And Still the Cart has Precedence.' American cartoon from March 1919, on the resistance to the League of Nations

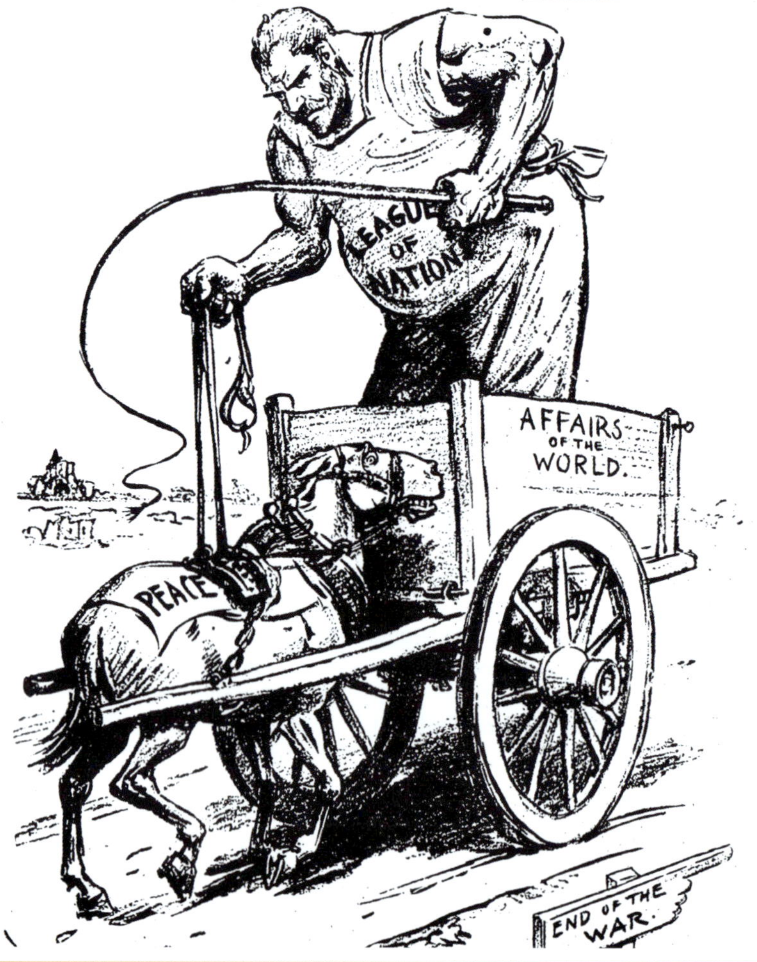

ACTIVITY

Copy and complete this table to summarize the League's agencies/commissions.

Commission	Improvements/successes	Weaknesses/failures

KEY DEBATE

WAS THE LEAGUE OF NATIONS DOOMED TO FAIL?

Historians question whether the League was doomed from the start. It certainly suffered a serious, perhaps irreparable blow when the USA refused to join. It also lacked any effective **executive power**. There was, of course, the Council of the League, but this could function only if the Council was united, and often two of its key members, Britain and France, had diametrically opposed ideas about the shape of the post-war world and the role of the League. Britain wanted a flexible League that would mediate rather than enforce decisions, while France wanted to strengthen the League's obligations and make them requisite on each member. It was this division of opinion that stopped the Geneva Protocol from being implemented in 1924. There were also contradictions in the League's constitution. Some historians have pointed out that Article 10, with its commitment to protecting the 'territorial integrity' of member states, appeared to preserve the status quo, while Article 19 raised the possibility of revising treaties and considering action in the case of 'international conditions whose continuance might endanger the peace of the world.' The League was created in a world where **power politics** were dominant. Major issues such as Germany's reparations, the frontiers of the new states, and revision of the peace treaties were dealt with either by the Supreme War Council or its successor, the Conference of the Ambassadors, or at a specific conference of the relevant powers, as at Lausanne in 1922 and 1923 or London in 1924.

Yet was the League already doomed to failure in the 1920s? There were clear-cut cases where it acted successfully as an arbitrator: the Aaland Islands, the future of Mosul, and the Greco-Bulgarian dispute of 1925. When Britain and France were unable to agree on the frontiers of Upper Silesia, the League was entrusted with the task of examining the question and coming up with a solution. The British commentary on the Covenant in 1919 observed that the League would be successful if it managed to influence public opinion and make 'peaceful co-operation easy and hence customary.' There were some signs of this. The League of Nations Union, which was formed to promote the causes of the League, was immensely popular in Britain and by 1931 had nearly half a million members in the UK, with branches in the Dominions and in the other former Allied countries. The Western world also enthusiastically welcomed the Kellogg–Briand Pact, although this was drawn up independently of the League. So maybe if it had not been for the financial crash of 1929 and the Great Depression of 1931–33, peaceful co-operation might have become 'more customary.'

Above all, we should also not forget the League's social, economic, and humanitarian activities, which turned out to be far more successful than was originally anticipated and were incorporated into the new United Nations in 1946.

KEY TERMS

Executive power The power of a government or other organization to put into effect the laws or decisions it makes.

Power politics A form of international politics in which countries threaten to use their military or economic strength against their rivals in order to further their national interests.

Why was the League of Nations created and what challenges did it face in the 1920s?

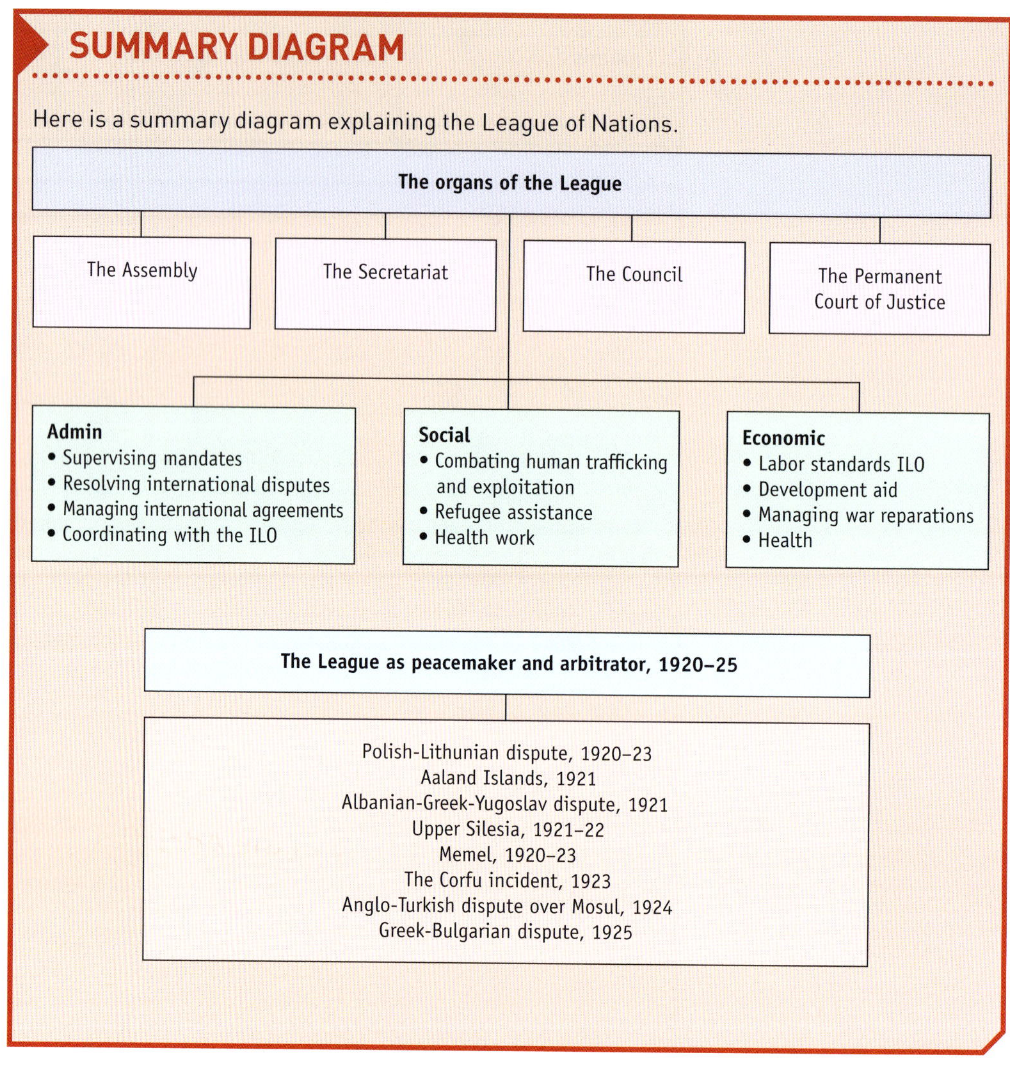

3 How and why did international tensions remain high after the Versailles settlement?

Once the peace treaties had been signed, the wartime Allies were faced with a new and complex world. Germany had reluctantly signed the Treaty of Versailles, yet deeply resented it and exploited every opportunity to prevent its implementation. The USSR, as Russia was now called, was hostile towards the West and was hoping to encourage revolution in Germany, while the USA had retreated into isolation. A new, assertive Turkey had also emerged from the ruins of the old Ottoman Empire. Above all, both Britain and France had conflicting ideas about how best to ensure that Germany carried out the Treaty of Versailles. Essentially, Britain, at the center of a worldwide empire, wanted to see a balance of power in Europe that would prevent either France or Germany dominating and leave it free to deal with the growing challenges to its authority from nationalist movements in India, Egypt, and Ireland. Britain was also convinced that only a prosperous and peaceful Germany could pay reparations and play its part in Europe as one of the main engines of the European economy. French policy swung between occasionally exploring the possibilities of economic co-operation with Germany and, more usually, applying forceful measures designed permanently to weaken Germany and to force it to fulfil the treaty.

Crises and tensions

To understand the nature of these international post-war pressures, it is helpful to look at the following crises and sources of tension:

- the Fiume and Corfu crises
- the Chanak crisis
- Germany and the reparations issue
- ethnic, political and economic problems in the successor states.

International tensions in the Adriatic: the Fiume and Corfu crises

KEY FIGURE

Gabriele d'Annunzio (1863–1938) Italian nationalist poet, writer and leader of the coup in Fiume.

KEY TERMS

Nationalism A patriotic belief in the superiority and power of someone's own nation.

National Fascist Party The National Fascist Party was formed in Italy by Mussolini in 1919. Its program was a mix of radical and reactionary ideas. Initially, it called for Italy to become a republic and campaigned against the control of the Catholic Church. When it was in power, its policies were more focused on intense nationalism and economic and social reforms.

Italian disappointment with the peace treaties led to both the Fiume and Corfu crises. The Corfu crisis was a major challenge to the authority of the League of Nations. Both crises ended in compromise, but showed the power of **nationalism** in post-war Italy.

The Fiume crisis

Italy was intent on making the Adriatic an 'Italian sea' by acquiring not only Trieste but also northern Dalmatia, the port of Fiume, and the city of Vlorë on the Albanian coast (see Figure 2.2). These claims were rejected by President Wilson, but a compromise seemed possible when Vittorio Orlando was replaced as Italian prime minister by Francesco Nitti in June 1919. However, an attack on nine French troops in Fiume by an Italian mob in July and then the seizure of the city in September by the Italian nationalist poet **Gabriele d'Annunzio** prevented any settlement and increased the international tension. It had been d'Annunzio who had coined the term 'mutilated victory' to highlight the lack of territorial gain from the war compared to the economic and military sacrifices given by Italy. It was not until November 1920 that Yugoslavia and Italy agreed on a compromise and signed the Treaty of Rapallo: Istria was partitioned between the two powers and Fiume was to become a self-governing free city, while the rest of Dalmatia went to Yugoslavia. In December Italian troops enforced the treaty by clearing d'Annunzio and his supporters out of Fiume.

The Corfu crisis

Italian nationalism and anger over the 'mutilated victory' were given a powerful voice when Benito Mussolini became leader of the Italian **National Fascist Party**. In October 1922 he became prime minister of Italy and gave fresh impetus to Italian nationalism. On August 27, 1923 an Italian general and his staff, who were part of an Allied team demarcating the new Albanian frontiers, were ambushed and killed by Greek bandits. Mussolini immediately seized the chance to issue a deliberately unacceptable ultimatum to the government of Greece in

ACTIVITY

Draw up a list of reasons explaining why there was international tension in the Adriatic between 1920 and 1923.

Athens. When Greece rejected three of the demands, Italian troops occupied Corfu, thereby significantly increasing international tension.

Greece wanted the League to intervene, but bowed to French and Italian pressure to have the incident referred to the Conference of Ambassadors. The Conference, while initially accepting some assistance from the League, ultimately settled the case itself by insisting that Greece should pay 50 million lira in compensation to Italy.

The Chanak crisis

The growing crisis in Turkey also contributed to international tension. By December 1921 it was becoming clear that the Treaty of Sèvres was no longer viable. After settling the dispute over the Russo-Turkish frontier in the Caucasus with Russia, Kemal was able to concentrate his troops against the Greek force in Smyrna without fear of Russian intervention from the north. By August 1922, he was poised to enter Constantinople and the Straits zone, which were still occupied by Allied troops. The Italian and French troops rapidly withdrew, leaving the British isolated. France rejected outright Britain's appeal for diplomatic support, and the British Dominions were also not prepared to provide assistance.

On September 22 Kemal sent a detachment of troops to Chanak, in the neutral zone between the British and Turkish forces. The cabinet in London sent General Harrington, the British commander, an ultimatum to deliver to Kemal demanding the withdrawal of his troops. War between Britain and Kemal's forces was now a very real possibility. The situation was all the more dangerous because Kemal would have been backed by the USSR. However, Harrington wisely did not deliver the ultimatum and Kemal was able to avoid direct confrontation with the British forces. Instead, both sides negotiated on October 11 the Armistice of Mudanya, which gave Kemal virtually all he wanted: Greece withdrew from eastern Thrace and Adrianople, and Britain recognized Turkish control over Constantinople and the Straits (see Figure 2.3). The Treaty of Sèvres was now redundant and a new settlement with Turkey was to be negotiated at Lausanne.

Germany and the reparations issue

KEY FIGURE

Walther Rathenau (1867–1922) The son of the founder of the German electrical company AEG. In 1914–15 he enabled Germany to reduce the impact of the British blockade by setting up the War Raw Materials Department. He was murdered by German Nationalist extremists in 1922.

It was, however, the reparations question that caused most international tension. At the end of April 1921 the Reparation Commission at last fixed a global total for Germany's reparations of 132 billion gold marks to be paid over a period of 42 years. When this was rejected by Germany on the grounds that the sum was too high, an ultimatum was dispatched to Berlin giving Germany only a week to accept the new payment schedule, after which its industrial heartland of the Ruhr would be occupied.

To carry out the ultimatum, a new government was formed by Joseph Wirth on May 10. Assisted by **Walther Rathenau**, his Minister for Reconstruction, he was determined to pursue a policy of negotiation rather than confrontation. The first instalment was paid, and Rathenau made some progress in persuading the French government to accept the payment of a proportion of reparations in the form of industrial goods and coal, but opposition from German industrialists prevented this plan from being implemented. By the end of the year the German government gave the shocking announcement that, as a consequence of escalating inflation, it could not raise sufficient hard currency to meet the next instalment of reparation payments.

The Ruhr crisis

KEY TERMS

Moratorium Temporary suspension of payments.

Productive pledges The possession of mines and factories as pledges or guarantees of German payment of reparations.

With the failure of the Genoa Conference in April–May 1922 to find a solution to the reparations problem, a major confrontation between France and Germany now seemed inevitable. In July the German government requested a three-year **moratorium**. At the same time, Britain announced that, as the USA was demanding the repayment of British wartime debts, it must in turn insist on the repayment of money it had loaned to other Allies, particularly France.

To France, Britain's demand for these repayments contrasted awkwardly with the concessions Lloyd George was ready to offer Germany. On November 27, 1922 the French cabinet decided finally that the occupation of the Ruhr and the seizure of its coal mines and key factories as **productive pledges** was the only means of forcing Germany to pay reparations. The Ruhr coal mines were of particular importance to France, as their own coal industry had been badly damaged in the war.

KEY TERMS

Benevolent passivity Favoring one side while not officially supporting them.

Passive resistance Refusal to co-operate, stopping short of actual violence.

On January 11, 1923 French and Belgian troops moved into the Ruhr. Significantly, Britain did not join in but adopted a policy of '**benevolent passivity**' towards France. In the opinion of the government after the proclamation of passive resistance, there was German patriotic enthusiasm and acts of civil disobedience against the French occupiers. If Germany had had the strength, French troops would have been repulsed by force, but Germany was virtually disarmed, and so for nine months the French occupation of the Ruhr was met by **passive resistance** and strikes by the German workers, which were financed by the German government.

Who do you think the audience was for Source 2.16? Why do you think this was created, and by whom? How is each side in the dispute portrayed, and how has the artist achieved this? Identify specific elements of the poster to support your answer.

SOURCE 2.16

A German poster from 1923 showing a German worker refusing to work for the French occupation authorities in the Ruhr. He says to the soldiers: 'No, you won't force me!'

ACTIVITY

Using the further reading section, find out more details on the Ruhr crisis of 1923–24. Consider why war did not break out between France and Germany over the Ruhr.

German hyperinflation

Passive resistance certainly hindered French operations in the Ruhr and raised international tensions still higher, but it also triggered **hyperinflation** in Germany. To subsidize the strikers and compensate for the lost tax revenues from the Ruhr, the government printed ever larger sums of money. The value of the German mark continued to sink rapidly, and by August 1923 it was worthless. From 4.2 marks to the dollar in July 1914 the exchange rate had risen to 4.2 trillion by November 15, 1923. This worsened the financial hardship of many middle-class people who relied on fixed incomes, war bonds, and pensions. In November the devalued and useless German mark was replaced by a new, temporary currency until the value of the currency was fully restored in August 1924.

KEY TERM

Hyperinflation
Massive daily increases in the prices of goods and in the amount of money being printed.

What do you think was the purpose of the photograph in Source 2.17? What message or perspective might the photographer have intended to convey?

SOURCE 2.17

A German woman using banknotes as fuel for a stove during the hyperinflation crisis.

The end of passive resistance

In September 1923 Germany was on the brink of economic collapse, and the new chancellor, Gustav Stresemann, called off passive resistance. The cost of the occupation also seriously weakened the French franc. France's attempts to back **Rhineland separatism** and to create an independent Rhineland currency were unsuccessful. Separatist leaders were assassinated by nationalist agents from unoccupied Germany or attacked by angry crowds. **Raymond Poincaré**, the French prime minister, had little option but to accept an American initiative for setting up a commission chaired by the US financier **Charles G. Dawes**. Two committees of experts, one to study Germany's capacity for payment of reparations, and the other to advise on how it could best balance the budget and restore the currency, began work in early 1924. Its recommendations are discussed below (see pages 119–121).

KEY TERM

Rhineland separatism
A movement favoring separation of the Rhineland from Germany.

KEY FIGURES

Raymond Poincaré (1860–1934) French president (1913–20) and three-time prime minister (1912–13, 1922–24 and 1926–29), who adopted a firm line towards Germany.

Charles G. Dawes (1865–1951) US banker and politician. He chaired the committee that proposed what came to be called the Dawes Plan.

GUSTAV STRESEMANN

1878	Born in Berlin
1907	Elected to the *Reichstag*
1917	Became leader of the National Liberals
1919	Set up the German People's Party
1922	Announced support for the Weimar Republic
1923 August–November	Served as Chancellor
1923–29	Served as German foreign minister
1929	Died

Gustav Stresemann started his career in business in Saxony and was elected to the *Reichstag* in 1907 as a National Liberal. During the First World War he was an ardent nationalist and fully supported the aims of the extreme nationalist organization the Pan-German League (see page 34). After the war, when the National Liberal Party was disbanded, he founded the German People's Party. He voted against the constitution of the newly formed **Weimar Republic** in 1919, but gradually he began to support it and, after Walther Rathenau's assassination in 1922, announced his backing for it. He was chancellor of the republic from August to November 1923 and ended passive resistance in the Ruhr. As foreign minister, he negotiated the Locarno Treaties and secured Germany a seat on the Council of the League of Nations. His great aim was the revision of the Treaty of Versailles. He wanted to restore German power, but he was ready to do it peacefully.

KEY TERM

Weimar Republic
Germany's first federal republic, proclaimed upon the abdication of Kaiser Wilhelm II at the end of the First World War and lasting until March 1933.

ACTIVITY

Write a brief explanation of the following terms: plebiscite, moratorium, Reparation Commission, the Ruhr, productive pledges, passive resistance, hyperinflation, benevolent passivity, Rhineland separatism.

KEY DEBATE

HOW SUCCESSFUL WAS FRANCE'S POLICY TOWARDS GERMANY BETWEEN 1919 AND 1924?

After the Treaty of Versailles was signed, France took every chance to fix what they saw as its flaws, making the Ruhr occupation a logical result of French policy. The Ruhr was the largest industrial region in Europe and contained most of Germany's coal resources. Its occupation was the most drastic weapon France could use against Germany. Which state benefited most from the crisis? Britain, by its refusal to participate in the occupation, was effectively marginalized and unable to influence or control France until France's finances were weakened by the cost of the Ruhr occupation. The German government was forced to abandon passive resistance in September 1923 and had to agree to French supervision of its industries in the Ruhr. So can it be argued that the French emerged as the victors from the Ruhr crisis? The French prime minister, Raymond Poincaré, and the French army believed they could effectively weaken Germany by backing Rhineland separatism and setting up an independent state. They were mistaken: the German government defeated the separatists as most Germans showed a loyalty to the Reich of 1871. However, Germany was faced with other destabilizing threats: hyperinflation, the Munich Putsch led by Adolf Hitler, and a communist uprising in Hamburg, as well as plans for revolts in the states of Saxony and Thuringia. Although these uprisings failed and inflation was brought under control, together these events showed the fragility of the Weimar Republic. On the other hand, without British and US support France lacked the power to capitalize on the temporary victory that it achieved with the German suspension of passive resistance. The growing chaos in the Rhineland, the steep decline in the value of the franc and France's increasing dependence on loans from Britain and the USA eventually forced its government to agree to the Dawes Plan. Some have seen the Ruhr crisis as a 'turning point' in the history of post-war Europe, but the real turning point was the Dawes Plan, as it led to greater involvement of the USA in European (and global) affairs, as well as to the Locarno Treaties.

Ethnic, political and economic problems in the successor states

With the partial exception of Czechoslovakia, the successor states that emerged following the war were fragile and vulnerable.

Czechoslovakia

Czechoslovakia had an industrial base and a stable democratic government. However, its frontiers were artificial and the state was composed of two historic but very different areas: the Czech lands (Bohemia and Moravia) and Slovakia. Many Slovaks rapidly came to resent what they believed to be the domination of the Prague government by Czechs. There was also a large German-speaking majority in the Sudetenland, which in 1930 made up 22.3 per cent of the population of the entire country. In the 1930s it increasingly looked to Nazi Germany for protection and ultimately provided Hitler with the excuse to annex the Sudetenland.

Poland

In response to Polish attempts in 1920 to annex Ukraine, which had been controlled by Poland in the sixteenth and seventeenth centuries, Soviet Russia invaded Poland. Only after the Bolshevik Red Army was decisively defeated in the Battle of Warsaw in August 1920 was it possible to determine Poland's eastern frontiers by the Treaty of Riga. Poland annexed a considerable area of Belorussia and western Ukraine (see Figure 2.2), all of which lay well to the east of the frontier that had been proposed in 1919 – the so-called **Curzon line**.

KEY TERMS

Curzon line The proposal made by Lord Curzon, the British foreign minister, for Poland's eastern frontier with the Soviet Union.

Volksdeutsche Ethnic Germans who lived in, and were citizens of, the states next to Germany.

Polish annexations came at a considerable price. In the new territories Polish people formed a minority. Tension remained high along these borderlands, and groups of Ukrainians frequently crossed the border to attack isolated Polish farms. There were also tensions between Polish people and Germans who had to live in the newly created state of Poland, which were only partly solved by the plebiscite of 1921 and the League's subsequent judgment of 1922 (see page 98). Some 700,000 Germans continued to live, for the most part unwillingly, within the new Polish frontiers. The loyalty of the great majority of these ***Volksdeutsche***, as they called themselves, was to Germany rather than to Poland, and when German troops invaded Poland in September 1939, most rallied enthusiastically to support them.

Armenia, Georgia and Azerbaijan

The Allies and the USA also recognized the new states of Armenia, Georgia, and Azerbaijan, which, in the power vacuum created by the defeat of the Ottoman Empire and revolution and civil war in Russia, had managed to establish a fragile independence. However, with the victory of the Bolsheviks in Russia and the revival of Turkey under Mustafa Kemal in 1923, these states rapidly lost their independence, as they were subjected to a Turkish invasion from the south and a Bolshevik one from the north.

The successor states to Austria–Hungary

In their efforts to create homogenous nation states out of the former Austro-Hungarian Empire, the victorious powers faced almost impossible problems as the populations of these states were ethnically very diverse and had been scattered throughout the Empire. In March 1919 communists temporarily seized control of Hungary and were defeated by the intervention of Romanian troops. In Yugoslavia there was tension and often clashes between Serbs and Croats, while the Treaty of Trianon ensured that 3 million Hungarians found themselves living in Romania, Yugoslavia, or Slovakia.

KEY TERM

Minority rights treaties Agreements guaranteeing the rights of ethnic minorities that the successor states had to sign as a condition of their independence.

In Romania, Hungarians were discriminated against despite the League's **minority rights treaties**. For example, in Cluj, the former capital of Transylvania, the Hungarian university was closed down and the professors and students dispersed. In an age of heightened nationalism these minorities were often viewed with suspicion in their new countries, and in turn minorities still held passionate loyalties to their old homelands. Integrating the often hostile minorities in the successor states was made more difficult by the way the peace treaties disrupted eastern Europe as an economic and political unit.

In Hungary, centuries of, assimilation, migration, and internal colonization by different nationalities resulted in large areas of mixed populations ranging in size from the half a million Magyar-speaking Szekely in Transylvania through to many small ethnic communities of a hundred thousand and villages of just a thousand people. It was consequently impossible to draw a frontier that did not leave some ethnic minorities on one side or another.

This was made worse by inflation and mounting post-war economic and political chaos. In 1922 both Austria and Hungary seemed on the verge of economic collapse and were saved only by the intervention of the League of Nations, which arranged international loans and advised on a program of financial reform.

ACTIVITY

Copy and complete this chart to summarize the situation in the successor states after the peace treaties.

State	Nature of the problems confronting it	Efforts to solve them

Aims and impact of international treaties and conferences

As we have seen, the post-war world during the years 1921–23 faced numerous problems, which increased international tensions:

- The First World War had decisively weakened the European states.
- Conversely, the USA had become the financial center of the world and potentially its strongest military power, yet it had at this very point retreated into isolation and was focusing primarily on its regional interests in East Asia, the Caribbean, and South America.
- At the same time, Bolshevik Russia, now called the USSR, had emerged victorious from the civil war, but was isolated and faced a hostile Western world.
- Japan remained a regional power mainly concerned with increasing its influence in China.
- Britain and France faced the task of implementing the peace treaties in Europe and the Middle East virtually alone. United, the two countries might just have been successful, but they had rival aims and were deeply distrustful of each other.

In such a fragmented and disunited world, the restoration of peace and prosperity was difficult to achieve. Nevertheless, at Washington, Genoa, and Lausanne, efforts were made to reduce international tensions. The Washington and Lausanne conferences achieved real but limited success, while the more ambitious aims of the Genoa Conference ended in failure and ultimately led to the occupation of the Ruhr.

KEY FIGURE

Charles I (1887–1922)
King of Austria and (as Charles IV) of Hungary. He succeeded to the Austro-Hungarian throne in 1916, but was banished in 1919 when his empire collapsed and Austria and Hungary became republics.

Little Entente, 1921

The Little Entente consisted of the following series of treaties between Czechoslovakia, Romania, and the Kingdom of the Serbs, Croats, and Slovenes (Yugoslavia):

- the treaty of April 1921 between Czechoslovakia and Romania
- the treaty of June 1921 between Romania and the Kingdom of Serbs, Croats, and Slovenes
- the treaty of August 1922 between Czechoslovakia and the Kingdom of Serbs, Croats, and Slovenes.

The main aims of these treaties were to protect the signatory states against a revival of Austrian and Hungarian power and ensure that the Treaty of Trianon was carried out. Briefly, there had seemed a danger of this when **Charles I**, the former emperor of Austria–Hungary

KEY FIGURE

Edvard Beneš (1884–1948) A leader of the Czechoslovak independence movement before 1918, then Minister of Foreign Affairs, 1918–35, prime minister, 1921–22, and president, 1935–38 and 1939–48 (in exile 1939–45).

returned to Budapest in March 1921. Although he was forced by the Allies to return to his exile in Switzerland, the threat of his presence had led to the signature first of the Czechoslovak-Romanian treaty and then of the other two treaties. Between them, the three treaties ensured that in the event of a Hungarian attack against any one of the signatory powers, the other two powers would provide military assistance.

In October of the same year, Charles returned to Hungary and with an army of his supporters marched on Budapest, where he was defeated by government troops. Under the leadership of **Edvard Beneš**, the Czechoslovak prime minister, the Little Entente threatened military intervention 'to avert once and for all the danger created by the **House of Habsburg** in central Europe.' Facing renewed pressure from the Conference of Ambassadors, the Hungarian government agreed to exclude permanently any member of the Habsburg dynasty from power and to carry out the Treaty of Trianon. The result was a major victory for the Little Entente.

KEY TERM

House of Habsburg The dynasty of the Austro-Hungarian emperors, including Charles I.

France and the Little Entente

Before 1914 France relied on its alliance with Russia to keep Germany in check, but this was no longer in force as a consequence of the Russian Revolution. Therefore, to protect itself against a re-emergence of Germany, it signed in 1921 a defensive alliance with Poland. By signing treaties of friendship with Romania, Czechoslovakia, and Yugoslavia, France also associated itself with the Little Entente. The treaties were not military alliances, but they did oblige the signatory members to consult each other on foreign policy and defense.

The Washington Conference, 1921–22

The Washington Conference of 1921–22 was one of the key post-war conferences and indicated the shape US policy was to take in the 1920s. The USA refused to join the League of Nations, but it was willing to play a major role in promoting disarmament and post-war financial stability. At Washington its main achievement was to stop a dangerous arms race developing between Britain, the USA, and Japan and to improve US-Japanese relations.

KEY FIGURE

President Warren Harding (1865–1923) Republican president of the USA, 1921–23. He was an opponent of President Wilson's interest in international diplomacy, which to him seemed to place international concerns above American ones.

Naval disarmament and the future of the Anglo-Japanese Treaty of 1902

By 1920 the USA was alarmed by the rise of Japanese power in the Pacific. Japan, already possessing the third largest navy in the world, had begun a major naval construction program. The USA responded by embarking on its own formidable building program, which, when completed, would make the US navy the largest in the world.

In turn this pushed Britain in early 1921 into announcing its own naval program, but privately it told Washington that it desired a negotiated settlement as it could not afford a naval race. **President Harding** would negotiate with Britain only if it agreed to terminate the 20-year-old Anglo-Japanese Alliance, which, theoretically at least, could have involved Britain as Japan's ally in a war against the USA. As the treaty was due for renewal in July 1921, Britain and Japan agreed under pressure from Washington to replace it with a new Four-Power Treaty, which committed Britain, France, Japan, and the USA to respecting each other's possessions in the Pacific and to referring any dispute arising out of this agreement to a conference of the four signatory powers, joined by Italy. The four powers then went on to sign the first Washington Naval Convention in February 1922, which halted the building of any new **capital ships** for ten years and laid down rules for the relative strength of the four navies: a ratio was established of three capital ships for Japan and one and two-thirds each for Italy and France to every five for Britain and the USA. In 1929 Britain, Japan, and the USA in the London Naval Treaty agreed to extend the main principle of this agreement to smaller fighting ships.

KEY TERM

Capital ships The most powerful warships in a navy.

Consider Source 2.18. To what extent does this photograph support the view that the Washington Naval Convention was a successful international agreement?

SOURCE 2.18

A photograph from December 1923 showing scrapped guns from the USS *Kansas* and other naval ships, and the USS *South Carolina* being dismantled in the background. (From the US Navy Historical Center.)

The Chinese question

KEY TERMS

Open door The policy of keeping China open to foreign trade.

Warlords Individuals who are able to control large areas through military strength rather than formal government.

The USA hoped to create a new framework for international trade with China that would reconcile the treaty port rights of the Western powers with the rapid growth in Chinese nationalism. In November 1921 the countries attending the Washington Conference agreed to 'respect the sovereignty, the independence and the territorial and administrative integrity of China' and in February 1922 signed the Nine-Power Treaty, which committed them to upholding the '**open door**' in China. Japan also agreed to evacuate all its troops from the Shandong peninsula and to allow China the right to buy the former German railway lease, which Japan had acquired by the Treaty of Versailles.

The decisions made at the Washington Conference improved Sino-Japanese relations during the 1920s, but did not help to stabilize China, which suffered from growing conflicts between local **warlords**.

The Genoa Conference, 1922

By calling the Washington Conference in 1921, the USA had shown that it had the power to compel Britain, France, and Japan to agree to limiting the size of their navies. It also played a major role in attempts to stabilize the political and economic situation in China. However, it still followed a policy of non-involvement in relation to the acute international tensions in Europe. In the absence of the USA, Lloyd George took the initiative in an attempt to break the Franco-German deadlock over reparations and create the conditions for a European economic recovery.

KEY TERM

Consortium An association of states with a common aim.

He believed that Germany needed a temporary suspension of its reparation payments to give it time to put its economy in order. In the longer term the key to the payment of reparations and a European economic revival would lie in rebuilding the Russian economy through the formation of a European **consortium**, which would include Germany. This would generate an

ACTIVITY

Produce a presentation to explain the key features of each of the conferences and treaties discussed in this section. Which would you choose as the most important overall? Is it important because of its success or its failure or because of other repercussions?

international trade boom, enable Germany to pay reparations, and reduce international tensions. Poincaré grudgingly consented to an international conference to be held in April and May 1922 in Genoa, to which both the USSR and Germany would be invited to discuss these plans, but he vetoed any concession on reparations. The government of the USSR agreed to attend, but was highly suspicious of Lloyd George's plans for opening up the Soviet economy to foreign capital, which it feared was a subtle attempt to destroy Bolshevism.

The Rapallo Pact, 1922

Suspicion of Lloyd George's motives prompted the USSR to negotiate the Rapallo Pact in secret with Germany during the conference, and both countries agreed not to seek any financial compensation from each other for the damages caused during the war. Germany also pledged to consult Moscow before participating in any international plans for exploiting the Soviet economy. Rapallo led to the collapse of the Genoa Conference and effectively stopped Lloyd George's plans for restoring the European economy. Why then did Germany sign the Rapallo Pact with the USSR? Poincaré's veto on the discussion of reparations was certainly a major cause, but the German government also feared that France and Britain were attempting to re-establish the pre-war Triple Entente with the USSR.

The pact was a mistake for Germany. While it helped Germany to escape from isolation, it did so at the cost of intensifying French suspicions of its motives and so increasing international tensions. In many ways, these suspicions were justified, as a secret **annex** signed in July allowed Germany to train its soldiers in Soviet territory, thereby violating the terms of the Treaty of Versailles. It is worth noting also that the Rapallo Pact did not stop the USSR from supporting communist groups in Germany who were plotting to overthrow the German government.

KEY TERM

Annex An addition to a treaty.

The Treaty of Lausanne, 1923

Of all the international conferences between 1920 and 1923, Lausanne was the most successful. At the Lausanne Conference, held between November 1922 and July 1923, Britain and France accepted the military and political realities of Kemal's successes and realized that the Treaty of Sèvres was unenforceable. Turkish control of Anatolia and Thrace up to the Maritsa River was recognized, but Turkey's former provinces in the Middle East remained under the control of Britain and France as League of Nations mandates. Kemal, not wanting to rely on the USSR, agreed to create small demilitarized zones on both sides of the Straits and let Britain, France, Italy, and Japan navigate freely through them. In return, he insisted on the abolition of the **capitulations**, which had given foreign states, particularly France, considerable powers over Turkish finances and trading policy. This was a serious blow to France's hopes of re-establishing its pre-war influence over Turkish finances, and arguably France lost more than any other power, apart from Greece, as a consequence of the Treaty of Lausanne.

KEY TERM

Capitulations Exemption of foreign merchants and their agents from Turkish taxation and law.

Changing relations between the major powers

Britain and France

Up to 1922 Britain reluctantly supported France in its efforts to carry out the Treaty of Versailles, but with the collapse of the Genoa Conference Anglo-French differences over German reparations created major international tensions and brought the Entente to the verge of collapse. In the absence of a general inter-Allied debt settlement, the French were determined to refuse any German requests for a moratorium unless they could occupy the Ruhr as a 'productive pledge.' Consequently, in January 1923 French and Belgian troops advanced into the Ruhr, while Britain stood aside, powerless to influence events with its policy of 'benevolent passivity.' Effectively, the Entente was at an end.

Germany

In the early post-war years Germany was essentially on the receiving end of decisions made by the Entente rather than an independent country that could make its own decisions.

German foreign policy therefore swung between despairing opposition and more constructive attempts to modify Versailles. For Germany, since the USA was unwilling to get involved in European politics, there were two main options for revising the treaty: one was to exploit Anglo-French differences to weaken the Entente and gain concessions from Britain; the other, supported by the army, diplomats, and some industrialists, was to form an understanding with the USSR to strengthen Germany's position against the Entente. The Rapallo Pact was the consequence of this policy, but a full alliance with the USSR was never going to be viable for the German government, as the ultimate aim of the USSR was to create a communist Germany. The greatest hope for Germany was that the USA might come forward with a financial settlement that could break the reparations deadlock. It was thus to Washington that Germany (and Britain) looked during the Ruhr occupation.

Italy

When Mussolini seized power in Italy in October 1922, there was no sudden radical change in Italian foreign policy. Like most Italians, Mussolini believed that Italy had been cheated of its just rewards in the peace treaties of 1919. He wanted to remedy this and build up an Italian empire in the Mediterranean. As Italy lacked both the economic and military resources of a great power, Mussolini's only hope of implementing this ambitious program was to win the backing of strong allies or else to exploit international crises and rivalries to extract valuable concessions.

In the course of 1922–23 the weakness of Italy's position was made very clear. Mussolini failed to gain any substantial concessions in Africa or the Middle East from Britain or France when they negotiated a new peace treaty with Kemal at the Lausanne Conference. He was also unable to derive any benefit for Italy from the international crisis caused by the French occupation of the Ruhr. He veered from trying to mediate between France and Britain, which opposed the occupation, to proposing at one point a potentially anti-British trading bloc composed of the main states of continental Europe. Not surprisingly, both the French and British governments distrusted Mussolini.

BENITO MUSSOLINI

1883	Born in the northern Italian region of Romagna
1904–14	Worked as a journalist for *Avanti!*, the official newspaper of the Italian Socialist Party, of which he was a leading member
1915	Expelled from the Socialist Party for supporting the war against Germany
1919	Founded the Fascist Party
1922–43	Served as Italian prime minister, seizing power by manipulation of the king, in the 'March on Rome'
1943–45	Kept in power in northern Italy by the Nazis after the Allied invasion of Italy
1945	Captured and executed by Italian partisans

The son of a blacksmith, Benito Mussolini started his political life as a member of the Italian Socialist Party, from which he was expelled for his support for Italy's entry into the First World War. He created the Fascist Party in 1919 and successfully exploited the post-war economic crisis, fear of Bolshevism, and disappointment with the peace treaties to gain power in 1922.

By 1929 Mussolini had consolidated his position and established a one-party government. He was determined to rebuild the Roman Empire and turn the Mediterranean into an 'Italian lake.' In October 1935 Italian forces invaded Abyssinia, and in May 1936 Mussolini declared it part of the Italian Empire. Hitler had been a great admirer of Mussolini and in many ways regarded him as a role model. Mussolini's fatal mistake was to enter the Second World War as an ally of Hitler in June 1940 on the assumption that Germany would win. After a series of Italian defeats in Greece and North Africa, Germany had to send troops to stop Italy from being knocked out of the war. From that point on, Italy effectively became a German satellite state.

The USSR and the challenge of communism

The new Soviet Russia that emerged from the Russian Revolution and subsequent civil war had survived, but the war had led to extreme hardship for most of the population. Although ideologically it was a threat to central and western Europe, in reality it was only a shadow of the power Russia had been in 1914 or was to become in 1945. After its defeat in the Polish-Soviet War in 1920 it attempted to normalize its relations with the Baltic and Scandinavian states, Poland, Germany, Britain, and Turkey. It attended the Genoa Conference in 1922 and signed the Rapallo Pact with Germany, but the USSR never renounced its ultimate aim of global revolution aimed at creating a communist world in which **capitalism** and imperialism would be destroyed for ever. In September 1920 the Congress of the Peoples of the East was held in Baku in Azerbaijan to encourage Asian peoples to revolt against capitalism and imperialism. Through the **Comintern**, it also supported subversive activities in Germany, western Europe, and the European colonial empires. During the Ruhr crisis, **Leon Trotsky**, as Commissar for the Armed Forces, planned a series of uprisings in Germany, although only one poorly planned operation in Hamburg actually occurred.

KEY FIGURE

Leon Trotsky (1879–1940) Organizer of the October Revolution in Russia and creator of the Red Army. Murdered by Stalin's agents in 1940.

KEY TERMS

Capitalism An economic system in which the production and distribution of goods depend on the investment of private capital.

Comintern An international movement set up in 1919 by the Communist Party of the Soviet Union to organize a worldwide communist revolution.

The USA: isolation or involvement

The USA emerged from the **Great War** as a major international force. Yet it was unwilling to accept a binding commitment to the League of Nations or to guarantee French security. However, that did not mean that it retreated into complete isolation. This has been described by some historians as involvement without commitment. It took the initiative in naval disarmament, and it was prepared to intervene during the Ruhr crisis with a proposal for setting up a committee of experts to work out a solution to the reparations issue. Under the direction of Herbert Hoover, the American Relief Administration (ARA) was set up in 1919 with a budget of 100 million dollars to help financial reconstruction in Asia and Europe. However, the USA's desire to promote global economic recovery had its limits: it still insisted on the repayment of Allied war debts and protected its own trade through high tariffs.

KEY TERM

Great War
Term originally used to refer to the First World War.

ACTIVITY

How different were the situations confronting the USA and USSR, 1920–24?

The emergence of Japan – internal issues and the effect on international relations

The USA and the European Allies were unsure when Japan attended the Paris Peace Conference in 1919 as a member of the victorious coalition that had defeated Germany whether Japan counted as a great power. Modern Japan had emerged as a major power only in the early twentieth century. By 1919 it had the world's third-largest navy and a formidable army, which had been able to defeat Russia in 1905. Its military strength was complemented by its economic strength. Between 1895 and 1920 its **GDP** had nearly trebled, and the output of mining and manufacturing in Japan had increased by almost six times. On the other hand, it was still essentially a regional power focused on expanding into Korea, Manchuria, and China. In the First World War it had concentrated on seizing the German concessions in Shandong in China and the small German islands in the north Pacific and had refused to send troops to Europe.

To Asian nationalists, Japan was an inspiration and an example. The country had managed to modernize itself. It was able to resist Western imperialists and, as the negotiation of the Anglo-Japanese Treaty of 1902 showed, even to co-operate with them as equals. Yet by 1919 Japan's success made Britain and the USA increasingly concerned about its growing economic and military power in East Asia. Military circles in both Japan and the USA were uneasily aware of the potential for a future confrontation between the two powers.

KEY TERM

GDP An acronym standing for 'gross domestic product' – the financial value of all goods and services produced by a country.

Japanese strategists saw the possession of the German north Pacific islands as the key to blocking a future US advance into the area.

Despite its strength, Japan, as an Asian power, experienced considerable racial prejudice, particularly in its dealings with the English-speaking powers, Britain, the USA, and Australia, New Zealand, and Canada. For example, US politicians were worried about the impact of possible Japanese immigration on California and the rest of the West Coast.

The failure of Japanese democracy

Historians have highlighted that during the 1920s Japan seemed at a critical point between even tighter government control and the possibility of greater democracy. By 1918 it seemed as if a new kind of party politics was emerging with the formation of two new political groups, the Seiyūkai (Association of Political Friends) and the more liberal Kenseikai (Constitutional Association), and yet successive governments backed by both groups still failed to democratize Japanese politics. **Hara Kei**, the leader of the Seiyūkai, did manage to open up some political posts to members of his party, but he was too dependent on the House of Peers and the **genrō** to consider making any serious constitutional reform or extending the **suffrage**.

KEY TERMS

Genrō A term used to refer to a group of Japanese elder statesmen who were seen as the founding fathers of modern Japan.

Suffrage The right to vote.

Diet The national parliament of Japan.

KEY FIGURES

Hara Kei (1856–1921) Japanese politician who served as prime minister from 1918 until his assassination in 1921.

Katō Takaaki (1860–1926) Japanese politician and prime minister from 1924 to 1926.

In contrast, **Katō Takaaki**, the leader of the Kenseikai, agitated strongly for the introduction of representative government on the British model. In 1924 he won an election fought on this issue, and in 1925 he introduced the Universal Suffrage Act, which gave the vote to all men over 25. The Act did not, however, signal the start of a more liberal regime. It became law only because the **Diet**, under pressure from conservative and nationalist pressure groups such as the Kokuhonsha (National Foundation Society), passed the Peace Preservation Law. This sweepingly outlawed any organization that dared demand changes to Japan's imperial constitution or an end to private property.

During the 1920s, Japan suffered a series of economic crises, all of which triggered anti-democratic reactions from the government. In September 1923 the Kantō earthquake devastated Tokyo and killed over 100,000 people. The large sums needed to recover from this disaster led to inflation and the weakening of the banking system. In 1927 the Japanese financial system was in crisis as the banks had huge debts they could not cover. This led to the collapse of more than 20 banks and an economic recession. In 1928, when the first election was held under the new franchise, the Peace Preservation Law was used to make over a thousand arrests and dissolve three left-wing parties. At the same time a permanent police surveillance system was set up. The fear of communism and socialism had provoked a reaction from the nationalist right and the government. These crises inevitably had political repercussions and fuelled political protests from left-wing groups, which the government ruthlessly suppressed. The strengthening of the nationalist right helped fuel Japanese aggression in the 1930s.

ACTIVITY

Copy and complete this chart to summarize the changing relations between the powers, 1918–24.

Power	What changed?	What stayed the same?

How and why did international tensions remain high after the Versailles settlement?

SUMMARY DIAGRAM

Here is a summary diagram explaining how and why.

Aims and impacts of key post-war treaties and conferences	
Washington Conference, 1921	1 Agreed on halting building of capital ships (major warships) for ten years. Established ratio of capital ships comprising 3 for Japan, and 1.67 for Italy and France to every 5 for Britain and the USA 2 Four-Power Treaty replaced Anglo-Japanese Treaty, mutually guaranteeing possessions in Pacific
Little Entente, 1921–22	Treaties signed between Czechoslovakia, Romania, and the Kingdom of the Serbs, Croats, and Slovenes (Yugoslavia) aimed to protect the signatory states against a revival of Austrian and Hungarian power and ensure that the Treaty of Trianon was carried out
Genoa Conference, 1922	Failure to solve reparations problem and to create a European consortium to rebuild Russian economy caused by the Rapallo pact between Germany and USSR
Rapallo Treaty, 1922	USSR and Germany agreed to forgo mutual claims against each other for reparations and Germany agreed to consult with the USSR before participating in international plans which affected Soviet economy
Lausanne Conference, 1923	Successful renegotiation of the Treaty of Sèvres

Role of great powers and their changing relations	
Britain	Together with France, responsible for enforcing Treaty of Versailles, but increasing differences with France over reparations. Does not occupy Ruhr with France
France	Increasingly diverges from Britain over German policy. In 1923 acts independently of Britain to occupy Ruhr
Germany	Tries to divide Britain and France and seeks US support to revise Treaty of Versailles. Negotiates surprise treaty with USSR to prevent its co-operation with Western forces against Germany (Rapallo)
USSR	Still aiming in the long term for world revolution. In the short term ready to normalize relations with European states, but in 1923 unsuccessfully tries to exploit Ruhr crisis to encourage revolution in Germany
USA	Played no role in carrying out peace treaties but negotiated Washington Naval Convention and Four-Power Treaty, as well as proposing the Dawes Plan
Japan	Growing regional power in the Pacific and potential naval rival of the USA. Rejection of Racial equality clause in 1919 fuelled Japanese concerns about their standing in the international community

4 How and why did international relations improve from 1924 to 1929?

Between 1924 and 1929 international relations dramatically improved, although peace still remained fragile. American intervention ended the Ruhr crisis, and the Dawes Plan at least temporarily produced a structure for reparation payments that Germany could keep up with. Stresemann realized that Germany could regain its status as a great power through patient negotiation, while at the same time France abandoned its policy of ruthlessly exploiting the Treaty of Versailles to weaken Germany. The Locarno Treaties were the consequence of these new attitudes, and the so-called 'Locarno Spirit' inspired a brief period of international detente and optimism.

This section looks at this improvement in the following terms:

- economic recovery and the improvement in international relations
- the aims and impact of key international proposals and conferences
- how relations developed between the major powers
- whether the improved relations were real or illusory.

Economic recovery and improved relations

KEY TERM

Gold standard A system by which the value of a currency is defined in terms of the price of gold.

The Dawes Plan created a new and more optimistic climate in Europe and led to France withdrawing from the Ruhr. Germany took measures to stabilize the mark: in November 1924 the devalued currency was replaced temporarily by the *Rentenmark*, and then in August 1924 by the new *Reichsmark*, which was put on the **gold standard**. In 1927 German industrial production reached the level of 1913. German economic recovery led to an improvement in international relations in the period 1924–29 and opened the way to better relations between France and Germany. However, the recovery, particularly in Germany, was fragile and rested on US investment. If the flow of money stopped, Europe would again face an economic crisis with frightening political consequences.

The Dawes Plan

The Dawes Plan played a crucial part in ending the bitter conflict over reparations that had nearly escalated into open war during the Ruhr occupation. Its aim was to restore economic stability to post-war Europe.

The elements of the plan were as follows:

- The overall reparations total of 132 billion gold marks was not changed.
- It did recommend a loan to Germany of 800 million gold marks to be raised mainly in the USA.
- The amount of annual reparation payments was to start gradually and rise at the end of five years to its maximum level.
- These payments were to be guaranteed by the revenues of the German railways and several other key industries.
- A committee of foreign experts sitting in Berlin under the chairmanship of a US official was to ensure that the actual payments were transferred to Britain, France, and Belgium in such a way that the German economy was not damaged.
- The plan was provisional and was to be renegotiated over the next ten years.

The effect of the Dawes Plan on international relations

While Britain saw the Dawes Plan as a way to ending the escalating conflict between France and Germany, both France and Germany viewed it rather more sceptically.

Britain

The Dawes Plan was welcomed enthusiastically in April 1924 by the British Treasury as 'the only constructive suggestion for escape from the present position, which if left must inevitably lead to war, open or concealed, between Germany and France.' Britain also saw it as having the advantage of involving the USA in the whole process of extracting reparations from Germany.

France

There was much that the French disliked about the plan. For example, it was not clear to France how Germany could be compelled to pay if it again defaulted and refused to pay, as it had in 1922. However, with the defeat of Poincaré in the elections of June 1924, France's willingness to co-operate markedly increased. Essentially, if France was ever to receive any reparations payments and avoid isolation, it had little option but to go along with the Dawes Plan.

Germany

The German government also disliked the plan as it placed Germany's railways and some of its industry under international control and did nothing to scale down its reparations debts. Stresemann, who after the fall of his cabinet in November 1923 was now foreign minister in a new government, realized, however, that Germany had no alternative but to accept the plan if France was to be persuaded to evacuate the Ruhr quickly.

Stresemann and German recovery

Stresemann became the most effective and best-known Liberal German politician during the Weimar Republic. He was chancellor from August to November 1923 and then foreign minister from August 1924 to October 1929. During these years, he played a major part in normalizing relations between Germany, Britain, and France and in securing Germany a permanent place on the Council of the League of Nations. His aims are outlined in Source 2.19.

Summarize in your own words the key points in Source 2.19. How useful is it in explaining Stresemann's foreign policy?

SOURCE 2.19

From a letter by Gustav Stresemann to the former heir to the German throne, written in September 1925.

There are three great tasks that confront German foreign policy in the more immediate future. In the first place the solution of the reparations question in a sense tolerable for Germany, and the assurance of peace, which is essential for the recovery of our strength. Secondly the protection of the Germans abroad, those 10–12 millions of our kindred who now live under a foreign yoke in foreign lands. The third great task is the readjustment of our eastern frontiers: the recovery of Danzig, the Polish frontier, and a correction of the frontier of Upper Silesia.

The London Conference

The London Conference in August 1924 resulted in an agreement to implement the Dawes Plan and a commitment from France and Belgium to withdraw their forces from the Ruhr within 12 months. The new balance of power in Europe was clearly revealed when Britain and the USA devised a formula for effectively blocking France's ability to act alone against Germany in the event of another default in reparation payments:

- If Germany again refused to pay, it was agreed that Britain, as a member of the Reparation Commission, would have the right to appeal to the Permanent Court of International Justice at The Hague.
- A US representative would immediately join the Reparation Commission.

Joint Anglo-American pressure would then be more than enough to restrain France from reoccupying the Ruhr. Having been deprived of much of its influence on the Reparation Commission, France undoubtedly suffered a major diplomatic defeat at the London Conference.

Study sources 2.20 and 2.21 on the next page. How far do they explain why Britain welcomed the Dawes Plan?

SOURCE 2.20

From a communication to the Foreign Office on January 5, 1923 by Lord Crewe, the British ambassador to France, in which he describes the great divide between Britain and France over how to treat Germany. At a conference in Paris in early January the two powers argued over whether or not to give Germany a moratorium with or without 'pledges.' France was convinced that only the seizure of pledges in the form of the occupation of the Ruhr would ensure the payment of reparations.

There was a ditch between us that not only the views of the French government and of the French delegation, but the views of the French people made it impossible they could cross it. The ground of principle constituting that ditch was this simple question: is there to be a moratorium with pledges or without pledges?

SOURCE 2.21

From the concluding speech of the British prime minister, Ramsay MacDonald, at the London Conference, August 1924.

We are now offering Europe the first fully negotiated agreement since the war; every party here represented is morally bound to do its best to carry it out because it is not the result of an ultimatum; we have tried to meet each other as far as the public opinion of the various countries would allow us.

This agreement may be regarded as the first Peace Treaty, because we sign it with a feeling that we have turned our backs on the terrible years of war and war mentality.

ACTIVITY

Draw a spider diagram to summarize the Dawes Plan and the attitudes of Britain, France and Germany to it.

German entry into the League of Nations

The logical consequence of the new mood of co-operation established at Locarno was for Germany to be given a permanent seat on the Council of the League of Nations. Initially, the French government, backed by Britain, wanted also to give its ally Poland a permanent seat on the Council to act as a counter to German influence. Germany rejected this, arguing that Poland was 'a state which was so young and unstable,' and consequently the German delegation returned to Berlin in March 1926 without having secured entry into the League.

Significantly, Stresemann did not allow German nationalists to exploit this issue. He told the *Reichstag* that the deadlock over Germany's entry had been caused by the fact that Germany 'was no longer an instrument of the victorious powers.' However, he argued, Germany should not confront Britain and France. Rather, the task of the German government was to continue to work to change the climate of opinion abroad in favor of the Weimar Republic, and in that way Germany would achieve its objectives. By September 1926 a compromise was reached. Germany had to agree to Poland becoming a non-permanent member of the Council for three years with a right to re-election at the end of its term. When the German delegation made its first official appearance at the League on September 10, the German diplomat Hermann Pünder reported back to Stresemann that the occasion had been 'a total success' for Germany, whose delegates had become 'the centre of attention.'

The Young Plan

Three years later Stresemann achieved his greatest success when he managed to persuade Britain and France to agree to a permanent reduction in reparations and to evacuate their troops from the Rhineland five years before the Treaty of Versailles required it. In February 1929, under the chairmanship of the American **Owen D. Young**, talks on a new reparations settlement opened in Paris. Young gained **President Hoover**'s support to reduce the reparations Germany had to pay from 132 billion gold marks to 112 billion Reichsmarks (including interest) over a period of 59 years and to set up a Bank for International Settlements, which Young described as 'the economic arm of the Kellogg Pact.'

KEY FIGURES

Owen D. Young (1874–1962) US industrialist, lawyer and diplomat.

President Herbert Hoover (1874–1964) Republican president of the USA, 1929–33.

Dispute over the evacuation of the Rhineland

At the Hague Conference of August 1929 and January 1930, during which the Young Plan was adopted, negotiations on the evacuation of the Rhineland ran parallel to those on reparation payments. The Coblenz Zone in the Rhineland was due to be evacuated by French troops in 1930, but Stresemann was determined to link Germany's acceptance of the Young Plan to Allied withdrawal from the Wiesbaden Zone, which according to the Treaty of Versailles was not to take place until 1935. Briand was prepared to start the evacuation of the Coblenz Zone early, on September 15, 1929, but was not ready to make any concessions about the final evacuation of the Rhineland until the financial settlement was agreed. Compromise was eventually made possible when Briand dropped his demand for the setting up of a special Verification Commission, which would check that Germany did not try to remilitarize the Rhineland. If there were any complaints, these were now to be referred to the Conciliation Commission provided by Article 3 of the Locarno agreement.

The referendum on the Young Plan

The agreement to end the Rhineland occupation helped to make the Young Plan acceptable in Germany, but even so in December 1929 the government faced a referendum forced on it by the Nazi and National People's parties. The electorate was asked to vote for or against the declaration that any German official signing the Young Plan would be committing an act of high treason, on the grounds that the plan still committed Germany to paying reparations. Although an overwhelming majority of the people who voted agreed with this declaration, the **turnout** was too low for the result of the referendum to constitutionally count, and so the Young Plan was officially implemented on January 20, 1930. Given continued US loans and German economic growth, it might have been successful and decisively improved international relations, but the Great Depression made it unworkable.

KEY TERM

Turnout The proportion of eligible voters who actually turn out to vote. For the December 1929 German referendum, the turnout was just 15 per cent.

Aims and impact of international proposals, treaties and conferences

The aims of the various conferences held, and treaties negotiated, between 1924 and 1929 were to stabilize the post-war world economy and to improve international relations. The most important of these initiatives were:

- the Geneva Protocol
- the Locarno Treaties
- the Kellogg–Briand Pact.

The Geneva Protocol, 1924: support and opposition

The question of how the League should enforce the peace continued to be controversial. In September 1924 the new British prime minister, **Ramsay MacDonald**, whose reputation had been boosted by the successful London Conference (see page 120), attended the fifth League Assembly. In his speech to the Assembly he made a passionate appeal for member states to submit their disputes to arbitration. This encouraged the Assembly to vote for a motion that asked the League to consider what it would do in the event that it was confronted with an aggressor nation that refused to accept arbitration. France welcomed this as it wanted to define more clearly when and how the League should enforce the settlement of a dispute if one side refused to accept its ruling.

In the autumn of 1924 the League announced a new initiative called the Geneva Protocol for the Pacific Settlement of International Disputes. Its essence was that all international disputes concerned with legal or treaty matters such as the recognition of frontiers should be submitted to the Permanent Court of International Justice at The Hague, whose judgment would be enforced by the League. However, the Protocol would not come into force until the disarmament conference that was scheduled to meet in Geneva in June 1925 had drawn up a plan for international disarmament. The Protocol was welcomed by France, but it would inevitably mean that Britain, as one of the leading great powers, would be involved in both naval and military action on behalf of the League. This was a commitment that France desired as it would guarantee the League's armed support against any country that started a war of aggression.

In October 1924 Ramsay MacDonald's government was overwhelmingly defeated in the British general election, and a Conservative government with a large majority was formed. The new government was very conscious of the potential commitments signing the Protocol would involve. In a memorandum on the Protocol the British Admiralty had observed that it was 'opposed to portions of the Navy being practically at the disposal of the League for a series of campaigns of indefinite duration and magnitude.' Not surprisingly, the British government rejected the Protocol, which was effectively its death warrant as it could not work without British participation. In the words of the British Foreign Secretary, **Austen Chamberlain**, Britain favored 'special arrangements to meet special needs.' When he used these words, he would have been aware of Stresemann's alternative proposals for the mutual recognition of

KEY FIGURES

Ramsay MacDonald (1866–1937) The first British prime minister from the Labour Party, January–October 1924 and 1929–35.

Austen Chamberlain (1863–1937) A member of Lloyd George's government, 1919–21, and then Foreign Secretary under Stanley Baldwin, 1924–29. He was the half-brother of future prime minister Neville Chamberlain.

the Franco-German border, which would form the basis of the Locarno Treaties. Inevitably, the Protocol's rejection made France more reluctant to make concessions to Germany.

ACTIVITY

Write a paragraph about the failure of the Geneva Protocol. Include a supported judgment of which factor was the most significant in its failure.

The Locarno Treaties, 1925: achievements and failures

KEY TERM

Cologne Zone
Area around Cologne occupied by the British, December 1918–26.

The Dawes Plan did not solve the problem of French security. Without any alliance with Britain, France was still left facing a potentially strong and aggressive Germany. Initially, therefore, France had little option but to continue to insist on the literal implementation of the Treaty of Versailles. For example, it refused to agree to the evacuation of the **Cologne Zone** of the Rhineland, which was due in January 1925 (see page 123), on the grounds that Germany had not yet carried out the military clauses of the treaty 'either in the spirit or in the letter.'

To reassure France that Germany's intentions were peaceful and so secure the evacuation of Cologne, Stresemann, on the unofficial advice of the British ambassador in Berlin, put forward a complex scheme for an international guarantee by the European great powers of the Franco-German border and of the status quo in western Europe. Austen Chamberlain at first suspected the proposal of being an attempt to divide France and Britain. Then he grasped that it was an opportunity to achieve both French security and the evacuation of Cologne without committing Britain to a military pact with France, which the British government would never tolerate. Aristide Briand, now back in office in France, was aware that only within the framework of an international agreement on the lines put forward by Stresemann could he in any way commit Britain to coming to the assistance of France if it were again attacked by Germany.

In the ensuing negotiations Briand successfully persuaded Chamberlain and Stresemann to widen the international guarantee to cover the Belgian-German frontier. He also attempted to extend the guarantee to Germany's eastern frontiers, but this was rejected by both Stresemann and Chamberlain. However, Stresemann did undertake to refer disputes with Poland and Czechoslovakia to arbitration, although he refused to recognize their frontiers with Germany as permanent. Chamberlain was quite specific that it was in Britain's interests to guarantee the status quo only in western Europe. He told the House of Commons in November 1925 that extending the guarantee to the Polish borders would not be worth 'the bones of a British grenadier.' Essentially, he believed that Britain would not be willing to make significant military commitments to defend Poland's frontiers.

The negotiations were completed at the Locarno Conference, October 5–16, 1925, and seven treaties were signed in London on December 1. The most important of these were agreements confirming the inviolability of the Franco-German and Belgian-German frontiers (meaning that the borders would not be changed) and the demilitarization of the Rhineland.

The treaties were underwritten by an Anglo-Italian guarantee. If a relatively minor incident on one of the frontiers covered by Locarno occurred, the injured party (for example, France) would first appeal to the Council of the League of Nations, and if the complaint were upheld, Britain and Italy (the guarantors) would assist the injured state to secure compensation from the aggressor (for example, Germany). In the event of a serious violation of the treaty, the guarantors could act immediately, although they would still eventually refer the issue to the Council of the League.

What does Source 2.22 show about the improvement in international relations in 1925?

SOURCE 2.22

The signing of the Locarno Treaties, London, December 1, 1925. (British prime minister, Stanley Baldwin, is on the far right; French foreign minister, Aristide Briand, is in the front row, center; behind him, third from left, is German foreign minister, Gustav Stresemann; and Winston Churchill, the Chancellor of the Exchequer, is in the back row, on the right.)

French, British and German views on Locarno

To assess the achievements and failures of Locarno, it is important to view the treaties from the French, British, and German perspectives.

KEY TERM

Locarno Spirit
The optimistic mood of reconciliation and compromise that swept through Europe after the signing of the Locarno Treaties.

Throughout western Europe and the USA, the Locarno Treaties were greeted with enormous enthusiasm and optimism, which was characterized as the '**Locarno Spirit**'. It appeared as if real peace had at last come. There was a sense that France might now have achieved the security it had for so long been seeking. However, of all the great powers, France gained least from Locarno. It is true that France's frontier with Germany was now secure, but under Locarno it could no longer threaten to occupy the Ruhr in order to put pressure on Berlin in the event of Germany breaking the Treaty of Versailles. Britain had managed to give France the illusion of security, but the provision for referring all but major violations of the Locarno agreements to the League before taking action ensured that the British government would in practice be able to determine, through its own representative on the Council, what action, if any, should be taken.

For Britain, there were two main advantages to Locarno: it tied France down by preventing it from repeating the Ruhr occupation. Also, by improving relations between Germany and the western Allies and by holding out the prospect of German membership of the League, it discouraged any close co-operation between Germany and the USSR, which briefly seemed possible when the Rapallo Pact was signed in 1922.

Locarno was deeply unpopular with German nationalists, but for Stresemann it was the key to the gradual process of revising the Treaty of Versailles. By assuring Germany of peace in the west, while not placing its eastern frontier under international guarantee, Locarno left open the eventual possibility of revision of the German-Polish border. Stresemann's aims were therefore diametrically opposed to Briand's, but both desired peace and therein lay the real importance of Locarno. It was a symbol of a new age of reconciliation and co-operation.

Locarno, as Ramsay MacDonald observed, brought about a 'miraculous change' of psychology on the continent, and in the short term significantly improved international relations. This change of mood was the real achievement of Locarno, and it made possible the improvement in international relations in Europe for the rest of the decade.

The Kellogg–Briand Pact, 1928: purpose and limitations

KEY FIGURE

Frank B. Kellogg (1856–1937) US lawyer and senator, and Secretary of State from 1925 to 1929. For his part in negotiating the Kellogg–Briand Pact, he was awarded the Nobel Peace Prize in 1929.

In June 1927 Briand wrote an open letter to the American people proposing a **bilateral** treaty outlawing war. Briand's purpose was to strengthen France's ties with the USA and strengthen France's position in relation to Germany by ensuring that disputes would be settled through diplomacy rather than war. Initially, the US government ignored the proposal, but the American peace movement organized a massive campaign to have war outlawed. In reaction to this **Frank B. Kellogg**, the US Secretary of State, suggested a general pact between as many countries as possible, rejecting war 'as an instrument of national policy.' This did not please Briand at all, as it would have opened up the pact to German membership. For that exact reason, Germany enthusiastically accepted Kellogg's proposal. In a contrast to the original French intentions, it hoped that the proposal would improve US-German relations and lead to the USA revising the Dawes Plan. Germany also believed that a **multilateral** peace pact would make it more difficult for France to build up anti-German alliances in the future. Consequently, in the complex negotiations that led to the signing of the pact on August 27, 1928 the German Foreign Office used all its skills in support of the project, while France raised difficulty after difficulty. Britain was happy to join the pact, believing that it would, by protecting the status quo, help preserve the British Empire.

KEY TERMS

Bilateral Describing an agreement or action between or by two states.

Multilateral Describing an agreement or action between more than two states.

Summarize in your own words the contents of Source 2.23. Do they indicate that the Kellogg–Briand Pact would act as an effective deterrent to war?

SOURCE 2.23

From the Kellogg–Briand Pact.

1 The high contracting powers solemnly declare in the names of their respective peoples that they condemn recourse to war for the solution of international controversies, and renounce it as an instrument of national policy in their relations with one another.

2 The high contracting parties agree that the settlement or solution of all disputes or conflicts of whatever nature or of whatever origin they may be, which may arise among them, shall never be sought except by peaceful means.

3 This treaty ... shall remain open ... for adherence by all other powers of the world.

ACTIVITY

Create a list of US involvements in international affairs in the period 1920–29. To what extent do you think US Foreign policy should be described as isolationist in this period?

Optimists saw the Kellogg–Briand Pact as complementing the Covenant of the League. The pact outlawed war, while the League had the necessary machinery for setting up commissions of inquiry and implementing cooling-off periods in the event of a dispute. Pessimists stressed its limitations in that it was just a general declaration of intention, which meant that it did not commit its members and would certainly not stop war.

ACTIVITY

Compare the Geneva Protocol, Locarno Treaties, and Kellogg–Briand Pact. Which of these was the most significant for improving international relations?

Developing relations between the major powers

The Locarno Treaties led to a dramatic improvement in Anglo-French-German relations. Britain, France, and Germany agreed that Locarno required goodwill and concessions, yet the scope and timing of these concessions were a matter of constant and often bitter debate.

KEY TERMS

Fulfillment A policy which aimed to show that Germany was willing to comply with the Treaty of Versailles in order to gain international trust and eventually seek revisions to its terms.

Detente A process of lessening tension between two or more states.

Dawes bonds Bonds sold by Germany on the international markets (mostly in the USA) to raise money to stabilize its economy. These were a form of loan, which Germany finally paid off in 2010.

France and Germany: the role of Stresemann and Briand

Both Stresemann and Briand had to convince their compatriots that their Locarno policy was working. Briand had to show that he was not giving too much away, while Stresemann had to satisfy German public opinion that his policy of **fulfillment** of the Treaty of Versailles was resulting in real concessions from the ex-Allies. It can be argued that the survival not only of Stresemann's policy but also of the German Republic itself depended on evermore ambitious diplomatic successes.

The atmosphere of **detente** created by Locarno quickly led to the evacuation of the Cologne Zone in January 1926, and in September 1926 Germany at last joined the League of Nations and received a permanent seat on the Council. Stresemann exploited every opportunity both inside and outside the League to accelerate the revision of the Treaty of Versailles. Briand was also ready to consider a 'general settlement' involving the evacuation of the Rhineland, the end of military control and the return of the Saar (see Figure 2.1). He knew that according to the Treaty of Versailles in ten years France would have to make both of these concessions anyway. So to strengthen the 'Locarno Spirit' he was ready to make a grand gesture by bringing forward the evacuation of the Rhineland and the termination of the work of the inter-Allied disarmament commissions.

In September 1926, a week after addressing the League, Stresemann invited Briand to a gourmet dinner in a small restaurant in the French village of Thoiry, where he attempted to exploit France's financial weakness by proposing that Germany would pay France nearly 1.5 billion gold marks, which were to be raised in the USA through the sale of **Dawes bonds**. This would help stabilize the value of the French franc, and in return France would evacuate the French Rhineland zone and hand back the Saar and its coal mines to Germany. Briand approved of the plan, as indeed did the German cabinet, but it met with opposition in France from Poincaré, who had returned to power, and from the US government, which refused to approve the sale of the bonds. Poincaré also, contrary to expectations, had managed to stabilize the franc without any outside help.

Stresemann secured more concessions from Britain and France. In January 1927, the inter-Allied disarmament commission left Germany, and by August, 10,000 troops from Britain, France, and Belgium were withdrawn from the Rhineland. The last Allied troops left the Rhineland in 1930 after the Hague Conference.

Briand's proposals for European integration

With the evacuation of the Rhineland, Germany's restoration to the status of a great European power was virtually complete. Briand, like his successors in the 1950s, appears to have come to the conclusion that Germany could be peacefully contained only through some form of European federation. At the tenth meeting of the Assembly of the League of Nations in 1929, he outlined an ambitious, but vague idea for creating 'some kind of federal link between … the peoples of Europe.'

What is the key message of Source 2.24? What additional knowledge could you use to consider its significance?

SOURCE 2.24

From Aristide Briand's speech to the Assembly of the League of Nations, Plenary Session, September 5, 1929.

I believe there should be some kind of federal link between peoples who are grouped together geographically, like the peoples of Europe. These peoples should be able to come into contact at any time to discuss their common interests, and to make a joint resolution ... Obviously the association will function most of all in the economic field ... this is the most immediate necessity ... I am also sure, however, that from the political or social point of view, the federal link could be beneficial, without interfering with the sovereignty of any of the nations which might form part of an association of this kind.

Stresemann reacted favorably, but was interested primarily in a European customs union and a common currency. Briand was then entrusted by the 27 European members of the League with the task of formulating his plan more precisely; but by the time it was circulated to the treasuries of Europe in May 1930, the whole economic and political climate had dramatically changed. Stresemann had died and the political crisis in Germany caused by the onset of the

Great Depression brought to power a government under **Heinrich Brüning** that was more interested in a customs union with Austria than in a European **federation**. The German cabinet finally rejected the memorandum on July 8, 1930. A week later it was also rejected by the Labour government in Britain.

It is tempting to argue that Briand's plan for a European federation, which were killed off by the economic crisis that was eventually to bring Hitler to power, was one of the lost opportunities of history. However, it would be a mistake to view the proposal through the eyes of early twenty-first century European federalists, who wish to create a European super-state, although his ideas did influence the development of the **European Economic Community** in the 1950s. Essentially, Stresemann hoped that the plan would lead to an accelerated revision of the Treaty of Versailles, while Briand calculated that it would have the opposite effect and strengthen the position of Poland and the other newly created eastern European states. Perhaps under favorable circumstances it could at least have provided a framework within which Franco-German differences could have been solved.

Italy and the impact of Mussolini's ambitions on international relations

The Corfu crisis gave Mussolini the reputation of being a dangerous aggressor, but in reality, given the powerful position of Britain and France in the Mediterranean, he had to follow a relatively cautious line. Italy thus participated in the Locarno Treaties and joined Britain as one of the guarantors of the demilitarized Rhineland and the Franco-Belgian-German frontiers. Up to 1925 Italy's only chance of modifying the peace treaties was to co-operate with Britain and France, but with the return of Germany to the ranks of the European great powers, Mussolini could potentially play off one state against another to gain concessions. However, for the next five years it was British friendship that enabled Mussolini to gain concessions in Africa, and, despite French suspicions, pursue an active policy in the Balkans. At the end of 1925 Austen Chamberlain, an admirer of Mussolini, supported Italy's annexation of Jaghbub on the Libyan-Egyptian border. He also recognized Italy's interest in Abyssinia. This did not, of course, stop Mussolini from encouraging anti-British activity in Egypt and elsewhere in the Middle East.

Relations with France

Relations with France were less friendly. France resented Italian claims to be a great power and also the constant stream of Mussolini's propaganda stressing the need to revise the peace treaties and to pursue an active foreign policy in the Balkans. This clashed with France's determination to uphold the post-war settlement. Good relations were also made more difficult when a left-wing government was elected in France in 1924 that was highly critical of fascism. In his attempt to play off Germany against France, Mussolini also exaggerated the importance of the German-Italian arbitration treaty of 1926, which was in fact nothing more than an expression of goodwill between two friendly states.

SOURCE 2.25

From Mussolini's monthly propaganda periodical, *Gerarchia* (quoted in Lowe, C., and Marzari, F., Italian Foreign Policy, 1870–1940, London: Routledge, 1975, p. 213).

... the brotherhood of arms between Italy and France is ... now lost ... Italy has now returned to her traditional ties with Germany.

Italian policy in the Balkans

Initially, Mussolini pursued a peaceful policy in the Balkans. He acquired Fiume from Yugoslavia by a treaty that pledged 'mutual support and cordial collaboration,' but two years later he was attempting to undermine Yugoslav unity by subsidizing Macedonian and Croat **separatist movements**. In defiance of France, he also supported Hungary's claims against Yugoslavia, supplying weapons over the frontier to help Hungary evade the restrictions imposed upon it by the Treaty of Trianon.

KEY TERMS

The Great Depression A severe worldwide economic downturn that began in 1929 and lasted until about 1939. It started in the USA with a dramatic decline in stock prices on the US Stock Exchange in New York.

Federation A system of government in which several countries or regions form a unity but still manage to remain self-governing in internal affairs.

European Economic Community A regional organization founded in 1958 and a forerunner of the current European Union.

KEY FIGURE

Heinrich Brüning (1885–1970)
Leader of the German Center Party, and chancellor of Germany from 1930 to 1932.

How does Source 2.25 explain the aims behind Italian policy from the signing of the Treaty of London in 1924 through to 1926? Research Italy's 'traditional ties' with Germany. What evidence can you find for the existence of earlier Italian-German co-operation? Also consider historical relations between Italy and Austria. Using your research of the context, consider the validity of Mussolini's statement.

KEY TERM

Separatist movements Political movements seeking the separation of a region from a country.

He also expanded Italian influence in Albania by:

- backing the claims of a local chieftain, Ahmed Zog, to the throne
- investing in the economy
- sending in Italian officers to train the Albanian army.

By 1928 Albania was effectively an Italian colony, and Mussolini ordered plans to be drawn up for settling Italian peasants in the most fertile regions of the country and driving the native Albanian population into the mountains.

Italian colonial policy

Mussolini claimed that the colonization of Albania was the 'first stage of our imperial journey.' At the same time he was tightening Italy's grip on its existing overseas territories. He waged military campaigns to strengthen Italy's power in both Somalia and Libya and also began to plan the conquest of Abyssinia. From 1929 onwards Italian troops began to exploit the absence of clearly marked frontiers to occupy areas actually inside the Italian frontier.

What can we learn from Source 2.26 about Italian colonial policy in the 1920s?

SOURCE 2.26

Ascari (local soldiers serving in the Italian imperial army) engaged in road construction in Italian Somaliland.

Shifting relations with the USSR

The Soviet government viewed the progress made in stabilizing western Europe through the Dawes Plan and the Locarno Treaties with both dismay and hostility, as it feared that this would strengthen the anti-Bolshevik attitudes in Europe and delay revolution in Germany. The USSR attempted to deflect Stresemann from his Locarno policy, first with the offer of a military alliance against Poland, and then, when that did not work, with the contradictory threat of joining with France to guarantee Poland's western frontiers.

Stresemann, aware of the USSR's revolutionary activities in Germany in 1923, did not want to abandon the Locarno policy. However, he aimed to maintain ties with Moscow and strengthen the Rapallo Pact of 1922 as a potential safeguard against Anglo-French pressure.

Thus, the USSR was able to negotiate a commercial treaty with Germany in October 1925. Then in April 1926, at a time when Poland and France were trying to delay Germany's membership of the League Council, it persuaded Stresemann to sign the German-Soviet Treaty of Friendship (the Treaty of Berlin). Essentially, this was a neutrality pact in which the two powers agreed to remain neutral if either party were attacked by a third power.

Anglo-Soviet relations

Relations between the USSR and Britain sharply deteriorated when a Conservative government was elected in October 1924. The outgoing Labour government had just negotiated the Anglo-Soviet General Treaty, which covered trade matters and the settlement of pre-war debts. The Conservatives, however, suspicious of attempts by the USSR to stir up a revolution in the UK, as suggested by the **Zinoviev letter**, refused to ratify the treaty. Three years later, after raiding the offices of Arcos, the official Soviet trading company, to find evidence of espionage, the British government cut all official ties with the USSR. Ambassadors were exchanged again only in 1929, when Labour returned to power. This outbreak of what could be called the first Anglo-Soviet cold war strengthened the determination of the new Soviet leader, Josef Stalin, to cut the USSR off from the West. Increasingly, the main thrust of Soviet foreign policy in the late 1920s was to exploit anti-Western feeling in the Middle East, China, and India.

KEY TERM

Zinoviev letter A letter supposedly from Grigory Zinoviev, the head of Comintern, to the leader of the British Communist Party urging him to stage strikes and other subversive activities, which was published in the *Daily Mail* a few days before the October 1924 general election. The letter was a forgery and the information was false, but it helped the Conservatives win the election.

KEY DEBATE

WHAT MOTIVATED STRESEMANN'S FOREIGN POLICY?

Stresemann's foreign policy is the subject of considerable debate by historians. Was he an early advocate of the policy followed by post-war West Germany of close co-operation with France, leading eventually to European integration along the lines that developed in the 1950s? When Stresemann became German chancellor in August 1923, he had no other option but to end passive resistance in the Ruhr and hope that the USA would intervene with a solution to the reparations problem. The subsequent London Conference and Dawes Plan created opportunities for Stresemann. Working with the British ambassador, he persuaded France to accept the Locarno Treaties. Stresemann's critics have argued that, as passive resistance had failed in the Ruhr, he had no alternative to launching his diplomatic offensive, which at least resulted in the Allies quitting the Cologne Zone and guaranteeing Germany's western frontiers. Why did Stresemann not agree to extending the border guarantee in Locarno to cover the Polish-German frontier? Was he just giving in to intense nationalist pressure in Germany or was this a masterpiece of ***realpolitik***? He gave a clear insight into his thinking when he told the German Crown Prince Wilhelm in a letter in 1925 that the 'most important thing' was to remove 'the strangler from our neck' (by which he meant ending the Rhineland occupation), and that this could be done only through diplomacy. Stresemann followed the path of negotiation brilliantly and by the time of his death in 1929 had restored Germany to the status of a major European power. It does seem that he also came to believe in a peaceful revision of the Treaty of Versailles and an understanding with France.

KEY TERM

Realpolitik A German term meaning literally 'realistic politics.' This is a political approach that favors pragmatism over idealism.

ACTIVITY

Draw up a list of Stresemann's policies from 1923 to 1929 and explain the intentions behind each of them. Come up with criteria to rate how significant each policy was and use these to decide which was the most significant policy in Germany's international relations during this period.

Were improved international relations a reality or an illusion?

There were promising signs that relations had improved between the major powers. However, problems remained.

European powers

Compared to the years 1920–23, relations between the key powers in Europe – Germany, France, and Britain – had improved dramatically:

- The Dawes and Young plans had provided practicable frameworks for the payment of reparations.
- The Locarno Treaties had provided guarantees for the Franco-German-Belgian borders.
- By 1930 Allied troops had evacuated the Rhineland, and the inter-Allied disarmament control commissions had been withdrawn from Germany.

France and Germany

Despite the improvement in France and Germany's relations, underlying tensions still existed. France still feared a German revival, and most Germans wanted the return of the land they had lost to Poland – Danzig, Upper Silesia, and West Prussia (see Figure 2.1). Stresemann never lost sight of his aim to restore Germany to its pre-war position in Europe. For example, he signed the Treaty of Berlin in 1926 to maintain a balance between France and Russia. In the hands of a less skilled statesman, German foreign policy could again have become aggressive and threatening. Briand certainly trusted Stresemann. On hearing of Stresemann's death in October 1929, Briand is reported to have said, 'Order a coffin for two. We have two deaths to lament.' By this he meant that the peaceful post-war reconstruction of Europe centring around a detente between France and Germany was now seriously threatened. This indeed was proved correct. The Wall Street Crash, which happened just three weeks after Stresemann's death, and the subsequent Great Depression, radicalized politics in Germany and contributed to the rise of the Nazi Party.

In southern Europe Italy pursued its own policy, attempting to play off France against Germany and stirring up unrest in the Balkans. As long as Franco-German relations were good, the Italian threat to European peace could be contained. Above all, however, the new European settlement established by the 1924 Treaty of London, the Locarno Treaties, and the Hague Conference was dependent on American finance. Without this, it would crumble.

Japan and the USA

To Japanese nationalists, American policy and the Treaty of Versailles seemed to be designed to preserve the status quo and check the rise of new developing nations, such as Japan itself. It was this perception that caused Japan to place so much importance on its unsuccessful demand for racial equality (see page 75). The Washington Conference, on the other hand, seemed to offer the prospect of a new world order, which would accept Japan as an equal. Japan was ready to accept naval disarmament in return for its recognition as a major power in the Pacific. However, two important factors combined to damage Japan's relations with the USA:

- US immigration policy continued to discriminate against Asians, particularly Japanese immigrants.
- The emergence of Japan as a great power was made possible by the expansion of its economy. If trade with the USA and East Asia drastically declined, the Japanese economy would be badly hit and fresh markets would need to be found in China, just at a time when China was anxious to abolish the privileges granted to the European powers and America. In the view of many in the Japanese army and nationalist parties, what Japan needed to do in this situation was strengthen its position in China, possibly by expanding into Manchuria.

The immediate impact of the Wall Street Crash

A key provision of the Dawes Plan was an international loan to Germany. Apart from this loan to the German government, American finance houses in Wall Street played a big role in raising some $3.9 billion to invest in other projects in Germany. The money was raised from ordinary Americans looking for somewhere safe to invest their money. The loans went to the German regional governments for rebuilding projects, to cities, and even to small companies and local councils. For example, a Bavarian town might borrow $125,000 to build a swimming pool. In the short term, pumping in money on this scale led to a temporary and fragile prosperity in Germany.

Towards the end of the 1920s investment in Germany slowed down as Americans began to put their money instead into the rapidly expanding home economy. By 1929 a huge and unsustainable stock market boom had developed, but in September of that year, believing that the stock market had reached its peak and would from now on decline, investors began to sell their shares. Over the following weeks the selling gathered pace. On October 24, which became known as 'Black Thursday,' 12.9 million shares were sold at a loss, and this extreme panic selling continued for another week. The economic consequences were disastrous. In the USA the crash abruptly stopped investment in industry. All plans for industrial expansion were dropped, and many people in the American middle and working classes were made considerably poorer.

What impression of the Wall Street Crash is given by Source 2.27?

SOURCE 2.27

A crowd gathering outside the New York Stock Exchange on Wall Street after the 1929 financial crash.

Impact on Germany and Japan

The Wall Street Crash also had a major impact on both Germany and Japan. To a great extent, the economic recovery that took place after 1924 not only in Germany but also throughout Europe had been dependent on short-term US loans. After the New York Stock Exchange crashed, US investors abruptly terminated these loans and no more were forthcoming. This was a devastating blow to the European and world economies.

How and why did international relations improve from 1924–29?

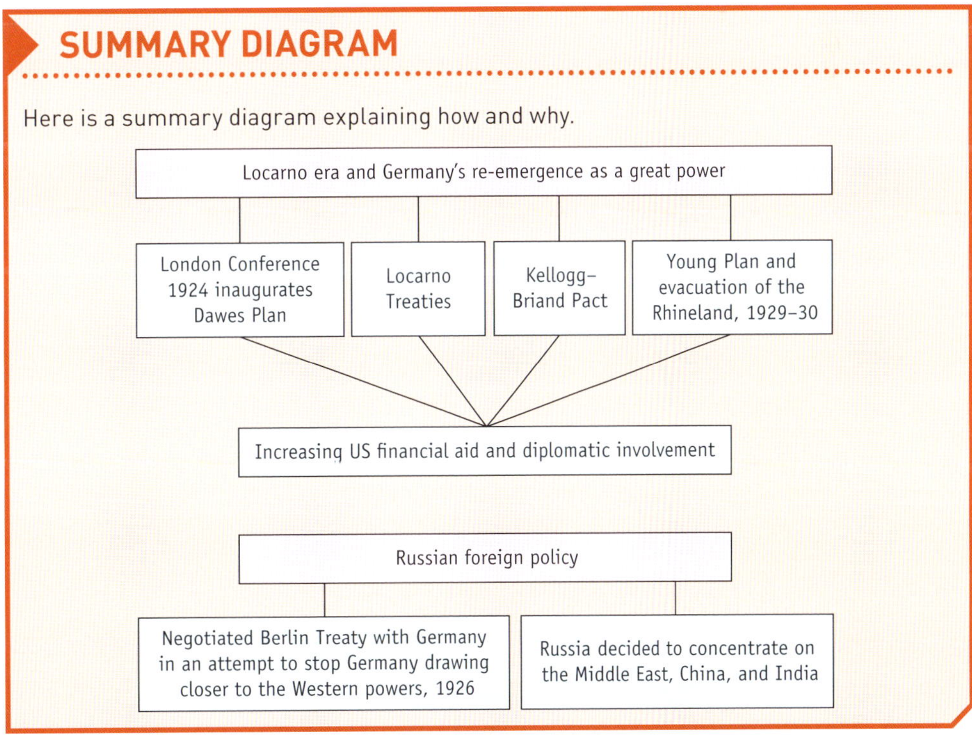

CHAPTER SUMMARY

In 1919 and 1920, the treaties of Versailles, Saint Germain, Trianon, and Neuilly were signed. Each contained the Covenant of the League of Nations. Germany lost its colonies, about 13 per cent of its territory, and was required to pay reparations and drastically disarm. The Allies and the USA were committed to creating independent nation states out of the ruins of the Austro-Hungarian Empire, but in reality seeds of much resentment and ethnic tension were sown through the weaknesses of the treaties and their attempts to re-draw borders.

Although the Ottoman Empire signed the Treaty of Sèvres in 1920, Kemal forced the Allies to make major concessions in the Treaty of Lausanne three years later. Germany was less successful in winning concessions from the Allies, even though Britain became increasingly sympathetic to its demands for a moratorium on reparations payments. In 1923 France occupied the Ruhr in an effort to break the reparations deadlock. Germany replied with passive resistance, which triggered hyperinflation. The stand-off was broken by US intervention, notably in the form of the Dawes Plan. The acceptance of the Dawes Plan and the signature of the Locarno Treaties marked a fresh start after the bitterness of the immediate post-war years, but these developments were viewed with suspicion by the USSR, which feared an anti-Bolshevik alliance. The Locarno years witnessed a strengthening of the League by Germany's entry and the Kellogg–Briand Pact.

REFRESHER QUESTIONS

1. What were the aims of the Allies and the USA at the Paris Peace Conference?
2. To what extent were the Fourteen Points implemented by the peace treaties?
3. Why was Turkey successful in revising the peace treaty imposed on it?
4. What problems faced the ex-Allies and the USA in the years 1920–23?
5. To what extent was the Ruhr occupation the turning point in the history of post-war Europe?
6. To what extent did the Dawes Plan and the Locarno Treaties create a more peaceful Europe?
7. To what extent did the USA pursue an isolationist foreign policy, 1920–29?
8. How effective was the League of Nations in solving international disputes, 1920–25?
9. To what extent could the great powers ignore the League and take unilateral action whenever it pleased them, 1920–29?
10. Why was the Kellogg–Briand Pact signed and what was its significance?

Study skills

Source questions

Evaluating sources considering provenance

Once you are sure what the source is saying about the issue in the question (not just what the source is saying generally), there are certain questions you need to ask yourself about its provenance (that is, who wrote it, when it was written, where it was written, and why).

You will be presented with a variety of sources in assessments. These may include extracts from written material such as speeches and memoirs, and visual sources such as cartoons, posters, and photographs. They need to be evaluated carefully to decide how strong or weak they are as evidence in response to the question.

It is dangerous to assume that all diaries kept by the people directly involved in the historical events in question are reliable, or that all newspaper articles are unreliable because you believe that journalists are more concerned with selling papers than getting to the truth, or that all records of conversation are useless because the person might not remember the exact words. Try not to generalize about evidence by 'type' – your response needs to be tailored to each source rather than be a stock response to the type of source. All sources need to be viewed with a critical eye and not accepted at face value.

After looking to see what the source is, ask yourself some key questions. The nature of the source, its origin, and its purpose will provide a good basis for your analysis.

- Why was it written? For example, if it is a speech, why was it delivered? What was the author's motive? How has that impacted what has been said/written?
- Who is the intended audience? A diary or a letter will have a different audience from a published report or a newspaper. Bear in mind, though, that not all letters will be 'private.'
- When was it written? Something written in the middle of a historical development, when it is not clear what will happen, is very different from something written later, when the outcome is known. Memoirs by central figures in the events may still be strong evidence even if they were written well after the events occurred.
- Is the source written by someone directly involved in events? Do you know some contextual information about this person? Remember that eyewitnesses might not be reliable or may withhold details for various reasons. You will need to use your own contextual knowledge to assess how accurate the details are from your knowledge of events.
- How representative is it? The source will give opinions by the author, but those ideas might not be typical of opinions at the time.
- What is the weight or value of this source as evidence in response to the question? What opinions are held? Does the source strongly support one side over another?

Let's consider one source, Source A (below), in relation to the question.

Read all of the sources. 'The main aim of the post-war peace settlements was to punish Germany and its allies.' How far do the sources support this view? (25 marks)

Is this a strong or weak source of evidence in response to the question?

Answer the following questions to analyze the source:

- Who wrote the source?
- When was it written?
- Why was it written?
- Who is the intended audience?
- What are the main points (focused on the question) in the source?
- What are the tone and emphasis of the source? Does it use 'loaded language' that shows a particular view?
- How likely is it to be a reliable source of information? What might make it unreliable?
- What is the context? What do you know from your contextual knowledge about what was happening when this source was written?

SOURCE A

Extract from Part VIII, Section 1 [I], Article 231, of the Treaty of Versailles, 1919.

The Allied and associated governments affirm, and Germany accepts, the responsibility of Germany and her allies for causing all the loss and damage to which the Allied and associated governments and their nationals have been subjected as a consequence of the war imposed upon them by the aggression of Germany and her allies.

Analyzing visual sources

You may be presented with a visual source. These should be analyzed and evaluated in the same way as written sources, but you will need to make inferences based on the way the image presents information.

Many visual sources are cartoons, although photographs, paintings, or posters could also be used. The nature of visual sources means that you will have to ask yourself different questions when considering context and provenance.

ACTIVITY

Look at the visual sources 2.15, 2.16 and 2.17 on pages 102, 107, and 108. Use the questions below to analyze each of these sources in terms of its content and provenance.

- Who created the source?
- When was it produced?
- Why was it produced? What was its purpose?
- Who is the intended audience? Was it aimed at local people or people in other countries?
- What are the main points (focused on the question) in the source?
- Are there captions on the image? What is their message?
- What are the tone and emphasis of the source? What is the focal point of the image? Is it satirical? How does the portrayal of people or events show this?
- Are there symbols or messages in the portrayal? Are features or clothing emphasized for effect? Why?
- How likely is it to be a reliable source of information? What might make it unreliable? For example, is it a staged photograph or a re-enactment after the event?
- What is the context? What do you know from your contextual knowledge about what was happening when this source was created?
- Do you recognize the name of the creator of the source? If so, what would you expect their opinion to be? Does the content of the source match your expectation?

Essay questions

Writing an introduction and writing essays analytically

Writing an introduction

Having planned your answer to the question, as described in the previous chapter (pages 70–71), you are now in a position to write your crucial opening paragraph. This should set out your main line of argument and briefly refer to the issues you are going to cover in the main body of the essay. It might also be helpful, depending on the wording of the question, to define in this paragraph any key terms mentioned in the question.

In the case of analytical essays, you will need to reach a judgement about the issue in the question, and it is a good idea to state in this vital opening paragraph what overall judgment you are going to make.

Writing analytically and avoiding descriptive answers

Causal essay questions

These questions are not asking you to describe events or developments but are asking you to explain causes. The most successful answers will distinguish between the relative importance of different causes.

Look at these two extracts from sample answers. One describes and one explains.

Explain the importance of the Washington Conference of 1921. **(10 marks)**

Commentary
The answer in Sample A is factually correct, but it merely narrates events rather than analyzing them.

Sample A

The USA had not joined the League of Nations nor had it any alliance with the Entente powers. By 1920 it was concerned by the rise of Japanese naval power in the Pacific and responded by building more warships, which, when completed, would make the US navy the largest in the world. In 1921 Britain, France, the USA, and Japan met at Washington. They agreed to a new Four-Power Treaty. By this, Britain, France, Japan, and the USA would respect each other's possessions in the Pacific and, if any dispute arose, the four powers would call another conference to solve it. The four powers plus Italy then went on to sign, in February 1922, the first Washington Naval Convention, which halted the building of any new battleships for ten years and laid down rules for the relative strength of the four navies: a ratio was established of three capital ships for Japan, and one and two-thirds each for Italy and France, to every five for Britain and the USA. In the London Naval Treaty of 1929, Britain, Japan, and the USA agreed to extend the main principle of this agreement to smaller fighting ships.

Commentary
Sample B not only avoids telling the story but makes a distinction between long- and short-term causes and begins to argue about the relative importance of the Washington Conference over time.

Sample B

The Washington Conference of 1921 was one of the key post-war conferences and indicated the shape US policy was to take in the 1920s. The USA would not join the League, but it was willing to play a major role in promoting disarmament and post-war stability. At Washington its main achievement was to stop a dangerous arms race developing between Britain, the USA, and Japan and to improve US-Japanese relations. In early 1921 the powers with interests and territorial possessions in the Pacific faced two problems that could have escalated into war: naval rivalry and deteriorating US-Japanese relations. One issue that particularly worried both London and Washington was what Britain would do in the event of a naval war between the USA and Japan. By the 1902 Anglo-Japanese Treaty, Britain would, at best, be neutral – and if another country intervened on the side of the USA, then Britain would be committed to fighting on the side of Japan.

To solve these problems, the US president, Harding, called a conference of the main naval powers in Washington. As a result of this initiative, it was agreed that Britain, the USA, France, and Japan would halt the building of capital ships for ten years, scrap a number of existing battleships and stop the construction of bases in Guam, Singapore, and Hong Kong. This was regarded as a significant achievement as it was believed that arms races ended in war – as they had done in 1914. The accord made Japan the strongest naval power in the west Pacific and made it easier to persuade it to replace the Anglo-Japanese Treaty of 1902 by a vaguer agreement that the four powers would respect each other's territory in the Pacific.

Essentially, under US leadership, the great imperial powers now recognized Japan as a major power as well. The Washington Conference therefore cleared the way for better relations between the USA and Japan. However, the onset of the global financial crisis in 1929 was to lead to a much more aggressive Japanese foreign policy and ultimately the invasion of Manchuria.

Analytical essay questions

These types of questions require an analytical answer and not a narration of events. This means you must focus on the key words and phrases in the question and link your material back to them. Therefore, your essay plan (see pages 70–71) is crucial as it allows you to check that you are doing this. You can avoid a narrative answer by referring back to the question as this should prevent you from just providing information about the topic. To keep focused on the question, ensure that the last sentence of each paragraph links back directly to the question.

How far did the Locarno Treaties mark the end of post-war instability in Europe? (20 marks)

In order to answer this question, you would need to consider the following issues about the situation in post-war Europe to judge whether the Locarno Treaties really solved the problem of post-war instability:

- the economically destabilizing reparation demands on Germany
- France's apparent determination to weaken Germany at every opportunity
- the growing disagreements between Britain and France
- the absence of the USA
- the Ruhr crisis.

Then you would need to consider other factors such as:

- the Dawes Plan
- the nature of the security offered to France by Locarno
- Stresemann's cautious revisionism
- co-operation between Stresemann and Briand
- the impact of the Wall Street Crash and Great Depression.

A very strong answer would weigh up the relative importance of each factor as it is discussed; a weaker answer would not reach a judgement until the conclusion; and the weakest answers would either just list the reasons or, worst of all, just describe the events of the period.

The following is part of a descriptive answer for the question above:

In December 1925 the Locarno Treaties were signed by Germany, Belgium, Britain, France, and Italy. They confirmed the existing Franco-German-Belgian frontiers and were guaranteed by Italy and Britain. If the treaties were violated, the injured party could appeal to the Council of the League, which could then help it to gain compensation from the aggressor. The Cologne Zone of the Rhineland was evacuated in January 1926, and a year later the last inter-Allied disarmament commission left Germany.

Commentary
This paragraph outlines some of the facts about the Locarno Treaties and is quite well informed, but there is little explanation. Why were France and Germany ready to accept such an agreement, which on the face of it marked a fresh start for Europe? Was it because the Ruhr occupation had weakened both of them? What was the significance of the Dawes Plan for the reparation problem?

The crucial importance of the opening sentence of each paragraph

One way that you can avoid a narrative approach is to focus on the opening sentence of each paragraph. A good opening sentence will offer a view or an idea about an issue relevant to the question, not describe an event or person. In a very good answer you should be able to read the opening sentence of each paragraph and see the line of argument that has been taken throughout the essay. It is therefore worth spending time practicing this skill.

ACTIVITY

How far did the Locarno Treaties mark the end of post-war instability in Europe?

Look at the following ten paragraph openers. Which of these offer an idea that directly addresses the question above and which simply give facts?

1. The Locarno Treaties were signed in 1925.
2. The Locarno Treaties were greeted with relief as they seemed to mark the beginning of a new era.
3. The Locarno Treaties did not in themselves mark the end of post-war instability.
4. It was really the Dawes Plan that gave Europe stability.
5. The Locarno Treaties guaranteed the German-French-Belgian frontiers.
6. Stresemann first proposed the Locarno Treaties.
7. The failure of the Ruhr occupation ultimately made possible the Locarno Treaties.
8. A US banker chaired the committee that proposed the Dawes Plan.
9. The reparations deadlock between France and Germany needed to be solved before any solution to the Rhineland could be found.
10. From 1919 to 1924 the USA played hardly any part in European diplomacy.

3 International history 1929–39: the rise of extremism and the road to war

Introduction

This chapter explains how the Great Depression unleashed forces that destroyed the peace settlement of 1919 and led to the rise of Hitler and more militant policies in Italy and Japan, and ultimately to the outbreak of the Second World War. It analyzes these problems by considering the following questions:

- How did the rise of extremism affect international relations?
- Why did the League of Nations fail to keep the peace in the 1930s?
- Why, and with what effects, did Britain and France pursue a policy of appeasement?
- Why did war break out in 1939?

KEY DATES

1929	**October**	Wall Street Crash
1929–33		Great Depression
1931	**September**	Japan invades Manchuria
1933	**January 30**	Hitler appointed chancellor of Germany
	October	Germany leaves both the League of Nations and the World Disarmament Conference
1934	**January**	German-Polish Non-Aggression Pact
	July	Nazi uprising in Austria fails
1935	**March**	Hitler reintroduces conscription
	April	Stresa Conference
	May	Franco-Soviet Pact
	June	Anglo-German Naval Agreement
	October	Italy invades Abyssinia
1936	**March**	Rhineland remilitarized
	July	Spanish Civil War starts
	October	Rome–Berlin Axis
	November	Anti-Comintern Pact
1937	**July**	Sino-Japanese War starts
	November 5	Hitler reveals his foreign policy plans
1938	**March 12**	Germany occupies Austria (*Anschluss*)
	September 8	Sudeten Germans break off negotiations with Prague
	September 29–30	Munich Conference
1939	**March 15**	Germany occupies Bohemia and Moravia in Czechoslovakia
	March 31	Anglo-French guarantee of Poland
	April 13	Anglo-French guarantee of Greece and Romania
	May 22	Pact of Steel signed in Berlin
	August 23	Nazi-Soviet Pact
	September 1	Germany invades Poland
	September 3	Britain and France declare war on Germany

1 How did the rise of extremism affect international relations?

In understanding how the rise of extremism affected international relations, the following factors are of crucial importance:

- the impact of the Great Depression on political ideologies and intentions
- the failure of the World Disarmament Conference
- changing relationships between the powers
- the changing nature of relations with the USSR and their impact on foreign policy.

The impact of the Great Depression on political ideologies

It is hard to exaggerate the international impact of the Great Depression. As we saw in the previous chapter, Europe's economic recovery after 1924 had been, to a large extent, dependent on short-term US loans, of which $4 billion went to Germany. After the New York Stock Exchange crashed in 1929, US investors abruptly terminated these loans. This was a devastating blow to the European and global economies. Between 1929 and 1932 the volume of world trade fell by 70 per cent. Unemployment rose to 13 million in the USA, to 6 million in Germany and to 3 million in Britain. Japan was particularly hard hit: some 50 per cent of its mining and heavy industrial capacity was forced to close, and the collapse of the US market virtually destroyed its large and lucrative export trade in silk.

The Depression alone did not bring about political extremism. In Japan nationalism had been growing since the First World War and had its origins in resentment at foreign influence since 1854. In Germany defeat in the First World War and resentment at the Treaty of Versailles had already led to the rise of nationalist parties, while economic hardship provided suitable conditions for the growth of communism. However, the effects of the Depression intensified loss of faith in the democratic system. The Depression also had a major effect on international affairs. It saw the rise of nationalist policies: Japan invaded the Chinese province of Manchuria in 1931 to gain raw materials and open up new markets; and in Germany **Adolf Hitler** rose to power with clearly stated aims for expansion and overturning the provisions of the Treaty of Versailles. The USA became more isolationist and imposed tariff restrictions to protect its economy. Powers like Britain and France became more concerned with looking after their economies than spending money on defense or supporting international order through the League of Nations. Thus, the Depression changed the whole way that international relations were conducted.

ADOLF HITLER

1889	Born in Braunau am Inn in Austria–Hungary, near the German border
1914–18	Served in the German army during the First World War
1921	Became chairman of the NSDAP (Nazi Party)
1923	Played a key role in the Munich Putsch, for which he was imprisoned for a year
1925–29	Rebuilt the Nazi Party
1933	Became chancellor of the German Reich
1936	Launched the Four-Year Plan to prepare the German economy for war
1939	Ordered the German invasion of Poland, which unleashed the Second World War
1945	Took his own life in Berlin

KEY TERM

NSDAP The National Socialist German Workers' Party (Nationalsozialistische Deutsche Arbeiterpartei), or Nazi Party. The party was banned after the Munich Putsch in 1923, but re-founded in February 1925. On July 14, 1933 it was declared the only legal political party in Germany.

Putsch An attempt to take over power.

Mein Kampf Literally, 'My Struggle:' Hitler's major political work, in which he outlined his beliefs and political intentions.

Reichstag The German parliament.

Adolf Hitler, the son of an Austrian customs official, left school without any qualifications in 1905. Convinced of his artistic gifts, he tried unsuccessfully to gain a place at the Academy of Fine Arts in Vienna. Up to 1914 he lived the life of an increasingly penniless artist in Vienna and Munich. He showed great interest in the current social Darwinist, nationalist, and racist thinking of the time, which was to form the basis of his future foreign policy.

In August 1914 Hitler volunteered for the German army and worked in dispatches for the next four years, delivering messages from headquarters to the front line. He was awarded the Iron Cross (First Class). In 1919 he joined the German Workers' Party, which was subsequently renamed the **NSDAP** (Nazi Party) and became its chairman or leader in July 1921. Inspired by Mussolini's successful march on Rome, Hitler attempted to seize power in Germany in the Munich **Putsch** of November 1923, which was a disastrous failure for the Nazi movement. Hitler was imprisoned and wrote ***Mein Kampf***. On his release, he rebuilt the Nazi Party.

During the Depression, the NSDAP became the largest party in the ***Reichstag***. When Hitler became chancellor in 1933, the other, more moderate political leaders were convinced (wrongly) that they could control him. However, by August 1934 he had destroyed all opposition and was able to combine the posts of chancellor and president and call himself '*Führer* of the German Reich' ('leader of the German Empire').

By 1937 Hitler had laid the foundations for 'rearmament in depth' and had dismantled the Versailles system. From 1938 onwards his foreign, domestic, and racial policies became increasingly radical. He annexed Austria and much of Czechoslovakia, and invaded Poland, which caused Britain and France to declare war. In June 1941 he made the major error of attacking the USSR and then, in December, of declaring war on the USA while leaving Britain undefeated in the west. Hitler killed himself on 30 April 1945 when the Soviet Red Army had reached Berlin.

The collapse of support for democracy and the rise of Nazism in Germany

As hardship increased in Germany – with unemployment, hunger and despair for the future – the attractions of extreme groups who promised a completely new system rather than just the usual domestic policies increased. Neither communism nor Nazism had much electoral support by 1928, but after the Wall Street Crash in 1929 both parties attracted more voters as the moderate politicians seemed unable to cope with the crisis. The Nazis offered a national revival based on their ideas of the unity of a 'German race,' ending the hated restrictions of the Treaty of Versailles and promoting Germany as a great power. The communists offered a social revolution that would give workers power and end the effects of the discredited world capitalist system.

As one historian has observed, the economic crisis of 1929–33 was 'Hitler's oxygen.' By January 1930 the number of unemployed people in Germany had reached 3 million, and this figure doubled the following year. Small businesses, farmers and the middle class were badly hit. Fear of bankruptcy and unemployment affected all classes. This was the background to the Nazis seizing power in Germany.

What different types of people are shown in Source 3.1? What additional knowledge could you use to make inferences from the photograph about the Depression? Then think about the political situation in Germany at the time. Who would be associated with the German army and why is this important between 1931 and 1933?

SOURCE 3.1

German soldiers serving food from their soup kitchen to unemployed and destitute civilians in 1931. The Nazi Party successfully exploited the Great Depression to gain political support.

How Hitler became chancellor

The years 1930–33 saw the rise to power of Hitler and the Nazi Party in Germany. As this was to have a profound impact on Europe and on international relations as a whole, it is important to understand how it happened.

In March 1930 **Heinrich Brüning** was appointed chancellor by the German president, **Paul von Hindenburg**. The German government was struggling with very high expenses caused by the Depression. Brüning tried to resolve this with a finance bill that included tax increases, cuts in welfare spending, and an 'emergency contribution' that people on a fixed income would have to pay. The bill was defeated in the *Reichstag*. He then attempted to use the emergency powers contained in **Article 48** of the Weimar Constitution to force the opposition to accept the bill, but was again defeated.

Consequently, on September 14 a general election was held. The result was a huge change to the make-up of the *Reichstag*. The Nazis increased their number of seats from 12 to 107, becoming the second-largest party. They particularly attracted the votes of the peasantry, white-collar workers, and shopkeepers, and owners of small businesses that were facing bankruptcy. However, their message of aggressive nationalism and the creation of a new people's community that would unite all Germans regardless of class resonated with many voters.

Brüning remained in power until the beginning of June 1932 and despite his **deflationary** policies was 'tolerated' by the **SPD**, the German Labour Party, which feared that if his government collapsed, the Nazis might come to power. Nevertheless, he had to use Article 48 – effectively ruling without democratic consent – 109 times just to keep the country running. Brüning cleverly exploited the **banking crisis of 1931** to persuade the ex-Allied powers to scrap reparations, but this won him little support as the effects of the Depression intensified. His ruthless deflationary policy, which cut salaries and benefits, led to him being called the 'hunger chancellor' and ultimately brought about his downfall – and the rise of Hitler.

KEY TERMS

Article 48 An emergency provision in the Weimar Constitution which allowed the president to pass laws without the consent of the *Reichstag*.

Deflationary A term relating to policies or events that bring about a fall in prices.

SPD The German Social Democratic Party (Sozialdemokratische Partei Deutschlands).

Banking crisis of 1931 A financial crisis triggered in May 1931 by the failure of the Kreditanstalt bank in Vienna. Fears of a similar crisis spreading to Germany were self-fulfilling as panic-stricken customers rushed to withdraw their deposits.

KEY FIGURES

Heinrich Brüning (1885–1970) Leader of the Center Party and chancellor of Germany, March 1930–June 1932. He emigrated to Britain and then the USA in 1934.

Paul von Hindenburg (1847–1934) Leader of the German army during the First World War and widely seen as a war hero. He was president of Germany from 1925 until his death in 1934.

By May 1932 there were plans drawn up by the German Center Party politician **Franz von Papen** and **General von Schleicher** in the Ministry of Defense to persuade President Hindenburg to sack Brüning and replace him with a nationalist right-wing coalition to be led by Papen himself. Crucially, it was assumed that Hitler, whose popularity was steadily increasing, would also join the coalition. Hitler had stood as a candidate in the presidential election in the spring of 1932, gaining some 37 per cent of the total votes cast, although Hindenburg was re-elected with 52 per cent of the vote. The Nazis had also achieved impressive results in a series of local elections.

Hitler initially agreed to support Papen provided a general election was called first, as he was convinced that the Nazis would win it. When the election was held on July 31, 1932, the Nazi Party emerged as the largest party, with 230 seats, but did not have an overall majority. Hitler refused the offer of vice-chancellorship, remaining in opposition while he decided what to do next.

On September 12 Papen's minority government was defeated in a **confidence vote**, and another election was held on November 6. This time the Nazis lost 2 million votes, and their number of seats fell to 196. However, Papen still did not have a majority. He was replaced by General von Schleicher as chancellor, who hoped to win the support of the SPD and the German trade unions by reversing some of the cuts made to government expenditure and setting up large-scale job creation projects. However, his position deteriorated rapidly: the SPD was not won over by his concessions, and he also lost the support of the great landowners in eastern Germany because he refused to introduce tariffs on imported food. Schleicher's request to dissolve the *Reichstag* and hold yet another election was rejected by Hindenburg, and he resigned on January 28, 1933.

Hitler's chance to become chancellor had at last arrived. Papen was ready to serve in a Hitler cabinet as vice-chancellor and persuaded Hindenburg to appoint Hitler as chancellor. The Nazis had only a minority of the cabinet seats, but crucially Hitler insisted on Nazis being appointed to the key position of Minister of the Interior in both the Reich and its largest state, Prussia, which gave the party control of the police. Papen assumed that the reliable establishment figures in the other cabinet seats would keep Hitler in check. He was proved wrong.

Although the Nazis gained only 44 per cent of the vote in yet another election, held on March 5, 1933, Hitler exploited the ***Reichstag* fire**, which had happened six days earlier, to stir up fears of a communist coup and give him an excuse to arrest the Communist Party members of the *Reichstag*. He then secured approval for the Enabling Act. This gave him a four-year period of emergency powers, which he exploited to create a Nazi dictatorship. On the death of Hindenburg in August 1934, Hitler combined the posts of chancellor and president and became ***Führer*** of Germany.

Election date	Vote share (%)
May 4, 1924	6.5
December 7, 1924	3.0
May 20, 1928	2.6
September 14, 1930	18.3
July 31, 1932	37.3
November 6, 1932	33.1
March 5, 1933	43.9

Table 3.1 Vote share for the Nazi Party in German national elections, 1924–33

ACTIVITY

What can we learn from Table 3.1 about Hitler's rise to power in Germany? What additional knowledge can you use to interpret these statistics?

KEY FIGURES

Franz von Papen (1879–1969) German soldier, diplomat and politician who became chancellor, June–December 1932. Later he was German ambassador to Austria and then Turkey.

Kurt von Schleicher (1882–1934) German soldier and statesman. He served in the Ministry of Defense and as an adviser to President Hindenburg before being appointed as chancellor, December 1932–January 1933. He was murdered by the Nazis in 1934.

KEY TERMS

Confidence vote
A vote held to decide whether parliament has confidence in the government.

***Reichstag* fire**
A devastating arson attack on the German parliament building on February 27, 1933. Dutch communist Marinus van der Lubbe was found at the scene and was arrested and executed for this crime, although there is ongoing debate about whether this was part of a plot to consolidate Nazi power.

Führer A new title for a role which combined the posts of chancellor and president of Germany, and emphasized absolute authority and control over the state and the Nazi Party.

ACTIVITY

Create a timeline or diagram showing the process of change in democracy in Germany between 1930 and 1934. Then research how many times Article 48 was used during the Weimar Republic. Make a judgement – how democratic was the Weimar Republic? Then assess the process of change from your timeline. How much change was there by 1934?

KEY DEBATE

WHY DID THE NAZIS GAIN CONTROL OF GERMANY?

Few historians dispute that the Great Depression played a key part in the rise of the Nazi Party as a mass movement. The political leaders and parties working within the democratic system seemed to have no answers to the crisis, so voters turned to more extreme parties, such as the Communists and particularly the Nazis. Historians argue about whether the electoral success of the Nazi Party was just a temporary expression of protest. By the end of 1932 the party seemed to be in decline. It was running short of money and losing voters. The view of many historians is still that Hitler gained power at the very moment that the voters were turning away from the Nazis. However, the party offered a popular message of national unity and recovery that was in tune with public opinion, and it was an established, permanent force in German politics.

Between 1930 and 1933 major mistakes were made by party leaders, which gave Hitler his chance to seize power. In retrospect, it was a serious error by the SPD to oppose Brüning's finance bill as this led to the election of September 1930, which saw the Nazis' share of the vote increase dramatically (from 2.6 per cent in 1928 to 18.3 percent just two years later). Again, it was a mistake for von Papen to form a coalition with Hitler in 1933 believing that he would be able to manipulate him.

The collapse of democratic government and rise of militarism in Japan

Rural Japan was the main source of the militarism and nationalism that were to dominate the country from 1931 to 1945. The peasants' bitterness and belief that their misery and poverty were not understood by big business or politicians were exploited politically by the various right-wing pressure groups, such as the Imperial Reservists' Association, for whom the countryside and its inhabitants embodied the traditional virtues of Japan. Economic despair fuelled the growth of nationalism and militarism, and increasingly it was to the army that the victims of the Great Depression looked to reform Japan, restore its ancient warlike qualities and increase Japanese influence in China so that new export markets could be opened up.

The growth in ultra-nationalist groups

Ultra-conservatives and Japanese nationalists had accepted that, to defend itself against Western imperialism, Japan had itself to industrialize and to model itself in many ways on the West. This threatened important traditions. Japanese patriots relied on the army to win battles and dominate East Asia, which they believed would restore national pride in Japanese traditions and also make Japan prosperous. By 1936 well over half a million Japanese people belonged to ultra-nationalist organizations. It was these groups that were to mobilize mass support for expansionist military activities in China in the 1930s (see page 155) and weaken the government's ability to control the army.

KEY FIGURE

Kita Ikki (1883–1937)
The leading ultra-nationalist philosopher, whose ideas inspired the Kōdō faction's failed coup in 1936, for which he was executed.

KEY TERM

Shōwa restoration
Attempts in the 1930s to restore the power of the Japanese emperor. Shōwa was the name given to Emperor Hirohito's reign, 1926–89.

Attempts to bring about the 'Shōwa restoration'

After 1930 the influence of the army and navy in Japanese politics increased to the point where effectively they controlled Japan. They never created an actual dictatorship, but they had the power to veto government policies and bring about the dismissal of ministers they considered hostile to their interests. The military, both in Japan, and in China and Manchuria, was the driving force behind Japanese expansionism.

Ultra-nationalist ideas were particularly strong in the army among junior officers, who were influenced by the ideas of **Kita Ikki** for a **Shōwa restoration**. By assassinating corrupt civilian politicians, they would destroy what they regarded as 'decadent' democracy and restore the power of the emperor. The Shōwa restoration failed, but the five plots against the government and assassinations of its members, 1931–36, nevertheless succeeded in strengthening the power of the armed forces over the government:

KEY FIGURE

General Kazushige Ugaki (1868–1956)
Japanese general and cabinet minister. He was governor general of Korea and later foreign minister.

KEY TERMS

Kwantung Army
A Japanese army guarding the South Manchuria Railway and stationed on the Liaodong peninsula since 1907.

Manchukuo
The name given to the Japanese-dominated state created in 1932, comprising the territory Japan seized in its invasion of Manchuria (see page 155).

- In 1931 there were two unsuccessful attempts by the nationalist Sakurakai, or Cherry Blossom Society, to assassinate the prime minister and install **General Ugaki**, the Minister of War, as the head of a new government.
- On May 15, 1932 members of the Ketsumeidan, or Blood League, who were predominantly young peasants, co-operated with military and naval cadets in a plan to destroy the government and declare martial law. Although they assassinated the prime minister, they failed to achieve a military government. Instead, a 'cabinet of national unity' was appointed.

In August 1935 and February 1936, fighting broke out between two rival groups within the army: the Kōdō ('Imperial Way') faction and the Tōsei ('Control') faction. The former believed in direct action to bring about the Shōwa restoration, while the latter believed that this was a distraction from preparing for an all-out war against China. The Kōdō faction was comprehensively defeated in 1936 when the navy, the key military authorities and Emperor Hirohito himself all turned against its plotters.

The army and Japanese expansion, 1931–37

The constant threats by ultra-nationalist officers against the government made it increasingly difficult for ministers to control the army. Even though they knew in advance of the **Kwantung Army**'s plans to occupy Manchuria in September 1931, they were unable to stop them, as the army simply ignored instructions from Tokyo. The anti-government plots of October 1931 and May 1932 failed, but nevertheless they intimidated the government into supporting the Kwantung Army's policy in Manchuria and recognizing the creation of the Japanese-dominated state of **Manchukuo**. The government now had no option but to defend the army's conquest of Manchuria in the League of Nations, even though it had not planned the conquest.

What is the message of Source 3.2? What additional knowledge of events in Japan could you use to explain the message?

SOURCE 3.2

A photo from the 1930s titled 'Off to the Wars.'

Draw a spider diagram to show the reasons for the failure of democracy in Japan, 1919–33.

Pressure on Mussolini for a change of policy in Italy

KEY FIGURE

Engelbert Dollfuss (1892–1934) An Austrian politician who was chancellor from 1932 until his assassination during a failed Nazi coup in 1934.

KEY TERMS

Corporate state A state where most of the economy is controlled by the government.

Satellite state A state that is officially independent but that is dominated by another state.

Buffer state A neutral state positioned geographically between two rival powers.

Under Mussolini, Italy initially tried to mediate between Germany and Britain/France while pursuing territorial ambitions in the Balkans and North Africa. Mussolini hoped that this would result in concessions from both sides. Initially, he welcomed Hitler's success on becoming chancellor in 1933. He claimed that Germany was following the example of fascist Italy, and Hitler was given what was usually unwanted advice on how to build a **corporate state** and govern Germany. Hitler responded by sending his 'homage and admiration' to Mussolini and expressed his hope for an alliance with Italy. In June 1933 Mussolini proposed a four-power pact between Britain, France, Germany, and Italy to achieve a peaceful but limited revision of the Treaty of Versailles.

However, the situation in Austria was to prove a source of tension between Germany and Italy. In February 1934 the differences between the Austrian Social Democrats and the government escalated into a brief civil war, which resulted in the defeat of the Austrian socialists. In May the Austrian chancellor, **Engelbert Dollfuss**, created a one-party state, which was effectively a dictatorship, and began to round up Austrian Nazis and those who wanted unification with Germany.

Hitler, alarmed by these events, met Mussolini in Venice in June and tried to convince him that Austria should become a German **satellite state**. Mussolini rejected this, as he was determined to keep Austria as an independent **buffer state** between Italy and Germany. The prospect of again having a major power on its northern frontier threatened to undo Italy's major gain from the 1919 peace treaties. Hitler then gave the Austrian Nazis strong unofficial encouragement to launch a coup in Vienna in July. Dollfuss was assassinated, but the uprising was quickly defeated.

Mussolini immediately mobilized troops on the Brenner Pass, a route through the Alps mountain range that forms the border between Italy and Austria, and forced Hitler to disown the coup. The incident brought about a sharp deterioration in German-Italian relations and appeared to rule out any prospect of an alliance. Hitler was not strong enough to offer support for the Austrian Nazis at this stage. The unsuccessful Nazi putsch in Vienna in July 1934 and the German announcement of conscription in March 1935 led Italy to align itself firmly with France.

Isolationist pressures on the USA

KEY FIGURES

Herbert Hoover (1874–1964) Republican president of the USA, 1929–33.

Franklin Roosevelt (1882–1945) Democratic president of the USA, 1932–45. He countered the effects of the Great Depression by investing in a massive program of public works.

During the 1920s, the USA participated in efforts to preserve the peace and bring about international disarmament, but the Great Depression devastated its economy. By 1933 nearly 13 million Americans were unemployed. Its GNP (gross national product) fell by 50 per cent, manufacturing output by 25 per cent and investment in business and industry by 98 per cent. This led many Americans to look inwards, focusing on domestic recovery and not international relations. Also, under **President Hoover**'s administration immigration policy tightened dramatically in response to the fear of many Americans that immigrants would compete for the scarce employment opportunities. The previous optimism had given way to despair, and the internationalism of the 1920s was replaced with a new wave of isolationism, which reinforced the USA's decision in 1920 not to join the League of Nations.

The USA was certainly alarmed by the Japanese occupation of Manchuria, but did nothing to stop it. Indeed, the mood among US voters remained strongly isolationist. Under pressure from the 'yellow press' and public opinion, the US Senate in January 1935 rejected any move for the country to join the Permanent Court of International Justice. Later in the year the Temporary Neutrality Act empowered **President Roosevelt** to ban the supply of arms to all belligerents – whether aggressors or victims of aggression – in the event of the outbreak of war, which further strengthened the US policy of non-involvement and neutrality.

SOURCE 3.3

Unemployed workers queuing for free soup during the Great Depression in the USA.

Look at sources 3.3 and 3.4 concerning the Great Depression. How far does source 3.3 support source 3.4?

SOURCE 3.4

US unemployment rate, 1910–60.

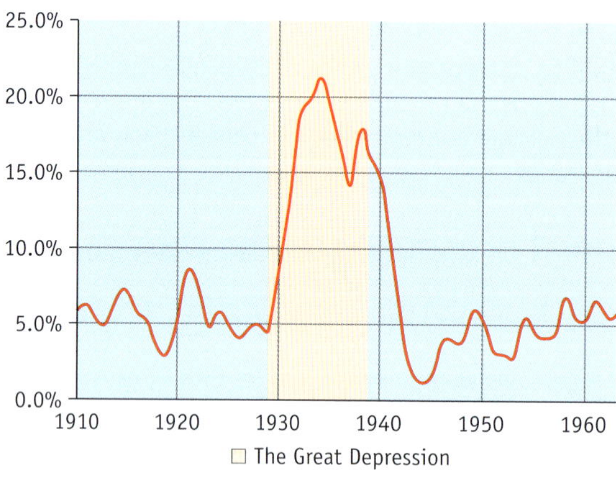

Failure of the World Disarmament Conference, 1932–34

One of the international initiatives that came about as a response to the devastation caused by the First World War was the World Disarmament Conference. It was widely believed that the enormous increase in armaments manufactured by the great powers of Europe before 1914 had been a major contributing factor to the outbreak of war. When the League Council called the long-awaited World Disarmament Conference in February 1932, millions of people from all over the world sent in petitions strongly supporting peace, and prayers were held in churches for the success of the conference. However, largely due to international events and the attitudes of major powers, the conference was a failure.

This section looks at:

- the reason why the conference was held
- the effect of international events on the conference
- the attitude of the major powers, especially France and Germany, towards the conference.

Reasons for the conference

One of the League of Nations' main tasks was to create a global disarmament program. In May 1926, a preparatory commission was formed to plan a disarmament conference. By 1930, after lengthy discussions, the commission produced a final draft for an international disarmament convention. It recommended:

- setting a budgetary control on the money spent on armaments
- limiting the number of personnel in the armed services
- creating a permanent disarmament commission to ensure that any agreed disarmament measures were carried out
- banning chemical and bacteriological weapons
- accepting the decisions taken to limit naval power at the 1930 London Naval Conference.

Representatives from 59 states met at the conference in Geneva to discuss these recommendations.

Who do you think is the intended audience for Source 3.5?
Read pages 146–148 and then draw up a plan to answer the question: To what extent is this source 'wishful thinking'?

SOURCE 3.5

'Mars Tied Down:' a 1932 cartoon referring to the World Disarmament Conference of 1932. Mars was the Roman god of war.

The effect of international events on the conference

The World Disarmament Conference could not have been convened at a more unfortunate time. In September 1931 the League of Nations had been powerless to prevent the Japanese invasion of Manchuria, while in Germany the Nazi Party, which was committed to rearmament, was growing rapidly, and in January 1933 Hitler would be appointed chancellor. This ominous rise of nationalism in Germany made France and Poland less likely to compromise over German demands for equality in armaments. Above all, the impact of the Depression on the USA strengthened its isolationist tendencies. Long before Germany withdrew from the conference, it was clear that it would fail.

The attitude of the major powers

The British and American governments supported disarmament. The strength of their navies had already been agreed by the Washington and London treaties (see page 149), and their armies were small compared to those of some of the other great powers. The USSR proposed the idealistic but impractical idea of banning armaments altogether. The real issues at stake were clear from the attitudes of the French and German governments.

The position of France

KEY TERM

Internationalized (A place or country) put under international control.

France wanted to give the League 'teeth' by adopting the following proposals:

- All civil aviation should be **internationalized** to prevent it from being used for military purposes.
- Armaments above a certain size should be banned to prevent Germany from developing larger weapons.
- An international police force under the League of Nations should be created to enforce disarmament.
- Arbitration over disputes between countries should be compulsory.

Until these suggestions were adopted, France would insist that Germany should be subject to the Treaty of Versailles.

The position of Germany

The German government under Chancellor Brüning demanded equality in armaments with the other powers. Having seen the strongly pro-rearmament Nazi Party increase its seats from 12 to 107 in the election of September 14, 1930, the government simply could not afford to make any concessions unless equality were achieved. A collision between France's need for security and Germany's demands for equality of armaments with the other powers now seemed unavoidable.

In July 1932 Germany withdrew from the conference in protest at its demand for equal armament rights not being accepted. However, in December it was persuaded to return when agreement was reached that it would have 'equality of rights in a system that would provide security for all nations.' For France, the problem with this formula, particularly after Hitler came to power in January 1933, was how 'security for all nations' would be provided when neither Britain nor the USA was ready to guarantee French security or to strengthen the League of Nations' ability to intervene in international disputes.

Hitler had no intention of agreeing to any disarmament proposals, but in May he stressed that Germany was committed to peace and even agreed to join the four-power pact with France, Britain, and Italy that Mussolini had proposed. In October 1933 Germany rejected a Franco-British proposal whereby a general armament plan for all the powers would come into force only after a delay of eight years, as this would prevent Germany from starting its rearmament program before 1941. That same month Hitler also walked out of the disarmament conference on the grounds that France and Britain were still insisting on the one-sided disarmament of Germany. This effectively brought to an end any hope of disarmament; the conference was adjourned on June 11, 1934 and did not meet again.

Changing relationship between the powers

Between 1930 and 1937 the relationship between the powers dramatically changed. This was primarily caused by the emergence of new aggressive regimes in Germany and Japan. It was above all German rearmament that led initially to attempts to contain Nazi Germany.

London Naval Conference, 1930

Unlike the ill-fated World Disarmament Conference, which met two years later, the London Naval Conference did manage to reach an agreement. However, this settlement was only partial and was soon to be ignored by Japan.

KEY FIGURE

Hamaguchi Osachi (1870–1931) Leader of the liberal Constitutional Democratic Party and prime minister of Japan, 1929–31.

The ten-year agreement limiting the size of the British, American, Japanese, Italian, and French navies, which was signed in Washington in 1922, was due to expire in 1932. The Washington Naval Convention had applied to capital ships and did not limit the construction of smaller warships – cruisers, frigates and submarines. The five powers that had signed the Washington agreement met in London in January 1930 to consider not only renewing restrictions on battleships but also extending them to smaller ships.

The Japanese government under **Hamaguchi Osachi**, despite intense hostility from its navy and army, agreed to accept a ratio that would allow Britain and the USA to build ten cruisers and smaller ships to Japan's seven. France and Italy were asked to accept the same ratio as Japan, but they refused on the grounds that each needed a large fleet in the Mediterranean to protect its interests. France would agree only if one of the following two conditions were satisfied:

- either Italy should agree to a permanent French naval superiority
- or there should be a security pact along the lines of the Locarno Treaties specifically to cover the Mediterranean.

ACTIVITY

How successful was the London Naval Conference? Could it be described as more successful than the World Disarmament Conference four years later? Create criteria to make a judgement about how important these conferences were. Take into account success over time in your assessment. You could consider:

- profundity: how deeply each participant was affected
- quantity: how many armaments were restricted
- durability: how long any agreements lasted.

Italy would not agree to the first demand, and Britain would not commit to a Mediterranean security pact. France and Italy consequently refused to accept the ratios set, the key part of the London Naval Treaty, but they did agree to a five-year pause in the construction of capital ships and a limitation of tonnage and gun calibre for submarines.

The Rome Agreement and Stresa Front

At first, Hitler tried to reassure the other European powers of his peaceful intentions, but his policies and actions alarmed his neighbors and led to the agreements signed at Rome in January 1935 and at Stresa in April. Essentially, these agreements were a response to:

- Hitler's support for the attempt by the Austrian Nazis to stage a coup against their government in July 1934
- the German rearmament program of 1935, which also involved the introduction of conscription.

The Rome Agreement

In January 1935 France and Italy signed the Rome Agreement, by which the two states undertook not to meddle in the affairs of the Balkan countries and to act together in the event of German rearmament or another threat to Austrian independence. In June direct Franco-Italian military **staff talks** started to discuss joint action in the event of a German attack on Austria, Italy or France.

KEY TERM

Staff talks Strategic discussions between officers of the planning and administrative departments of two or more national armies.

The Stresa Front

The Rome Agreement was reinforced by the Stresa Front, which was negotiated in April 1935 between Britain, France, and Italy to condemn German rearmament and resolve to maintain the peace settlements. The three powers agreed to reaffirm the Locarno Treaties and oppose any further German breaches of international treaties. Confidentially and away from the business of the conference, the British delegate Sir Robert Vansittart, a senior official at the Foreign Office, discussed with Mussolini Italian plans for the annexation of Abyssinia; these discussions gave Mussolini the impression that Britain would not oppose him. Some historians see Stresa as the last chance of halting escalating German aggression, but the Anglo-German Naval Agreement and the strength of the hostility of British public opinion

How did Mussolini react to the growing aggression of Nazi Germany, 1933–35? Create a list of your ideas.

towards the Italian invasion of Abyssinia eventually weakened the Stresa Front and arguably drove Mussolini into Hitler's arms.

The Rome–Berlin Axis, 1936

The Rome Agreement and the Stresa Front seemed to indicate that Mussolini had moved on from his policy of mediating between France and Germany and had firmly come down on the side of Britain and France, but this did not mean that Italy had given up its imperial ambitions. On the contrary, Mussolini was still interested in annexing Abyssinia and from January to October 1935 worked to gain French and British support for his plans. However, when Italian forces invaded Abyssinia in October 1935, he did not receive the backing he had hoped for. Even though Britain and France were initially ready to make concessions, ultimately both powers approved the ineffective sanctions taken by the League, and consequently Mussolini began to align Italy more closely to Nazi Germany. He did not protest when German forces re-entered the demilitarized Rhineland (see page 173), and he also softened his position on Austria. In return, Germany defied the League's sanctions and exported coal to Italy, which was vital for the Italian economy.

The summer of 1936 saw increasingly friendly relations develop between Germany and Italy. While Britain pointedly refused to recognize the king of Italy as the 'emperor of Abyssinia.' Germany rapidly did so. Hitler and Mussolini also co-operated in blocking a new British initiative to update the Locarno Treaties. Italy's growing hostility towards Britain, France, and especially the USSR, with which it had enjoyed fairly good relations until the Spanish Civil War (see pages 162–66), also ensured that it had to be more tolerant of German influence in Austria. In January 1936 Mussolini let it be known to the German ambassador in Rome that, 'If Austria, as a formerly independent state, were ... in practice to become a German satellite, he would have no objection'.

Thus, after being a major block to Hitler's plans for Austria and rearmament in 1934–35, Mussolini became more co-operative. He and Hitler began to work together to prepare the ground for the October Protocols of 1936.

The signature of the October Protocols and announcement of the Rome–Berlin Axis

The understanding between Italy and Germany over Austria prepared the way for a German-Italian agreement, the October Protocols, which were signed in Berlin in October 1936. Mussolini announced this new alignment, known as the Rome–Berlin Axis, to the world at a mass meeting in Milan on November 1 (see Source 3.6).

What is the message of Source 3.6 and how does it explain the change in Mussolini's policy towards Germany? Who was the intended audience of this speech?

SOURCE 3.6

From Mussolini's speech in Milan, November 1, 1936 (quoted in Noakes, J. and Pridham, G. eds., Nazism 1919–1945, Volume 3, Liverpool: Liverpool University Press, 2001, p. 672).

The meeting at Berlin resulted in an agreement between the two countries on certain questions, some of which are particularly interesting in these days. But these agreements, which have been included in special statements and duly signed – this vertical line between Rome and Berlin – is not a partition, but rather an axis round which all the European states animated by the will to collaboration and peace can also collaborate. Germany, although surrounded and solicited, did not adhere to sanctions [against Italy] ... And may I remind you that even before the Berlin meeting [in October 1936] Germany had practically recognised the Empire of Rome.

The Anti-Comintern Pact, 1936–37

Three weeks after the announcement of the Rome–Berlin Axis, Hitler overrode advice from his professional diplomats and signed the Anti-Comintern Pact with Japan, which was worried about growing Russian influence in China. The pact was more of symbolic than practical importance as it was aimed against the Comintern rather than the USSR itself, although, of course, the Comintern was run by the USSR. For Hitler, coming as it did so soon after the Rome–Berlin Axis, the pact trumpeted to the world that Germany was no longer isolated, as it had appeared to be in the spring of 1935. In November 1937 the pact was further strengthened by Italy's accession to it.

ACTIVITY

Create a diagram to show the process of change in Germany's international relations from when Hitler came to power in January 1933 until the end of 1936.

KEY TERM

New Economic Policy
A Soviet economic policy introduced by Lenin as a temporary measure in 1921. It contained elements of capitalism.

Changing nature of relations with the USSR and the impact on foreign policy

Bolshevism was perceived to be a deadly threat to capitalism, the Western democracies, and the whole peace settlement negotiated in 1919–20. The former wartime Allies and the USA had sent troops into Russia to assist the White Russians in their campaign against the Bolshevik forces (see pages 63–64). When this failed and the Red Army advanced into Poland, France assisted Poland by sending military advisers and equipment. The Red Army's defeat outside Warsaw in August 1920 was widely seen as a miracle that saved the Western world. The fear of Bolshevism played a major part in the rise of Italian fascism and German Nazism, and communist parties in western Europe were regarded as the 'enemy within'. Yet, once the Bolshevik regime had stabilized itself by 1921 and introduced its **New Economic Policy**, Russia (now the USSR) began to play a greater role in European great power diplomacy, without ever – thanks to the Comintern (see page 152) – entirely abandoning its revolutionary principles.

The Soviet response to the rise of Nazism

The Soviet leader, Joseph Stalin, like the other European leaders, reacted cautiously to the Nazi takeover of power. His distrust of the West was at least as great as his fear of Nazi Germany.

Stalin negotiated a defensive agreement with France, signing the Franco-Soviet Treaty of Mutual Assistance in May 1935. He also sought collective security by joining the League of Nations in September 1934. He aimed, with French co-operation, to build up a regional eastern European defense agreement similar to the Locarno Treaties. The USSR signed a pact with Czechoslovakia. Neither pact, however, was backed up with actual military agreements.

However, Stalin also attempted to maintain good relations with Germany despite such setbacks as the German-Polish Non-Aggression Pact. The Soviet negotiations with France in the spring of 1935 were counterbalanced by a series of secret talks with Germany, which mirrored the French strategy of trying for a settlement with Hitler in the summer of 1935. Soviet-Nazi talks continued intermittently right up to February 1936. Only with the ratification of the Franco-Soviet Treaty of Mutual Assistance by the French parliament were they broken off, but they were renewed in the summer of 1939 (see page 188).

JOSEPH STALIN

1878	Born in Georgia
1903	Joined the Bolshevik Party
1917	Assisted Lenin in the Russian Revolution
1922	Became general secretary of the Communist Party
1924	Took over as unofficial leader of the USSR after Lenin's death
By 1929	Had effectively become dictator of the USSR
1936–38	Conducted the Great Purge to remove his perceived opponents
1939 August 23	Signed the Nazi-Soviet Pact
1939 September 17	Ordered the Soviet occupation of eastern Poland
November 30	Ordered the invasion of Finland
1941	Took over as supreme commander of the Soviet war effort following Germany's invasion of Russia
1953	Died

Joseph Stalin, whose family name was Djugashvili, was born in Georgia, the son of a shoe repairer. He originally intended to become a priest, but in 1899 was expelled from the training academy for his revolutionary views. He was twice sent to Siberia, but each time managed to escape. At various times he was in exile in Paris and Vienna, and in 1912 he became the Bolshevik Party's expert on racial minorities. He edited *Pravda* in 1917 and became Commissar for Nationalities in the first Soviet government. In 1922 he became General Secretary of the Communist Party.

By 1929 Stalin had taken firm control of the Communist Party and was in a position to launch the first of his Five-Year Plans, which involved the collectivization of agriculture and the massive expansion of heavy industry. He defended himself from the criticism that followed the ruthless implementation of these policies through a lengthy campaign of mass arrests, show trials, imprisonments, and executions known as the Great Purge. In 1941 he became Chairman of the Council of Ministers and took over supreme control of the Soviet war effort. The Soviet victory in 1945 was celebrated as his crowning achievement and enabled the USSR to control most of eastern Europe. After 1945, until his death in 1953, Stalin's position in the USSR was unchallenged.

The Comintern and the fear of communism

The USSR had a **Janus face**: looking in one direction, it was ready to negotiate treaties with Germany and France, while, looking the other way, it tried to stir up revolution within these countries through the Comintern. This explains why, among governments in western Europe and the USA, the fear of communism was always an important factor. In the USA Robert Lansing, the most important of President Wilson's advisers, called communism 'the most hideous and monstrous thing the human mind has ever conceived,' showing how fearful the Americans were about the potential of Soviet ideology.

Unlike the pre-war Socialist International, which was a federation of independent and democratic socialist parties, the Comintern followed the Leninist principle of **democratic centralism**. As its chairman, **Grigory Zinoviev** explained, it was in fact a single entity with sections in various different countries. To maintain absolute control, the Soviet Communist Party had five seats on the executive in each country, while the country concerned had just one.

KEY TERMS

Janus face An expression named after the Roman god of lies and deception Janus, who had two faces and was, therefore, associated with duality.

Democratic centralism An organizational system introduced by Lenin in which policy was decided centrally and had to be carried out by all government bodies and members.

KEY FIGURE

Grigory Zinoviev (1883–1936) A key Bolshevik politician during the early years of the USSR, including as chairman of the Comintern, 1919–26. He later fell out of favor and was sentenced to death in 1936 during Stalin's Great Purge.

By maintaining the fiction that the Comintern was an independent organization, the Soviet government was able to negotiate economic and even military treaties with Germany and other European states while at the same time helping local communist parties. In Turkey and India the Comintern was a useful tool to undermine Western influence. When the Ruhr crisis occurred in Germany in 1923–24, the Comintern drew up a timetable for a series of armed uprisings in Germany, which was discovered by Western intelligence agents. This confirmed one of the main fears of British officials: that the economic chaos caused by the passive resistance of German workers to the French occupation of the Ruhr would result in a communist revolution in Germany.

ACTIVITY

Write a paragraph about the work of the Comintern. Consider its role in international affairs. Include a supported judgement about its significance.

ACTIVITY

Produce a presentation to show how Britain, France, the USSR, and Italy reacted to the new Nazi Germany, 1933–36.

How did the rise of extremism affect international relations?

SUMMARY DIAGRAM

Here is a summary diagram explaining how.

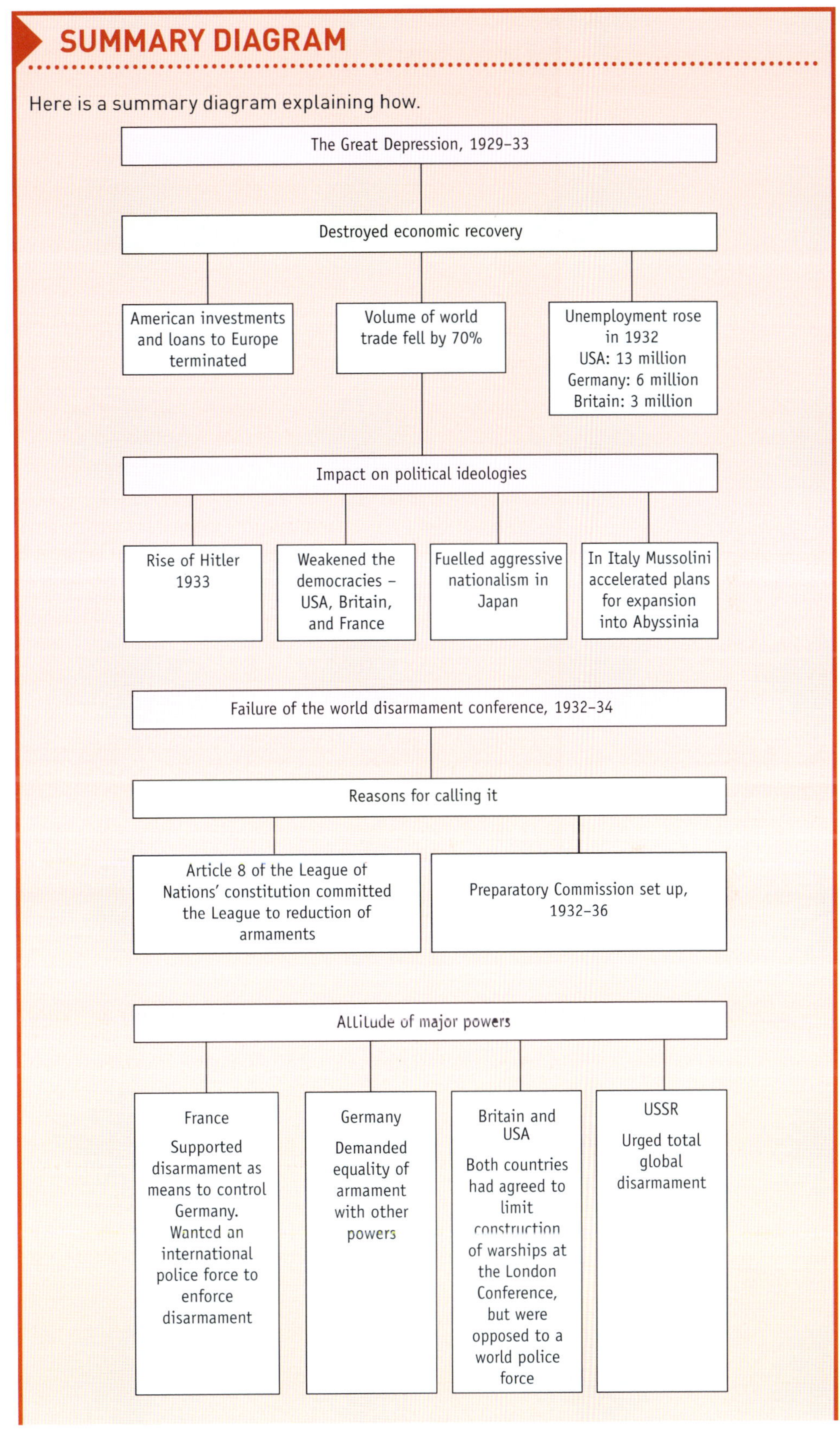

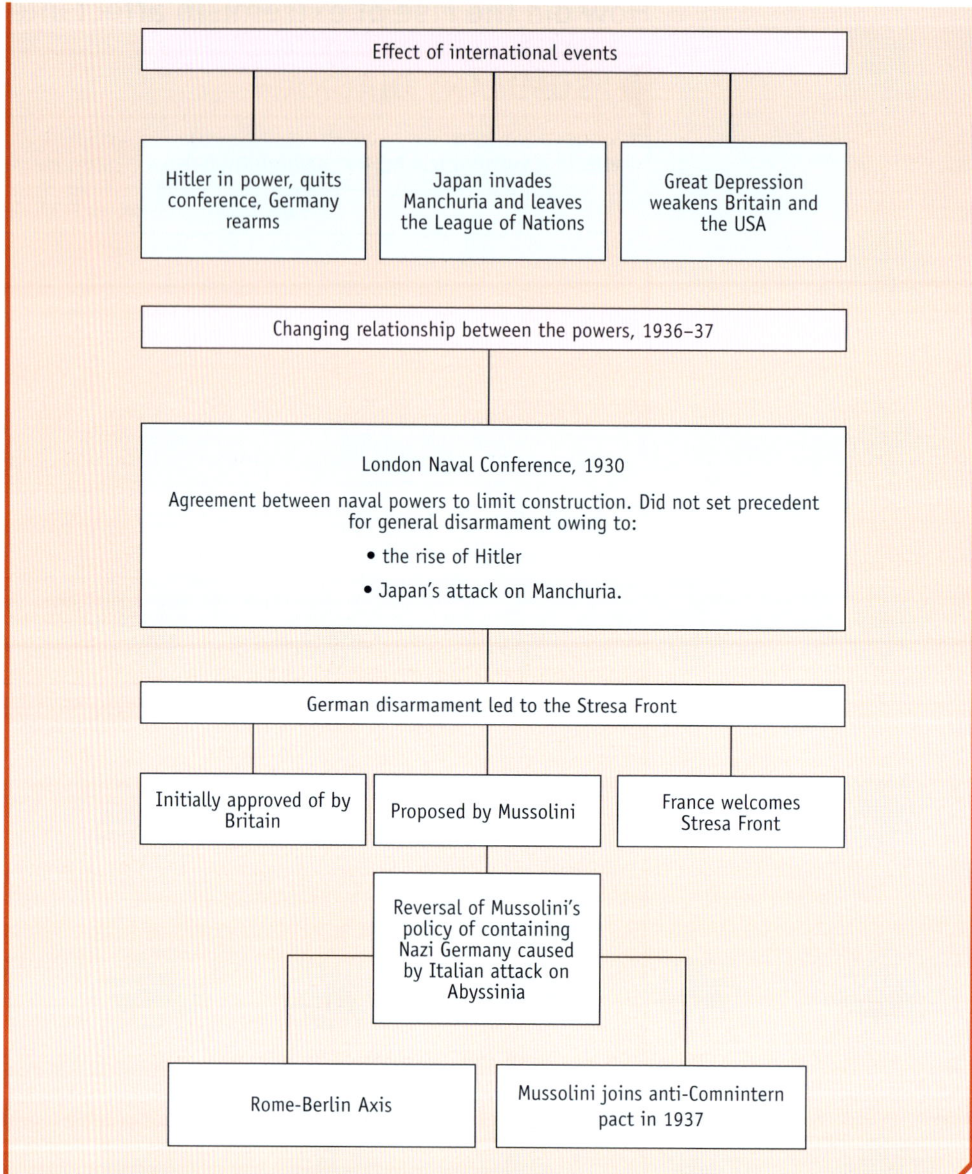
Effect of international events
Hitler in power, quits conference, Germany rearms
Japan invades Manchuria and leaves the League of Nations
Great Depression weakens Britain and the USA
Changing relationship between the powers, 1936–37
London Naval Conference, 1930
Agreement between naval powers to limit construction. Did not set precedent for general disarmament owing to:
• the rise of Hitler
• Japan's attack on Manchuria.
German disarmament led to the Stresa Front
Initially approved of by Britain
Proposed by Mussolini
France welcomes Stresa Front
Reversal of Mussolini's policy of containing Nazi Germany caused by Italian attack on Abyssinia
Rome-Berlin Axis
Mussolini joins anti-Comnintern pact in 1937

2 Why did the League of Nations fail to keep the peace in the 1930s?

To understand why the League failed to keep the peace in the 1930s, it is necessary to look at its responses to the major international crises in Manchuria and Abyssinia and how it responded to the Spanish Civil War. It is also important to consider how the attitudes of the major powers towards the League changed and other reasons for its failure, such as the effects of the Great Depression.

Response of the League to major crises

In the 1920s the League of Nations made efforts to solve disputes and promote an atmosphere of international co-operation. This had not been attempted on such a scale before, and the achievements were promising. Although there were regimes that were nationalistic in outlook, they were prepared to take part in the League's activities and meetings. However, in the 1930s the rise of nationalism and the introduction of more extreme policies by powers discontented with the post-war peace settlements made the League's task even more difficult. The intense economic depression brought a change of regime in Germany, which decided to leave the League in 1933, ignore the restrictions of the Treaty of Versailles, and expand German territory. Economic pressures resulted in Japanese expansion into China from 1931 onwards. In Italy the growing imperialism of Mussolini's fascist regime brought about a colonial war of conquest in Abyssinia.

There was no effective international action to prevent these threats to peace, and the League was bypassed by France and Britain in their attempts to deal directly with Germany and Italy. By the time of the outbreak of war in 1939, the League had become irrelevant. Its failure to intervene decisively in the Manchurian and Abyssinian crises destroyed its credibility as a peacekeeping organization. The League's prestige might just have survived its mishandling of the Manchurian crisis, but its failure to stop Italian aggression in Abyssinia effectively destroyed it.

Manchuria, 1931–33

The failure of the Japanese government to deal with the impact of the Depression on the economy convinced the Japanese officer corps that it would have to act decisively and occupy the whole of Manchuria. This would then enable Japan to control the region's valuable coal and iron resources at a time when economic nationalism was already hampering its efforts to purchase these vital raw materials elsewhere. Consequently, Japanese officers in Manchuria decided to devise an incident that would provide the pretext for intervention. On September 18, 1931 a bomb exploded on the railway line just outside the city of Mukden (modern-day Shenyang), where both Chinese and Japanese troops were stationed. This was immediately blamed on Chinese insurgents and provided the Japanese forces with the desired excuse to occupy not only Mukden but also the whole of southern Manchuria.

What we can we infer from Source 3.7 about the nature of the occupation of Mukden? What additional knowledge could you use to explain the context of the source?

SOURCE 3.7

Japanese troops enter Mukden, the largest city in Manchuria, in 1931.

KEY FIGURE

Lord Lytton (1876–1947)
British governor of Bengal, 1922–27, who chaired the Lytton Commission in Manchuria in 1931.

The response of the League

China immediately appealed to the League of Nations, but the Council responded cautiously. It first asked Japan to withdraw its troops back into the railway zone and, when this request was ignored, sent a commission of inquiry under the chairmanship of **Lord Lytton**. Japan was able to complete the occupation of Manchuria, turn it into a satellite state and rename it Manchukuo while the Lytton Commission was conducting a leisurely fact-finding operation in the spring of 1932.

Refusal of Britain and the USA to use force

It is easy to criticize the League for not responding more decisively, but without the commitment of the great powers it was not in a position to take effective action. Neither of the two most important naval powers, Britain and the USA, was ready to use force against Japan. From the Japanese point of view, the timing of the Mukden incident could not have been better. Britain was facing a major economic crisis, which threatened to force the pound off the gold standard and trigger a currency devaluation. To protect the pound, a national government had been formed under the Labour prime minister, Ramsay MacDonald, who agreed to immediate pay cuts for teachers, civil servants, and servicemen. On September 15, 1931 a minor mutiny at the naval base at Invergordon in Scotland, which was caused by a cut in sailors' wages, threatened temporarily to shut down the Royal Navy; and five days later the pound did leave the gold standard. The USA, shell-shocked by the Depression, was unwilling to do more than denounce Japanese aggression. President Hoover argued that using economic sanctions against Japan would be like 'sticking pins in tigers' and would run the risk of leading to war.

KEY TERMS

Chinese Civil War
A conflict fought intermittently from 1927 to 1949 between the nationalist government of the Republic of China and the forces of the Chinese Communist Party.

It is sometimes suggested that the British government and powerful financial interests in the City of London secretly supported Japan. It is true that Britain did have some sympathy with Japanese action in Manchuria. Like Japan, it had commercial interests in China, which it felt were threatened by the chaos brought about by the **Chinese Civil War**. Britain also recognized Japan's potential role in impeding the spread of Bolshevism from the USSR into northern China. Nevertheless, the main reason why Britain was not ready to urge more decisive action against Japan was that neither the government nor the people desired to fight a war on an issue that was not central to British interests (see Source 3.8).

How does Source 3.8 explain Britain's attitude to the Manchurian crisis? Consider whether Simon's view is justified.

SOURCE 3.8

From a speech by Sir John Simon, the Foreign Secretary, to the House of Commons on the subject of the situation in Manchuria, February 1933.

I think I am myself enough of a pacifist to take the view that, however we handle the matter, I do not intend my own country to get into trouble about it ... There is one great difference between 1914 and now and it is this: in no circumstances will this government authorise this country to be party to this struggle.

The report of the Lytton Commission

It was not until September 1932 that the League received the Lytton Commission's report. Although it conceded that the treaty rights that Japan had enjoyed in Manchuria since 1905 had made Sino-Japanese friction unavoidable, it nevertheless observed that 'without a declaration of war a large area of what was indisputably Chinese territory has been forcibly seized and occupied by the armed forces of Japan and has in consequence of this operation been separated from and declared independent of the rest of China.' It proposed that Japanese troops should withdraw back into the railway zone, and then both China and Japan should negotiate not only a treaty guaranteeing Japan's rights in Manchuria but also a non-aggression pact and a trade agreement.

Essentially, the report was based on the incorrect assumption that Japan had no territorial designs in China and was ready to compromise over Manchuria. When it was adopted unanimously, with the single exception of Japan, by the League Assembly on February 24, 1933, Japan withdrew from the League in protest. It was obvious that only armed intervention by the great powers would now be able to force Japan out of Manchuria, and that option was not politically realistic in 1933.

The consequences of the occupation

The Japanese occupation of Manchuria changed the balance of power in the Pacific. Japan had broken free from the restraints that had been imposed on it at the Washington and London conferences by Britain and the USA and had guaranteed its access to valuable coal and iron ore resources. Above all, Japan was now in a favorable strategic position to plan a large-scale military invasion of China, which was launched in July 1937.

Abyssinia, 1935–36

In Abyssinia the League was to face its greatest challenge since its creation. The Italian fascist dictator Mussolini wanted to build up a large empire in North Africa, which would have the added advantage of distracting his people from the impact of the Depression on the Italian economy. By 1932 he had begun to plan in earnest the annexation of Abyssinia. Not only would Abyssinia provide land for Italian settlers, but it would also connect Eritrea with Italian Somaliland and thus put most of the Horn of Africa under Italian control. Abyssinia was also believed to be rich in raw materials, especially oil, and would provide Italy with export markets (see Figure 3.1).

What can you infer from Source 3.9 about the nature of Haile Selassie's coronation? What do you think the elaborate robes and crown and Christian symbols signify about the role of the emperor? Undertake some research about the Abyssinian empire to support your ideas.

SOURCE 3.9

Emperor Haile Selassie of Abyssinia in his coronation robes in 1930.

The border between Abyssinia and Italian Somaliland was uncertain and disputed, and in December 1934 a clash occurred between Italian and Abyssinian troops at the small oasis of Wal-Wal, some 50 miles (80 km) on the Abyssinian side of the border. About 150 Abyssinian soldiers were killed, and the Abyssinian force had no option but to retreat. This incident brought matters to a head. **Haile Selassie** seized the chance to challenge Italy's illegal occupation by appealing to the League, which attempted in vain to find an acceptable compromise. Like the Japanese three years earlier in Manchuria, Mussolini was determined on war, and he used this and subsequent minor incidents to provide a pretext to provoke hostilities. In the following October the long-expected invasion of Abyssinia began.

KEY FIGURE

Haile Selassie (1892–1975) Emperor of Abyssinia (now Ethiopia), 1930–74.

Make a short summary of the key issues raised by Haile Selassie to the Assembly in Source 3.10. Compare this to your knowledge of the Geneva Protocol.

SOURCE 3.10

From Haile Selassie's address to the Assembly of the League of Nations, May 12, 1936.

It is my duty to inform the Governments assembled in Geneva, responsible as they are for the lives of millions of men, women and children, of the deadly peril which threatens them, by describing to them the fate which has been suffered by Ethiopia. It is not only upon warriors that the Italian Government has made war. It has above all attacked populations far removed from hostilities, in order to terrorise and exterminate them ... Special sprayers [of poison gas] were installed on board aircraft so that they could vaporise, over vast areas of territory, a fine, death-dealing rain. Groups of nine, fifteen, eighteen aircraft followed one another so that the fog issuing from them formed a continuous sheet. It was thus that, as from the end of January 1936, soldiers, women, children, cattle, rivers, lakes and pastures were drenched continually with this deadly rain. In order to kill off systematically all living creatures, in order more surely to poison waters and pastures, the Italian command made its aircraft pass over and over again. That was its chief method of warfare ...

Apart from the Kingdom of the Lord there is not on this earth any nation that is superior to any other. Should it happen that a strong Government finds it may with impunity destroy a weak people, then the hour strikes for that weak people to appeal to the League of Nations to give its judgment in all freedom. God and history will remember your judgment.

Study sources 3.10 and 3.11. Compare the evidence in Source 3.10 and Source 3.11 about the Italian invasion and its methods of warfare. Compare this evidence with the Geneva Protocol from 1925 which had been ratified by Italy. What do you think would be a likely response from the League of Nations?

SOURCE 3.11

A cartoon by David Low, which appeared in the British newspaper the *Evening Standard* on April 3, 1936. The containers carried by Mussolini have 'poison gas' written on them.

KEY FIGURE

Pierre Laval (1883–1945)
French prime minister, 1931–32, and again in 1935–36, when he also served as foreign minister. During the German occupation of France in the Second World War, he was head of the collaborationist government based in Vichy and was executed for treason in 1945.

The failure of Anglo-French attempts to compromise

Mussolini was convinced that neither Britain nor France would raise serious objections. In January 1935 **Pierre Laval**, the French foreign minister, had verbally promised him a free hand, while the British Foreign Office was desperate to avert the crisis either by offering Mussolini territorial compensation elsewhere or by helping to negotiate an arrangement, comparable to Britain's own position in Egypt, that would give Italy effective control of Abyssinia without **formally annexing** it.

Study Source 3.12. What is the attitude of Vansittart towards the League of Nations?

SOURCE 3.12

From a Foreign Office memorandum by Sir Robert Vansittart, a senior British diplomat, June 8, 1935.

The position is as plain as a pikestaff [obvious]. Italy will have to be bought off – let us use and face ugly words – in some form or other, or Abyssinia will eventually perish. That might in itself matter less, if it did not mean that the League would also perish (and that Italy would simultaneously perform another **volte-face** into the arms of Germany).

KEY TERMS

Formal annexation The taking over of full control of a territory by another power.

Volte-face An about turn; a sudden and complete change of policy.

Why then could such a compromise not be negotiated? The scale and brutality of the Italian invasion, particularly the use of poison gas, confronted both the British and French governments with a considerable dilemma. The British government was facing an election in November 1935 and was under intense pressure from the electorate to support the League. In an unofficial 'peace ballot' in June 1935 organized by the League of Nations Union, which was formed in 1918 to win public support for the League, 10 million out of 11 million replies backed the use of economic sanctions by the League in a case of aggression. In France public opinion was more evenly divided, with the left supporting the League and the right supporting Italy. However, both powers feared the diplomatic consequences of alienating Italy over Abyssinia. In particular, Britain's persistent refusal to join France in guaranteeing the status quo in central and eastern Europe inevitably increased the importance for France of its friendly relations with Italy.

On October 18, the League Council condemned the Italian invasion of Abyssinia and, under Article 16 of the League's constitution, voted for a gradually escalating program of sanctions. In the meantime both Britain and France continued to search for a compromise settlement. In December Laval and the British foreign minister, Sir Samuel Hoare, produced a secret plan that involved placing some two-thirds of Abyssinia under Italian control (see Figure 3.1). There was a strong possibility that it would have been acceptable to Mussolini, but it was leaked to the French press, and an explosion of rage among the British public forced Hoare's resignation and the dropping of the plan. In January 1936 Laval himself resigned, having seen the thwarting of one of his main foreign policy aims: to co-operate closely with Mussolini to prevent Italy's alignment with Germany.

The failure of diplomacy did not then ensure vigorous action against Mussolini. While the League imposed some sanctions on Italy, including embargoing arms and denying credit, it put no embargo on oil exports, and Britain refused to close the Suez Canal to Italian shipping on the grounds that this might lead to war with Italy. Mussolini was thus able to step up his campaign and by May 1936 had overrun Abyssinia.

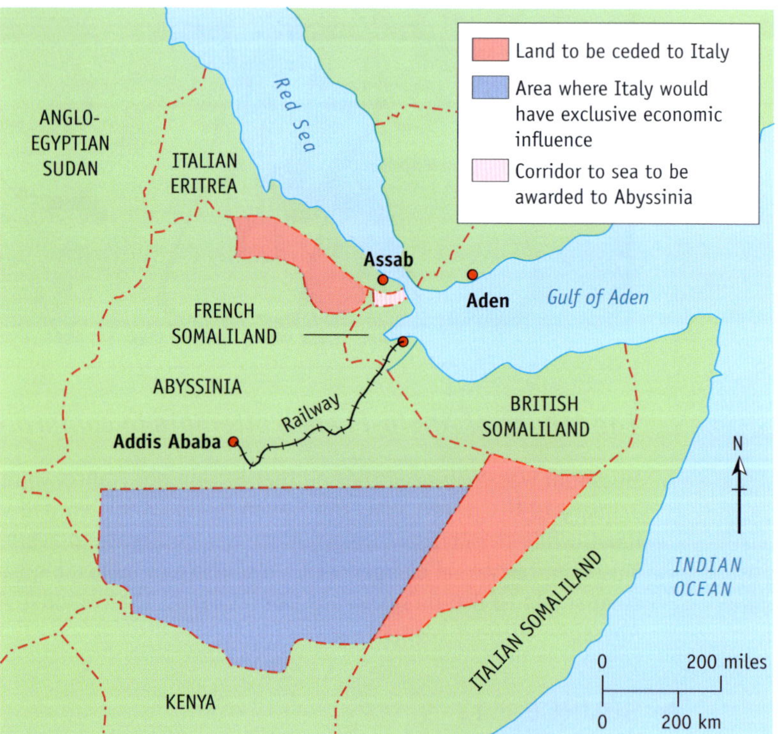

Figure 3.1 The Hoare–Laval plan for the partition of Abyssinia, which was dropped

The consequences of the Abyssinian war

The Abyssinian crisis was a crucial turning point in the 1930s. Not only did it irreparably weaken the League and provide Hitler with an ideal opportunity for the illegal remilitarization of the Rhineland, but it also effectively destroyed the Franco-Italian friendship and ultimately replaced it with the Rome–Berlin Axis (see page 150). This realignment of Italy and Germany eventually enabled Hitler in 1938 to absorb Austria without Italian opposition. The 'Axis' was also to threaten vital British and French lines of communication in the Mediterranean with the possibility of hostile naval action and thus seriously weaken their potential response to future German – or indeed Japanese – aggression.

Produce a presentation to show the reasons why the League failed to solve the Abyssinian and Manchurian crises. Then write two paragraphs indicating how the two crises differed.

What is the attitude of the cartoonist towards Mussolini and the League of Nations?

SOURCE 3.13

A cartoon by David Low, which appeared in the British newspaper the *Evening Standard* on February 15, 1935.

Changing attitudes of the major powers towards the League of Nations

On July 4, 1936 the League terminated sanctions against Italy. It had failed to halt Italian aggression in a situation where its two most powerful members, Britain and France, could easily have brought pressure on Mussolini through meaningful sanctions and a naval blockade. The consequence of this failure was an increasing lack of confidence in the League's capacity to protect the smaller countries and solve conflicts. In September 1936 the League Council invited member states to draw up proposals for reforming the League, but was reform possible and what was the attitude of the major powers?

Withdrawal of Japan, Germany, and Italy

As noted above, two of the major powers, Japan and Germany, withdrew from the League in 1933. Italy followed in 1937 after taking control of Abyssinia and drawing closer to Germany through the Axis agreements. All three would bypass the League from now on in their foreign policy. Germany totally ignored the League when it annexed Austria, the Sudetenland and Bohemia, and attacked Poland in 1939. Japan, despite appeals from the League Council, continued to wage all-out war against China.

Admission of the USSR

While some major powers were withdrawing from and/or ignoring the League, the Soviet Union joined the organization in 1934 and was the only major power to give it its full support. It saw the League as a means of rallying the smaller countries against Germany and insisted that the League had not 'broken down.' During the Sudeten crisis of September 1938, the USSR was ready to help Czechoslovakia as long as it secured the agreement of the League Council.

Negotiations taking place outside the League

As seen in Manchuria and Abyssinia, and in the Spanish Civil War, countries attempted to negotiate with each other directly for their national interest, rather than working through the League of Nations. The USA was still isolationist and increasingly believed that the League should confine itself to health, humanitarian, and economic issues. Britain and France initially hoped in 1936 that they could persuade Germany to rejoin a reformed League of Nations to work out a security system to replace the Locarno Treaties. After the German rejection of this, and in response to its increasingly aggressive foreign policy in central Europe, the two powers had little option but to ignore the League and prepare for war against Nazi Germany.

ACTIVITY

Consider the changes in the attitudes towards, and involvement in, the League of Nations by the major powers during the 1930s. Which of the changes would you choose as the most significant cause of the weakening of the League?

Responses to the Spanish Civil War

The extreme political ideas of the inter-war period were evident in Spain, which had also suffered from economic hardships. In June 1931 a socialist-republican coalition government was elected by a large majority. In the midst of the global economic depression, it embarked on a number of controversial reforms, which involved breaking up the great landed estates and ending the powerful political influence of the Church. This provoked an unsuccessful coup by monarchist general, José Sanjurjo in 1932. While it lasted less than 24 hours, the failed coup showed the government how unstable Spain was. In its aftermath the government accelerated the reforms, but in the opinion of the anarchists and the militant **anarcho-syndicalist** trade union the **CNT**, these were not sufficiently radical. The CNT then launched a nationwide strike, which was accompanied by bomb and arson attacks by the anarchists. The coalition government began to fall apart as the divisions between the republicans and socialists widened. In November 1933 the prime minister, Manuel Azaña, held another election, but this did not produce a majority for him and instead led to the polarization of Spain between conservative, pro-Catholic forces and the parties of the left. For the next 18 months a series of weak coalition governments failed to unify the country, which continued to be deeply divided between the forces of the left – anarchists, republicans, socialists, and communists – and the forces of the right, comprising traditional monarchists and conservatives, and a new fascist party called the Falange. The army was politically conservative and in July 1936 launched a coup that aimed to overturn the left-wing republican government. This led to the outbreak of a civil war, which came to have a major impact on international relations.

KEY FIGURE

General Francisco Franco (1892–1975)
A Spanish army general who became leader of the Spanish Nationalists and then head of the Spanish state, 1936–75.

The civil war in Spain was essentially a domestic matter, but it rapidly became an international issue that threatened to involve the major powers in a European conflict. The Nationalists, as the rebels called themselves, were led by **General Franco** and looked to Germany and Italy for help, while the Republicans approached Britain, France, and the USSR. Foreign aid was given to both sides.

KEY TERMS

Anarcho-syndicalism A belief that the state should be replaced by trade unions and similar organizations, which would negotiate directly with each other and exchange all the goods and services necessary to meet the needs of the population.

CNT The National Workers' Confederation (Confederación Nacional del Trabajo), a grouping of anarcho-syndicalist trade unions.

Figure 3.2 The geographical division of Spain between the Nationalists and the Republicans at the outbreak of the Spanish Civil War in July 1936

Intervention of Germany and Italy

The coup, which was planned by **General Mola**, was launched on July 17 in Spanish Morocco. Mola chose Francisco Franco to lead the Army of Africa – the Spanish army's elite force. Hitler quickly agreed to provide a fleet of transport aircraft to fly Franco's soldiers in Spanish Morocco across to Spain. He then followed this up with the dispatch of some 6,000 troops. Hitler certainly wanted to stop Spain becoming communist, but he also wanted to distract the European powers so that he could continue to rearm without fear of intervention. Spain was also seen by the Nazi leaders as a testing ground for their military strategies and weaponry. Hitler was aware of the advantages of having a friendly government in Madrid, which would not only supply Germany with Spanish mineral resources but also in wartime possibly provide bases for German submarines.

KEY FIGURE

Emilio Mola (1887–1937) Spanish general who commanded the Nationalist army in the War in the North during the Spanish Civil War. He was killed in a plane crash in 1937.

Mussolini also agreed to assist Franco for the same mixture of ideological and strategic reasons: he hoped to defeat the left in Spain, gain a new ally in Franco, who might grant Italy a naval base on one of the Balearic Islands, and 'strengthen' the Italian character by exposure to war. As the Italian invasion of Abyssinia had been opposed, admittedly ineffectually, by Britain, France, and the League of Nations, he was also anxious to draw closer to Germany.

KEY FIGURE

Léon Blum (1872–1950) France's first socialist prime minister. He led the Popular Front government, 1936–37 and March 1938–April 1938, before being imprisoned by the Vichy regime in 1940.

Lack of commitment of France and Britain, and the Non-Intervention Agreement, 1936

With Germany and Italy openly supporting Franco, there was a risk of a European war if France and Britain joined the Republicans. When the French prime minister, **Léon Blum** (whose power rested on a left-wing coalition), was first asked for help by the Republic, he was tempted to give it – if only to deny potential allies of Germany a victory in Spain. However, two factors forced him to have second thoughts.

Firstly, the actual dispatch of French military aid to the Republicans would have polarized French society, which was already deeply divided between right and left, and risked plunging France into a civil war of its own (see pages 171–72). Secondly, the British government came out strongly against intervention. The British ambassador in Paris even threatened neutrality should French assistance to the Republicans lead to war with Germany. Despite the strategic dangers for Britain's position in the Mediterranean in the event of a Nationalist victory, the cabinet viewed the civil war as essentially a side issue that must not be allowed to prevent the continued search for a lasting settlement with Germany. In addition, there were powerful voices within the ruling Conservative Party who actively sympathized with the Nationalists.

To prevent the war spreading, Britain and France proposed a non-intervention agreement. This was signed by 27 other European powers, including Italy, Germany, and the USSR in 1937. An international committee was set up, and a naval patrol shared by Britain, Italy, France, and Germany was to monitor any violations of the agreement, but it did not have the legal powers to stop any shipping. This policy seriously weakened the Spanish Republican government as it deprived them of the necessary weapons to strike against the rebels. After a German patrol boat was bombed by the Spanish Republican forces, Italy and Germany withdrew and supplied Franco with weapons and troops.

Intervention of the USSR

The Republican government now had little option but to approach the USSR for help. Despite agreeing to the Non-Intervention Agreement, Stalin saw the ideological importance of supporting the communist factions in Spain through secret work by Comintern agents supporting activists in Catalonia. Donations were given through national communist parties to support humanitarian relief and to enable international volunteers to go to Spain to fight against the Nationalists. In September 1936 Stalin sent hundreds of military advisers and large quantities of military equipment. He took precautions to ensure that the entire aid operation would be carried out as far as possible in strict secrecy. Spanish gold reserves were sent to the USSR in payment for combat planes, tanks, rifles, food, and fuel. In October 1936 the Soviet Union shipped material aid to the new Popular Front Republican government led by Prime Minister Francisco Largo Caballero, which included two communist ministers.

On October 23 the Soviet ambassador to the United Kingdom, Ivan Maisky, appeared before the Non-Intervention Committee to defend these actions. He did so by denouncing the aid previously sent by Italy and Germany to Nationalist forces, which, of course, also constituted a violation of the Non-Intervention Agreement.

Stalin, like Hitler, saw the civil war as a way to divide his enemies. He wanted to avoid a Nationalist victory in Spain, fearing it would strengthen fascism and increase the likelihood of a German attack on the USSR. However, by early 1937, when he realized that the Republicans could not win, he reduced the supply of arms to a level that was just sufficient to prolong the conflict. In this he was successful, as it was not until March 1939 that Franco at last occupied Madrid.

The International Brigades and other volunteers

Although a few foreigners initially joined the militia created by the CNT, the decision to recruit an international volunteer force was taken by a branch of the Comintern in Prague. This meant that direct Soviet involvement with ground troops could be avoided, although the USSR did send military experts to train the Spanish Republican army. Volunteers were mainly recruited by the local communists and left-wing parties from all over the world. They were convinced that their mission was to fight fascism in all its forms.

The initial group of British volunteers was organized by two communists from London's East End. The majority were workers, many of them unemployed, but they were joined by a scattering of intellectuals such as **George Orwell** and the poet **John Cornford**. France contributed the largest number of volunteers. Volunteers from Italy also fought on the side of the Republicans. At the Battle of Guadalajara, Italian troops sent by Mussolini were defeated, suffering 2,000 dead and 4,000 wounded. Embarrassingly, their humiliation was brought about by the Garibaldi Battalion, anti-fascist Italians serving in the International Brigade. Eventually, the volunteers in the International Brigades totalled about 35,000 men and women.

KEY FIGURES

George Orwell (1903–50) British writer best known for his books *Animal Farm* and *1984*. A socialist, who became disillusioned with communism.

John Cornford (1915–36) British poet and communist who was killed in the Spanish Civil War.

KEY TERM

Blueshirts A fascist organization founded in Ireland to bring about Irish unity by creating a corporate state along Italian lines.

Not all volunteers supported the Republic: some of them, such as the French Jeanne d'Arc Battalion, fought for the Nationalists; and 700 Irish **Blueshirts** under the fascist **Eoin O'Duffy** joined to fight the communists.

There were also volunteers who were primarily interested in helping Spanish civilians by providing food and medical care. The Quakers, the Save the Children Fund and the League of Nations Union were active in fundraising and providing refuge in Britain for children and their mothers. In May 1937 nearly 4,000 Basque children arrived in Britain and were then divided into smaller groups and sent to camps throughout the country. The Red Cross and other organizations also sent out volunteers. For example, in March 1937 **Violetta Thurstan**, who had previously supervised refugee camps in North Africa, travelled to Spain to set up a British ambulance station in Almería.

KEY FIGURES

Eoin O'Duffy (1890–1944) Irish nationalist leader, who took control of the fascist Blueshirt movement in the 1930s.

Violetta Thurstan (1879–1978) Nurse who served during the First World War, Spanish Civil War, and Second World War. As well as tending to the wounded, she worked in naval intelligence and helped to evacuate and resettle displaced children.

Equipment	Republicans	Nationalists	
	USSR	Germany	Italy
Aircraft (all types)	648	621	632
Tanks and armoured vehicles	407	250	150
Artillery units	1,186	700	1,930
Machine guns	20,486	31,000	3,436
Rifles	497,813	157,309	240,747
Ammunition (rounds)	862,000,000	250,000,000	325,000,000
Submarines	0	0	4

Table 3.2 Military equipment supplied to Spain by the USSR, Germany, and Italy during the civil war

The consequences of the Spanish Civil War

It was undoubtedly Germany who benefited most from the conflict since it diverted the attention of the other powers away from the Nazi rearmament program during the crucial period of April 1936–February 1938. For the democracies, the civil war could not have come at a worse time. It polarized public opinion between right and left, threatened France with encirclement, and cemented the Italo-German rapprochement. In October 1936 Germany and Italy, after a visit by the Italian foreign minister, signed the October Protocols, which were in effect an Italo-German entente and eventually led the way to the Pact of Steel in May 1939.

The Republic's defeat was a blow for the cause of democracy and could have led to France being surrounded, but Franco's Spain was too war-weary to support Germany and Italy in another conflict.

The war brought about a feeling among some people that fascism was on the move and needed to be stopped. It also showed the destructive power of modern war, as in the well-publicized bombing by German and Italian aircraft of the Republican town of Guernica, immortalized in a painting by Picasso (see Source 3.14). The conflict also revealed to Hitler and Mussolini the weaknesses of Britain and France. It showed, too, that Stalin's communists were more intent on fighting their internal opponents than the forces of fascism and so generally encouraged Hitler to risk greater expansion.

Look up Picasso's painting, *Guernica*, online and compare it to the photograph. What does the painting tell you about Picasso's attitude to the bombing of *Guernica*?

SOURCE 3.14

Survivors of the Condor Legion's bombing survey the wreckage of Guernica.

ACTIVITY

Copy and complete this chart to summarize the actions taken by the great powers in response to the Spanish Civil War.

Country	Action(s) taken	Result	Assessment of action(s)

Why did the League of Nations not respond more effectively to the Spanish Civil War?

The Non-Intervention Agreement was negotiated independently of the League. When Italy and Germany resigned from the Non-Intervention Committee and began to supply Franco with weapons and troops, the Spanish government appealed to the League Council and Assembly for support, but with little effect. The USA, the one great power that could have made a difference, was not in the League, and American public opinion was still fiercely isolationist. For example, when in October 1937 President Roosevelt in a speech in Chicago did propose a vague scheme for 'quarantining aggressors,' public opinion moved sharply against him. The Spanish Republican government frequently appealed to the Council and Assembly to stop Italy and Germany supplying Franco, but all the League could do was to advise its members to comply with the Non-Intervention Agreement.

KEY DEBATE

WHAT CAUSED THE SPANISH CIVIL WAR?

The causes of the Spanish Civil War have been much discussed by historians and Spanish politicians. Once he won the war, General Franco claimed that the struggle was a crusade against the 'Godless' and communism. Because the Franco regime in Spain exercised strict censorship, the first studies of the war were written by foreign historians, who initially argued that the war was a straight fight between communism and fascism, but this was a simplification of complex facts and also ignored Spanish history. What sort of war was it? The conflict wasn't about communism vs. fascism or democracy vs. fascism. Britain and France wanted to avoid a European war, so they created the Non-Intervention Committee, while the USA stayed isolated. The USSR did intervene essentially for defensive reasons as it wanted to prevent Spain from becoming a fascist power and also wanted to divide its potential enemies.

The civil war was also not a simple struggle between revolution and reform on the one side and reactionary Spanish forces on the other, as there was in effect 'an undeclared civil war' between the communists and the anarcho-syndicalists. Detailed historical research since the Spanish archives were opened after the death of Franco in 1975 has shown that it was largely a result of the tensions in Spanish history between the great landowners and the peasantry, between the industrialists and between the workers, and between the Catholic Church and the supporters of liberalism and socialism.

It is also important to remember that as the war developed it was not just a Spanish civil war, since Germany, Italy, and the USSR were all involved, as indeed were thousands of volunteers from all over Europe and the USA. One historian has called it 'an episode in a greater European civil war that ended in 1945.'

Causes of the failure of the League of Nations

After 1936 the League was virtually ignored by the great powers. Important negotiations such as the Non-Intervention Agreement, and the Munich Agreement of 1938 had to take place outside the League because many of the key powers were not members. The last session of the League's Council met in May 1939. It did not discuss the gathering crisis between Nazi Germany and Poland that was to lead to war. Instead, it dealt with purely technical matters such as the standardization of signalling at railway level crossings. Ironically, its last significant action was to expel its most loyal member, the USSR, from the League after it had invaded Finland in November 1939. In May 1946 the League was officially replaced by the United Nations.

In conclusion, the following factors all contributed to the failure of the League to prevent war:

- The Great Depression played a crucial role. It seriously damaged the economies of Europe, Japan, and the USA, driving the USA into isolation just at the time its influence was needed in Europe and Asia.
- With the USA pursuing isolationist policies during the 1930s, the burden of keeping the peace fell on Britain and France, which lacked the strength to act as the 'world police.'
- Increasing nationalism, strengthened by economic hardship, led to Hitler coming to power in Germany and the army gaining a decisive influence in Japan. Both powers walked out of the League in 1933 and subsequently ignored it.
- Consequently, it was impossible to achieve any agreement at the World Disarmament Conference.

However, it is important not to forget the League's less controversial work such as the ILO and its health committees, which were more successful and were incorporated in the United Nations in 1946.

Below are five factors that affected the failure of the League of Nations. Award each factor a mark out of 6. The higher the mark, the greater the importance. Explain in detail why you have given it the mark.

- The constitution of the League
- The Great Depression
- The rise to power of Hitler
- The Japanese annexation of Manchuria
- The Italian invasion of Abyssinia

What led to the failure of the League of Nations?

SUMMARY DIAGRAM

Here is a summary diagram explaining why.

The failure of disarmament, 1933–35

- Germany withdraws from Disarmament Conference, 1933, and begins to rearm
- Japan renounces treaties controlling naval construction, 1935

The Manchurian crisis

Causes

- Threats to Japanese interests in Manchuria through Chinese Civil War
- Impact of the Great Depression
- Weak Japanese government
- Pressure from the army

↓

Mukden incident, September 18, 1931

↓

Japanese occupation of Manchuria

↓

China appealed to League of Nations

↓

Lytton Commission sent

↓

Recommended withdrawal of Japanese troops and then a negotiated settlement

↓

Japan quit League of Nations when the Assembly adopted the recommendations, February 1933

The Abyssinian crisis

October 1935: Italian troops invaded Abyssinia

↓

Britain and France sought a compromise to keep Italy as a potential ally against Nazi Germany

↓

Hoare–Laval Pact

↓

Leaked to French press and dropped

↓

League pursued an ineffective policy of sanctions against Italy

↓

Mussolini became increasingly dependent on German help

↓

Hitler exploited the crisis to remilitarize the Rhineland

↓

Rome–Berlin Axis

Changing attitudes of major powers towards League of Nations, 1937–39	
Germany and Italy	Ignored League and carried out independent and aggressive foreign policies
Britain and France	Unable to persuade Germany to rejoin League, they became focused on appeasement policies, to try to avoid war
Japan	Despite appeals from League, continued to wage war in China
USA	Believed League should only focus on health, economic, and humanitarian issues
USSR	Increasingly saw League as means of building an alliance against Germany. Argued it had not 'broken down'

3 Why, and with what effects, did Britain and France pursue a policy of appeasement?

The policy that Britain and France followed towards Germany from 1933 to 1939 has become known as appeasement. Today this word has negative connotations – meaning the giving in to the demands of a bully. However, at the time 'appeasement' was seen as a positive policy. The term was used by **Winston Churchill** when he spoke in the 1920s of the need 'for the appeasement of European hatreds.' In the 1930s it came to mean a readiness to listen and respond to legitimate demands to maintain peace. Until 1937 appeasement meant doing nothing to endanger peace, but after Neville Chamberlain became British prime minister in that year it meant taking active steps to reduce tensions to keep peace – being, in modern terms, 'proactive' even when Britain's direct interests were not involved. That policy became controversial when Britain and France, in their determination to keep peace, pressured Czechoslovakia to accept German territorial demands.

KEY FIGURE

Winston Churchill (1874–1965) British politician and prime minister, best known as an inspiring war leader, 1940–45.

NEVILLE CHAMBERLAIN

1869	Born in Birmingham
1915–18	Served as lord mayor of Birmingham
1918	Entered parliament
1923–29	Served as Minister of Health
1931–37	Served as Chancellor of the Exchequer
1937–40	Served as prime minister
1940	Died six months after resigning as prime minister

Neville Chamberlain was a politician who had been a very successful Minister of Health and Chancellor of the Exchequer. When he became prime minister, he was determined to avoid Europe plunging into war. Marginalizing the Foreign Office, he took personal control of British foreign policy. He was convinced that German grievances could be met through a policy of appeasement and believed that he would be able to come to an agreement by a direct man-to-man discussion with Hitler. Even though he reluctantly accepted that war was probable after Hitler's seizure of Bohemia in March 1939, he never completely abandoned appeasement – a policy he inherited from his predecessors Stanley Baldwin and Ramsay MacDonald.

The impact of economic, military and social considerations on foreign policy

It was not until 1935–36 that the scale of German rearmament became clear. Inevitably, the pace of German military expansion created concern in France and Britain, and caused both powers to start their own major rearmament programs, the economic and military implications of which influenced their foreign policy.

Unlike in 1914, there was no calm assumption that the next war would soon be over. All three countries, learning from the First World War, expected a long struggle. Even though tanks and aeroplanes had made battlefields more mobile, most military experts still thought in terms of First World War trench warfare tactics. France built the **Maginot Line**, which was an enormous series of concrete fortifications along its frontier with Germany, while Germany built the **Westwall** fortifications along the east bank of the Rhine.

An important lesson from the First World War was that a future conflict would be a **total war**: the armed forces needed so much equipment that the economy and the workforce had to be totally mobilized in order to supply them. The nation that could most efficiently supply and finance its armed forces in a long war would eventually win. The heavy financial burden of rearmament, and the considerable social problems that came with it, made the appeasement of Germany an attractive proposition for Britain and France.

KEY TERMS

Maginot Line A line of concrete fortifications that France constructed along its eastern borders, particularly those with Germany, in the 1930s. It was named after André Maginot, the French Minister of War who had the initial idea.

Westwall Also known as the Siegfried Line, a German line of fortifications stretching from its Dutch border to Switzerland, started in 1936.

Total war The mobilization of a whole population to contribute to a war effort, whether that be by fighting, producing food or manufacturing and supplying equipment.

KEY TERM

Ten-Year Rule British government guidelines for reducing military spending after the First World War, assuming that Britain would not be involved in a significant war for the next ten years.

Britain

The **Ten-Year Rule** was abandoned by the British cabinet on March 23, 1932 at the height of the Great Depression, but this did not immediately lead to a big increase in armaments. The government specifically warned that the decision to give up the Ten-Year Rule 'must not be taken to justify an expanding expenditure by the Defence Services without regard to the very serious financial and economic situation' that the country was in. By 1935 the British economy had recovered from the effects of the Depression except for a continued decline in the coal mining, steel, and textile industries in Scotland, South Wales, and northern England, but it was not until 1936 that defense spending began to rise. Despite the economic recovery, rearmament did cause considerable financial strain, which Prime Minister Neville Chamberlain feared might 'break our backs.'

Pacifism and the Oxford Union

KEY TERMS

Pacifism and pacificism are terms with similar, but different meanings:

Pacifism The belief that violence should <u>never</u> be used to settle disputes.

Pacificism The belief that violence should be used <u>only</u> when there is no alternative.

Oxford Union The students' debating club at Oxford University.

While the government was becoming increasingly concerned about the pace of German rearmament, both **pacifism** and **pacificism** remained strong in the country. A large number of war memoirs published in the 1920s, which stressed the horrors of modern conflict, helped create this mood. So many families had experienced the death or maiming in battle of their family members that there was a deep revulsion against war in all classes. Unlike pacifists, believers in pacificism did not entirely rule out the use of force.

Pacifism, was an influential ideology, particularly among students and younger people. In February 1933 the **Oxford Union** held the notorious 'King and Country' debate. The result was a vote of 275 against 153 that 'in the event of a declaration of war, the house would not support the government,' and in October 1934, just a few days after the collapse of the World Disarmament Conference, the Peace Pledge Union was launched by **Canon Dick Sheppard**. After a broadcast on the BBC he asked men to write on a postcard the following pledge: 'I renounce war and never again will I support or sanction another.' Within two years 100,000 men had signed the pledge. It was women who had traditionally been associated with the peace movement, but this initial appeal only to men was aimed at making the point that men too supported the cause. From 1936 membership was opened to women as well. The peace ballot held by the League of Nations Union showed immense support for the League and the hope that it could prevent war.

KEY FIGURE

Canon Dick Sheppard (1880–1937) An Anglican priest, the Dean of Canterbury and an influential Christian pacifist.

Fascism as a bulwark against Bolshevism, and sympathy for Nazi policies

The first British fascist party was founded by **Rotha Lintorn-Orman** in 1923. Her hero was Mussolini, whom she believed had saved Italy from Bolshevism. A more dynamic pro-Nazi fascist party was founded by **Sir Oswald Mosley** when he launched the British Union of Fascists (BUF) in October 1932. By 1934 there were 400 branches of the BUF in the UK and a membership of 20,000. Mosley also enjoyed the support of the newspaper tycoon **Lord Rothermere**, who shared his hostility towards communism. The increasing violence and fanaticism of the BUF and its black-shirted paramilitary uniform soon alienated most people in Britain. In October 1936 the Blackshirts, as they were known, marched into the East End of London and were met in Cable Street and elsewhere by a strong force of anti-fascists (a combination of local trade unionists, communists, anarchists, Labour Party members, and local Jewish people). A large force of police intervened, and the march was rerouted to the West End of London. In January 1937 the Public Order Act gave police greater powers to deal with demonstrations and banned the wearing of unauthorized uniforms.

KEY FIGURES

Rotha Lintorn-Orman (1895–1935) Founder of the British Fascisti movement in 1923.

Sir Oswald Mosley (1896–1980) British politician who, after leaving the Labour Party, founded the British Union of Fascists in 1932. He was imprisoned, 1940–43, and lived in France and Ireland for most of the rest of his life.

Lord Rothermere (1868–1940) Owner of the *Daily Mail* newspaper and a supporter of the British Union of Fascists.

What impression of Mosley's BUF does Source 3.15 give?

SOURCE 3.15

A photograph showing Sir Oswald Mosley on the day of the 'Battle of Cable Street,' October 5, 1936

However, hostility towards communism remained a strong force in the Conservative Party, which feared revolution and the brutal class war that communists had waged in Russia. The purges and show trials conducted by Stalin in the 1930s did little to improve the image of Soviet Russia in their eyes. Many Conservatives even believed that Hitler was 'the principal guardian of Europe against the spread of communism.' When asked why they thought Nazism was any better than communism, they argued that Nazism would ultimately reform itself and become more democratic. Neville Chamberlain himself deeply distrusted Russia and until 1939 believed that the USSR was a greater threat to European peace than Germany. The BUF was banned in July 1940 by the British government, who feared that its remaining supporters might undermine the war effort. Some of the BUF's most prominent members were arrested and interned under defense regulations.

France

Initially, France appeared to have weathered the Great Depression better than either Britain or the USA, but by 1933 this was shown to be an illusion: unemployment rose to 1.3 million and the franc was greatly overvalued. A succession of governments failed to stabilize France's finances and bring down unemployment. Distrust of the political system led to a series of riots in Paris culminating in large-scale disturbances in February 1934 by right-wing groups, including French fascists. A few days later there were communist riots at the other end of Paris. This led to a regrouping of parties on the left to form the **Popular Front**, led by Léon Blum, which won the election in 1936.

Neither Blum nor his successors managed to stabilize French politics, and the Popular Front collapsed in June 1937. However, it did manage to pass some important social reforms as well as nationalizing the armament and military aviation industries. Unfortunately, this initially disrupted the production of armaments just three years away from the beginning of war in September 1939. The franc had to be **devalued** three times between 1936 and 1938 to help pay for rearmament. In November 1938 a general strike was called in Paris in protest against wage cuts and the decline in living standards caused by diverting resources to rearmament. The pace of French rearmament was slowed by the weakness of the economy, but even so military expenditure increased by six times between 1936 and 1939.

KEY TERMS

Popular Front A coalition of French left-wing parties, including the Communist Party, to face up to the threat of fascism.

Devaluation A deliberate decision taken by a government to lower the value of its currency in order, for example, to boost exports and thereby stimulate the economy.

EXTENSION

French fascism

Like the Blackshirts in Britain, France had its own fascist-style movement, the Croix-de-Feu ('Cross of Fire'), which was founded in 1927 by Maurice d'Hartoy. Initially composed of First World War veterans, later it was joined by many French Catholics and was particularly strong among French settlers in Algeria. It was very antisemitic. In 1930 the movement was taken over by **François de La Rocque**, and it took part in the large demonstration in 1934 that led to the downfall of the governing left-wing coalition known as the Cartel des Gauches. Having grown into a mass movement with somewhere between 300,000 and 400,000 members, the Croix-de-Feu was dissolved in 1936 by the Popular Front government. La Rocque then formed the more moderate French Social Party (the PSF), a right-wing conservative movement that by 1939 had some half a million members.

KEY FIGURE

François de La Rocque (1885–1946) A soldier and the leader of the Croix-de-Feu and later the PSF. During the war, de La Rocque was a member of the French Resistance against the German occupation of France.

French grand strategy: creation of the Maginot Line

French strategy was based on the assumption of a long war with Germany and the total mobilization of all economic resources. There would be two stages:

1. The first stage would be defensive. Carrying out the plans of the Minister of War, **André Maginot**, a defensive line with underground fortifications to make it invulnerable to air attack and artillery bombardment would be built along France's frontiers with Italy, Switzerland, Germany, Luxembourg, and Belgium.
2. The second stage would consist of building a large mechanized army and a bomber force, which would in time enable France to break out from behind the Maginot Line. The French government calculated that a British naval blockade like the one that had worked so well in the First World War would enable France to produce twelve times as much weaponry as Germany because the blockade would cut Germany's access to vital raw materials.

KEY FIGURE

André Maginot (1877–1932) A French civil servant and politician who in 1926 succeeded in persuading the French parliament to allocate funds for the construction of the defensive line that bore his name.

ACTIVITY 

What were the main economic, social, and military factors that influenced the foreign policies of Britain and France? Which considerations do you think were the most important: economic, social, or military? Why do you think this?

Actions taken to appease Hitler, 1935–38

Essentially, appeasement was a realistic policy for the rulers of the large and vulnerable British Empire. It was based on the assumption that a willingness to compromise would avert conflict and protect the essential interests of the Empire. There was also the argument that the Treaty of Versailles had been too punitive and now was the time to make further concessions, which would make Hitler less aggressive in his intentions. It was in this spirit that Britain signed the Anglo-German Naval Agreement of 1935 and tolerated the remilitarization of the Rhineland. However, appeasement failed to achieve any lasting settlement with Germany.

ACTIVITY

Create a timeline of key events and agreements as you read through the rest of section 3 on Anglo-French appeasement. For each one, record how Britain and France responded to the event and their reasons for this response.

The Anglo-German Naval Agreement, 1935

In reaction to the introduction of German conscription, the British, French, and Italian heads of government had met in April 1935 at Stresa in Italy to condemn German rearmament and resolve to maintain the peace settlements. Hitler responded by attempting to reassure the powers of his peaceful intentions. He proposed a series of non-aggression pacts with Germany's neighbors, and promised to observe the agreements at Locarno (see page 123) and to accept an overall limitation on armaments. He also offered Britain an agreement limiting the German fleet to 35 per cent of the total strength of the Royal Navy. Britain accepted this offer in June without consulting the other Stresa powers, which did much to undermine the unity of the Stresa Front and unilaterally revised the Treaty of Versailles.

Remilitarization of the Rhineland, 1936 and Anglo-French inaction

German troops marched into the Rhineland on March 7, 1936. In order to reassure France that they did not intend to violate the Franco-German frontier, they were, initially, few in number and lightly equipped. So why did the French army not immediately intervene? The French general staff, who since the late 1920s had been planning for a defensive war against Germany based on the fortifications of the Maginot Line on France's eastern frontier, refused to invade the Rhineland unless they had full backing from Britain. The most the British government was ready to do was to promise France that, in the event of an unprovoked German attack on French territory, it would send two divisions of troops across the Channel. Essentially, British public opinion agreed with **Lord Lothian**, who said that Hitler was merely walking into 'his own back garden.'

KEY FIGURE

Lord Lothian (1882–1940) A British politician, diplomat, and newspaper editor who was a committed supporter of appeasement.

The crucial element here, it seemed, was that Germany was not occupying new territory. It was putting forces into German territory and allowing for a legitimate defense of its frontiers, which was the right of any state, yet was denied to Germany by the Treaty of Versailles. Given that Britain and France had accepted German rearmament and that Britain had even signed a naval treaty with Germany, it would have seemed illogical to take military action to stop this remilitarization. Also, in an age of air power, where planes could attack targets deep inside enemy territory, arguably the shifting of border defenses an extra 50 miles (80 km) or so had little real military significance. In itself the remilitarization would have made an unconvincing case for war. However, the consequences were to make war more likely.

The remilitarization of the Rhineland was a triumph for Hitler, as it marked a decisive shift in power from Paris to Berlin. It was also a considerable gamble. German rearmament had not got very far by 1936, and any decisive French resistance would have driven the German forces out and possibly toppled the Hitler regime. All at once, Hitler had violated both the Treaty of Versailles and the Locarno Treaties without any effective response from Britain and France.

What can we learn from Source 3.16 about the international consequences of the German remilitarization of the Rhineland?

SOURCE 3.16

From an internal French foreign ministry memorandum on the consequences of the German action in the Rhineland, March 12, 1936.

A German success would likewise not fail to encourage elements which, in Yugoslavia, look towards Berlin ... In Romania this will be a victory of the elements of the right which have been stirred up by Hitlerite propaganda. All that will remain for Czechoslovakia is to come to terms with Germany. Austria does not conceal her anxiety. 'Next time it will be our turn' ... Turkey, who has increasingly close economic relations with Germany, but who politically remains in the Franco-British axis, can be induced to modify her line. The Scandinavian countries ... are alarmed.

Acceptance of *Anschluss* by Britain and France

Almost exactly two years after the remilitarization of the Rhineland, Hitler decided to realize his long-held ambition of annexing Austria. The *Anschluss*, or 'joining,' of Austria and Germany in March 1938 violated the Treaty of Versailles, which specifically forbade the union of Germany and Austria. In taking this step, Hitler had for the first time invaded an independent state, even though the Austrian army did not oppose him, and put himself in a position from which to threaten Czechoslovakia.

Why then did this not bring about a revival of the Stresa Front, which was briefly formed in 1934 against German aggression? Although British Prime Minister Chamberlain was in contact with the Italian government, and in April had concluded an agreement aimed at lowering the tension in the Mediterranean, essentially Mussolini had decided as long ago as 1936 that Austria was part of Germany's sphere of interest. Not surprisingly, therefore, on March 11, 1938 he backed Hitler's decision to invade Austria. Both Britain and France protested to Berlin, but neither had any intention of going to war over Austria. Indeed, France was distracted by an internal political crisis caused by the resignation of **Camille Chautemps** as prime minister, and between March 10 and 13, did not even have a government.

KEY FIGURE

Camille Chautemps (1885–1963) A center-left French politician who served in several French governments and was, briefly, prime minister three times: in 1930, 1933–34 and 1937–38.

Figure 3.3 Central Europe showing German expansion from 1935 to August 1939

Study sources 3.16 and 3.17. Compare the views in each source about the threat from Nazi Germany.

SOURCE 3.17

From a letter by Neville Chamberlain to Mrs Morton Prince, an American citizen, January 16, 1938.

... as a realist I must do what I can to make this country safe ... [The British people] are perfectly aware that until we are fully rearmed our position will be one of great anxiety. They realise that we are in no position to enter light-heartedly upon a war with such a formidable power as Germany, much less if Germany were aided by Italian attacks on our Mediterranean possessions and communications. They know that France, though her army is strong, is desperately weak in some vital spots ...

KEY TERM

Sudeten Germans
German-speaking people who had been settled in the Sudetenland since the thirteenth century.

The Sudetenland crisis

The annexation of Austria with minimal international protest greatly exposed Czechoslovakia to Nazi pressure, as it was now surrounded on three sides by German territory (see Figure 3.3). Above all, in its Sudeten territories in Bohemia, which had until 1919 been part of the Austro-Hungarian Empire, there were 3 million **Sudeten Germans**, many of whom wanted to have the Sudetenland integrated into Nazi Germany. In the aftermath of the *Anschluss* both Britain and France were acutely aware of this growing threat to Czechoslovakia. Chamberlain was unwilling to guarantee Czechoslovakia and yet realized that Britain might well not be able to remain detached from the consequences of a German attack on it.

Who was the intended audience of Source 3.18? What impact might this have had on the content, tone, and attitudes shown in the source? What additional knowledge could you use to consider whether this view of Hitler's threat to Czechoslovakia was justified?

SOURCE 3.18

From a speech by Neville Chamberlain to the House of Commons on the prospect of a German invasion of Czechoslovakia, March 24, 1938.

It would be well within the bounds of possibility that other countries, besides those which were parties to the original dispute, would almost immediately become involved. This is especially true in the case of two countries like Great Britain and France, with long associations of friendship, with interests closely interwoven, devoted to the same ideals of democratic liberty and determined to uphold them.

KEY FIGURE

General Joseph Vuillemin (1883–1963) First World War fighter ace promoted to commander of the French air force in 1939.

France, unlike Britain, was pledged by two treaties signed in 1924 and 1925 to consult and assist Czechoslovakia in the event of a threat to their common interests. In reality, though, France was in no position to help. The Chief of the French Air Staff, **General Vuillemin**, who was in charge of operational planning, made no secret of his fears that the French air force would be destroyed within two weeks of an outbreak of war with Germany. The French government was therefore ready to follow the British lead in seeking a way of defusing the Sudeten crisis before it could result in war. The urgency of this was underlined by the war scare of the weekend of May 20–21, 1938 – the so-called May crisis – when the Czech government suddenly partially mobilized its army in response to false rumours that a German attack was imminent. Hitler, warned by both Britain and France of the dangerous consequences of any military action, rapidly denied having any such plans. Meanwhile, France and Britain were redoubling their efforts to find a peaceful solution. The Anglo-French peace strategy aimed to put pressure on both the Czechs and the Sudeten Germans to make concessions, while continuing to warn Hitler of the dangers of a general war.

Chamberlain intervenes

On September 12, 1938 Hitler's campaign moved into a new phase when, in a speech at the annual Nazi Party rally in Nuremberg, he violently attacked the Czech government and assured the Sudeten Germans of his support. Both Britain and France desperately attempted to avoid war. Military assistance from the USSR seemed unlikely. Maxim Litvinov, the Soviet foreign minister, had made it clear that the USSR would assist Czechoslovakia only once France had done so. Chamberlain deeply distrusted the USSR and believed that it was trying to involve Britain in a war with Germany.

KEY FIGURE

Édouard Daladier (1884–1970) A center-left French politician who served three terms as prime minister: in 1933, 1934, and 1938–40.

Édouard Daladier, the French prime minister, suggested that he and Chamberlain should meet Hitler, but Chamberlain seized the initiative and flew to see Hitler on September 15 at Hitler's holiday home, the Berghof, in Bavaria, southern Germany. There he agreed, subject to consultation with France, that Czechoslovakia should cede to Germany all areas that contained a German population of 50 per cent or more. This would be supervised by an international commission. Hitler also demanded that Czechoslovakia should renounce its pact with the USSR.

When Chamberlain met Hitler again, at Bad Godesberg on September 22, after winning French backing for his plan, Hitler demanded that the German occupation of the Sudetenland should be speeded up so that it would be completed by September 28. Nor was it to be supervised by any international commission. At this stage Chamberlain's peace initiative seemed to have failed. France and Britain reluctantly began to mobilize, although both powers still continued to seek a negotiated settlement.

The Munich Conference and its outcome

In retrospect, it is often argued that France and Britain should have gone to war and called Hitler's bluff. Chamberlain's critics particularly stress that the USSR was ready to come to the aid of Czechoslovakia, but at the time offers of Soviet help seemed to Britain, France, and even Czechoslovakia to be unconvincing. As neither Poland nor Romania would allow Soviet troops through their territory, how could they help Czechoslovakia? It is thus not surprising that Chamberlain and Daladier warmly welcomed Mussolini's last-minute proposal on September 28 for a four-power conference in Munich. Mussolini was anxious to avoid the outbreak of a war that might eventually involve Italy as a potential ally of Germany. Italy had a huge budget deficit because of the war in Abyssinia and its intervention in the Spanish Civil War. It was also militarily unprepared as a result of those two campaigns. The German generals, too, were convinced that Germany was neither economically nor militarily prepared for war at this point.

KEY FIGURE

Joachim von Ribbentrop (1893–1946) German ambassador to Britain, 1936–38, and then foreign minister, 1938–45. He was sentenced to death by the victorious Allies in 1946.

Consequently, the next day, under pressure from both his generals and Mussolini, Hitler reluctantly agreed to:

- delay the occupation of the Sudetenland until October 10 and allow an international commission to map the boundary line
- guarantee, jointly with Britain, France, and Italy, the independence of what remained of Czechoslovakia
- sign a declaration affirming the desire of Britain and Germany 'never to go to war with one another again' (which was supplemented by a similar declaration with France signed by **Joachim von Ribbentrop**, Hitler's foreign minister, in Paris in December).

At the time many in Britain saw Munich as a great victory for Chamberlain. Arguably, he did buy more time for rearmament, but to the outside world Munich seemed to be a major defeat for Britain and France. The British ambassador in Tokyo reported that 'the Japanese reaction … is that we are prepared to put up with almost any indignity rather than fight. The result is that, all in all, our prestige is at a low ebb in the East.'

In practice, Britain and France began to recognize Czechoslovakia as a German sphere of influence. The German representatives were allowed to dominate the international commission that was to map out the new frontiers after the secession of the Sudetenland, and neither power protested when Germany refused to participate in finalizing the terms of the joint guarantee of Czechoslovakia in February 1939.

What is the attitude of the cartoonist to the Munich Conference? Note down specific details to support your view.

SOURCE 3.19

***What, no chair for me?*: a cartoon by David Low that appeared in the British newspaper the *Evening Standard* on October 1, 1938. It depicts (from left to right) Hitler, Chamberlain, Daladier, Mussolini and Stalin.**

KEY FIGURE

Emil Hácha (1872–1945)
A lawyer and politician who was president of Czechoslovakia, November 1938–March 1939.

Responses to Hitler's occupation of Prague

On March 6, 1939, Germany seized the chance to break up Czechoslovakia after acquiring the Sudetenland. When the Czech government sent troops to suppress Slovak independence demands, which the Nazis had instigated, Hitler urged the Slovaks to seek help from Berlin. On March 14, 1939 the president of Czechoslovakia, **Emil Hácha**, was ordered to travel to Berlin, where he was ruthlessly bullied into putting the fate of his country into 'the hands of the *Führer*.' The next day German troops occupied Prague, and Slovakia was turned into a German protectorate. This action was to precipitate a major diplomatic revolution in Europe: Britain broke decisively with its traditional foreign policy of avoiding a continental commitment and together with France guaranteed Poland against a German attack. Appeasement was over.

List the reasons for the dismantling of the state of Czechoslovakia. Then choose the reason you think the most important and explain why.

KEY DEBATE

WAS CHAMBERLAIN RIGHT TO PURSUE APPEASEMENT?

In the first 20 years after the defeat of Hitler, historians scornfully dismissed Chamberlain's appeasement policy. They were heavily influenced not only by Winston Churchill's memoirs but also by a book, *Guilty Men*, which was written by three left-wing journalists, including Michael Foot, later a leader of the Labour Party. It was published in July 1940, just a few weeks after the fall of France and the **evacuations from Dunkirk**. It bitterly accused Chamberlain of pursuing a disastrous policy that had left Britain unprepared militarily for war. In the eyes of the general public and of historians on both the left and right, Neville Chamberlain rapidly became the scapegoat – and not only for his own countrymen. French historians and politicians claimed that he bullied them into appeasement, while some Germans were tempted to excuse their own support for Hitler by blaming Chamberlain for not standing up to the Nazis.

Only with the opening up of the British and French archives in the 1960s and 1970s did it gradually become possible to reassess the whole policy of appeasement and place Chamberlain's decision-making in the context of Britain's slow economic decline as well as the global challenges facing the British Empire. The speed at which Chamberlain could rearm was limited by his need to balance the budget, so that if war came Britain would have enough money to buy vital materials and equipment from the USA. By the end of the 1980s historians were arguing that Chamberlain's policy was essentially determined by Britain's economic weakness and that he had no other option but to attempt to appease Germany if the Empire was to be preserved. The logical consequence of that argument is to accuse those who wanted to fight Hitler of being 'guilty' of waging a war that could only end in the dissolution of the Empire and bankruptcy. However, this line can be strongly challenged by the argument that after the *Anschluss* in March 1938 Chamberlain could have secured sufficient support in Britain for a close alliance with France and a policy of containing and encircling Germany by claiming that he was acting in accordance with the Covenant of the League of Nations.

KEY TERMS

Evacuations from Dunkirk The retreat of the British Expeditionary Force to the northern French port of Dunkirk in May 1940 and subsequent rescue by a risky sea evacuation.

Successes of appeasement

Despite the failure of appeasement to produce a lasting peace, there were some successes brought about by the policy:

- It postponed war by a year. It also halted Hitler in his intention to seize the whole of Czechoslovakia and indicated that Britain and France would not automatically give him a free hand in central Europe. Hitler was forced to accept their right to intervene in central European questions.
- It gave Britain and France more time to rearm. In 1938 the Chiefs of Staff were convinced that if war had broken out, Britain would have lost it, but over the following year Britain made strong progress, particularly in aircraft manufacture.
- It gained popular consent for the war when it was eventually declared. There is no doubt that the Munich agreement, the most important consequence of appeasement, was widely welcomed. It was met with relief by many Germans (although they were proud of what Hitler had achieved), as well as by the vast majority of French and British people. In his monthly letter to parishioners, the Reverend Marshall Selwyn, an eminent churchman in the city of Bath, claimed that 'through Chamberlain God has worked a miracle.' In 1938 the majority of people in Britain and throughout the British Empire would not have supported a war that would have denied ethnic Germans the right to be part of Germany. The USA had also made it clear that it would not support Britain and France in a war over the Sudetenland. However, having made concession after concession to Hitler, only to see him occupy Prague in March 1939 and then invade Poland in September, Chamberlain had the backing of most people in Britain and the Dominions when he declared war on Germany in September 1939. By this point there appeared to be no alternative to war, a conclusion that the pacificist mood of the British public accepted. In that sense, there was a growing opposition to a seemingly futile policy of further appeasement.

Failures of appeasement

There were also many failures of appeasement:

- It allowed Germany and Italy one more year in which to rearm (even though for Italy this was still insufficient). France and Britain had overestimated Germany's ability to wage a successful war in 1938 – the German army was not strongly mechanized and Hitler's own generals had reservations about its operational ability. However, by 1939 Germany was stronger and better prepared for war.
- Up to a point, it emboldened the dictators. It did not deter Hitler from taking Czechoslovakia in March 1939. Indeed, it is arguable that he thought that the Munich settlement had given him the green light for expansion into eastern Europe. It gave clear signals to Hitler that the democracies were weak.
- It arguably stopped plans developed by a group of high-ranking German officers to have Hitler arrested if war broke out.
- Munich also became a byword for surrender and cowardice. Critics pointed out that the Czech government was not consulted and was simply told to hand over part of its country – the Sudetenland. Also, Jewish people, socialists, and communists were persecuted in the occupied areas.
- Any chance of co-operation with the USSR was lost, and Stalin eventually concluded that he had to ally with Hitler instead.
- The League of Nations was ignored.
- Having given up Czechoslovakia to Germany, the Western powers also gave up access to the country's 35 army divisions, thriving war industries, and strong defenses when war eventually broke out.

Why, and with what effects, did Britain and France pursue a policy of appeasement?

ACTIVITY

Create a presentation that gives an overview of appeasement between 1935 and 1938. What changed and what stayed the same between these dates? Your presentation should consider the pros and cons of appeasement as discussed above and should end with a statement of your own opinion on whether the policy could be justified in 1938.

SUMMARY DIAGRAM

Here is a summary diagram explaining why and the effects.

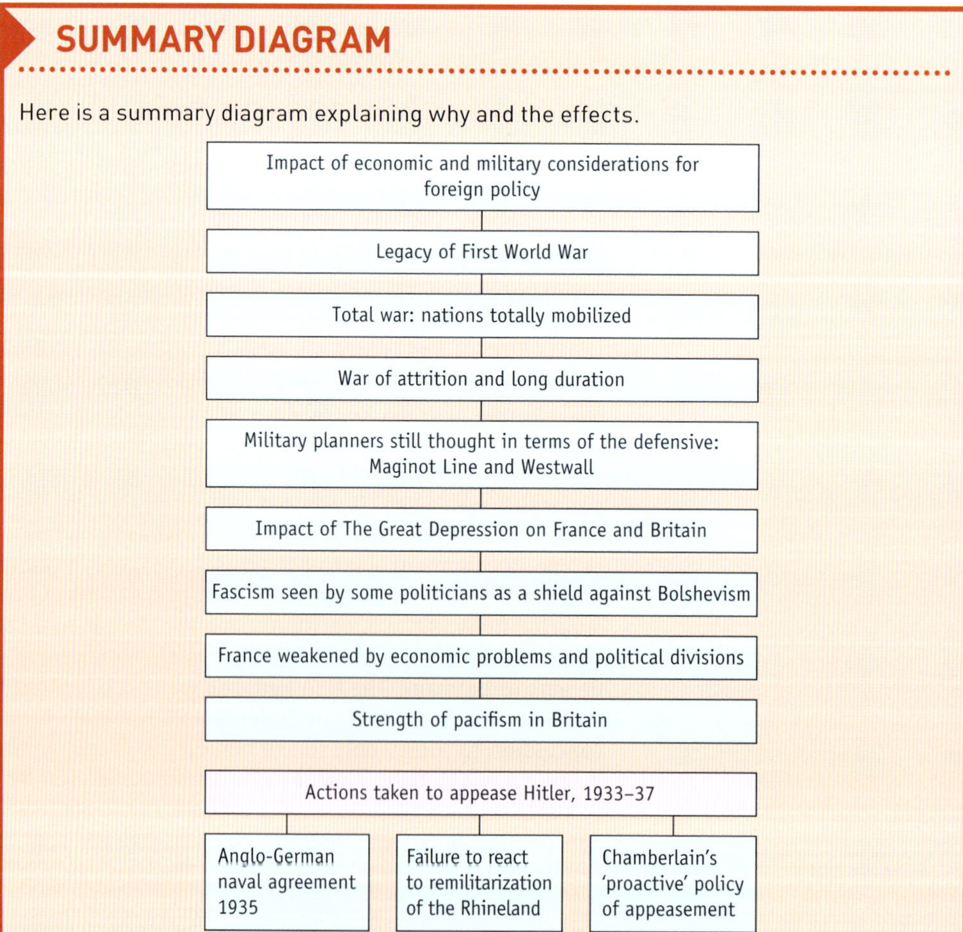

Anschluss and destruction of Czechoslovakia

Austrian and Czech crises, 1938

Anschluss
- Faced with threat of referendum on Austro-German Agreement, Germany annexed Austria, March 12
- Chamberlain accepted *Anschluss* and hoped talks with Germany on a comprehensive settlement would go ahead

Sudeten crisis
- Hitler intended to exploit Sudeten demands for independence to 'smash' Czechoslovakia
- Fearing war, Chamberlian negotiated Munich agreement with Hitler: Sudetenland ceded to Germany; rest of Czechoslovakia guaranteed by Britain, France, Italy, and Germany (September 29)

Successes of appeasement

- Won time for public opinion to accept need for war against Nazis
- Bought time to rearm
- British Dominions opposed to war in 1938

Failures of appeasement

- German occupation of Prague marked total failure of appeasement and enabled Hitler to strengthen Germany with Czech resources
- Increased distrust of USSR towards France and Britain
- Blocked plans by German army to depose Hilter
- Ignored League of Nations

4 Why did war break out in 1939?

In answering this question, it is necessary to look at:

- the aims and impact of Hitler's expansionist policies
- British rearmament in response to Germany's expansionism
- the development of German alliances
- the attack on Poland.

Aims and impact of Hitler's expansionist policies

In German domestic policy, Hitler was notorious for often failing to give a definite lead, but this was not the case in foreign policy. He was always well briefed at foreign policy meetings and according to his press secretary, Otto Dietrich, he would read a large number of foreign press reports daily. By 1937 at the latest, neither German foreign ministry officials nor senior officers of the armed services were able to exert decisive influence on him. His aims are the subject of considerable debate by historians and are discussed below.

Underlying aims of Hitler in foreign policy

In essence, Hitler revived the idea of a ***Grossdeutschland*** on an even greater scale. Hitler's ideas involved the creation of German ***Lebensraum*** in eastern Europe and the European provinces of Russia from which all Slavs, **Roma**, and Jewish people would be removed. His immediate priorities were to rearm, destroy the Versailles settlement, dismantle the French alliance system in eastern Europe, and negotiate alliances with Italy and Britain, which would give him a free hand in Europe. The impact of these policies is explored in the following section of this book.

KEY TERMS

Grossdeutschland The concept of a 'greater Germany' containing all German-speaking peoples in a single state. This idea first emerged during the nineteenth century in the German nationalist movement, which wanted the many individual states loosely bound in the German Confederation to become one country called Germany. However, the unified German state that did emerge in 1871 omitted Austria. This approach was known as *Kleindeutschland* ('lesser Germany').

Lebensraum A term meaning 'living space:' the idea of providing Germans with all the land and resources that they needed.

Roma A traditionally nomadic ethnic group originally from northern India but now living across Europe and the Americas.

KEY DEBATE

WHAT WERE HITLER'S AIMS IN FOREIGN POLICY?

The tempo of the German campaign against the Treaty of Versailles quickened once Hitler came to power in 1933, although for at least two years he appeared to pursue the same policy as his three predecessors. Was he, then, just following the traditional policy of making Germany the greatest power in Europe by exploiting every opportunity that presented itself to increase German power? In his book *Mein Kampf* ('My Struggle'), written in 1924, Hitler was quite specific about the main thrust of Nazi foreign policy. Germany was to turn its gaze towards 'the land in the east,' which meant above all Russia, which he regarded as territory to be colonized in the future by German settlers.

Was this still an aim in 1933 or was it just a dream long since forgotten? Some historians argue that Hitler had no consistent foreign policy of clear priorities and that his decisions were usually determined by economic pressures and demands for action from within the Nazi Party itself. Other historians, often called intentionalists, take the opposite view and argue on the strength of *Mein Kampf* and *Hitler's Secret Book* (published in 1928) that he had a definite program that he worked towards from the start. First of all, he planned to defeat France and the USSR, and then, after building up a large navy, he would make a determined bid for world power, even if it involved war against both Britain and the USA.

The history of Nazi foreign policy generates such controversy because Hitler's actions were so often ambiguous and contradictory. Despite this, there is currently a general consensus among historians that Hitler did intend to wage a series of wars that would ultimately result in a struggle for global domination. Many believe his goals stayed the same, but his methods and tactics changed based on the opportunities he encountered.

German rearmament, 1933–35, and the Anglo-German Naval Agreement of 1935

Without building up its arms and ending the restrictions imposed by the Treaty of Versailles, Germany would not be able to play a major role in European affairs. The Depression had not only helped to bring Hitler to power with this plan (see Source 3.1), but it also helped to explain why the other European powers took so little action to defend the Versailles agreement. German rearmament brought about a considerable change in international relations. Ultimately, Hitler's intention was to mobilize the whole German economy and society for war, as indicated by the measures that he took between 1933 and 1935:

- In July 1933 the decision was taken to create an independent ***Luftwaffe***.
- In December plans were announced for a peacetime army of 300,000 men.
- In March 1935 **conscription** was reintroduced, despite the fears of his advisers that this would lead to French military intervention.
- Plans were also being discussed by the German Admiralty to increase the size of the navy so that it would be able to safeguard vital supplies of iron ore from the Scandinavian states in the event of war.

KEY TERMS

Luftwaffe The German air force.

Conscription Compulsory military service.

Initially, the worst fears of the German foreign ministry, who anticipated an intervention by Britain and France, appeared to be confirmed by the Stresa Front and Franco-Soviet Treaty in April 1935. Together, these two agreements appeared to isolate Germany, but Hitler successfully broke up the unity of the Stresa Front with the Anglo-German Naval Agreement, which, by allowing Germany to build more ships than sanctioned by the Treaty of Versailles, implied British acceptance of German rearmament.

The agreement approved of German plans to construct over the coming decade a moderate-sized fleet of 8 battleships, 3 aircraft carriers, 8 cruisers, 48 destroyers, and 72 submarines. The total size of the German fleet would amount to 35 per cent of Britain's Royal Navy. This agreement had profound consequences, as it effectively halted the creation of an anti-Hitler coalition and enabled the **Third Reich** to escape from the threat of isolation.

KEY TERM

Third Reich

The name that the Nazis gave to their regime, thereby positioning it as the successor to the Holy Roman Empire (800–1806) and the German Empire (1871–1918).

Remilitarization of the Rhineland, 1936, and its consequences

The remilitarization of the Rhineland marked an important stage in Hitler's plans for rebuilding German power. The construction of strong fortifications there would enable him to stop any attempts by France to invade Germany. Hitler had originally planned to remilitarize the Rhineland in 1937, but the favorable diplomatic situation created by the Abyssinian crisis persuaded him to act in March 1936. He justified this by arguing that the Franco-Soviet Pact was contrary to the Locarno agreement and represented a direct threat to German security.

What can we learn about German foreign policy in 1936 from Source 3.20?

SOURCE 3.20

German soldiers cross the Hohenzollern Bridge in Cologne during Germany's remilitarization of the Rhineland in 1936, in direct violation of the Treaty of Versailles. Anglo-French failure to intervene was a turning point in international affairs.

Crucial to the success of his plan was the attitude of Italy. Mussolini, isolated from the other **Stresa powers** because of his Abyssinian policy, had little option but to reassure Germany that he would not co-operate with Britain and France to enforce Locarno if German troops entered the Rhineland.

KEY TERM

Stresa powers The states that attended the Stresa Conference in April 1935: France, Italy, and Britain.

German rearmament, 1936–39

After the remilitarization of the Rhineland the pace of German rearmament accelerated. Hitler appointed **Hermann Göring** to implement the Four-Year Plan, which was to prepare Germany for war by 1940. Through raising taxes and government loans and cutting public spending on other areas, military expenditure nearly quadrupled between 1937 and 1939. An ambitious program for the production of **synthetic materials** was also started to get round the impact of a future British blockade. By August 1939 the *Luftwaffe* had 4,000 front-line aircraft, and the strength of the army had risen to 2.75 million men. In January 1939 Hitler also announced plans for the construction of a major battle fleet to challenge Britain.

KEY FIGURE

Hermann Göring (1893–1946) First World War air ace who became a leading Nazi, overseeing the *Luftwaffe* and the Four-Year Plan.

KEY TERM

Synthetic materials Laboratory-created alternatives to natural resources such as rubber and oil.

The Four-Year Plan was over-ambitious. It had to be extended in 1940, and even then Germany failed to meet its production targets. In reality, the German rearmament program was scheduled to be ready by the mid-1940s. In the meantime Hitler's policy was to give the impression that Germany was armed in greater depth than it actually was.

Commodity	1936	1938	1942	Plan target for annual output
Mineral oil	1,790	2,340	6,260	13,830
Aluminium	98	166	260	273
Buna (synthetic) rubber	0.7	5	96	120
Explosives	18	45	300	223
Nitrogen	770	914	930	1,040
Gunpowder	20	26	150	217
Steel	19,216	22,656	20,480	24,000
Iron ore	2,255	3,360	4,137	5,549
Coal (black)	158,400	186,186	166,059	213,000
Coal (brown)	161,383	194,985	245,918	240,500

Table 3.3 The Four-Year Plan and output (in thousands of tons) (Source: Petzina, D., *Autarkiepolitik in Dritten Reich: Der nationalsozialistische Vierjahresplan*, Stuttgart: Deutsche Verlags-Anstalt, 1968, p. 182)

ACTIVITY

What can we learn from Table 3.3 about German rearmament?

Hitler considers his options, April 1936–February 1938

By the autumn of 1937 Hitler had virtually dismantled the Europe created by the Locarno and Versailles treaties. Owing to the following factors, he had also greatly strengthened Germany's position in Europe, even though he had given up the idea of an alliance with Britain:

- The Spanish Civil War and the outbreak of the Chinese-Japanese War had distracted his potential enemies.
- Italy was drawing ever closer to Germany, as the Rome–Berlin Axis of 1936 showed.
- In November 1936, Germany was further strengthened when Hitler signed the Anti-Comintern Pact with Japan. This was of more symbolic than practical importance, as it was aimed at the Comintern, the Soviet Communist Party's international movement, rather than the USSR itself. However, it did have a secret protocol in the event of a war between either Germany or Japan, and the USSR 'to take no measures which would tend to ease the situation of the USSR.'
- Both the Anti-Comintern Pact and Rome–Berlin Axis showed that Nazi Germany was no longer isolated. Potentially, Italy, Japan, and Germany were now capable of putting the democracies under great pressure.

Hitler was therefore in a favorable position to consider options for a new and more aggressive phase of foreign policy. On November 5, 1937 he outlined to his commanders-in-chief and foreign and war ministers possible scenarios involving civil war in France, or even a Franco-Italian war, that would enable him to annex Austria and destroy Czechoslovakia without fear of international intervention. He achieved these aims in 1938–39, even though the circumstances that he had predicted never in fact came about. Both the *Anschluss* and the eventual destruction of Czechoslovakia show Hitler's ability to adapt his tactics to the prevailing circumstances while steadily pursuing his overall aims.

Summarise in your own words the key points in Source 3.21. How does it help us to understand Hitler's foreign policy?

SOURCE 3.21

From the minutes of Hitler's address to his senior ministers, November 5, 1937.

The aim of German policy was to make secure and to preserve the **racial community** and to enlarge it. It was therefore a question of space [*Lebensraum*] ... The question for Germany was: Where could Germany achieve the greatest gain at the lowest cost? German policy had to reckon with two hate-inspired antagonists, Britain and France, to whom a German colossus in the centre of Europe was a thorn in the flesh ... Germany's problem could only be solved by the use of force ... If the resort to force with its attendant risks is accepted ... there then remains still to be answered the questions 'When?' and 'How?'

KEY TERM

Racial community
Here, Hitler is referring to the 'German race' and any other peoples deemed acceptable in Nazi race theory.

Anschluss, 1938

The annexation of Austria had long been a key aim of Nazi foreign policy as part of the creation of *Grossdeutschland*. Hitler himself was Austrian and, with the dissolution of the Austro-Hungarian Empire in 1918, many of his compatriots hoped that Austria would be incorporated into Germany, but this had been forbidden by Article 80 of the Treaty of Versailles.

As we have seen, Hitler was sympathetic to attempts by the Austrian Nazis to seize power in 1934, but failed to persuade Mussolini to agree to the German annexation of Austria. Hitler did not plan the actual events that enabled him to achieve it. The crisis was ultimately triggered when **Kurt von Schuschnigg**, the Austrian chancellor, alarmed by the activities of the Austrian Nazis, requested an interview with Hitler in February 1938. Hitler welcomed the chance to achieve an easy diplomatic success by imposing on Schuschnigg an agreement that would not only subordinate Austrian foreign policy to Berlin but also give the Austrian Nazi Party complete freedom. However, Schuschnigg then decided unexpectedly to regain some room for manoeuvre by calling a referendum, which he planned to hold on Sunday March 14 and in which he would ask Austrians to vote for a 'free and German, independent and social, Christian and united Austria.'

KEY FIGURE

Kurt von Schuschnigg (1897–1977) Chancellor of Austria, 1934–38. He was imprisoned by the Nazis after the *Anschluss*.

The German army occupies Austria

The immediate danger for the German government was that if Schuschnigg's appeal was endorsed by a large majority, he would be able to renounce his agreement with Hitler. Confronted by this challenge, Hitler rapidly dropped his policy of gradual absorption of Austria and not only forced Schuschnigg to cancel the referendum but on March 12 also ordered the German army to occupy Austria. Then Hitler decided, apparently on the spur of the moment after a highly successful visit to the Austrian city of Linz where he had attended secondary school as a boy, to incorporate Austria into the *Reich* rather than install a satellite Nazi government in Vienna.

The Sudetenland, 1938

Hitler had long regarded Czechoslovakia, with its alliances with both France and Russia, as a strategic threat to Germany that would eventually have to be eliminated. However, he was not sure how this could be achieved. He certainly played with the idea of launching a sudden attack on Czechoslovakia if a major crisis were to be triggered, by, for example, the assassination of the German ambassador in Prague. An easier and safer way of bringing about the disintegration of Czechoslovakia was to stir up the nationalism of the Sudeten Germans. Czechoslovakia was a fragile state undermined by an ethnically divided population. Its unity was particularly threatened by the 3 million Sudeten Germans and the 2 million Slovaks who lived within its borders. Hitler therefore specifically instructed **Konrad Henlein**, the Sudeten German nationalist leader, to keep making demands for concessions that the Prague government could not possibly grant if it wanted to preserve the unity of Czechoslovakia.

KEY FIGURE

Konrad Henlein (1898–1945) Leader of the Sudeten German Party and later Nazi *Gauleiter* (regional leader) of the Sudetenland.

The May crisis

Henlein was so successful in following Hitler's instructions that on the weekend of May 20–21, 1938 the Czech government suddenly started mobilizing its army, believing that a German attack was imminent. In response to warnings from Britain and France, Hitler denied that he was mobilizing the German army. However, far from making him more reasonable, this incident appears to have had the opposite effect, as he immediately stepped up military preparations for an invasion and set October 1 as a deadline for 'smashing Czechoslovakia.' Was this just a bluff? Was Hitler waiting for Britain and France to take the initiative and come up with proposals for the future of Czechoslovakia? There were certainly, as we have seen, powerful forces working for the dismantling of the Czechoslovak state, but most historians do not dismiss Hitler's plans for the invasion of Czechoslovakia. It is more likely that he was just waiting to see whether force or diplomacy would be the better option.

Hitler and Chamberlain negotiate, September 15 and 22, 1938

In early September Edvard Beneš, the Czechoslovak prime minister, responded to Anglo-French pressure and granted almost all Henlein's demands. As this threatened to remove the justification for the Nazi campaign against Czechoslovakia, Hitler immediately instructed Henlein to provoke a series of incidents that would enable him to break off talks with Beneš. After Hitler's inflammatory speech at the Nuremberg Rally in which he promised German support to the Sudetens, Chamberlain, to avoid the war that a German invasion of Czechoslovakia would almost certainly have brought about, flew to Germany to meet Hitler.

On September 15 Chamberlain seemed to have negotiated an agreement with Hitler on the Sudetenland: Czechoslovakia would hand over to Germany those regions in the Sudetenland where there was a German population of 50 per cent or more. Czechoslovakia would also cancel its defensive alliance with the USSR. In the meantime Hitler assured Chamberlain that he would take no military action.

After gaining French support for this agreement and persuading the Czechoslovak government to accept it, Chamberlain met Hitler again on September 22. The only concessions Chamberlain and Daladier made to Czechoslovakia were that there would be an Anglo-French guarantee of the new border, which would be mapped out by an international commission, and there would be a Czechoslovak-German non-aggression pact.

Hitler's reaction

Instead of confirming the agreement, Hitler presented Chamberlain with what was in effect an ultimatum: the German occupation of the Sudetenland was to be completed by September 28 without any supervision by an international commission. Why Hitler should suddenly have changed his mind has puzzled historians. Was he anxious to avoid accepting Chamberlain's plan in the hope that Hungary and Poland would step in with their own demands for the Czechoslovakian territory that they had claimed back in 1919 at the Paris Peace Conference? This would give him the opportunity to move in and occupy the whole country under the pretext of being a 'peacemaker' revising the 1919 Treaty of Saint Germain with Austria. On the other hand, it is possible that Hitler had no such elaborate plan in mind and merely wanted to eliminate Czechoslovakia once and for all through war.

The Munich agreement

On September 28 Mussolini intervened with a proposal for a Four-Power Conference in Munich. As we have already seen, in the Munich agreement Hitler reluctantly agreed to delay the occupation of the Sudetenland and to allow an international commission to map the boundary line, as well as guaranteeing independence to the remainder of Czechoslovakia. The signed declaration that Britain and Germany would never go to war again made headlines across the world.

It is too simple to call Munich a triumph for Hitler. He had, it is true, secured the Sudetenland, but arguably he had not achieved his real aim, the destruction of Czechoslovakia, which apparently was now about to be protected by an international guarantee. Germany seemed to be in danger of being involved in just the sort of international agreement Hitler had always hoped to avoid.

Czechoslovakia, 1939

KEY TERM

Czecho-Slovakia
Short for the Second Czecho-Slovak Republic, the name by which what was left of Czechoslovakia was known from September 1938 until March 1939.

The argument that Hitler merely responded to events is hard to sustain when his foreign policy from October 1938 to March 1939 is analyzed. His main priority remained the destruction of **Czecho-Slovakia**, as it was now called. On October 21, 1938 the German army was ordered to draw up fresh plans for military action, and on November 1 the German navy was instructed to speed up its construction program. Hitler tempted Hungary, Poland, and Romania with territorial gains from Czecho-Slovakia to gain their support. German agents were also sent into Slovakia to create anger against Prague. Quite apart from the political reasons, there were important economic reasons for the occupation of Czecho-Slovakia. Czech industry, military equipment, raw materials, and gold reserves were all urgently needed for German rearmament. Strategically, it would also strengthen Germany's southern boundaries and open up the Balkans to German influence.

KEY FIGURE

Jozef Tiso (1887–1947)
Prime minister of the autonomous Slovak region that was created within Czecho-Slovakia following the Munich agreement.

Hitler saw his opportunity when the tensions between the Czech and Slovak communities came to a head as a result of the central government in Prague forcing the Slovakian prime minister, **Jozef Tiso**, out of office. Tiso was summoned to Berlin, where he was told by Hitler that he should declare Slovakian independence. Otherwise, he risked Slovakia being partitioned between Poland, Hungary, and Romania, who all had claims to parts of its territory. The next day Tiso announced the meeting of a Slovak National Assembly, and a German naval flotilla was sent down the Danube River to Bratislava. Meanwhile President Hácha was forced to agree to the German occupation of Bohemia and the establishment of a German protectorate in Slovakia.

Czecho-Slovakia was becoming a German sphere of influence.

ACTIVITY

How similar were the reasons and factors to consider in German policy relating to the following countries and regions between 1936 and 1938: the Rhineland, Austria, the Sudetenland, and Czechoslovakia as a whole? What were the key similarities and key differences?

British rearmament in response to Germany's expansionism

As a consequence of German rearmament and Hitler's increasingly aggressive foreign policy, in 1936 Britain drew up a four-year plan for rearmament in which priority was given to the navy and air force. In a future war with Germany the navy would play a key role in blockading Germany to ensure that it could not import vital raw materials for its war industries. An important part of the rearmament program was also the construction of a bomber strike force. Using British bases, bombers could attack German cities and factories.

Despite his support for appeasement, the program was accelerated when Chamberlain became prime minister in 1937, and increased funds were also made available for the army. Between 1936 and 1939 expenditure on armaments increased from £185.9 million to £719 million. On February 22, 1939 the government authorized aircraft production 'to the limit' regardless of cost. British (and French) rearmament preparations were planned to reach their peak in the period 1939–40. Thereafter the sheer cost of rearmament would begin to cause political and economic problems. Consequently, viewed from Paris and London it was better for war to come in 1939–40 rather than a few years later – if it was to come at all.

	Britain	France	Germany
1935	1,140	785	3,183
1936	1,877	890	5,112
1937	2,153	743	5,606
1938	2,827	1,382	5,235
1939	7,940	3,163	8,295
1940	15,049	2,133	10,247

Table 3.4 Annual aircraft production in Britain, France and Germany, 1935–40

ACTIVITY

What do the statistics in Table 3.4 tell you about the arms race between Britain and France on one side, and Germany on the other?

Preparation for air raids

In November 1932 Prime Minister Stanley Baldwin told the House of Commons that the single most feared aspect of modern war was the bomber. 'A man,' he observed, feared above all 'seeing his wife and children killed from the air.' He then made the notorious comment that 'the bomber will always get through.' There was a general assumption in Britain that almost within minutes of the declaration of war, bombs would rain down on London and other large British cities.

Summarise Fuller's observation in Source 3.22 and then explain how the fear of bombing influenced both British public opinion and the British government's policy towards Germany.

SOURCE 3.22

In 1936 the military strategist Major General John Fuller painted an alarming picture of what would happen in London once air raids began (quoted in Heffer, S., *Sing As We Go: Britain Between the Wars*, London: Hutchinson Heinemann, 2023, p. 567).

London for several days will be total chaos, the hospitals will be stormed, traffic will cease, the homeless will shriek for help, the city will be a pandemonium. What of the Government of Westminster? It will be swept away by an avalanche of terror. Then the enemy will dictate his terms ...

By the summer of 1936, in response to Germany's rearmament program, the British government informed the local authorities that they needed to prepare 'precautionary measures, which would be necessary for safeguarding the civil population against the effects of air attack.' In an attempt to avoid the panic that such measures might cause, it added reassurance that it did not believe war to be imminent (see Source 3.23).

To what extent does Source 3.22 explain the tone of the message in Source 3.23?

SOURCE 3.23

From a letter sent by the Home Office to local councils throughout the UK, July 9, 1936.

The need for these measures in no way implies a risk of war in the near future; nor does it imply any relaxation of effort on the part of His Majesty's Government to ensure the promotion and maintenance of peace by all means in their power and to use to the full the machinery of the League of Nations.

Town councils slowly began to draw up plans for implementing Air Raid Precautions, or ARP, as they were called. Initially, lack of money meant that little progress was made beyond drawing up plans and sending officials to conferences. At first there was also considerable opposition from pacifist movements, local branches of the Labour Party, teachers, and clergy. Many teachers above all were concerned that ARP measures would be traumatic for small children. Nevertheless, by 1938 with the help of more generous government grants councils were able to make more adequate preparations. These involved:

- instructing the public in using gas masks
- providing air raid shelters (both communal shelters and, for those with gardens, small **Anderson shelters**)
- appointing air raid wardens, who would be responsible for ensuring that their street was properly prepared for air raids and had **blackout blinds** over their windows
- making provision for the treatment of casualties and the provision of mortuaries for those killed by the bombs
- holding regular exercises with simulated bombing attacks on cities.

What impression of Britain's war preparations are given by Source 3.24?

SOURCE 3.24

An Anderson shelter in a small garden. This photograph is from a newspaper, and was originally captioned: 'Mrs Alice Prendergast of 3 Western Lane, Balham, is not at a disadvantage through building an Anderson shelter where her vegetables grew. She planted her vegetables on top of the shelter, and now has lettuce, beetroots and marrows growing. Mrs Prendergast is seen watering the vegetables on the top of her shelter.'

KEY TERMS

Anderson shelters Named after Sir John Anderson, the government minister who commissioned their development, these were steel shelters installed in gardens to provide protection against air raids.

Blackout blinds Blinds that would cover windows to prevent light from inside attracting the attention of enemy bomber crews, who would be targeting large industrial cities.

Targets and progress by 1939

KEY FIGURE

John Anderson (1882–1958) Scottish civil servant and politician who was put in charge of ARP measures by Chamberlain.

By the outbreak of war Britain had made considerable progress in its rearmament efforts. Preparations for war ran parallel with Chamberlain's appeasement policies. Under **Sir John Anderson**, a dynamic politician and administrator, the government more than quadrupled its expenditure on ARP measures. Some 300,000 hospital beds were made ready for an emergency, and plans were drawn up for the evacuation of children from the big cities to safer rural areas.

In May 1939 limited conscription was introduced for 20- to 22-year-old men, and the army was planned to expand by 800,000 within three years; anti-aircraft defenses were to be manned permanently in both peace and war. However, the regular army remained under-equipped. Shipyards, many of which had been closed during the Depression, were now producing warships as quickly as possible. To counter future German U-boat attacks, cruisers and destroyers were being built. Impressive progress was made in building up the RAF (see Table 3.4). Pressure was put on aircraft manufacturers to build even more factories and to have plans for increasing production in the event of war.

Create a diagram showing how Britain prepared for war, 1936–39. What were the main successes and limitations of the preparations?

Development of German alliances

By 1939 Germany was not isolated. Hitler had signed the October Protocols, or Rome–Berlin Axis, and through the Anti-Comintern Pact it was linked to both Italy and Japan. Neither pact had any military content. They were rather ententes, or expressions of goodwill. Hitler failed to convert them into military alliances, but they did indicate that potentially Japan and Italy in a future war involving Germany and the Western powers would remain benevolently neutral.

Pact of Steel

In May 1939 Hitler further strengthened Germany's links with Italy by concluding the Pact of Steel. The treaty committed the two powers to assisting each other if either went to war. The treaty gave Hitler complete freedom of action, but he assured Mussolini that he had no intention of going to war for at least three years. Mussolini believed that he had gained two important advantages: an alliance with the strongest power in Europe and several more years of peace in which he could build up his forces and exploit the political advantage of his alliance with Germany to extract territorial concessions from Britain and France.

The Nazi-Soviet Pact

After the occupation of Czechoslovakia Hitler was determined to force Poland to agree to the return of Danzig to Germany after being a free city under the League of Nations since 1919 and to reduce Poland to the status of a German satellite state. However, given the British guarantee of Poland in March 1939, this could be achieved only at the risk of war with Britain and France (see page 189). Neither the Anti-Comintern Pact nor the Pact of Steel would protect Hitler from a war on two fronts in which Germany would have to fight Britain and France to the west, and the USSR to the east. This was a growing possibility as Britain and France were attempting to build up a 'peace front' in eastern Europe composed of Greece, Romania, Turkey and, it was hoped, the USSR, with which negotiations had started in April 1939.

Once the decision was taken, on May 23, to prepare for war against Poland, Hitler began to consider the possibility of an alliance with the USSR. Right through to the middle of August, Moscow continued to keep both options open, but by then the slow pace of the military discussions with Britain and France seemed finally to have convinced Stalin that an agreement with Hitler would be preferable. Stalin distrusted Russia's former First World War allies as much as he did Germany; he feared that secretly Britain and France were encouraging Hitler to attack the USSR. With only days to go before the start of the military campaign against Poland, Hitler was ready to accept Stalin's terms, and the Nazi-Soviet Pact was signed on August 23. It contained the following terms:

- If either the USSR or Germany were attacked by a third power, neither the USSR nor Germany would offer 'in any form' support to this third power or join a hostile alliance.
- Both powers agreed to keep in close contact with each other and inform each other about questions 'affecting their mutual interests.'
- The pact was to last for ten years, with automatic renewal for a further five unless either power raised objections.
- A separate secret protocol outlined the German and Russian spheres of interest in eastern Europe: the Baltic states and Bessarabia in Romania would be part of the Russian sphere, and Poland was to be divided between the two powers.

To many Nazis, the idea of an alliance with the USSR was hard to accept as communist Russia was seen as Germany's real enemy. Hitler had always stressed that the Bolsheviks were 'Jewish agents' intent on the destruction of the Western world. Above all, Hitler had ambitions to create living space for German settlers in the western USSR. Initially, he had hoped that Poland, once it had handed over Danzig, would, together with Germany, seek territorial compensation in Russia. However, there was support for an agreement with the USSR in the German foreign ministry and the army. They argued that if war broke out with Britain and France, the USSR could supply Germany with vital raw materials, and consequently defeat a British blockade.

The German attack on Poland and the outbreak of war

KEY TERM

Pomorze A narrow strip of Polish territory giving Poland access to the Baltic Sea and separating the main body of Germany from the German province of East Prussia (see Figure 3.3).

In September 1939 war in Europe broke out because Poland had refused German demands for a return of former German territory called **Pomorze** in Poland, the so-called 'Polish Corridor' – Posen, West Prussia, and the city of Danzig. The name 'corridor' was used by Germans who resented the loss of this territory, implying that the land was merely a passageway and was not rightfully Polish. Germany accused Poland of hostile acts against the German population and invaded on September 1, 1939. This was a culmination of German actions contrary to the Treaty of Versailles, which began with rearmament and the remilitarization of the Rhineland and continued with the *Anschluss* and the dismantling of Czechoslovakia. The lack of resistance by the signatories of the peace treaties encouraged Hitler to think that there was limited will to prevent German expansion.

German-Polish issues including Danzig and the Pomorze/Polish Corridor

In October 1938 and then again in January and March 1939 the German foreign minister, Ribbentrop, unsuccessfully approached the Polish government about the return of Danzig and the construction of a road and rail link through Pomorze. In return, Poland was offered the eventual prospect of acquiring land in Ukraine. Essentially, Hitler wanted to turn Poland into a reliable satellite, but, given the fate of Czechoslovakia, it was precisely this status that the Poles rejected in March 1939.

The Anglo-French guarantee to Poland and the end of appeasement

In the 1920s there was no commitment to defending Poland, yet on March 31, 1939 Britain broke decisively with its traditional foreign policy of avoiding a continental commitment and, together with France, guaranteed Poland against a German attack. In many ways, it appeared a foolhardy gesture as both Britain and France lacked the military power to defend Poland.

This change can to a great extent be explained by the speed and brutality of the German occupation of the Czech province of Bohemia, which clearly indicated that Hitler could no longer be trusted to respect treaties and guarantees. Hitler had previously assured Chamberlain that his aim was just to bring all the Germans in the Sudeten area of Czechoslovakia into the German Reich, but Germany had now effectively conquered the whole of Czechoslovakia, which contained nearly 9 million Czechs and Slovaks. It is also important to stress that, in the spring of 1939, the French economy, and with it French self-confidence, had made a strong recovery. Thus, a tougher policy towards Hitler increasingly appeared to the French government to be a realistic option.

Britain was initially stampeded into its guarantee of Polish independence by the following events:

- On March 17 there were panic-stricken and inaccurate rumours that Hitler was about to occupy Romania and seize its oil wells. Access to these would greatly strengthen the German war industry and enable it to survive any future British naval blockade.
- At first Britain aimed to contain Germany by negotiating a four-power pact with France, the USSR, and Poland, but, given the intense suspicion with which the USSR was viewed by Poland and the other eastern European states, this was not a practical policy.
- When Hitler went on to force Lithuania to hand back the former German city of Memel to the Reich on March 23, it became even more vital to deter Hitler by any means possible.
- Thus, Chamberlain and Daladier had little option but to announce on March 31, 1939 an immediate Anglo-French guarantee of Poland against external attack.
- However, the Polish guarantee was seen as merely the first step towards constructing a comprehensive security system in eastern Europe. Chamberlain hoped to buttress it with a series of interlocking security pacts with other eastern European and Baltic states.

ACTIVITY

List the reasons why Britain guaranteed Poland's independence in March 1939.

Anglo-French guarantees of Greece and Romania and the peace bloc

When, on April 7, Mussolini invaded Albania, a wave of panic among the eastern Mediterranean states led Britain and France to guarantee both Greece and Romania. In May Britain considerably strengthened its position in the eastern Mediterranean by negotiating a preliminary agreement with Turkey for mutual assistance 'in the event of an act of aggression leading to war in the Mediterranean area.' By July both Bulgaria and Yugoslavia were beginning to gravitate towards the Anglo-French '**peace bloc**.'

KEY TERM

Peace bloc A group of states committed to opposing an aggressor power.

Failure to secure an Anglo-French alliance with the USSR

Britain and France needed a pact with the USSR to build up their 'peace front.' This put Stalin in the enviable position of being able to play off Hitler against Chamberlain and Daladier. Protracted negotiations between the USSR, Britain, and France began in April 1939, but, as we have seen, the two sides deeply mistrusted each other. Stalin's demand that Russia should have the right to intervene militarily in the affairs of the small states on its western borders if they were threatened with internal subversion by the Nazis, as Austria and Czechoslovakia had been in 1938, was rejected outright by Britain. They feared that the Russians would use the threat of Nazi indirect aggression as an excuse to seize territories for themselves. Stalin, on the other hand, was equally suspicious that the democracies were attempting to manoeuvre the USSR into a position where it would have to do most of the fighting against Germany. Consequently, he was ready to conclude the Nazi-Soviet Pact in August. The Anglo-French failure to secure an effective alliance with the USSR was an important reason why Hitler felt Germany was free to attack Poland in September 1939.

Summarize in your own words the key points in Source 3.25. To what extent does this source reveal why Stalin's policy towards Nazi Germany changed between 1935 and 1939?

SOURCE 3.25

From a report of March 20, 1939 by Sir William Seeds, the British ambassador in Moscow, on Stalin's speeches to the Congress of the Soviet Communist Party.

M. Stalin and various other speakers at the Congress emphasise Soviet readiness to defend the frontiers of the Soviet Union ... should they be attacked, the line taken by all of them is that the chief care of those responsible for Soviet foreign policy must be to prevent the Soviet Union from being dragged into the struggle now taking place between the fascist states and the so-called democracies ... Those innocents at home who believe that Soviet Russia is only awaiting an invitation to join the Western democracies should be advised to ponder M. Stalin's advice to his party: 'To be cautious and not allow Soviet Russia to be drawn into conflicts by warmongers who are accustomed to have others pull the chestnuts out of the fire.'

KEY FIGURES

Lord Halifax (1881–1959) Viceroy of India, 1926–31, and British foreign minister, 1938–40.

Georges Bonnet (1889–1973) French foreign minister, 1938–39, and a leading supporter of appeasement.

Possible concessions to Hitler

In June, **Lord Halifax**, the British Foreign Secretary, stressed that while Britain would defend Poland against any threat to its independence, this did not necessarily mean that its existing frontiers could not be altered or the status of Danzig changed. He went on to repeat a message that was frequently to come out of London in the summer of 1939: namely that, once trust was re-established, 'any of Germany's claims are open to consideration round a table.' In June and July there were also occasional talks between British and German officials on economic collaboration in Europe and Africa. In France, too, the mood seemed increasingly for a compromise settlement, and **Georges Bonnet**, the French foreign minister, was suggesting that France should 'push Warsaw into a compromise.' Appeasement was not quite dead after all.

ACTIVITY 

Create a diagram showing the process of change in relations between the major powers in the late 1930s. Include Britain, France, Germany, Italy, Japan, and the USSR. How did attitudes towards Germany change over time?

Hitler's intentions

By August Hitler aimed first to destroy Poland and only then to negotiate a settlement with Britain and France. On August 25 he even offered Britain an alliance and a guarantee of its empire provided it consented to the destruction of Poland and to German supremacy in eastern Europe. The response from London continued to be that only after a freely negotiated Polish-German agreement could the future of Anglo-German relations be discussed.

In October 1939, after Poland had been defeated and divided between Germany and the USSR, Hitler briefly considered setting up a small Polish satellite state, but once it was clear that both Britain and France were intending to continue the war against Germany, he drew up the following plans for the future of Poland:

- All the territory lost to Germany in 1919 would be returned, in addition to a large area in west and north-west Poland with a population of some 10 million.
- The rest of German-occupied Poland would be administered by the German General Government in Krakow.
- The Polish elites would be murdered or imprisoned, and Polish Jews would be 'ethnically cleansed', in other words, murdered.

War delayed by a week

On August 23 Hitler ordered the army to prepare to attack Poland in three days' time, but then two days later, on August 25, these orders were cancelled because, contrary to his expectations, Britain had reacted to the news of the Nazi-Soviet Pact by ratifying its guarantee of Poland. Mussolini also announced that he could not fight without impossibly large deliveries of German armaments and equipment. Was there now a chance for a compromise? Superficially, it might seem that there still was. During the next few days, Britain and France utilized all the diplomatic channels they could to avoid war. Theoretically, some sort of compromise on Poland might eventually be possible, but in the final analysis they were not ready to sacrifice Poland's independence to achieve it. They were unwilling to repeat Munich. They wanted a settlement with Hitler, but only one that Allied rearmament forced him to accept.

Belatedly, it looked as if Hitler was ready to make some concession:

- On August 29, he suddenly demanded that Britain should instruct Poland to send a minister with full negotiating powers to Berlin by the following day.
- Fearing that Hitler would treat him as he had Schuschnigg and Hácha (see pages 183 and 185), the British government refused to press the Polish government to send a negotiator to Berlin and instead argued that such a deadline was impracticable since time was needed to prepare for negotiations.

Was a last-minute chance to save the peace lost? Should, as some historians argue, Hitler have made this demand a few days earlier, so that Britain and France could have put pressure on Poland to agree to send a negotiator with full powers? However, it is more likely that Hitler was aiming to isolate Poland and manoeuvre it into a position where its 'stubbornness' could be blamed for starting the war, and so give Britain and France an excuse not to intervene.

Why, according to Source 3.26, did Hitler think that Germany would be able to defeat Poland in isolation?

KEY TERM

Autarky Economic self-sufficiency.

SOURCE 3.26

From a speech made by Hitler to his military commanders on August 22, 1939, the eve of the signature of the Nazi-Soviet Pact (quoted in Adamthwaite, A., *The Making of the Second World War*, London: Allen and Unwin, 1979, p. 219).

To be sure a new situation has arisen. I experienced those poor worms, Daladier and Chamberlain, in Munich. They will be too cowardly to attack. They won't go beyond a blockade. Against that we have **autarky** and the Russian raw materials. Poland will be depopulated and settled with Germans. My pact with the Poles (the 10 year non-aggression Pact signed in 1934) was merely conceived of as a gaining of time ... After Stalin's death – he is a very sick man – we will break the Soviet Union. Then there will begin the dawn of German rule of the earth.

Disagreement between Hitler and the German high command

The one force that could still stop Hitler was the German army. The generals who listened to Hitler's speech were not particularly inspired by the prospect of war, but they did not openly object. The army was far more cautious than Hitler and did not believe that Germany was ready for war. In 1936 the army's high command had initially been critical of Hitler's plans to remilitarize the Rhineland, as it feared that France would intervene to stop this happening. In 1938 plans to overthrow Hitler were drawn up by General Beck, head of the German army's general staff, and four of his colleagues, but they were thwarted by Hitler's success in negotiating the Munich agreement.

By August 1939 most in the army felt that it was far too late to stop an invasion of Poland, and they could only hope that the war would be limited to the Polish campaign rather than escalating into a European or even global struggle. However, when Hitler postponed the invasion of Poland on August 25, the generals believed, briefly, that Hitler had lost so much prestige that, to quote **Major General Oster**, he was 'finished.' **Admiral Canaris** optimistically argued that 'peace has been saved for the next 20 years.' **General Thomas** remained pessimistic and was convinced that a war against Poland would escalate into a general European war, which Germany economically was not strong enough to win. However, his arguments were brushed aside by the German high command. Only on the Rhine was a high-ranking German general ready to act. At the army's headquarters in Cologne **General von Hammerstein**, whose task was to defend western Germany from a possible attack, hoped to persuade Hitler to visit his headquarters, where he could be seized and killed, but Hitler's attention was focused on Poland, and so he had no reason to visit Cologne.

KEY FIGURES

Major General Hans Oster (1887–1945) Deputy head of the German security service (*Abwehr*) and one of the most determined opponents of Hitler. He was executed by the Nazis in 1945.

Admiral Wilhelm Canaris (1887–1945) Head of the German security service; arrested and executed by the Nazis after being accused of involvement in a failed plot against Hitler in July 1944.

General Georg Thomas (1890–1946) Chief economic strategist of the German army. He was arrested for plotting against Hitler, but escaped execution.

General Kurt von Hammerstein (1878–1943) Chief of the German High Command from 1930 until 1934, when he resigned from the army because of his anti-Nazi views. In September 1939 he briefly returned to service, and then continued to plot against Hitler until his death in 1943.

War breaks out

What message is Source 3.27 communicating to the German people?

SOURCE 3.27

German troops demolish a Polish frontier barrier during the invasion of Poland, which began in September 1939. Poland was rapidly defeated and partitioned between Germany and Russia.

Even when, on September 1, 1939, Germany at last invaded Poland, frantic efforts to avert war still continued. Mussolini urged a four-power European conference, and only when it was absolutely clear that Hitler would not withdraw his troops from Poland did Britain and France declare war on Germany on September 3. Italy, despite the Pact of Steel, remained neutral until France was defeated in June 1940 as Mussolini was initially unsure of a speedy German victory and Italy was not prepared economically for a war.

Unlike in 1914, news of the declaration of war was greeted with fear and resignation by the majority of the German population. Many were ready to support a limited war against Poland, but they dreaded the prospect of another world war. The American journalist William Shirer wondered how a nation could go to war 'with a country so dead against it.' Only with Hitler's spectacular successes against France and Britain in 1940 did German public opinion change.

KEY DEBATE

WHAT CAUSED THE SECOND WORLD WAR?

From 1945 to the early 1960s it was agreed that Hitler was the main if not sole cause of the Second World War. In 1961 this view was challenged principally by historians in Britain and Germany, who argued that Hitler's foreign policy aims were similar to his predecessors' both before 1914 and in the 1920s. This view caused furious debates, which ultimately resulted in a deeper understanding of the causes of the Second World War. Some historians have argued that the Treaty of Versailles, which humiliated but did not permanently weaken Germany, could be seen as the 'seedbed' of the Second World War. Arguably, the chain of crises that started with the German remilitarization of the Rhineland and culminated in the German attack on Poland owed its origins to the Versailles settlement. Others have placed emphasis on the Great Depression. This, at the very least, made the outbreak of the Second World War more likely. It weakened the democracies, helped bring Hitler to power in Germany, and strengthened militant nationalism in Japan. While the role of Hitler with his well-documented aims for territorial expansion cannot be overlooked, it does obscure the fact that the British and French governments went to war to maintain their position as great powers rather than to wage a crusade against the evil force of Nazism.

ACTIVITY

Create a presentation showing why war broke out between Britain, France, and Germany in September 1939.

Why did war break out in 1939?

SUMMARY DIAGRAM

Here is a summary diagram explaining why.

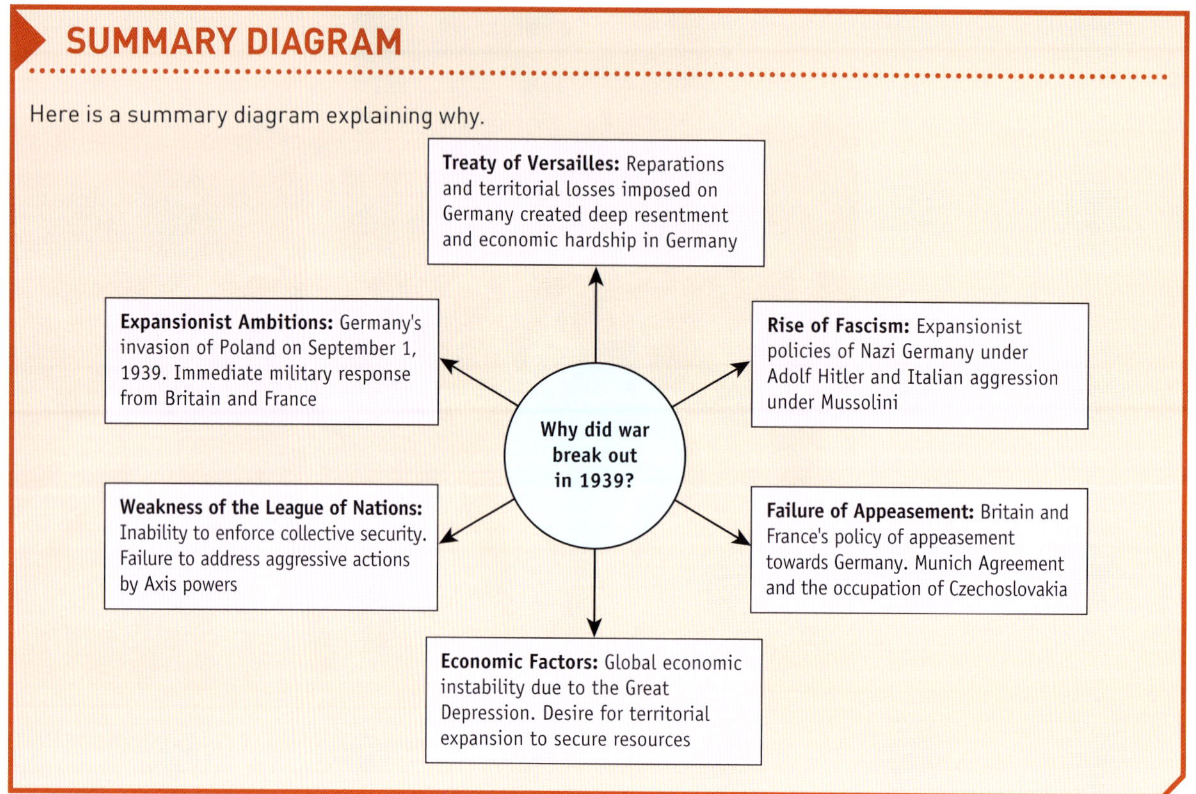

CHAPTER SUMMARY

In 1930 Britain and France, thanks to their victories in 1918, still dominated Europe. By 1937 all this had changed. The Great Depression had weakened the Western democracies. This, combined with German hatred of the Treaty of Versailles and the structural faults in the Weimar Constitution, brought Hitler to power in Germany in 1933. Economic hardship caused by the Depression also strengthened the power of the army in Japan, which had occupied Manchuria in 1931.

In reaction to German rearmament, France, Britain, and Italy formed the Stresa Front in 1935, but this was destroyed by the Abyssinian crisis, which Hitler exploited to remilitarize the Rhineland in March 1936. In July 1936 Italy and Germany intervened on behalf of the Nationalists in the Spanish Civil War, and in October and November the Rome–Berlin Axis and the Anti-Comintern Pact were signed. It was now the democracies and not Germany that were on the defensive. Owing to its failure to solve the Manchurian and Abyssinian crises, the League of Nations had become an irrelevance. In 1937 Chamberlain launched his appeasement campaign. At Munich he persuaded Hitler to compromise over Czechoslovakia, but in March 1939 Germany occupied Bohemia. This led to the Anglo-French guarantee of Poland, Greece, and Romania. An attempt to negotiate an alliance with the USSR failed when Stalin instead signed the Nazi-Soviet Pact. On September 1, 1939 Germany invaded Poland. Britain and France declared war on Germany two days later.

REFRESHER QUESTIONS

1. What was the impact of the Great Depression on international affairs?
2. How did France, Britain, and Italy respond to the rise of Hitler, 1933–35?
3. Why did France and Britain propose to the European powers an agreement not to intervene in the Spanish Civil War and why did this fail?
4. Why did Italy in the spring of 1935 align itself with Britain and France, but in October 1936 form the Rome–Berlin Axis with Hitler?
5. Why did the League of Nations fail to halt aggression in Manchuria and Abyssinia?
6. How many of his foreign policy aims had Hitler achieved by October 1939?
7. Why did appeasement fail?
8. How did Germany, France, and Britain prepare for war, 1936–39?
9. What was the main aim of British policy towards Germany?
10. Why did the USSR sign the Nazi-Soviet Pact in August 1939?

Study skills

Source questions

Using contextual knowledge effectively

Using contextual knowledge to explain similarities and differences

Some source questions give you the opportunity to use your own knowledge to explain the similarities and differences between sources. Consider the following question.

Read sources A and B. Compare these two sources as evidence about Hitler's intentions for German foreign policy. (15 marks)

First, read the sources carefully and identify the similarities and differences between the attitudes in each source.

SOURCE A

Hitler speaking to representatives of the Associated Press in Berlin, May 17, 1933.

Speaking deliberately as a German National Socialist, I desire to declare, in the name of the National Government and of the whole movement of national regeneration, that we in this new Germany are filled with a deep understanding for the same feelings and opinions and for the rightful claims to life of the other nations. The present generation of this new Germany, which so far has only experienced the poverty, misery and distress of its own people, has suffered too deeply to be able to contemplate treating others in the same way. Our boundless love for and loyalty to our own national traditions make us respect the national claims of others and makes us desire from the bottom of our hearts to live with them in peace and friendship.

SOURCE B

From the minutes of Hitler's address to his senior ministers, November 5, 1937.

The aim of German policy was to make secure and to preserve the racial community and to enlarge it. It was therefore a question of space [*Lebensraum*] ... The question for Germany was: Where could she achieve the greatest gain at the lowest cost? German policy had to reckon with two hate-inspired antagonists, Britain and France, to whom a German colossus in the centre of Europe was a thorn in the flesh ... Germany's problem could only be solved by the use of force ... If the resort to force with its attendant risks is accepted ... there then remains still to be answered the questions 'When?' and 'How?'

ACTIVITY

Write a paragraph explaining the differences between the two sources using the provenance of the two sources together with your understanding of the historical context.

Then, consider **why these sources have different attitudes.**

First, look at the intended audience – why would this affect the views expressed in each source? What was Hitler's purpose in each of these sources? What details of the historical context do you know that might explain the difference?

Analyzing sources to reach a judgment

In other source questions there is a hypothesis or view, and you need to assess how far the sources support or challenge this view. The sources selected will give opportunities to support or challenge, and sometimes there will be a nuanced source, where the content partly supports and partly challenges the view. You should aim to establish what the sources say about the issue in the question, analyzing the source material by considering the nature, origin and purpose of the source in its historical context. Then you need to reach a judgement that addresses the 'How far' element of the question. Which side of the argument is stronger?

Consider this question and its view of appeasement. Then read the sources.

Read all of the sources. 'The importance of Chamberlain's appeasement policy in 1938 was that it gave the British government and people time to prepare for war.' How far do the sources support this view? (25 marks)

SOURCE A

From a letter by Neville Chamberlain to Mrs Morton Prince, an American citizen, January 16, 1938.

... as a realist I must do what I can to make this country safe ... [The British people] are perfectly aware that until we are fully rearmed our position will be one of great anxiety. They realise that we are in no position to enter light-heartedly upon a war with such a formidable power as Germany, much less if Germany were aided by Italian attacks on our Mediterranean possessions and communications. They know that France, though her army is strong, is desperately weak in some vital spots ...

SOURCE B

***What, no chair for me?*: a cartoon by David Low that appeared in the British newspaper the *Evening Standard* on October 1, 1938. It depicts (from left to right) Hitler, Chamberlain, Daladier, Mussolini, and Stalin.**

SOURCE C

From Winston Churchill's speech in the House of Commons debate on the Munich Agreement, October 5, 1938.

France and Great Britain together, especially if they had maintained a close contact with Russia, which certainly was not done, would have been able in those days in the summer, when they had prestige, to influence many of the smaller States of Europe, and I believe they could have determined the attitude of Poland. Such a combination, prepared at a time when the German dictator was not deeply and irrevocably committed to his new adventure, would, I believe, have given strength to all these forces in Germany, which resisted this departure, this new design. They were varying forces – those of a military character, which declared that Germany was not ready to undertake a world war, and all that mass of moderate opinion and popular opinion, which dreaded war ...

SOURCE D

From a speech by Neville Chamberlain in the House of Commons, September 1, 1939.

It now only remains for us to set our teeth upon this struggle, which we ourselves earnestly endeavoured to avoid, with determination to see it through to the end. We shall enter it with a clear conscience, with the support of the Dominions and the British Empire, and the moral approval of the greater part of the world. We have no quarrel with the German people, except that they allow themselves to be governed by a Nazi government. As long as that government exists and pursues the methods it has so persistently followed during the last two years, there will be no peace in Europe. We shall merely pass from one crisis to another, and see one country after another attacked by methods which have now become familiar to us in their sickening technique.

ACTIVITY

Write a sample response to the source question above which evaluates the sources in context and includes a conclusion that gives a judgment about which side of the argument is stronger.

Writing introductions and conclusions when considering how far sources support a view

An introduction for a judgment-based source question is just setting out understanding of the question and can be brief. The conclusion is the substantiated judgment – the question is looking for a considered judgment about the extent to which the sources agree and/or disagree about a particular view. The conclusion is the judgment about which side of the argument is stronger – do the sources mostly support or challenge the view in the question, and if they mostly favor one side, is that because the content of some of the sources can be given more weight because of their authorship?

Essay questions

Writing effective essays with supported judgments in your conclusion

Writing a conclusion

What is the purpose of a conclusion? A conclusion should come to a judgment that is based on what you have already written and should be supported. It should not introduce new ideas – if those ideas were important, they should have been discussed in the main body of the essay. You must also take care to avoid offering a contrary argument to the one you have pursued throughout the rest of the essay as that will suggest that you have not thought through your ideas and are unclear as to what you think.

It might be that you are largely restating the view you offered in the vital opening paragraph, or in stronger answers there might be a subtle variation to the judgment – you confirm your original view, but suggest, with an example, that there were occasions when this was not the case.

If the question has named a factor, then you should give a judgment about that factor's relative importance, explaining why it either is or is not the most important and the role it played in the events you have discussed. If the question asks you to assess a range of factors, the conclusion should explain which you think is the most important and should support the claim. At first sight, a claim might appear to be a judgment, but without supporting material it is no more than an assertion.

Consider the following essay question:

'The foreign policy and intentions of the Nazi government under Adolf Hitler were the main reasons for the outbreak of war in 1939.' How far do you agree? (20 marks)

In order to answer this question, you would need to consider:

- Hitler's ideas and program for restoring German power and the ways in which they helped cause war with France and Britain
- the significance of Chamberlain's appeasement policy in causing the war
- the Anglo-French guarantee to Poland
- the Nazi-Soviet Pact.

Now consider this sample conclusion:

While German nationalists wished to make Germany as great a power as it had been before 1914, it was the dynamism of Hitler and his intentions that were the main reason for war in 1939. There is plenty of evidence stretching from 'Mein Kampf' to Hitler's speeches to his military commanders in the summer of 1939 that indicates that Hitler had plans for seeking 'living space' in eastern Europe and Russia. He stressed unambiguously in November 1937 that Germany had a right to enlarge its 'living space.' On the other hand, Hitler's ambitious plans could have been contained if Britain, France, and Italy had consistently worked together and intervened decisively in the early stages to stop Nazi Germany breaking the Versailles and Locarno treaties.

Chamberlain's appeasement policy, instead of leading to a settlement with Nazi Germany, convinced Hitler that he could risk the destruction of what remained of Czechoslovakia. This in turn set in motion a train of events that ended in war. The Anglo-French guarantee of Poland would have been effective only if Germany could have been contained by an alliance of eastern and southern European states, containing above all the USSR. By avoiding a war on two fronts, the Nazi-Soviet Pact made it safe for Hitler to invade Poland and risk war with Britain and France.

Commentary

This is an excellent conclusion because:

- It focuses immediately on the issue in the question.
- It provides a clear judgment on the issue.
- That judgment is supported with good argument and evidence.
- It briefly summarizes what the author believes was the main reason.

Further reading

General texts

Brogan, H. (2001), *The Penguin History of the USA*, London, Penguin

James, L. (2016), *Empires in the Sun: the Struggle for the Mastery of Africa*, London, Weidenfeld and Nicolson

Kitchen, M. (1988), *Europe Between the Wars*, London, Longman

Lowe, C.J. (1994), *The Great Powers, Imperialism and the German Problem, 1865–1925*, London, Routledge

Lowe, C.J., and Marzari, F. (1975), *Italian Foreign Policy, 1870–1940*, London, Routledge

Rich, N. (1992), *Great Power Diplomacy, 1814–1914*, Columbus, OH, McGraw Hill

Taylor, A.J.P. (1971), *The Struggle for Mastery in Europe, 1848–1918* (paperback edition), Oxford, OUP

Wesseling, H.L. (2004), *The European Colonial Empires, 1815–1919*, Harlow, Pearson/Longman

Wiskemann, E. (1970), *Europe of the Dictators*, London, Fontana

Chapter 1

Badawai, Z. (2024), *An African History of Africa*, London, Penguin

Beasley, W.G. (2000), *The Rise of Modern Japan* (third edition), Basingstoke/London, Palgrave Macmillan

Brand, H.W. (2002), *The Reckless Decade: America in the 1890s* (new edition), Chicago, University of Chicago Press

Chamberlain, M.E. (2010), *The New Imperialism* (new edition), Historical Association pamphlet

Chamberlain, M.E. (2010), *The Scramble for Africa* (third edition), London, Taylor Francis

Ferrell, R.H. (1985), *Woodrow Wilson and the First World War, 1917–1921*, New York, Harper and Row

Gordon, A. (2003), *A Modern History of Japan*, New York, OUP

Gott, R. (2011), *Britain's Empire: Resistance, Repression and Revolt*, London, Verso

Herring, G.C. (2008), *The American Century and Beyond*, New York, OUP

Hopkins, A. (2018), *American Empire: A Global History*, Princeton, Princeton University Press

Jansen, M., and Duus, P. (eds), (1989), *The Cambridge History of Japan* Vols. V and VI, Cambridge, CUP

Joll, J. (1992), *The Origins of the First World War* (second edition), Harlow, Longman

Langer, W.L. (1951), *The Diplomacy of Imperialism, 1890–1902* (revised edition), New York, Knopf

Lowe, J., and Pearce, R. (1998), *Rivalry and Accord: International Relations, 1870–1914* (second edition), London, Hodder

Pakenham, T. (1992), *The Scramble for Africa*, London, Abacus

Robinson, R. (1979) 'The Partition of Africa' in Hinsley, F.H. (ed.), *The New Cambridge Modern History XI*, Cambridge, CUP, (reprinted) pages 593–640

Robinson, R., and Gallagher, J. (1961), *Africa and the Victorians*, London, Macmillan

Rodney, W. (2018), *How Europe Underdeveloped Africa*, London, Verso

Siollum, M. (2021), *What Britain Did To Nigeria*, London, Hurst and Co

Stevenson, D. (1998), *The First World War and International Politics*, Oxford, OUP

Williams, W.A. (2009), *The Tragedy of American Diplomacy* (new edition), New York / London, Norton Publishing

Veevers, D. (2023), *Defiance*, London, Ebury Press / Penguin

Chapter 2

Fischer, C. (2002), *The Ruhr Crisis*, Oxford, OUP

Hathaway, O.A. (2017), *The Internationalists*, New York, Simon and Schuster

Henig, R. (1995), *Versailles and After, 1919–33* (second edition), Oxford, Routledge

Henig, R. (2010), *The League of Nations*, London, Haus Publishing

Jordan, W.M. (1971), *Great Britain, France and the German Problem, 1918–39* (new impression), London, Cass

Macmillan, M. (2001), *Peacemakers*, John Murray

Maier, C.S. (1988), *Recasting Bourgeois Europe*, Princeton University Press

Mayer, A.J. (1968), *Politics and Diplomacy in Peacemaking: Containment and Counter-Revolution at Versailles*, London, Weidenfeld and Nicolson

Northedge, F.S. (1986), *The League of Nations: Its Life and Times*, Leicester, Leicester University Press

Schulz, G. (1972), *Revolutions and Peace Treaties, 1917–20*, London, Methuen

Sharp, A. (ed.), (2009), *Makers of the Modern World: The Paris Peace Conferences 1919–23*, Haus Publishing

Steiner, Z. (2005), *The Lights That Failed, 1919–1933*, Oxford, OUP

Tooze, A. (2014), *The Deluge: The Great War and the Remaking of Global Order, 1916–1931*, London, Allen Lane

Williamson, D.G. (1997), *Mussolini, From Socialist to Fascist*, London, Hodder

Williamson, D.G. (2017), *The British in Interwar Germany, 1918–30*, London, Bloomsbury

Wright, J. (2002), *Gustav Stresemann: Weimar's Greatest Statesman*, OUP

Chapter 3

Adamthwaite, A. (1977), *France and the Coming of the Second World War*, London, Cass

Bell, P.M.M. (1986), *Origins of the Second World War in Europe*, London/New York, Longman

Boyce, R. (1989), 'World Depression, World War: Some Economic Origins of the Second World War' in Boyce, R., and Robertson, E.M. (eds), *Paths to War: New Essays on the Origins of the Second World War*, London, Macmillan

Bullock, A. (1971), 'Hitler and the Origins of the Second World War' in Robertson, E. (ed.), *The Origins of the Second World War*, London, Macmillan

Carr, W.M. (1972), *Arms, Autarky and Aggression*, Arnold

Dutton, D. (2001), *Neville Chamberlain*, London, Hodder

Evans, R.J. (2003–2009), *The Third Reich in Power*, London, Penguin

Hannemann, M. (2001), *Japan Faces the World, 1925–1952*, Harlow, Longman

Heffer, S. (2023), *Sing as we go: Britain between the wars*, London, Penquin

Kershaw, I. (1998–2000), *Hitler, Vol. I, Hubris; Vol. II, Nemesis*, London, Allen Lane

Lamb, M., and Tarling, N. (2002), *From Versailles to Pearl Harbor*, London, Palgrave

Mallett, R. (2003), *Mussolini and the Origin of the Second World War*, London, Macmillan

Overy, R.J. (1987), *The Origins of the Second World War*, Longman

Parker, R.A.C. (1993), *Chamberlain and Appeasement: British Policy and the Coming of the Second World War*, London, Macmillan

Parker, R.A.C. (2000), *Churchill and Appeasement*, London, Palgrave

Roberts, G. (1995), *The Soviet Union and the Origins of the Second World War, 1933–41*, Macmillan

Robertson, E. (1979), *Mussolini as Empire-Builder: Europe and Africa, 1932–1936*, London, Macmillan

Shay, R. (1977), *British Rearmament in the Thirties: Politics and Profits*, Princeton, Princeton University Press

Taylor, A.J.P. (1961), *The Origins of the Second World War*, London, Arnold

Thorne, C. (1972), *The Limits of Foreign Policy: The West, the League and the Far Eastern Crisis of 1931–1933*, London, Hamilton

Weinberg, G. (1970–1980), *The Foreign Policy of Hitler's Germany, Vol. I, Diplomatic Revolution in Europe, 1933–36, and Vol. II, Starting World War II*, Chicago, University of Chicago Press

Wright, J. (2007), *Germany and the Origins of the Second World War*, London, Palgrave

Internet sources

- Michael Duff's First World War.com: **www.firstworldwar.com** Contains a vast amount of material relevant to the causes, course and consequences of the First World War.
- Fordham University's Modern Internet History Sourcebook: **https://sourcebooks.fordham.edu/mod/modsbook.asp** A mine of source material including treaties, speeches, etc.
- Both the British National Archives and the US National Archives contain an enormous volume of material on the events covered by this book: British National Archives: **www.nationalarchives.gov.uk** and US National Archives: **www.archives.gov**
- Yale Law School, the Avalon Project, Documents in Law, History, and Diplomacy, **Avalon.law.Yale.edu/** Useful for treaties and other historical documents covering the period of this book.

Glossary

Alliance system A mutual agreement between two or more countries, possibly involving defending each other in the event of an attack.

Allies An international coalition of countries fighting in the First World War led by Britain, France, and Russia and also including Japan and Italy.

Anarchist A supporter of anarchism, a political theory advocating small, self-governing societies.

Anarcho-syndicalism A belief that the state should be replaced by trade unions and similar organizations, which would negotiate directly with each other and exchange all the goods and services necessary to meet the needs of the population.

Anderson shelters Named after Sir John Anderson, the government minister who commissioned their development, these were steel shelters installed in gardens to provide protection against air raids.

Annex An addition to a treaty.

Anschluss The union of Austria with Germany.

Anthropologist Someone who studies human beings and their societies, customs, and beliefs.

Apartheid The system of racial segregation and discrimination against non-white people in South Africa in the second half of the twentieth century.

Arbitration A form of dispute resolution through mediation by a third party.

Article 48 An emergency provision in the Weimar Constitution which allowed the president to pass laws without the consent of the *Reichstag*.

Associated power A status held by the USA when it entered the First World War which meant it was free, if necessary, to pursue its own policies.

Autarky Economic self-sufficiency.

Balfour Declaration A 1917 communication by Arthur Balfour, the British foreign secretary, declaring British support for establishing a national home for the Jewish people in Palestine.

Balkan crisis (1875–78) When revolts against Ottoman rule occured in Bosnia, Serbia, and Montenegro, Russia threatened to support the rebels and advanced to Constantinople (modern-day Istanbul). This worried Britain, which feared Russia gaining access to the Mediterranean. The crisis was resolved when German chancellor Bismarck called the Berlin Congress.

Balkan Prussia A descriptive phrase by which Bulgaria was compared to Prussia, which in the eyes of the Allies had an aggressive, militarist reputation.

Banking crisis of 1931 A financial crisis triggered in May 1931 by the failure of the Kreditanstalt bank in Vienna.

Battle of Sedan A traumatic defeat of France by Prussia in September 1870.

Battle of Waterloo An 1815 battle in Belgium in which Britain defeated France.

Benevolent passivity Favoring one side while not officially supporting them.

Bessemer process A new process to mass-produce steel from molten pig iron, primarily by removing impurities from the iron by oxidation.

Bilateral Describing an agreement or action between or by two states.

Black Dragon Society Also the Kokuryukai or Amur Society; an ultranationalist association founded in 1901 with the aim of extending Japan's 'imperial mission' to Manchuria, Mongolia, and Siberia.

Blackout blinds Blinds that would cover windows to prevent light from inside attracting the attention of enemy bomber crews, who would be targeting large industrial cities.

Blueshirts A fascist organization founded in Ireland to bring about Irish unity by creating a corporate state along Italian lines.

Boers Descendants of Dutch settlers who had originally colonized South Africa.

Bolshevism A term associated with the Bolsheviks, a faction of the Russian socialist movement led by Vladimir Lenin. The Bolsheviks believed in radical, revolutionary methods to overthrow the existing government. This ideology laid the foundation for the Russian Revolution of 1917, leading to the creation of the Soviet Union.

Bond A means for a government or large company to borrow money, which they promise to repay at a fixed rate of interest by a specified date.

Boxers The English name for a secret Chinese patriotic and nationalist organization, which instigated an anti-Western uprising in 1899–1901. The literal translation of the group's name is 'the Society of Righteous and Harmonious Fists.'

Buffer state A neutral state positioned geographically between two rival powers.

Cant and humbug Hypocritical nonsense.

Capital ships The most powerful warships in a navy.

Capitalism An economic system in which the production and distribution of goods depend on the investment of private capital.

Capitulations Exemption of foreign merchants and their agents from Turkish taxation and law.

Central Powers An international coalition fighting in the First World War, consisting of Germany and Austria–Hungary, the Ottoman Empire, and Bulgaria.

Chinese Civil War A conflict fought intermittently from 1927 to 1949 between the nationalist government of the Republic of China and the forces of the Chinese Communist Party.

Civil war in Mexico A conflict that lasted from 1910 to 1920 which started as a revolt against the regime of President Porfirio Díaz.

CNT The National Workers' Confederation (Confederación Nacional del Trabajo), a grouping of anarcho-syndicalist trade unions.

Coaling station A base where steamships can be fuelled with coal.

Coalition A term commonly used to refer to a government made up of two or more minority parties who agree to work together to form a majority.

Collective security Security gained through joining an alliance where each member state agrees to defend the others.

Cologne Zone Area around Cologne occupied by the British, December 1918–26.

Colonization Taking control of a territory through settlement and military force.

Comintern An international movement set up in 1919 by the Communist Party of the Soviet Union to organize a worldwide communist revolution.

Conference of Ambassadors A standing committee of the principal Allied and associated powers set up to supervise the carrying out of the Treaty of Versailles. It succeeded the Supreme War Council.

Confidence vote A vote held to decide whether parliament has confidence in the government.

Confucian philosophy The ideas of an ancient Chinese philosopher, named Confucius. He wrote rules telling people how to live ethically and maintain a harmonious society.

Congregational Church A branch of the Protestant Church founded in England in the sixteenth century.

Congress The US parliament, consisting of a lower chamber, the House of Representatives, and an upper chamber, the Senate.

Conscription Compulsory military service.

Consortium An association of states with a common aim.

Consular courts Courts presided over by foreign officials to protect the interests of their countrymen who were trading or working in a country such as Japan or China.

Continentalist strategy A policy that was primarily concerned with matters occurring on the North American continent.

Corporate state A state where most of the economy is controlled by the government.

Council of Ten The controlling committee of the Paris Peace Conference, consisting of the head of government and foreign minister from each of Britain, France, Italy, Japan, and the USA.

Counter-revolutionary A person who opposes a revolution and wants to reverse its results.

Court martial A court in which members of the armed forces can face trial under military law.

Covenant A general term meaning 'agreement' or the specific document laying out the agreed rules and constitution of the League of Nations.

Cowrie Type of sea snail or mollusc.

Creditor An individual, organization, or country to whom money is owed.

Curzon line The proposal made by Lord Curzon, the British foreign minister, for Poland's eastern frontier with the Soviet Union.

Czecho-Slovakia Short for the Second Czecho-Slovak Republic, the name by which what was left of Czechoslovakia was known from September 1938 until March 1939.

Dawes bonds Bonds sold by Germany on the international markets (mostly in the USA) to raise money to stabilize its economy.

Decolonization This refers to the process by which colonies gained independence from their colonial powers, often after years of struggle and negotiation.

Deflationary A term relating to policies or events that bring about a fall in prices.

Deliberative chamber An assembly appointed to debate or discuss issues.

Demilitarized Having all military defenses removed.

Democratic centralism An organizational system introduced by Lenin in which policy was decided centrally and had to be carried out by all government bodies and members.

Détente A process of lessening tension between two or more states.

Devaluation A deliberate decision taken by a government to lower the value of its currency in order, for example, to boost exports and thereby stimulate the economy.

Dictated peace A peace treaty that is dictated to the defeated party rather than negotiated.

Diet The national parliament of Japan.

Dollar diplomacy The furthering of diplomatic aims by using economic pressure or incentives, including the offer of loans.

Domain lords Provincial noblemen who were in control of large estates and who owed their loyalty to the Emperor.

Dominions Self-governing countries within the British Empire and Commonwealth.

Donghak A nationalist neo-Confucian movement in Korea that was strongly opposed to Western culture.

Elite The ruling class.

Entente A friendly understanding between states rather than a formal alliance.

Entente powers Another term given to the Allied countries fighting Germany and Austria–Hungary: Britain, France, Italy, and Russia.

Eupen and Malmedy Western German territories integrated into Belgium in 1925 after the League of Nations consulted the local populations about their wishes.

European Economic Community A regional organization founded in 1958 and a forerunner of the current European Union.

Evacuations from Dunkirk The retreat of the British Expeditionary Force to the northern French port of Dunkirk in May 1940 and subsequent rescue by a risky sea evacuation.

Evangelical Referring to Christians who are determined to spread their beliefs through the Gospels.

Executive committee A committee that can take key decisions.

Executive power The power of a government or other organization to put into effect the laws or decisions it makes.

Fascist Party A party formed in Italy by Mussolini in 1919. Its program was a mix of radical and reactionary ideas. Once in power, its policies focused on intense nationalism and economic and social reforms.

February Revolution An uprising in Russia February 1917, which installed the Provisional Government. The Bolsheviks seized power later that year in the October Revolution.

Federation A system of government in which several countries or regions form a unity but still manage to remain self-governing in internal affairs.

First Opium War A war fought between Britain and China from 1839 to 1842, which was won by Britain.

Formal annexation The taking over of full control of a territory by another power.

Free city A self-governing city under the protection of the League of Nations.

Free trade Trade between nations unimpeded by tariffs.

Free trade zone An area where countries can trade without restrictions.

Führer A new title for a role which combined the posts of chancellor and president of Germany, and emphasized absolute authority and control over the state and the Nazi Party.

Fulfillment A policy aimed by Germany at extracting concessions from Britain and France by attempting to fulfill the Treaty of Versailles.

GDP An acronym standing for 'gross domestic product' – the financial value of all goods and services produced by a country.

General staff A group of officers responsible for administering the army and planning operations.

Genocide The deliberate killing of a large number of people from a national, ethnic, or religious group with the aim of destroying that group in whole or in part.

Genrō A term used to refer to a group of Japanese elder statesmen who were seen as the founding fathers of modern Japan.

German Confederation A loose grouping of the German states, including Austria, set up in 1815 and dissolved in 1866.

Gold standard A system by which the value of a currency is defined in terms of the price of gold.

The Great Depression A severe worldwide economic downturn that began in 1929 and lasted until about 1939. It started in the USA with a dramatic decline in stock prices on the US Stock Exchange in New York.

Great War Term originally used to refer to the First World War.

Grossdeutschland The concept of a 'greater Germany' containing all German-speaking peoples in a single state. This idea first emerged during the nineteenth century in the German nationalist movement.

Guerrilla warfare Tactics used by small groups of irregular troops, such as sabotage and assassination.

House of Habsburg The dynasty of the Austro-Hungarian emperors, including Charles I.

Hyperinflation Massive daily increases in the prices of goods and in the amount of money being printed.

Ideology A system and set of ideas and theories.

Imperial War Cabinet A co-ordinating body made up of representatives from Britain and the self-governing Commonwealth countries, which met from 1917 to 1919.

Imperialism The policy, carried out by a state, of acquiring and controlling dependent territories.

Impi A body of Zulu warriors.

Indirect government Control exercised by a colonial power indirectly through trading companies or local community leaders.

Industrial Revolution The process that enabled the mass production of goods in factories and their transportation by steam-powered trains and ships.

Inter-Allied commissions Allied committees set up to deal with particular tasks set by the conference.

International civil service A permanent administration made up of officials from all the member states.

International Congo Society An organization established by King Leopold II of Belgium to further his colonial interests in the Congo.

Internationalized When a place or country is under international control.

Inter-tribal slavery The practice of using captives from a rival tribe for slave labor.

Isolationists Those who argue in favor of remaining detached from international politics.

Jameson Raid An armed intervention in the Transvaal led by Leander Starr Jameson, a British politician in Cape Colony, over the New Year weekend of 1895–96.

Janus face An expression named after the Roman god of lies and deception Janus, who had two faces and was, therefore, associated with duality.

Jiaozhou A bay area on the Shandong peninsula in northern China, seized by Germany in 1897 in revenge for the murder of two missionaries.

Jingoism Extreme patriotism in support of an aggressive foreign policy. 'By jingo' was an expression of mild surprise in a popular British song of the 1870s. The term jingoism evolved from this song to describe extreme patriotism.

Khedive The title used by the governor and ruler of Egypt and Sudan.

Kwantung Army A Japanese army guarding the South Manchuria Railway and stationed on the Liaodong peninsula since 1907.

Lebensraum A term meaning 'living space:' the idea of providing Germans with all the land and resources that they needed.

Liberia A country founded in the early nineteenth century by the American Colonization Society as a refuge for African-Americans.

Locarno Spirit The optimistic mood of reconciliation and compromise that swept through Europe after the signing of the Locarno Treaties.

Lubricant A substance used to make movement smoother, on machines, for example.

Luftwaffe The German air force.

Lutheranism A German variant of Protestantism that followed the teachings of the sixteenth-century theologian Martin Luther.

Maginot Line A line of concrete fortifications that France constructed along its eastern borders, particularly those with Germany, in the 1930s. It was named after André Maginot, the French Minister of War who had the initial idea.

Magyar The ethnic Hungarian people.

Mahdi A Sudanese religious title meaning 'the redeemer of Islam.'

Malaria A potentially life-threatening disease carried by mosquitoes.

Manchukuo The name given to the Japanese-dominated state created in 1932, comprising the territory Japan seized in its invasion of Manchuria.

Mandated status A status given to former German and Ottoman territories by the League of Nations. It put Allied powers in charge, to govern on behalf of the League of Nations.

Mass industrial production Large-scale production of goods in factories.

Maxim gun A machine gun invented in the USA by Hiram Maxim and mass-produced from 1884.

Meiji regime The era, from 1868 to 1912, in which Emperor Mutsuhito ruled Japan under the title of Meiji.

Mein Kampf Literally, 'My Struggle'. Hitler's major political work, in which he outlined his beliefs and political intentions.

Merchant marine A fleet of cargo vessels.

Minority rights treaties Agreements guaranteeing the rights of ethnic minorities that the successor states had to sign as a condition of their independence.

Monroe Doctrine An American foreign policy position that opposed any intervention in the western hemisphere by colonial powers other than the USA.

Moratorium Temporary suspension of payments.

Multilateral Describing an agreement or action between or by more than two states.

Mutilated victory An Italian nationalist view of their country's victory in the First World War, which they saw as having been tarnished by the refusal of the Allies to give Italy what it had been promised.

Nationalism The belief that a nation is better and more important than all other nations.

Navy League A pressure group which agitated for a large German navy.

New Economic Policy A Soviet economic policy introduced by Lenin as a temporary measure in 1921.

New Imperialism Intensive colonization by the European powers, Japan, and the USA roughly in the period 1890–1914.

NSDAP The National Socialist German Workers' Party (Nationalsozialistische Deutsche Arbeiterpartei), or Nazi Party.

Open door The policy of keeping China open to foreign trade.

Ottoman Empire An empire centered on modern-day Turkey 1299–1922 that extended deep into south-east and central Europe, North Africa, and west Asia.

Oxford Union The students' debating club at Oxford University.

Pacificism The belief that violence should be used only when there is no alternative.

Pacifism The belief that violence should never be used to settle disputes.

Pandemic An epidemic on a global scale.

Pan-German League A German political society that believed that Germany should extend its frontiers to include all Germans – particularly in Poland, Switzerland, and Austria.

Partition Dividing up a continent or country into territories controlled by different powers.

Passive resistance Refusal to co-operate, stopping short of actual violence.

Peace bloc A group of states committed to opposing an aggressor power.

People's war A popular war fought by the mass of the people.

Perpetual sovereignty Lasting control, power, and authority.

Philanthropy The desire to help humanity.

Plebiscite A direct vote by the electorate on a single issue.

Pomorze A narrow strip of Polish territory giving Poland access to the Baltic Sea and separating the main body of Germany from the German province of East Prussia.

Polygamy Having more than one wife or husband.

Popular Front A coalition of French left-wing parties, including the Communist Party, to face up to the threat of fascism.

Power politics A form of international politics in which countries threaten to use their military or economic strength against their rivals in order to further their national interests.

Power vacuum A situation in which a territory is left ungoverned after the withdrawal or collapse of the original ruling power.

Pressure groups Associations formed to promote a particular interest by influencing government policy.

Productive pledges The possession of mines and factories as pledges or guarantees of German payment of reparations.

Protectionism Stopping foreign goods by levying tariffs or taxes on imports.

Protectorate A territory that is controlled and protected by another state without being a possession of that state.

Provenance The origin or source of a document or artifact. It is important to know a source's provenance so you can assess its authenticity and reliability by considering factors such as who created it, when and where it was created, and why it was created.

Provisional government A temporary government in power only until elections can be held.

Puppet ruler Someone who holds a title that suggests they have authority, but who is actually loyal to or controlled by an outside group or individual.

Putsch An attempt to take over power.

Quinine A chemical compound derived from the bark of the South American cinchona tree that was first discovered as a malaria treatment in the seventeenth century, and is sometimes used today.

Racial community Here, Hitler is referring to the 'German race' and any other peoples deemed acceptable in Nazi race theory.

Ratified Having received formal approval from the legislature.

Raw materials Unprocessed materials such as coal, iron ore, and crude oil.

Realpolitik A German term meaning literally 'realistic politics.' This is a political approach that favors pragmatism over idealism.

Recession A decline in economic productivity.

Reich The German Empire, formed in 1871 when the southern German states (not including Austria and Liechtenstein) formed a union with the North German Confederation.

Reichstag The German parliament.

***Reichstag* fire** A devastating arson attack on the German parliament building on February 27, 1933. Dutch communist Marinus van der Lubbe was found at the scene and was arrested and executed for this crime, although there is ongoing debate about whether this was part of a plot to consolidate Nazi power.

Reparations Compensation paid by a defeated power to make good the damage it caused in a war.

Rhineland separatism A movement favoring separation of the Rhineland from Germany.

Right-wing A general term to describe conservative politicians, parties, and policies. Right-wing politics uphold 'traditional' social hierarchies and argue that some level of social inequality is natural and acceptable. Extreme right-wing beliefs are referred to as 'far-right', and include fascism and Nazism.

Roma A traditionally nomadic ethnic group originally from northern India but now living across Europe and the Americas.

The Ruhr Germany's most important industrial region, centered around the Ruhr Valley in the west of the country.

Rump state What is left of a much bigger state after it has been reduced by factors such as annexation, occupation, or the breaking up of an empire.

Sabre rattling Inflammatory statements threatening military action.

Samurai A member of the Japanese ruling class or nobility.

Sanctions Penalties, usually of a commercial or economic nature, applied to bring pressure on a state that is failing to meet its international obligations.

Satellite state A state that is officially independent but that is dominated by another state.

Schlieffen Plan The German military strategist Alfred von Schlieffen envisaged that any war in Europe would be fought on two fronts, against France and Russia. He therefore created a plan for a swift attack through Belgium to defeat France in one month, allowing Germany's army to then focus on Russia.

Self-determination The right of a people to decide its own future.

Separatist movements Political movements seeking the separation of a region from a country.

Shogun Theoretically the Japanese emperor's military deputy, but in reality the ruler of Japan.

Shōwa restoration Attempts in the 1930s to restore the power of the Japanese emperor. Shōwa was the name given to Emperor Hirohito's reign, 1926–89.

Social imperialism A policy aimed at uniting all social classes behind plans for creating and expanding an empire.

South Slavs The main ethnic group in Bosnia and Herzegovina, which Austria had occupied since 1878.

SPD The German Social Democratic Party (Sozialdemokratische Partei Deutschlands).

Sphere of interest An area where a great power enjoys special privileges and rights.

Splendid isolation A term used to describe the determination of British governments from 1815 to 1902 to avoid forming permanent alliances.

Staff talks Strategic discussions between officers of the planning and administrative departments of two or more national armies.

Status quo A Latin term denoting the current state of affairs.

The Straits Two important Turkish waterways – the Bosphorus and the Dardanelles – which link the Black Sea to the Aegean Sea.

Strategic aims Aims intended to gain military or economic security for a state.

Stresa powers The states that attended the Stresa Conference in April 1935: France, Italy, and Britain.

Successor state A new country created when a larger country is divided up.

Sudeten Germans German-speaking people who had been settled in the Sudetenland since the thirteenth century.

Suffrage The right to vote.

Synthetic materials Laboratory-created alternatives to natural resources such as rubber and oil.

Tariffs Taxes placed on imported goods to protect the home economy.

Teller Amendment An amendment (or qualification) put forward in April 1898 to a joint resolution by the US Congress, calling for American forces to aid Cuban independence.

Ten-Year Rule British government guidelines for reducing military spending after the First World War, assuming that Britain would not be involved in a significant war for the next ten years.

Third Reich The name that the Nazis gave to their regime, thereby positioning it as the successor to the Holy Roman Empire (800–1806) and the German Empire (1871–1918).

Tokugawa dynasty A powerful Japanese dynasty established in 1603 after a period of civil war and not overthrown until 1868.

Total war The mobilization of a whole population to contribute to a war effort, whether that be by fighting, producing food, or manufacturing and supplying equipment.

Treaty of London The 1915 treaty that Britain, France, and Russia made with Italy to ensure that Italy would enter the First World War on the side of the Allies.

Treaty of Prague An 1866 peace treaty between Prussia and Austria, signed at Prague.

Treaty ports Chinese port cities that opened up to foreign trade as a result of treaties agreed between Western powers and China.

Triplice An alliance or agreement between three powers.

Tsetse fly A large insect that inhabits much of tropical Africa and lives by feeding off the blood of vertebrate animals and humans.

Turnout The proportion of eligible voters who actually turn out to vote. For the December 1929 German referendum, the turnout was just 15 per cent.

Twin infanticide The practice of killing twins at birth in the belief that they were unnatural and inhabited by evil spirits.

Union of South Africa A self-governing Dominion of the British Empire, which came into being in 1910 when the Cape, Natal, Transvaal, and Orange River colonies were unified.

Universal conscription A system in which all people, or all men, of a certain age have to serve for a period of time in the armed services.

Unrestricted submarine warfare Submarine attacks on any ships that were considered to be involved in the war effort, whether naval or merchant, including ships bearing the flags of neutral countries.

USSR The Union of Soviet Socialist Republics, the new Bolshevik name for the Russian Empire after 1922.

Volksdeutsche Ethnic Germans who lived in, and were citizens of, the states next to Germany.

Volte-face An about turn; a sudden and complete change of policy.

Wahhabist Referring to a fundamentalist Islamic reform movement founded by Muhammad ibn Abd al-Wahhab (1703–92).

War guilt Blame for starting a war.

Warlords Individuals who are able to control large areas through military strength rather than formal government.

Weimar Republic Germany's first federal republic, proclaimed upon the abdication of Kaiser Wilhelm II at the end of the First World War and lasting until March 1933.

Weltpolitik Literally 'world policy,' a political strategy designed to turn Germany into a global power.

Western civilization A term used to describe the culture, organization, and values of western European countries and the USA.

Westernizers Those who believed that the Japanese state should modernize along European and American lines.

Westwall Also known as the Siegfried Line, a German line of fortifications stretching from its Dutch border to Switzerland, started in 1936.

White Russians The name given to members and supporters of the counter-revolutionary 'White' armies, which fought against the Bolshevik 'Red' army in the Russian Civil War (1918–21).

Yellow journalism A style of sensationalist and often exaggerated reporting that emerged in the late nineteenth and early twentieth centuries. It was characterized by bold headlines and exaggerated stories. The term originated from the fierce competition between two New York City newspapers, Joseph Pulitzer's *New York World* and William Randolph Hearst's *New York Journal*.

Yugoslavia A country that came into existence in 1918 as the Kingdom of Serbs, Croats and Slovenes and changed its name to Yugoslavia in 1929. In 1992 it was dissolved and replaced by several independent states.

Zinoviev letter A letter supposedly from Grigory Zinoviev, the head of Comintern, to the leader of the British Communist Party urging him to stage strikes and other subversive activities, which was published in the *Daily Mail* a few days before the October 1924 general election. The letter was a forgery and the information was false, but it helped the Conservatives win the election.

Index

Y

Z

Photo credits

The Publishers would like to thank the following for permission to reproduce copyright material:

p.4 © INTERFOTO / Alamy Stock Photo; **p.6** © The Print Collector / Alamy Stock Photo; **p.13** © Zoom Historical / Alamy Stock Photo; **p.14** © The Print Collector / Alamy Stock Photo; **p.18** © Deutsches Bundesarchiv via Wikipedia Commons (public domain); **p.21** © Chronicle / Alamy Stock Photo; **p.22** © Granger, NYC / TopFoto; **p.32** LSE Library via https://flickr.com/photos/35128489@N07/22473779343 (public domain); **p.40** © MeijiShowa / Alamy Stock Photo; **p.42** © Chronicle / Alamy Stock Photo; **p.45** © DEA / BIBLIOTECA AMBROSIANA via Getty Images; **p.48** 帝国軍人教育会 編『大戦争写真帖』,帝国軍人教育会,大正4. 国立国会図書館デジタルコレクション https://dl.ndl.go.jp/pid/966291 (参照 2025-04-07); **p.51** © Collection of Chief Quartermaster John Harold. U.S. Naval History and Heritage Command Photograph. NH 106120-KN; **p.52** © The Granger Collection / Alamy Stock Photo; **p.55** © Everett Collection Inc / Alamy Stock Photo; **p.61** Library of Congress, Prints & Photographs Division, Detroit Publishing Company Collection / LC-DIG-det-4a26353; **p.75** © Harris & Ewing. Library of Congress, Prints & Photographs Division LC-USZ62-8054; **p.85** © Bettmann via Getty Images; **p.95** © Harlingue / Roger Viollet via Getty Images; **p.98** © ullstein bild / Gircke / Topfoto; **p.101** © Stan Pritchard / Alamy Stock Photo; **p.102** © GRANGER - Historical Picture Archive / Alamy Stock Photo; **p.107** © Chronicle / Alamy Stock Photo; **p.108** © World History Archive / Alamy Stock Photo; **p.109** © Lebrecht Music & Arts / Alamy Stock Photo; **p.113** U.S. Naval History and Heritage Command; **p.115** Library of Congress, Prints & Photographs division, Washington / LC-DIG-ggbain-37463; **p.124** © Davis Jr / Stringer / Hulton Archive via Getty Images; **p.128** © DEA / A. DAGLI ORTI / Contributor; **p.131** © Glasshouse Images / Alamy Stock Photo; **p.140** © Illustrated London News; **p.141** © Popperfoto / Getty Images; **p.144** © MeijiShowa / Alamy Stock Photo; **p.146** © US National Archives (NARA) 541927; **p.147** © Mary Evans Picture Library; **p.151** Library of Congress, Prints & Photographs division, Washington / LC-USW33-019081-C; **p.156** © World History Archive / Alamy Stock Photo; **p.158** © Pictorial Press Ltd / Alamy Stock Photo; **p.159** © David Low / The Evening Standard; **p.161** © David Low / The Evening Standard; **p.166** © ullsteinbild / TopFoto; **p.169** © Wikipedia Commons (public domain); **p.171** © Heritage Image Partnership Ltd / Alamy Stock Photo; **p.176** © David Low / The Evening Standard; **p.182** © Fox Photos / Getty Images; **p.187** © piemags / ww2archive / Alamy Stock Photo; p.193 © Rolls Press / Popperfoto / Getty Images; **p.197** © David Low / The Evening Standard;

Acknowledgements

Every effort has been made to trace all copyright holders, but if any have been inadvertently overlooked, the Publishers will be pleased to make the necessary arrangements at the first opportunity.

Although every effort has been made to ensure that website addresses are correct at time of going to press, Hachette Learning cannot be held responsible for the content of any website mentioned in this book. It is sometimes possible to find a relocated web page by typing in the address of the home page for a website in the URL window of your browser.